ENVISIONING ABOLITION

Edited by
David Gordon Scott and Emma Bell

First published in Great Britain in 2026 by

Bristol University Press
University of Bristol
1–9 Old Park Hill
Bristol
BS2 8BB
UK
t: +44 (0)117 374 6645
e: bup-info@bristol.ac.uk

Details of international sales and distribution partners are available at bristoluniversitypress.co.uk

© Bristol University Press 2026

British Library Cataloguing in Publication Data
A catalogue record for this book is available from the British Library

ISBN 978-1-5292-3477-0 hardcover
ISBN 978-1-5292-3478-7 paperback
ISBN 978-1-5292-3479-4 ePub
ISBN 978-1-5292-3480-0 ePdf

The right of David Gordon Scott and Emma Bell to be identified as editors of this work has been asserted by them in accordance with the Copyright, Designs and Patents Act 1988.

All rights reserved: no part of this publication may be reproduced, stored in a retrieval system, or transmitted in any form or by any means, electronic, mechanical, photocopying, recording, or otherwise without the prior permission of Bristol University Press.

Every reasonable effort has been made to obtain permission to reproduce copyrighted material. If, however, anyone knows of an oversight, please contact the publisher.

The statements and opinions contained within this publication are solely those of the editors and contributors and not of the University of Bristol or Bristol University Press. The University of Bristol and Bristol University Press disclaim responsibility for any injury to persons or property resulting from any material published in this publication.

Bristol University Press works to counter discrimination on grounds of gender, race, disability, age and sexuality.

Cover design: Liam Roberts Design
Front cover image: Getty/calvindexter

Bristol University Press' authorised representative in the European Union
is: Easy Access System Europe, Mustamäe tee 50, 10621 Tallinn, Estonia,
Email: gpsr.requests@easproject.com

Contents

Notes on Contributors		v
Preface		x
1	Abolitionism in Red and Black *Emma Bell and David Gordon Scott*	1
2	The Embryonic Abolitionist Ideas of William Godwin in the Late 18th Century *Ruby Tuke*	33
3	Robert Owen and the Owenites: Abolitionist Ideas in the Early British Socialist Movement *Ophélie Siméon*	50
4	'Do What Is Right, and Let Come What May': Tolstoy and Penal Abolition *Andrei Zorin*	66
5	Arthur St John: Tolstoyan Abolitionism in Practice *Peter Cox and Paul Taylor*	87
6	Edward Carpenter's Realist Utopian and Contingent Abolitionism *Jonathan Baldwin*	108
7	William Morris' Utopian Case for Prison Abolition *Owen Holland*	125
8	Beyond Sanction: Jean-Marie Guyau between Penal Abolition and Social Defence *Federico Testa*	146
9	Pyotr Kropotkin: Foundations of Anarchist Prison Abolition *Robert D. Weide*	169
10	Anarchism and the Abolition of the Criminal Justice System: The Struggle for the Discourse on Evolution and Social Order in Spain *Alejandro Forero Cuellar*	189
11	Fear or Freedom? Errico Malatesta on Crime and Punishment *Davide Turcato*	207

12	Envisioning a New Society: Pietro Gori and the Problem of Criminal Justice *Marco Manfredi*	226
13	'Cemeteries of the Living Dead': Eugene V. Debs, Prison Abolitionist *Lisa Phillips*	242
14	Altgeld's Protégé: Clarence Darrow and the Abolition of Prisons and Capital Punishment in the United States *Andrew E. Kersten*	259
15	Emma Goldman: The Making of a Prison Abolitionist *Penny A. Weiss*	276
16	Seeing through the Game: Alexander Berkman and the Modern Prison Abolition Movement *Søren H. Hough*	301

Index — 323

Notes on Contributors

Jonathan Baldwin completed his PhD at Royal Holloway, University of London. His thesis examined the meeting between the conceptualizations of crime and the varied formations of utopian projections in late 19th and early 20th-century socialist and anarchist discourse in Britain. He has a passion for widening participation in higher education and works with young people from disadvantaged backgrounds and groups in his role as Higher Education Outreach Network Officer for the Office for Students Uni Connect programme.

Emma Bell is Professor of Contemporary British Politics at Savoie Mont-Blanc University in Chambéry. She has published widely in the UK and France on authoritarianism in the British state in journals such as the *British Journal of Criminology*, *Race and Class*, *Theoretical Criminology* and *Socialism and Democracy*. She is the author of *Criminal Justice and Neoliberalism* (Palgrave Macmillan, 2011) and *Soft Power and Freedom under the Coalition* (Palgrave Macmillan, 2015), and is a founding editor (with David Gordon Scott) of the journal *Justice, Power and Resistance*. Her current research focuses on radical democracy and challenges to state authoritarianism.

Peter Cox is former Professor of Sociology at the University of Chester. His primary teaching areas are in social change and social movements and in the politics of sustainability, together with core social and political theory. He has a longstanding interest in Tolstoyan activist networks in the late 19th and early 20th centuries that started when he was undertaking research for his undergraduate degree at Lancaster University in the 1980s. He will one day get round to finishing his monograph on the subject.

Alejandro Forero Cuellar has a PhD in law and political sciences from the University of Barcelona. He is a researcher at the Observatory of the Penal System and Humans Rights, and coordinator of the System for the Documentation and Communication of Institutional Violence (SIRECOVI) at the same university.

Owen Holland read English Literature at St Catharine's College, Cambridge, and subsequently took an MA in Critical Theory at the University of Sussex. He was awarded his doctorate from the University of Cambridge in 2015. He was Career Development Fellow in Victorian and Modern Literature at Jesus College, Oxford between 2016 and 2018, before he moved to University College London (UCL), where he was an associate lecturer in the English Department between 2018 and 2021. He joined the Department of English and Scottish Literature at the University of Edinburgh in 2022. His first book, *William Morris's Utopianism: Propaganda, Politics and Prefiguration*, was published with Palgrave Macmillan in 2017. His second book on British responses to the Paris Commune of 1871 was published by Rutgers University Press in 2022. He is also a former editor of the *Journal of William Morris Studies* and has edited a selection of Morris' political writings for Verso's 'Revolutions' series.

Søren H. Hough works as a science communicator and freelance journalist. He has served as an editor at a variety of media outlets, including *Science for the People* magazine, and has written for film publications such as RogerEbert.com. He has interviewed figures as varied as the political theorist Noam Chomsky, public health expert Michael Marmot and visual effects legend Douglas Trumbull. He currently serves as an editor at *The Commoner* and co-leads a historical research project focused on the life and work of the anarchist biologist, Marie Goldsmith (https://mariegoldsmith.uk/). He has published academic articles across the fields of science, film studies, history and bioethics. He completed his PhD in DNA repair at the University of Cambridge.

Andrew E. Kersten has been the Dean of the College of Arts and Sciences at Cleveland State University since 2022. He was previously at the University of Missouri–St. Louis and Dean of the College of Letters, Arts, and Social Sciences at the University of Idaho. Additionally, he was a faculty member, department chair and associate provost at the University of Wisconsin-Green Bay. As a faculty member, he taught courses in US history and courses on working class people and organized labour in the interdisciplinary programme Democracy and Justice Studies. He researches and writes about American history since Reconstruction. His books include an investigation of President Franklin D. Roosevelt's Fair Employment Practice Committee (*Race, Jobs, and the War*, University of Illinois Press, 2000), a history of the American Federation of Labor during the Second World War (*Labor's Home Front*, New York University Press, 2006), a biography of labour and civil rights leader A. Philip Randolph (*A Life in the Vanguard*, Rowman & Littlefield, 2006) and a biography of the famous defence lawyer Clarence Darrow (*Clarence Darrow: American Iconoclast*, Hill & Wang, 2011).

NOTES ON CONTRIBUTORS

Marco Manfredi is currently Assistant Professor in modern history at the University of Pisa. His research interests include the history of Italian *Risorgimento* and the history of social movements in the 19th and early 20th centuries. His publications include: *Emozioni, cultura popolare e transnazionalismo. Le origini della cultura anarchica in Italia (1890–1914)* (Mondadori Education, 2017); (with E. Papadia) 'Charisma and Revolution: A History of a Controversial Relationship', in «Memoria e Ricerca», 1, 2021; and 'Italian anarchism and popular culture: history of a close relationship', in I. Favretto and X. Itcaina (eds) *Popular Culture, Folk Traditions and Protest in 19th and 20th Century Europe* (Palgrave Macmillan, 2016).

Lisa Phillips is Professor in the History Department at Indiana State University, where she specializes in 20th century US labour, African-American, and women's and gender history. She researches and writes about labour unions that worked to improve the economic status of African-American, Jewish and recent immigrants (Italian and Puerto Rican) in the mid-20th century. Her first book, *A Renegade Union: Interracial Organizing and Labor Radicalism* was published by the University of Illinois Press in 2013. Her second book, now underway, is a labour history of Disney entitled *The Wonderful World of Service Work: Walt Disney and the Advent of Performance Labor*. In 2022, she published an article on Disney's involvement in subcontracted sweatshop labour in Haiti in the immediate post-Cold War era.

David Gordon Scott works at The Open University. He has edited/co-edited several books, including *Why Prison?* (Cambridge University Press, 2013), *International Handbook of Penal Abolition* (Routledge, 2021) and *Abolitionist Voices* (Bristol University Press, 2025). As well as authoring/co-authoring ten other books, including *Against Imprisonment* (Waterside Press, 2018) and *For Abolition* (Waterside Press, 2020) he is also a former co-editor of the *Howard Journal of Crime and Justice* and co-founding editor (with Emma Bell) of the international journal *Justice, Power and Resistance*. His current research is focused on meanings of justice and the history of socialist ethics.

Ophélie Siméon is a graduate from the Ecole Normale Supérieure (Lyons). She holds a PhD in British history and is an associate professor at the University Paris 3-Sorbonne nouvelle. Her research addresses early socialism in the context of the Industrial Revolution, notably in the writings and community experiments of Robert Owen. She has published a monograph on Owen (*Robert Owen's Experiment at New Lanark: From Paternalism to Socialism*, Palgrave Macmillan, 2017) and also an edited collection on Owen (*Contemporary Thought on Nineteenth Century Socialism*, Routledge, 2020) and his followers, known as the 'Owenites', in the 19th century.

Paul Taylor is Head of the School of Humanities and Social Sciences, University of Chester. His teaching and scholarly interests focus on punishments and penology, and the impact of detention in custodial environments on mental health and wellbeing. Most recently, he was lead editor of *Mental Health and Punishments: Critical Perspectives in Theory and Practice* (Routledge, 2021).

Federico Testa is Lecturer in Sociology and Humanities at Norwich Medical School, University of East Anglia (UEA), and holds a PhD in philosophy from the University of Warwick and Monash University. His work develops issues related to norms and critique in different domains of experience, from politics to health, passing through artistic creation and aesthetics. His recent monograph *On the Politics of the Living* (Bloomsbury, 2025) discusses the works of Foucault and Canguilhem, reopening the problem of life and the normative grounds of social criticism in order to reflect on biopolitical resistance. He is particularly interested in 19th and 20th-century French philosophy, as well as in modern receptions of ancient thought. He is the translator of Jean-Marie Guyau's *The Ethics of Epicurus* (Bloomsbury, 2021) and Pierre Hadot's *Selected Writings: Philosophy as Practice* (Bloomsbury, 2020).

Ruby Tuke is a Godwin scholar. Her previous writings include the chapter 'Gifts, Giving, Gratitude: The Development of William Godwin's Radical Critique of Charity in the 1790s' in *New Approaches to William Godwin* (Palgrave Macmillan, 2021). Her PhD thesis, awarded by Queen Mary University London, was entitled 'Gifts, gratitude, charity: representing indebtedness 1790–1834'.

Davide Turcato was born and raised in Italy, and lived for a long time in Canada before moving to Ireland. He works as a language engineer and has published extensively in the field of computational linguistics. As a historian, he has written articles and book chapters on the history and historiography of anarchism, including 'Italian anarchism as a transnational movement, 1885–1915' (*International Review of Social History*, 2007), the entry 'Anarchist communism' in the *Palgrave Handbook of Anarchism* (2019) and 'Interpreting the world, changing the world: the anarchist view' (*Journal for the Study of Radicalism*, 2021). He is the author of *Making Sense of Anarchism* (Springer, 2012) and edited the Malatesta reader *The Method of Freedom* (AK Press, 2014). He is the editor of Errico Malatesta's complete works, a ten-volume project currently underway in both Italian and English editions.

Robert D. Weide is Associate Professor of Sociology at California State University, Los Angeles. He has a PhD from the Department of Sociology at New York University. His subfield areas of expertise include criminology, race and ethnicity, penology and radical theory. He has published scholarship on graffiti, gangs, prisons, race, nationalism, identity and radical theory, including his 2022 book *Divide & Conquer: Race, Gangs, Identity, and Conflict* (Temple University Press) and numerous journal articles. He is currently working on a book-length critique of RICO cases involving gang allegations in California.

Penny A. Weiss is Professor of Women's and Gender Studies at Saint Louis University. She is author or editor of eight books, including *Feminist Reflections on Childhood* (Temple University Press, 2021), *Feminist Manifestos* (ed., NYU Press, 2018) and *Canon Fodder: Historical Women Political Thinkers* (Penn State Press, 2015). She is an avid gardener and relentless doodler, and owes her anarchist leanings in part to Emma Goldman. She is currently working on a two-volume history of political theory that expands the canon in its list of authors, its attention to systems of inequality and its sense of what matters to collective coexistence.

Andrei Zorin is Chair of Russian and a Fellow of New College, Oxford. He received his PhD and 'Habilitation' from Moscow State University, taught in the Russian State University for Humanities (Moscow) and was a visiting professor at Harvard University, Stanford University, the University of Michigan Ann Arbor, and New York University (NYU). He is the author of *By Fables Alone: Literature and State Ideology in Russia in the Last Third of the Eighteenth–First Third of the Nineteenth Centuries* (Academic Studies Press, 2014), *On the Periphery of Europe, 1762–1825: The Self-Invention of the Russian Elite* (co-authored with Andreas Schoenle, Cornell University Press, 2018), *Leo Tolstoy: A Critical Life* (Reaktion Books, 2020) and has edited several collected volumes and published more than 200 articles in English, Russian, German, French, Italian and Finnish, among other languages.

Preface

David Gordon Scott and Emma Bell

Envisioning Abolition is a collection of papers exploring the embryonic ideas and sentiments of penal abolitionist thought from the late 18th century to the early 20th century. To be sure, this was not the starting point for penal abolition. It is clear from our own research that abolitionist notions existed long before this time – they can probably be found for as long as there have been formalized punishments. There is obviously something intuitively problematic about the deliberate infliction of pain and the application of punishments and other forms of coercion.

The full history of penal abolitionism is yet to be written, but what is evident in this volume, and its companion *Abolitionist Voices* (Scott, 2025), is that the long and diverse history of abolitionism has been hidden or lost and that many people today, including those who identify as penal abolitionists, seem completely unaware of the longevity and historical roots of much abolitionist thought. While there have been some very significant attempts to shine a spotlight on the historical development of penal abolition – here we are thinking in particular of the work of Rene van Swaaningen, and especially his influential 1997 book *Critical Criminology: Visions from Europe* and also the abolitionist reflections of Vincenzo Ruggiero, most notably his 2010 book *Penal Abolitionism* – such detailed explorations of abolitionisms of the past are relatively rare (van Swaaningen, 1997; Ruggiero, 2010).[1]

There are probably many reasons why the diverse history of penal abolitionism has been lost to contemporary generations. This is not through conspiracy – we do not believe that abolitionist ideas have been expunged from memory or deliberately concealed by the actions of those in power. Rather, there is likely a combination of relatively mundane reasons for the absence of awareness of penal abolitionism in history. Abolitionism is a political doctrine and moral philosophy which is most likely to come from below, especially from those directly experiencing legal repression. When the powerful redefine their harms to avoid criminal classification, they may negate the impulse of punishment, but they are not working for abolition; they are simply exercising power. Penal abolition as a credo is not about avoiding responsibility or believing one can act with immunity and impunity. Instead, penal abolition questions power and demands that those who harm others are answerable and more broadly accountable for their actions. It questions the logic and rationale of penal sanctions, and in particular calls for the ending of the carceral punishment of the poor, disenfranchised and disempowered members of society. Thus, one of the reasons why it has become easy to make invisible is that history is written by the winners, whereas penal abolition is a struggle by those on the downside of history. Power is therefore a key aspect in shaping what knowledge is passed down the generations through official discourses, and penal abolition fundamentally questions such power.

A further rather mundane reason for the invisibility of earlier abolitionist sentiments and thought is that almost by definition penal abolition is not bound by the categories of a given academic discipline. Boundaries have closed in and around abolitionist thought throughout history. Yet recent trends towards the transcending of academic and other boundaries presents a unique opening for abolitionism. There are many different routes to abolitionist conclusions (Scott, 2025). Interdisciplinary scholarship may provide an opportunity for abolitionist synergies to emerge, making connections that have perhaps not been made before or at least for quite some time. *Envisioning Abolition* itself is a collection which reaches out to scholars in a number of different academic disciplines.

We too, as abolitionist thinkers, do not wish to claim that we have a full grasp of the diversity and complexity of penal abolitionism in the past, and perhaps even in the present. For the same reason as others, we, like everyone else, will be blind to what may later be revealed as a deep and profound tradition of abolitionist thinking, sentiments, reflections or inspired actions. In neither *Envisioning Abolition* nor its companion volume *Abolitionist Voices* (Scott, 2025) do we wish to claim a monopoly on the truth of the extent and nature of penal abolitionism in the past. On the contrary, like everyone else, we are working with fragments of knowledge. Our understanding is partial and limited and in need of revision. We simply claim that we are conscious of how little we know, despite many decades as students of abolitionist ideas. What we hope is that these two volumes collectively will inspire others to search deeper to find even further evidence of abolitionist thinking. *Envisioning Abolition* and *Abolitionist Voices* are thus stepping stones on a much bigger journey to uncover the breadth of abolitionist thinking in the past.

The first of these two volumes, *Abolitionist Voices*, focuses on what might be called the 'abolitionist rhizome' (Scott, 2025). Penal abolitionism has multiple interconnected roots, which means that there is no one single source of abolitionist ideas. The 14 chapters in *Abolitionist Voices* lay out the emergence of abolitionist thought as it has evolved and developed in various different philosophical and theological traditions, including Christianity, postcolonialisms, labelling theory (symbolic interactionism) and anti-slavery. The selection of traditions and thinkers is not comprehensive, but it does indicate that it is important to recognize that there are many different reasons why people propose abolitionist ideas and that we should note that there is not just one line of abolitionist thought, but rather a number of different 'abolitionisms', many of which interconnect as part of this 'abolitionist rhizome'. *Abolitionist Voices* gives the reader some sense that we need to search far and wide to uncover the full extent of abolitionist thinking and that a reductionist approach to claiming just one tradition as the basis of abolitionisms today is counterproductive.

However, it is recognized that within the abolitionist rhizome, abolitionist thought has prospered differently in different traditions. It is now well established, especially in the US, that the anti-chattel-slavery tradition is of enormous value in understanding the emancipatory logic that underscores penal abolitionism. Many abolitionists, especially in South and North America, frame their challenge against the penal law through the lens of the afterlives of slavery. In other countries around the world, the imposition of criminal and penal laws through colonization provides an equally powerful lens through which to critique the penal infamies of the present. Countercolonial projects and demands for the return to indigenous ways of handling conflict have again provided inspiration for abolitionist interventionism and activism in this present.

The goal of *Envisioning Abolition* is also to look in depth at one of the strongest branches in the abolitionist family tree. Our focus here is on penal abolitionist ideas and sentiments as they emerged and developed in the thought of anarchists and early socialist philosophers. Our goal here is once again modest. We wish to merely give a flavour of embryonic abolitionist thought from the late 18th to the early 20th centuries, and some of the key arguments with regard to abolition that were made at the time by socialists and anarchists. We therefore note the presence in the chapters in this volume of both significant contradictions and continuities in both abolitionist strategy and thought.

One small volume like this does not suffice to explore the diversity and complexity of abolitionist ideas which can be found among socialists and anarchists. We are therefore very conscious of omissions and absences among the contents list of this volume. We regret that only one woman is the focus of a chapter in this collection: the anarchist feminist Emma Goldman. This perhaps reflects the unfortunate reality that many women thinkers were sidelined at the time, even in radical circles. We very much hope that this book will inspire contemporary thinkers and biographers of early anarchists and socialists to aid the wider aspirations and hopes that we share of shining a detailed spotlight on the centrality of abolitionist thought to those who we describe here, perhaps aspirationally, as libertarian socialists. For us (and as we elaborate further in Chapter 1, the introduction) a libertarian socialist promotes a non-authoritarian form of socialism that rejects all coercive aspects of the state. We find these ideas in early socialism (sometimes referred to as 'utopian socialism'), anarchism, democratic socialism and autonomous Marxist traditions. In using the term 'libertarian socialism', we do not wish to obscure the very real contradictions, tensions and strategic differences between these distinct approaches to meeting human need and living in a free and just society for all. Rather, we believe that in order for socialism to fulfil its goals, it needs to achieve what the great Italian socialist Antonio Gramsci (1971) called hegemony. To do so, we believe that leftist thinkers need to find ground where they can work together. Through a focus on penal abolition, something which is present in all of these socialist-inspired approaches, we believe there is such common ground (Scott, 2016). At a time when the far right is gaining ground across Europe, North America and elsewhere around the world, the need for socialists and anarchists to work together as part of a collective leftist struggle for freedom is as great as ever.

This volume (and its companion volume) have been long in the making. We are both former coordinators of the *European Group for the Study of Deviance and Social Control* (EG), which is one of the most established and well-known criminological forums in the world today. In our time as coordinators (David Scott, 2009–2012 and Emma Bell, 2012–2015), we noted that the values and praxis underscoring the EG very much reflected those of the kind of libertarian socialism and abolitionism that we would like to see rolled out more broadly in society (Scott, 2016). Together, we further elaborated on how these ideas might inform a 'nonpenal real utopia', which was inspired by the libertarian socialist thinker Erik Olin Wright, in the foundation volume of the EG journal, *Justice, Power, and Resistance*, which we co-founded in 2016 (Bell and Scott, 2016).

The long history of nonpenal real utopias, as well as that of abolitionist ideas more broadly, also became obvious to us in our teaching of critical issues relating to crime and punishment. When looking at historical figures and their ideas, we asked the following question: why was the work of Jeremy Bentham, Immanuel Kant and Cesare Beccaria so prominent, but not that of, say, Robert Owen, William Godwin or Peter Kropotkin? The latter match the former in terms of coherent and well-developed intellectual ideas, but whereas the former leave hierarchies of power unscathed, the latter offer a radical questioning of power and the penal rationale. Indeed, in preparatory work on the formulation of ideas around the development of an 'abolitionist real utopia' (Scott, 2013), one of us was introduced to the early abolitionist writings of Owen and Godwin by Barbara Goodwin in her book *Social Science and Utopia* (1978). This book, which also detailed the embryonic critical views of Charles Fourier and Saint-Simon on punishment, was influential in the development of this edited collection. This understanding of in-depth critical engagement between early socialists and what would now be known as abolitionism resulted in profuse readings of not only the key works of Owen and Godwin, but also of several other British socialists, notably the 'Owenites' and the imprisoned Chartists in the 1840s, and, perhaps most crucially of all, the complete works of anarchist thinkers like Peter Kropotkin.[2]

It is one thing for contemporary penal abolitionists to read early socialist and anarchist literature for inspiration; it is quite another to deliver an authoritative text which details the commitments, nuances and embryonic emergence of abolitionist sentiments in libertarian socialism. The authors of the chapters in this volume were all approached because of their expertise on a given anarchist or socialist thinker. We were conscious that if we were to propose a new set of readings on abolitionism, then any claims on its emergence must be fully understood with the context of that given thinker. We hope that you as a reader will be as delighted as we are to discover in the following chapters a detailed account of how people envisioned abolition long before the 'penal abolitionisms' of today. We hope that this modest contribution will lead to greater acknowledgement of penal abolitionism before the late 20th century and demonstrate how these embryonic formulations can help with the continued promotion and consolidation of abolitionist ideas.

We would like to take this opportunity to thank all the authors who have contributed to this volume for their hard work and willingness to reflect upon the contemporary relevance of a given thinker's work for penal abolitionist scholars and activists today. We would also like to thank all at Bristol University Press for their help in the production of this volume. We of course though take responsibility for any remaining errors.

Notes

[1] We also note several important papers on abolitionist history at the 'Abolitionism in history' ICOPA conference in Warsaw, Poland. These papers were later edited into a book published by Warsaw University Press in 1991.

[2] It is perhaps notable of his influence that Kropotkin is the only thinker with a dedicated chapter in each of the two volumes.

References

Bell, E. and Scott, D. (eds) (2016) *Non-penal Real Utopias: Foundation Volume of Justice, Power and Resistance*, Bristol: EG Press.

Goodwin, B. (1978) *Social Science and Utopia*, London: Harvester.

Gramsci, A. (1971) *Selections from the Prison Notebooks*, London: Lawrence & Wishart.

Kropotkin, P. (1924) *Ethics*, London: George Harrap & Co Ltd.

Ruggiero, V. (2010) *Penal Abolitionism*, Oxford: Clarendon Press.

Scott, D. (2013) 'Visualising an abolitionist real utopia: principles, policy and praxis', in M. Malloch and W. Munro (eds) *Crime, Critique and Utopia*, Basingstoke: Palgrave Macmillan, pp 90–113.

Scott, D. (2016) *Emancipatory Politics and Praxis: Essays for the European Group for the Study of Deviance and Social Control*, Bristol: EG Press.

Scott, D. (ed.) (2025) *Abolitionist Voices*, Bristol: Bristol University Press.

Van Swaaningen, R. (1997) *Critical Criminology: Visions from Europe*, London: Sage.

1

Abolitionism in Red and Black

Emma Bell and David Gordon Scott

Introduction

Socialists have long highlighted the harms of the prison place and the need for a different kind of world where human interactions and collective responses to human wrongdoing are grounded in a socialist ethic. When looking backwards, it is immediately evident that the writings of early socialist and anarchist thinkers – an *abolitionism in red and black*[1] – can, and do, speak to the present. Our aim in this volume is to 'to retrieve lost socialist voices, their histories, and their continuing legacy and relevance' in order to 'inspire political action today' (Bevir, 2011: 3). Abolitionist ideas and reasoning that originated in the 18th and 19th centuries[2] continue to speak to us because prisons and punishment are counterintuitive and stand in contradiction to many of our most cherished values and principles. When looking backwards at early socialist thought, there can be no doubt that similar moral values are central to objections to the penal rationale.

Critiques of iatrogenic penal harms and radical visions of a more just and equitable society can be found in the writings of socialists, anarchists and others engaged in emancipatory politics and praxis and the struggle for freedom and liberative justice the world over today (Coyle and Scott, 2021). Indeed, interest in penal abolitionism has had something of a revival in the 2020s, with many new books, articles and thinkers promoting its virtues. Yet, at the same time, many of these new advocates of penal abolitionism seem unaware of both its recent and its more ancient history. This is not to say that there were always organized movements, activists and scholars who self-defined as abolitionists as some do today, but rather that embryonic abolitionist ideas and sentiments date back many centuries and can be found in many different places. Those fixated on the present, and the writings of a small number of abolitionist thinkers who have become well known globally in the last couple of decades, to the exclusion of those who came before, are missing out on much wisdom from the past. This volume is intended for penal abolitionist activists and scholars engaging in emancipatory struggles today. It aims to help address a significant gap in abolitionist literature by turning back the clock so that we can read with fresh eyes some of the earliest abolitionist formulations.

Of course, we do not wish to pretend that by 'looking backwards', abolitionists today will find ready-made toolkits and theoretical concepts that will be a perfect fit for the present. The focus and content of abolitionisms at any moment in time will clearly reflect the given socioeconomic, political, geographical and institutionalized forms of legal coercion and state punishment. For example, many thinkers discussed in this volume were influenced by positivism (especially social positivism), which later became regarded in critical circles as morally problematic. Nonetheless, we remain convinced that learning about the sentiments, ideas and critical evaluative frameworks of abolitionists in the past can provide enormous inspiration in the present moment. Thinking critically about punishment has always entailed: the rejection of judgements rooted in blameworthiness; the identification of the relationship in practice between poverty and criminalization; and the questioning of state violence and the recognition that the state is the biggest facilitator of harm, suffering and premature death in a capitalist society. Looking backwards can help us to further strengthen penal abolitionism by acknowledging that many others in the past came to the same conclusions about the need to reject state coercion and its penal apparatus.

While there are different 'abolitionisms' (Scott, 2025), undoubtedly one of the most important historical 'roots' of penal abolitionism can be found in socialist and anarchist thought. Yet, as several of the chapters in the volume attest, the ideas of socialists and anarchists from the past are not always credited as such by penal abolitionist thinkers today. This volume aims to trace and place back in the spotlight these early embryonic abolitionist ideas. We hope that this will provide a stark reminder to radicals and ordinary rebels today that the critique of the penal rationale is a central plank in a 'libertarian socialist' project. The prison and, indeed, other forms of penal sanctions and legal coercion are anathema to socialist ethics and libertarian socialist visions of freedom. Commitment to the values of solidarity, kindness, love, mutuality and friendship in libertarian socialism means that the prison, as currently constituted, can have no place in a genuinely socialist society. The state should be stripped of its 'power to punish', and peace and safety should be achieved through alternative means that reflect socialist values, virtues and ethical principles.

This chapter is divided into four sections. The first section, 'Looking backwards', situates socialist, anarchist and penal abolitionist praxis within historical context, detailing some well-known examples of anti-prison protests and anarchist and socialist-inspired penal abolitionism from the 18th to the early 20th century. In section two, the chapter considers the argument that 'Punishment is a socialist issue'. This section explores not only how 'mainstream', statist and democratic socialism has a mixed relationship with penal abolitionism, but also the continuing significance of grassroots libertarian socialist and other penal abolitionist organizing today outside of the orbit of the state. The third section of the chapter explores 'The libertarian socialist tradition' by giving an overview of five key themes that are shared among anarchists, socialists and penal abolitionists: the critique of power; the critique of social and economic inequalities; the valorization of freedom; the importance of solidarity, mutual aid and cooperation; and a moral compass informed and evaluated by libertarian socialist ethics. Finally, the fourth section, 'Looking forward: socialist inspirations in red and black', concludes the chapter by arguing that socialists and anarchists working together is key to successfully challenging the penal rationale of the state in the future.

Looking backwards

One of the biggest concerns with the penal abolition movement today is that it has become susceptible to 'immediatism' – that is, an overfocus on the present at the expense of historical analysis. When the recent literature does engage with historical reflections, it largely focuses on the embedding of abolitionism in academia in Europe – as exemplified in the writings of Louk Hulsman, Nils Christie, Joe Sim, Barbara Hudson, Herman Bianchi and Thomas Mathiesen or in the more activist-orientated Quaker abolitionism in North America promoted by Ruth Morris and Faye Honey Knopp, among other notable figures. What is required to counter this tendency towards immediatism is something not so dissimilar to what Michel Foucault called the 'history of the present' – the consideration of historical abolitionist writings in the light of the present day.

Theories from 19th-century pioneers of socialism unequivocally demonstrate that problems like poverty and destitution are part and parcel of capitalism, and that when capitalism is rampant, it can subjugate, pillage and destroy whole nations in the name of 'civilization'. This much is well known, but what is less reflected upon is that many anarchist and socialist pioneers also identified similar aspects of domination, exploitation, alienation and dehumanization in state institutions of punishment. Though not all directly advocated immediate abolition of the prison (see Cox and Taylor, Chapter 5 in this volume; and Baldwin, Chapter 6 in this volume), many raised concerns that have been repeatedly rehearsed by abolitionists in the 21st century.

Developing a historical lens is crucial to understanding the present and imagining a better future because it is only by reflecting on testimonies, ideas and theories from the past that we can see clearly which harms of state punishment are enduring and permanent. In other words, an historical lens reveals to us what cannot be reformed and lays bare any claims to short-term exceptions. Just as libertarian socialists have over history called out the enduring and inherent harms of capitalist accumulation, they have also problematized the inherent and enduring harms of prisons, punitive detention and punishment.

Evidence abounds of direct action mobilized against the gaols, prisons and Houses of Correction in England in the 1700s. This was instigated by Jacobins and English radicals who made wider appeals to 'English liberty' and its associated rights and customs. Although predating fully fledged 'socialism', these interventions nonetheless indicate that popular justice movements have long been prepared to confront penal oppression head on.

For example, in February 1707 protesting handloom weavers broke into a common gaol at Taunton and released its prisoners; in 1731 extensive protests broke out at Fleet Prison after claims of cruelties and the removal of certain 'rights and privileges' of those detained; in May 1768 a crowd of hundreds attempted to break into Southwark Prison, London, in a failed attempt to free the imprisoned English radical parliamentarian John Wilkes; in June 1780 a crowd surpassing 500 broke into Clerkenwell Prison and successfully released all the prisoners during the infamous 'Gordon Riots' of that year (and indeed during these protests the crowd released prisoners from at least four other London prisons – New Prison, Surrey House of Correction, Kings Bench Prison and Borough Compter – while Newgate Prison, the Clink and the above-mentioned Fleet Prison were completely destroyed); in 1794 a debtors prison in Sheffield was broken open and all the prisoners released by anti-enclosure protestors; and in the late 1790s and early 1800s Sir Francis Burdett gained widespread popularity among the lower classes when he challenged the mass imprisonment of political radicals under repressive new laws, naming the prison the 'English Bastille'. His calls to 'pull down the Bastille' resulted in at least one attempt by a crowd of protestors to destroy the prison at Cold Bath Fields in August 1800.

The anti-prison protests continued well into the new century. A gaol at Rochdale was burned to the ground and its prisoners liberated in June 1808 by protesting Lancashire weavers. In 1816 more than 350 protestors broke into Bideford Prison, Dorset and released all the women prisoners held there. In May 1829, in an attempt to free 16 rebels imprisoned for attacking Rochdale cotton mills in a desperate attempt to raise wages, six protestors died instantly and it was believed at the time that a number of others died later of their wounds when soldiers guarding the Rope Street New Bailey Prison indiscriminately opened fire. Critiques of prisons, workhouses and the new police as unjust 'bastilles' endured well into the 1800s, perhaps the most well-known being those made by the English Chartists in the 1830s and 1840s. Bereft of the ideological veneer of reform and rehabilitation, prisons were clearly profoundly unpopular.

If there is still remarkably little scholarship or teaching courses which explore either penal abolitionist ideas or those of anarchist and early socialist thinkers which pre-date the late 20th century, this is understandable given that there are no easily accessible texts providing a detailed historically situated account of these ideas.[3] However, there are some accounts and reflections of the emergence of abolitionist-inspired social movements in Europe that are part of a libertarian socialist tradition. For example, from 1906 to 1917 an Anarchist Red Cross was formed to support anarchist political prisoners. In 1919 it was renamed the Anarchist Black Cross (ABC), which continues to function in several countries to this day. There are other examples too, with perhaps the most well-known being the promotion of explicitly penal abolitionist ideas by the Ukrainian peasant Nestor Makhno, who led the 'Makhnovist insurgency' from 1917 to 1921. The anarchist Makhnovist group famously declared in 1919 that all state forms of 'justice' were in fact unjust and should therefore be abolished (Skirda, 1982; see also Weide, Chapter 9 in this volume).

Further examples of abolitionist ideas can also be found among the anarchist collectives in Spain in the 1930s. From 1936 to 1939, their beliefs in mutualism and cooperation led them to look beyond statist responses to harmful behaviour in favour of community-based solutions. Of course, many anarchists had experience of prisons and their dire conditions, which may have also motivated their opposition. Even in the Republican militias, George Orwell was surprised to see that usual army discipline was rejected in favour of 'a democratic "revolutionary" type of discipline' which was more reliable since, rather than being based on fear, it was based on class loyalty. He noted that 'when a man refused to obey an order you did not immediately get him punished; you first appealed to him in the name of comradeship' (Orwell, 2002[1938]: 49).

In the US, socialist-inspired penal abolition was clearly intertwined with other struggles for liberation, notably the 'Black Radical Tradition' which encapsulates anti-slavery abolitionism, the civil rights and Black liberation movements (James, 2021). The Marxist-inspired Black Panthers and Black Liberation movement in the US in the 1960s and 1970s viewed the criminal justice system as inherently racist and regarded the prison system as a tool of oppression. True liberation and social justice could only be achieved by abolishing prison, thus reducing the power of the coercive state.

Scholarship of the preceding examples sadly remains underdeveloped, but the focus of this volume is somewhat different. It concentrates on abolitionist sentiments and ideas that either pre-date or emerge elsewhere to these well-known 20th-century socialist-inspired interventions. In so doing, it provides an even deeper insight into the history of penal abolition in the libertarian socialist tradition. Its aim is to bring together in one volume a collection of papers of key historical socialists and anarchists (or those closely associated with these traditions through their life, work or legal interventions) who have visualized a world without prisons and punishment as constituted and defended at the time of writing. Each of the thinkers has played a part in *envisioning abolition* – laying down the foundations for the development of penal abolition. The question we ask is not so much whether there were abolitionist ideas before self-proclaimed penal abolitionists, but rather why so many radical thinkers in the 19th and early 20th centuries came to advocate the abolition or radical transformation of prisons and punishment. In so doing, this volume helps to visibilize the currently hidden, long and nuanced history of penal abolitionism in socialist and anarchist thought, and calls for the ending of legal coercion, domination and repression.

Punishment is a socialist issue

It would perhaps come as no surprise to anarchists and other early socialists that the capitalist state in the 20th and 21st centuries continued to deepen its commitment to legal coercion. Nor would they be astonished by a greater recourse to the 'social evil' of state punishment in times of increasing social and economic inequalities. However, they might be bitterly disappointed when such penal rhetoric is advanced by ostensibly left-wing parties.

In 1993, under the headline 'Crime is a socialist issue', the British weekly news magazine the *New Statesman* published an article penned by future Prime Minister Tony Blair, in which he famously declared that the Labour Party 'should be tough on crime and tough on the underlying causes of crime' (Blair, 1993). In doing so, he borrowed from 'left realist' scholars in criminology who claimed that the left has often tended to play down the harmful effects of 'crime', particularly on the poorest communities, and that it was time that it directed more energy to tackling the problem (Lea and Young, 1993).

In practice, New Labour in government from 1997 to 2010 was to directly contradict the arguments of early anarchists and socialists that the 'crimes' of the poor were the result of an impoverished social environment and ignorance, and that socialists should be tough on social and economic inequalities rather than people. Indeed, it downplayed the emphasis on the structural causes of 'crime' (which had preoccupied the left realists) in favour of increasingly harsh punishment (Bell, 2011). Under Blair's leadership, the UK became one of the principal nations leading the so-called 'punitive turn' in penal policy across the Global North (Garland, 2001; Pratt et al, 2005. Scott, 2013b), characterized by a rapid expansion of the prison population, the displacement of proportionality as a guide to sentencing, the restriction of civil liberties, the return of the public shaming of offenders, increased police numbers and a halt to prison reform efforts.

There has been no reversal of this 'punitive turn', even if there has been a small drop in prison population rates in countries like the US in the past decade (World Prison Brief, 2024). Imprisonment rates in many countries remain considerably higher than they were 40 years ago, with the US continuing to have the largest prison population in the world. Globally, over 11 million people are currently incarcerated (World Prison Brief, 2024). In the UK Keir Starmer as current leader of the Labour Party shows no signs of reversing punitive trends, despite a landslide electoral win in June 2024. Indeed, he has echoed Blair in stating 'fighting crime is a Labour cause' because it is primarily 'working class communities who have to live under its shadow', and he promised to make 'law and order' a priority for the labour government. In the US too, while former Democratic President Joe Biden initially criticized over-incarceration, his record on tackling this issue has been judged disappointing (Grawert and Richmond, 2022) and the Democrats have been accused of 'sudden silence on criminal justice reform' in the face of accusations from the Republican Party that they were 'soft on crime' (Burns, 2024).

In continental Europe, the picture is similar. A 2013 survey of 12 European countries from Spain to Russia identified an intensification of punitive trends, even if these were selective, targeted at certain categories of the population, notably migrants (Ruggiero and Ryan, 2013). Even countries such as the Netherlands, once considered as 'a beacon of tolerance' witnessed the assertion of a more punitive attitude, not only towards serious 'crime' but also towards minor offences, and a shift away from social welfare measures towards those that tend to exclude and incapacitate (Boone and van Swaaningen, 2013). Across Europe, 'anxiety entrepreneurs' in politics and the media helped to lead a punishment boom fuelled by moral outrage against those deemed as 'other', regardless of the actual dangerousness of their behaviour (Ruggiero, 2013).

Over a decade later, these trends in the main have only magnified. There are of course some contradictions and anti-punitive countertrends, but while years of austerity could have encouraged trends towards decarceration in an attempt to drive down public spending, it would seem that they have instead intensified the political need to scapegoat marginalized groups, as 'security populism' (Hamilton, 2022) has become de rigueur. Migrants in particular have borne the brunt of authoritarian trends as penal populism has become 'bordered', even in countries such as Norway that might previously have been considered as outliers resisting the 'punitive turn' (Todd-Kvam, 2019).

The dominance of authoritarianism

Yet the story is not one that can be just reduced to that of betrayal by state socialists. The rise of the far right has undoubtedly played a role in fuelling these trends, whether or not far-right parties are actually in power. Even where left or centre-left politicians in government attempt to go against punitive trends, they face considerable opposition. In Spain, Prime Minister Pedro Sánchez faced not just far-right protests but also considerable judicial opposition to legislation introduced by his government in November 2023 to provide an amnesty for over 300 Catalan politicians, activists and protesters facing criminal charges for their involvement in the disputed Catalan independence referendum of 2017 (Gilmartin, 2023).

Self-proclaimed 'centrist' administrations, such as that of Emmanuel Macron in France, have placed particular emphasis on law and order in an attempt to snatch the issue from the right, particularly from Jordan Bardella's far-right Rassemblement national. In 2023, France's prison population reached its highest-ever peak at over 75,000 people incarcerated – over 11 per cent higher than a decade previously – leading to a crisis of overpopulation (148.5 per cent capacity) (Ministère de la justice, 2023). This rise has been driven primarily by increased criminalization, fast-track sentencing, the lengthening of prison sentences and the increased use of pre-trial detention (OIP, 2024). While the increase in the prison population pre-dates Macron's first election (in 2017), the current President has adopted a particularly tough stance towards law and order, notably during the *gilets jaunes* protests of 2018–2019 and the 'riots' which erupted following the fatal shooting of 17-year-old Nahel Merzouk in the Paris suburb of Nanterre in late June 2023. Police repression of the *gilets jaunes* movement was unprecedented, even during the disturbances of 1968. On a single day of protest (8 December 2018), 1,300 people were taken in for police questioning while 900 were held in custody (Bantigny, 2019: 51).

In February 2019, the United Nations (UN) High Commissioner of Human Rights denounced the heavy-handed police response to the *gilets jaunes* protests as a threat to the right to freedom of peaceful assembly. UN experts criticized in particular 'the high number of arrests and detentions, searches and confiscations of demonstrators' possessions' and the 'serious injuries [that] have been caused by a disproportionate use of so-called "non-lethal" weapons like grenades and defensive bullets or "flashballs"' (OHCHR, 2019). Following the 2023 'riots', 742 people were sentenced to prison (Dupond-Moretti, 2023), fines for young people violating curfews were increased from €150 to €750, and municipal police powers were strengthened (France Info, 2023).

Mainstream socialist voices

It would seem that right-wing discourses on the application of the criminal law are dominant, drowning out alternative approaches that push for decarceration, justice divestment and welfare investment. Nonetheless, alternative voices have not been entirely silenced and can still be detected, in other places, in anarchist and socialist-inspired grassroots movements and academic work. Even in the political mainstream, a few isolated voices are challenging punitive state responses to 'crime', seeking to shift the focus from 'crime' to punishment. In doing so, they are (largely unwittingly) unearthing a long socialist tradition which regards punitive state reactions to what is commonly understood as 'crime' as the problem rather than the solution to harmful behaviour. This is important. Not only can these socialist voices, even if marginalized, light a candle for justice in the present; their words and actions can also be a spark for a socialist fire to come.

For instance, Democratic Congresswoman Alexandria Ocasio-Cortez has questioned punitive responses to 'crime' that focus on policing and incarceration, notably supporting 'The People's Justice Guarantee' introduced to the House of Representatives in 2019 by Democratic member Ayanna Pressley which called for the decriminalization of sex work and drug use, an end to the death penalty, and to mandatory minimum sentences and life sentences without parole (Ocasio-Cortez, 2024). In voicing support for prison abolition on Twitter (Ocasio-Cortez, 2019), Ocasio-Cortez was connecting with the movement for penal abolition which has been gaining in momentum over the past decade or more. Her position was not entirely at odds with the Democratic Party platform, although this fell short of calling for abolition. Indeed, the Party's 2020 platform promised to end mandatory minimum sentences and criticized police violence and high rates of imprisonment, notably for young people (ACLU, 2020).

Although the Democrats in power have been much less radical, this stance represents an encouraging shift in discourse from the 'tough on crime' Clinton years. It is a position supported by the Democratic Governor of California, Gavin Newsom. Since assuming office in 2019, he has closed two state prisons, plans to close two more by 2025 and has promised to transform San Quentin state prison into a rehabilitation centre in order to pursue 'true rehabilitation, justice, and safer communities' and create 'a new model for safety and justice – the California Model – that will lead the nation' (Newsom, 2023). Although this plan falls short of abolitionist campaign groups' demands to close ten state penitentiary institutions by 2025 (CURB, 2024), Newsom's discourse and policy nonetheless signal a recognition that punitive carceral logic is being challenged. Beyond the Democratic Party, in 2021 the National Committee of the United States Green Party voted to endorse the '#No New Jails' movement and to support campaigns for prison abolition (Green Party US, 2021).

There are also some further signs that abolitionist logics are gaining some traction in political parties in Europe, even though they remain marginal. In 2021 the Greens in the European Parliament organized a debate entitled 'Are prisons obsolete? From prison reform to prison abolition'. Although the issue is marginal to the political alliance's policies, this does at least demonstrate some awareness of the problematic nature of incarceration. The French Green Party, Europe écologie les verts, does not support prison abolition, but it is committed to policies that have a decarceral thrust – for instance, the decriminalization of offences linked to poverty and drug use, and the promotion of restorative justice and alternatives to prison (EELV, 2021). Jean-Luc Mélenchon, the left-wing presidential candidate from the left-wing party La France Insoumise, promised in his 2022 electoral manifesto to 'look beyond the carceral horizon towards reparation and rehabilitation' (Mélenchon, 2022). Alongside this was a debate in Houses of Parliament at Westminster in June 2019 calling for the abolition of child imprisonment. Sponsored by Emma Lewell-Buck, a Labour Party MP, the parliamentary debate was televised live on BBC Parliament, but was poorly attended by members of Parliament. Significantly, Lewell-Buck proposed in the debate that prison should be an option of absolute last resort for children and young people.

Voices from below

There are also dissenting voices from socialists, anarchists and others promoting the principles of penal abolition who are also (perhaps unwittingly) echoing voices from the past. These voices are situated outside the state, challenge reformist agendas and call for progressive social transformation. Prison abolition is not a single issue, but rather is part of a wider struggle for freedom, dignity and justice. The very legitimacy of state punishments and legal coercion are brought into question by abolitionists, and they are found wanting.

Operating beyond conventional politics, abolitionist activism is present in new social movements and in academia. In terms of social movements, this recent revival was first propelled by the launch of *Critical Resistance* and other anti-violence and abolitionist grassroots movements in the US in the late 1990s, and in more recent times by global campaigns relating to Black Lives Matter following the killing of George Floyd in May 2020. These protests not only inspired a new generation of abolitionist activists and scholars, but also led to real change, especially with regard to the police. Following the killing of Floyd, Camden, NJ police chief Joseph D. Wysocki not only joined Black Lives Matters protests against racist policing but also effectively abolished the Camden Police Department. While the intervention of Wysocki was merely a 'starting over' and a 'resetting reform' of the state police, it sent a message that radical change in policing policy and practice, and thus the wider coercive apparatus of the capitalist state, was conceivable.[4]

Encouragingly, there are other important sites of activism in the US. For example, the Incarcerated Workers Organizing Committee (IWOC) is an outreach organization of the Industrial Workers of the World (IWW). The IWW (the Wobblies) was conceived in 1905 as 'one big union' for all workers around the world and is firmly grounded in the politics and praxis of revolutionary socialism. The IWW is of course closely associated with one of its founders, the famous socialist campaigner Eugene V. Debs, who promoted prison abolition (see Phillips, Chapter 13 in this volume). One of the tactics of the IWW was to question the exclusive recourse of the powerful to the language of 'law and order', calling for workers to closely adhere to rules and regulations in the workplace as a way of resisting capitalist exploitation. There was a minor revival of the IWW in the US and elsewhere in the mid-2010s, resulting in the formation of the IWOC (Incarcerated Workers Organizing Committee). IWOC initially attempted to form a prisoner union in the US, and similar attempts were made elsewhere, including the UK. The IWOC aims to further the revolutionary goals of the IWW on global emancipation, amplify the voice of the incarcerated, foster class solidarity and connect to the struggles of the incarcerated against penal slavery, encourage prisoners to challenge other forms of oppression (such as patriarchy and white supremacy) and challenge the overcriminalization of marginalized groups (such as Black people) and the workings of the 'prison industrial complex'.

The Committee to Abolish Prison Slavery (CAPS) in the US is also an abolitionist activist campaign group grounded in socialist principles. Making direct connections between penal labour, servitude and slavery, CAPS point out that while prison labour is not often described as slavery, it shares many of its characteristics: coerced labour; threat of violence and intimidation; little or no financial renumeration for labour; and physical constraints or severe restrictions on freedom of movement. Prison labour cannot be voluntary or chosen and the workers are exploited in the interests of large companies and corporations. CAPS also hypothesizes that prisons and other forms of state detention are a way of managing the relative surplus population – that prisons are a way of containing the unemployed and other nonproductive members of the wider population.

As in the US, penal abolitionism rarely features in formal political debate in Europe, but there are pan-European grassroots campaigns against prisons. For example, in 2016 the European Prison Observatory published a 'Manifesto for a new penal culture' in which it called for a replacement of retributive justice with preventative justice, the decriminalization of drug use and the use of alternative sentences which are 'freed from the necessity to simulate a retributive loss of freedom' (European Prison Observatory, 2016). Although the organization is not strictly an abolitionist organization, focusing as it does on human rights in prison, its work can help to inform abolitionist logic. Other small groups can be found around Europe, for example, the Forum for Prison Abolition in Copenhagen, Denmark,[5] which boldly asserts that 'humane prisons do not exist'. In the UK, the Empty Cages Collective/

Community Action on Prison Expansion campaigns against the existence of the prison, as well as more specifically against prison building across the four nations. Specifically in Scotland, prison expansion is being challenged today by the penal abolitionist group TAP (Together Against Punishment), whereas the English anti-slavery group Campaign Against Prison Slavery is inspired by the concept of the 'prison industrial complex', and works against labour exploitation in private prisons.[6] In the summer of 2024 a new penal abolitionist network was formed by activists and academics from both the North and Republic of Ireland, with the explicit intention of creating a new Irish abolitionist social movement.

While libertarian socialist organizing remains small, in a time when there has been a virtual collapse of mainstream leftist politics and a capitulation to the right-wing voices of law and order and legal repression, these grassroots movements provide a chink of light breaking through the punitive bleakness and a hope that a libertarian socialist revival is still possible.

Abolitionists in academia

Grassroots movements for abolition are complemented by anarchist and socialist-inspired scholarship. While socialist-inspired revolutionary abolitionist praxis remains on the margins, some libertarian socialist-, anarchist- and Marxist-inspired writings in academia have helped to fuel the growth of abolitionist grassroots activism in the last three decades (Scott, 2018).

Marxist- and anarchist-inspired 'abolitionism' began to emerge as part of academic disciplines from the late 1960s and early 1970s onwards. Thomas Mathiesen's (1974) *The Politics of Abolition* and Mike Fitzgerald and Joe Sim's (1979) *British Prisons* together highlighted the key foundational priorities of an explicitly Marxist abolitionism. Anarchist abolitionist ideas date back to a similar time, with influential criminologists such as Stanley Cohen reflecting on anarchist ideas in the late 1960s. Anarchist ideas were further popularized in academia in the 1970s and 1980s in the influential writings of Nils Christie (1977, 1981), Harold Pepinsky (1978) and a monograph by Larry Tift and Dennis Sullivan (1980) *The Struggle to Be Human,* which drew heavily upon the ideas of Kropotkin to question state coercion and violence.

Anarchist-inspired abolitionism in academia has continued to flourish (Cohen, 1988; Ferrell, 1998, 2021; Shantz, 2014), including from those addressing key issues such as nonpenal alternatives to domestic and sexual violence (Gaarder, 2009; see also Moore et al, 2014). The activism and later writings of Angela Y. Davis (2003) and Ruth Gilmore Wilson have also been hugely significant in influencing Marxist abolitionist scholarship across the globe.[7]

Academic scholarship grounded in libertarian socialist aspirations has not operated in a vacuum, but has often been directly connected to grassroots abolitionist movements. This has arisen in specific instances, but also in terms of organizing wider movements. As mentioned earlier, *Critical Resistance* arose through the interventions of Marxist and feminist scholars in the US (James, 2025). In Europe, the *Prison, Detention and Punishment Working Group* – an international network of academics, practitioners and activists working towards social justice, state accountability and decarceration – has also been grounded in emancipatory politics and praxis (Scott, 2016). Further, following a call for prison abolition in 2012 by Livio Ferrari and Massimo Pavarini in their manifesto entitled 'No prison', a book of papers by abolitionist scholar-activists was subsequently published translated into seven European languages, notably into English in 2018 by the EG Press, the publisher of the *European Group for the Study of Deviance and Social Control* (Ferrari and Pavarini, 2018). This led to the launch of a European-wide abolitionist movement in 2019[8] which reflects socialist principles.

This left-wing focus on penal abolition has certainly helped to frame *punishment* rather than '*crime*' as a socialist issue, yet the movement and its literature tends to draw primarily on the recent past, thus neglecting important links to abolitionist writings of the earlier socialist traditions. By shining a light on this literature, this volume seeks to open a space for considerations on how such an approach to abolition can be used to inspire a new generation of abolitionist thinking grounded in these traditions. This would provide the greatest antidote to the punitive consensus that has spread its tentacles around parliamentary parties of all political hues, and remind us of what real socialism looks like. This likely embodies a very different form of political organization and conception of the true meaning of democracy than that found in liberal democracies. Revisiting the socialist thought of the 19th and early 20th centuries can help correct our course, reinvigorate the calls for socialist-inspired notions of freedom and justice, and remind us that real change comes from below rather than some self-proclaimed liberal political elite.

The libertarian socialist tradition

We consider that the 'lost socialist voices' that have most relevance to penal abolition are those which can be associated with the tradition which can be termed as libertarian socialism.[9] We understand libertarian socialism as a non-authoritarian form of socialism that has drawn inspiration from democratic socialism, anarchism and Marxism. This is a plural tradition that brings together both anarchists and those who were often disparagingly referred to (notably by Engels) as 'utopian socialists'. Rather than seeing this diverse inspiration for socialism as a weakness, we consider it to be a strength. Despite their differences, anarchists such as Willam Godwin, Peter Kropotkin, Errico Malatesta, Leo Tolstoy and Emma Goldman shared much in common with early socialists such as Robert Owen and William Morris.[10] Their key areas of concern were hierarchies and elitism: the centralization of power and the corruption of the powerful; domination and authoritarianism; dehumanized relationships, slavery and the negation of human spirituality; the coercion and violence of law and punishment; and the inevitable generation of harm, injury and death in the prison place and elsewhere. Consequently, they embraced the principles of association, cooperation and egalitarianism in seeking to advance individual freedom.

Libertarian socialist visions of freedom and justice are grounded in participatory democracy; community values of inclusion, tolerance, diversity and autonomy; human flourishing and dignity; reciprocal awareness, mutuality and ethical responsibility; and social transformations facilitating a more equitable redistribution of wealth. There is no contradiction between principles of mutualism and individualism. Many anarchists, for example, 'would find it quite acceptable to call themselves individualists in everyday life, syndicalists in wanting self-management at work, and communists in looking forward to a society in which goods are shared in common' (Marshall, 2008: 11). Both early socialists and anarchists could thus largely subscribe to Pinta and Berry's definition of libertarian socialism as:

> an anti-parliamentary disposition, rejecting the formal political democracy (as opposed to, and distinct from, economic democracy) of bourgeois parliaments or participation in electoral activity as effective methods for advancing social change; working-class self-activity and direct action as both a method for circumventing mediating bureaucracies, argued to stifle initiative and channel grievances into acceptable areas, and as a way to forge solidarities and create a sense of collective workers' power. (Pinta and Berry, 2012: 298)

Although a tension remains between interstitial strategies and those of exploiting contradictions in state policies, it is necessary to read early formulations of anarchism and socialism together rather than in isolation or as competing political philosophies. They both fit firmly into the tradition of libertarian socialism.

Libertarian socialism fits quite naturally with penal abolitionist perspectives. Indeed, both challenge privilege, power and social and economic inequalities; expose human suffering in its many different manifestations; provide a platform for those people whose voices are elsewhere denied; and work towards profound social transformations that can promote the genuine freedom and fulfilment of humanity for all. Abolitionism itself might be regarded as a broad-based socialist liberation movement aiming to emancipate the powerless and dehumanized.[11] Like 'utopian [early] socialism' and anarchism (and autonomist Marxists and even some thinkers categorized as democratic socialists), abolitionism entails the search for non-authoritarian ways in which the consequences of 'crime' and troublesome conduct can be minimized.

Furthermore, libertarian socialists are also likely to share a similar approach to human nature. No libertarian socialist would regard humans as being born naturally 'evil' and thus inevitably in need of repressive controls (though some might be tempted to occasionally deploy the theories of individual pathology in exceptional circumstances to explain the horrendous behaviour of a very small number of individuals – see also Forero Cuellar, Chapter 10 in this volume, for further discussion). Rather, they would emphasize the lack of radical differences between humans and the importance of social conditions in shaping human conduct and character. Sometimes referred to as the 'homo-duplex', human beings can be socialized into altruism and values of solidarity or individual selfishness depending on the environment (see, for example, the socialist writings of Émile Durkheim for the classic statement on this).

There are five key themes that indicate the intimacy and interconnections between the libertarian socialist tradition and the idea of penal abolition. It is important to note that the thinkers discussed in this book largely came to abolitionist conclusions from their commitment to the ethical and political frameworks of socialism and anarchism.[12] This implies two significant things: first, that there is considerable historical overlap between what we now refer to as abolitionism and the ethics and politics of libertarian socialism; and, second, that through grasping and understanding the key principles and ideas of libertarian socialism, a pathway opens up to the promotion of penal abolition. As indicated previously, if a return to the abolitionist ideas of the early socialists and anarchists is a way of shining a light on the corruption of socialism in mainstream liberal democratic leftist parties who have embraced the punitive consensus, reflections and engagement with the ideas of libertarian socialism might also help to strengthen the foundation and commitment to penal abolitionism and the realization of a genuine socialism.

The critique of power

The first key theme that links libertarian socialism to abolitionism is its critique of power. Libertarian socialism is inherently suspicious of power. As the anarchists warned, 'beware the trappings of power, beware bureaucracy, and ensure that authority is always distrusted' (Newman, 2005: 21). Power should neither be concentrated in the hands of the elites nor in the hands of the state. Indeed, forms of socialism that led to the latter were virulently denounced by anarchists such as Emma Goldman who regarded Stalin's dictatorship as more absolute than any tsar's had been (Marshall, 2008: 400; see also Weiss, Chapter 15 in this volume). The principal problem with concentrations of power is that it is almost always wielded in favour of those who hold it. As Kropotkin argued, legislation that is enacted by the elites who wield power through the state is always made in the interests of those elites (see Weide, Chapter 9 in this volume). As such, it entirely fails to prevent 'crime', ignoring the social harms, illegalities, corruption and wrongdoing of the powerful. As Ruby Tuke points out in this volume, William Godwin argued that legal institutions – through their support of private wealth and property – are criminogenic. Furthermore, far from preventing violence, the criminal law, as the instrument of the powerful, only serves to perpetuate it. This became very clear to William Morris, who regarded the law as a mere instrument of class domination and denounced the 'false universality of bourgeois law' (see Holland, Chapter 7 in this volume). After witnessing police brutality during the events of 'Bloody Sunday' in 1887 when four protesters demanding the release of Irish nationalist William O'Brien from jail were killed and 200 were hospitalized, Morris was horrified, writing: 'The greatest humbug which Sunday's events have laid bare is the protection afforded by the law to the humblest citizen' (quoted by Bevir, 2011: 93; see also Holland, Chapter 7 in this volume). He was also horrified by the violence demonstrated by Gladstone's liberal government in both Ireland and Alexandria (Bevir, 2011: 92).

Similarly, the state's repression of political opponents in the US served to galvanize influential thinkers like Emma Goldman, Eugene V. Debs and Clarence Darrow against the legal system of their time. Witnessing the violent repression of the striking factory workers in Haymarket, Chicago in 1886, and the subsequent refusal of politicians, even critics of the system such as Governor of Illinois John Altgeld, to pardon the leaders, both Goldman and Darrow became convinced that the law was wielded by the powerful in order to maintain their domination over the labouring classes (see Weiss, Chapter 15 in this volume; Kersten, Chapter 14 in this volume). Debs was also galvanized in his abolitionist convictions by the state's coercive response to the 1894 Pullman strike by railway workers (see Phillips, Chapter 13 in this volume).

The questioning of power is also central to contemporary abolitionist thought (Scott and Sim, 2023). Penal abolitionists not only question existing power structures that accept the state's 'truth' about 'crime' and punishment, which meant, in reality, working-class criminality to the exclusion of the harms of power, but also shine a spotlight on the institutionalized indifference of the state to pain and suffering of prisoners.

The critique of inequality

The libertarian socialists' critique of power necessarily led them to focus on a critique of social and economic inequalities and a commitment to greater equality and equity in society. The liberal democratic state which fails to challenge – and indeed facilitates – concentrations of power cannot possibly oversee an equal or equitable system of justice, rendering equality before the law a myth. Indeed, the anarchists noted that 'equality before the law ... does not mean the end of injustice, for all people could be treated with equal unfairness under unjust laws' (Marshall, 2008: 48). Such concerns are clear in the writings of Gori and Malatesta (see Manfredi, Chapter 12 in this volume; Turcato, Chapter 11 in this volume). Substantive equality can only be possible when power is diffused as far as possible throughout society, and the administration of justice taken out of the hands of the state. Before tackling inequality linked to material resources, early socialists and anarchists thus believed in the necessity of reorganizing power relations (Newman, 2005: 145). With notable exceptions (Godwin, Owen and Fourier advocated sexual freedom and rejected the institution of marriage), they tended to ignore the idea of gender equality, but they did play an important role in highlighting inequalities of class.

In common with contemporary abolitionists, the early libertarian socialists understood that law enforcement and mechanisms of social control play a decisive role in maintaining structural divisions. Anarchists seemed to be particularly well attuned to this (see Forero Cuellar, Chapter 10 in this volume; Turcato, Chapter 11 in this volume; Weiss, Chapter 15 in this volume; Hough, Chapter 16 in this volume). They saw how criminal justice reinforces the structural inequalities that characterize our socially unjust and unequal societies, given that its energies are focused predominately on controlling marginalized and powerless people whose 'crimes' are relatively harmless, while failing to exercise control over powerful actors who are responsible for many of the most harmful behaviours. For Gori, the injustices perpetrated by the law reflected perfectly the injustices of society (see Manfredi, Chapter 12 in this volume).

Also, in common with contemporary abolitionists, the early socialists and anarchists considered inequality and the conditions of poverty and human debasement that it entailed to be a source of 'crime'. The writings of Gori, Malatesta, Carpenter, Kropotkin, Owen and anarchists such as Mella, Goldman and Berkman show this (see Manfredi; Turcato; Baldwin; Weide; Siméon; Forero Cuellar, Weiss, and Hough, this volume). For Gori, 'the seed of crime was born from the property system' (Manfredi, Chapter 12 in this volume). Thus, the solution to criminality was not imprisonment, but the fundamental reordering of society to ensure that power (and thus wealth) was distributed more equally. Indeed, both of these cojoined traditions consider social inequalities and social injustice to be the most significant problems we face. Even when looking at interpersonal and relational conflicts, it is necessary to consider broader structural and political contexts and to propose solutions to harmful behaviour based on *equality, equity* and *social justice* rather than *penal repression*. Advocating change in the penal system cannot be disconnected from a demand for radical change at a societal level. New nonpenal ways of resolving conflicts, troubles and difficulties are needed not only for those problematic behaviours currently processed by the criminal law but also to address the harms of power and interpersonal abuses, such as sexual violence, corporate harms, environmental destruction and state-sanctioned killings – problems and conflicts which are largely neglected by the criminal law and the penal system (Hillyard and Tombs, 2004).

The commitment to equity and socialist diversity is also important here. Equity is enshrined in the socialist ideal of 'from each according to their ability, to each according to their need' (a notion which was perhaps first expressed by Étienne-Gabriel Morelly in 1755, but was popularized by Karl Marx more than a century later in his *Critique of the Gotha Programme*). Thus, whereas both libertarian socialists and abolitionists have questioned 'structural inequalities', the simple promotion of 'equality' as the solution – whether that be equality of opportunity or indeed the equal distribution of the social product – will not satisfy the demands of a libertarian socialist conception of freedom or justice. Libertarian socialists recognize that people are different and that they have different needs. Given the widespread nature of human diversity, treating everyone the same paradoxically means not treating them equally.

This diversity of human life is something which can strengthen a society and lead to new innovations and ways of thinking. For penal abolitionists, the necessity of equity and accepting that people have different and diverse needs is illustrated in the institutionalized response to 'crime'. Legal punishments, especially the prison, are on the face of it rooted in equality – the equal deprivation of liberty, services, goods, relationships and so on for everyone. Yet they systematically fail to rehabilitate because they are grounded in the 'batch' approach according to which one model or approach to rehabilitation is deployed for categories of prisoners irrespective or their subjective experiences and needs. When reflecting on what should be done in response to harms, wrongdoing, problematic and troublesome behaviours, the prison will always fail because it cannot meet the second aspect of the libertarian socialist motto 'to each according to their need'. The prison is a one-solution-fits-all approach (Scott and Codd, 2010). Indeed, for Emma Goldman, despite the boasts of reformers prisons failed on every count (see Weiss, Chapter 15 in this volume).

The commitment to freedom

A commitment to equality and equity goes hand in hand with a commitment to freedom, since freedom is considered as meaningless unless it is available to all. For the libertarian socialists, it was thus only genuine equality that could give true meaning to freedom: 'on this view a socialist was a liberal who really meant it' (Wright, 1987: 26). Their focus on freedom naturally led them to reject all forms of coercion (legal or otherwise), whether from the state or from public opinion. For example, the 'method of freedom' is central to the writings of Malatesta (see Turcato, Chapter 11 in this volume). Coercion arises when someone is forced to submit to the will of another without approval or consent. The use of coercive powers always raises moral questions because they harm people and threaten human rights, dignity and the socialist conceptions of freedom. The recipient of coercion is prevented from performing actions of their choice and (possibly also) compelled to act in ways which are not of their choosing. Coercive powers can be legal. Indeed, coercion is often considered an essential component of the criminal law and its enforcement. For Malatesta and Kropotkin and others committed to living a life without the threat or fear of coercion, this has led to calls for the abolition of the state itself (see Weide, Chapter 9 in this volume; Turcato, Chapter 11 in this volume).

It is important to recognize that when referring to the critique of coercion, the concern is with what might be termed 'negative freedoms'. 'Negative freedoms' are about the removal or constraints placed upon freedoms through (state) coercion. The idea of freedom is clearly something that requires the removal of oppression and domination (such as in historical systems of slavery). In contrast to this, there is also the notion of 'positive freedoms' (Berlin, 1958). Here freedom means the ability to choose and determine how we live our lives. To achieve this requires more than just the removal of something; it requires the fulfilment of socialist-inspired social policies and institutions. Freedom means the ending of all forms of subjugation, domination and exploitation, and the creation of a world which facilitates human wellbeing and opportunities for all people to realize their full potential (Scott, 2020).

While some early libertarian socialists such as Godwin and Morris thought that the weight of public opinion would be more efficient than the law to prevent deviant behaviour, this would not be experienced as coercion since, in a state of freedom and equality in which power was widely distributed, the individual interest would become synonymous with the social interest (see Holland, Chapter 7 in this volume). Moral education was frequently posited as an alternative to coercion (see, for example, Tuke, Chapter 2 in this volume; Cox and Taylor, Chapter 5 in this volume; Turcato, Chapter 11 in this volume; and Kersten, Chapter 14 in this volume). For instance, Godwin highlighted the need to 'involve the offender understanding and acknowledging the consequences of their actions on the victim, their community and on themselves' (Tuke, Chapter 2 in this volume). This entailed the acceptance of a responsibility to deal with harmful behaviour on the part of both society and the offender, demonstrating that freedom was not thought to be incompatible with responsibility – the exercise of individual freedom was to be constrained by the need to have regard to the welfare of the community as a whole. This perhaps chimes with the anarchist aspiration to 'communal individuality' (Marshall, 2008: 403; see also Siméon, Chapter 3 in this volume).

Solidarity and the belief in community cooperation and responsiveness

For libertarian socialists, cooperation and solidarity are to always be favoured over coercion. The commitment to solidary is abundantly clear in a number of chapters in this volume, both in those inspired by anarchism (such as Forero Cuellar, Chapter 10 in this volume) or socialism (such as the chapter by Phillips, Chapter 13 in this volume). It is through cooperation that power can be equally or equitably shared and the needs of individuals and the community reconciled. This entails adopting a positive view of human nature, as the Russian anarchist Peter Kropotkin did when he asserted that mutual aid was much more important than competition when it came to the evolution of species (Kropotkin, 1905; Spade, 2020; see also Weide, Chapter 9 in this volume). Indeed, Kropotkin believed that all societies were originally based on principles of mutual aid and that these were wholly compatible with individual freedom. As Marshall asserts, 'perhaps his most important insight was that only a genuine community can allow the full development of the free individual' (Marshall, 2008: 338). This entails a commitment to radical and participatory democracy which involves all members of society in decision-making processes.

The libertarian socialist belief in cooperation over competition has important implications for how societies should deal with problematic behaviour. It entails a move away from a focus on blame and exclusion towards understanding and inclusion. We find this idea in the work of early socialists such as Robert Owen (see Siméon, Chapter 3 in this volume) and pioneers of anarchism. Tolstoy and St John believed that the creation of a new society committed to communal utopianism would provide the opportunity for personal transformation (see Zorin, Chapter 4 in this volume; Cox and Taylor, Chapter 5 in this volume). Together with Carpenter and Morris, St John considered deterrence based on fear to be futile – the desire to participate fully in the community in a positive way would be a far stronger determinant of 'good' behaviour (see Cox and Taylor, Chapter 5 in this volume; Baldwin, Chapter 6 in this volume; and Holland, Chapter 7 in this volume). In his work on mutualism, anarchist Joseph Proudhon (1989) addressed the issue of justice and social harm. He grounded his notions of justice in respect, inherent dignity and guaranteed, mutually reciprocal relations. Citizens had a duty to protect the dignity of their neighbour and ensure that there was 'natural harmony'. However, Proudhon also recognized that conflict and troubles would be inevitable.

Proudhon, himself imprisoned for three years where he experienced solitary confinement and 'forced relationality' (Guenther, 2016), where his health was broken in the long term, was an early embryonic penal abolitionist. For him, no authority had the right to punish: punishment has nothing to do with justice; it is instead merely a barbaric form of vengeance. He was against penal servitude and argued that punishment was symbolic of the moral problems regarding inequality and injustice. He believed there was a need to replace penal discipline with the morality of justice (Hyman, 1979). The ethical demands of justice required that conflicts be handled through nonviolent methods, such as reparations.

'Utopian socialists' (or early socialists as they are now often referred to) such as Morris also advocated such responses to harmful behaviour, notably encouraging offenders who are deemed to have transgressed the ideal of free cooperation to accept therapeutic intervention and forms of reparations and redress to society (see Holland, Chapter 7 in this volume). Indeed, anarchists like Tolstoy firmly believed in the capacity of even the most violent criminals for moral redemption (see Zorin, Chapter 4 in this volume). For Guyau, this could never be achieved through the infliction of pain and coercion, but only through benevolence and what he described as 'grace', which would enable people to exercise free will on the path to salvation (see Testa, Chapter 8 in this volume).

Such thinking has been adopted by many contemporary abolitionists who favour minimally coercive community-based solutions to offending (see, for example, Bianchi, 1994). As Louk Hulsman (1986) highlighted, this entails learning to think beyond 'crime and punishment' – to decolonize ourselves of the language of penal repression, domination and authoritarianism. This of course has striking parallels with insights of Tolstoy (see Zorin, Chapter 4 in this volume). Though Hulsman does not seem to directly draw on the writings of Tolstoy, the moral sentiments of both are very similar. For Hulsman (1986), we must learn to take troubles, conflicts and individual and social problems seriously without falling into a punitive trap – to abolish the repressive state apparatus and replace it with assistance for conflict resolution and other 'radical alternatives' that help people in the real world.

In an important recent contribution, Dean Spade (2020) revisits Kropotkin's ideas about *mutual aid* in the 21st century. He argues that at a grassroots level, mutual aid is essential for building solidarity and an abolitionist liberation movement. Mutual aid is essential not only for libertarian socialist collective forms of organizing and protest, but it is also necessary if there is to be a sustained critical engagement that can effectively contest power. Mutual aid today means grounding abolitionist praxis, solidarity and ethics of care within struggles against penal injustice and the individualizing logic of neoliberal capitalism. Mutual aid is the social cement that can keep a movement together (Spade 2020). The work of Spade (2020) indicates that there is still much that Kropotkin (1905, 1924) has to offer when contemplating community responsiveness (see Weide, Chapter 9 in this volume).

The libertarian socialist belief in cooperation and mutualism certainly leads us to think about 'crime' differently. Dominant conceptions of 'crime' and 'criminal conduct' exclude many forms of harmful behaviour and provide legitimacy to existing power relations and the penal apparatus of the state. As Darrow noted, 'crime was a construction of the rich to oppress the poor' (cited by Kersten, Chapter 14 in this volume). Alternatively, the mutualist focus on what is best for society as a whole rather than on what is best for the state and the elites entails shifting one's gaze beyond those harms defined as 'crimes' by the state towards all forms of harmful behaviour that impact upon the collective. This allows for a focus on social harms rather than 'criminal harms', which in turn allows for consideration of social policy responses and welfare interventions in reducing the amount of harm in society. Ultimately this entails tackling all social, economic or psychological forms of harm. For contemporary abolitionists, it is more constructive to analyse all harms together rather than bracketing off and focussing exclusively on criminal harms. As Forero Cuellar (Chapter 10 in this volume) reminds us, this focus on the harms of the powerful was very much at the forefront of the anarchist abolitionist writings in Spain at the end of the 19th century and the beginning of the 20th century. For Morris and Tolstoy, the powerful who inflicted punishment were perpetrating harms that were more serious than the 'crime' committed by those they punished (see Zorin, Chapter 4 in this volume; Holland, Chapter 7 in this volume).

Consequently, it is important that the definition of 'crime' itself is questioned. The language of 'crime' has become embedded in our 'common sense' understanding of our world; it has, in a Gramscian sense, established its hegemony. But like much common sense, we only need to scratch the surface to see the contradictions, omissions and mystifications in real-life situations. By recognizing that the way in which acts can be interpreted is socially constructed – for example, by being classified as 'crimes' – abolitionists offer the opportunity of seeing these acts in a variety of different ways. This in turn leads to the opening up of the possibility of a wide range of solutions beyond those offered by the criminal law (Hulsman, 1986). The writings of William Godwin (see Tuke, Chapter 2 in this volume) indicate that the very notion of 'crime' (and the need for an alternative language) is something which has preoccupied the thoughts of libertarian socialists for nearly 250 years.

Ethical evaluation and the moral compass

Noncoercive solutions to harmful behaviour proposed in a spirit of mutualism and communal responsibility stem from libertarian socialist ethical commitments. As Tuke notes, 'perhaps the greatest lesson that Godwin's writing can impart to us is that the application of justice is as much a question of ethics as it is jurisprudence' (Tuke, Chapter 2 in this volume). For Malatesta (see Turcato, Chapter 11 in this volume), the creation of a socialist society required the development of a new moral order. Further, Kropotkin notably emphasized the superior moral sense of the community over that which might be imposed by authority (Marshall, 2008: 321; see Weide, Chapter 9 in this volume). He also rejected desert-based notions of justice in favour of a needs-based system compatible with the notion of mutual aid (Bevir, 2011: 265). These arguments were influential on libertarian socialists, whether from an anarchist or early socialist heritage (Bevir, 2011: 266). While this principle was primarily applied to theories of ownership and the distribution of wealth, needs-based justice might also be applied to how the perpetrators of harmful behaviour can be dealt with.

While deserts-based justice was considered to serve only the interests of the powerful, needs-based justice could serve the interests of both society as a whole and offenders. For St John, needs-based justice should be informed by an 'ethics of care' which would more effectively tackle the root causes of harmful behaviour (Cox and Taylor, Chapter 5 in this volume). Punitive solutions to harmful behaviour such as prison hardly fulfil this aim, given that they inflict considerable pain on offenders without addressing the causes of harmful behaviour and, in many cases, turn people out worse than they were before. Many thinkers discussed in this volume were clear that prisons were inherently anti-social and criminogenic, and this was one of the main observations that informed their abolitionist convictions. Godwin described prisons as 'seminaries of vice'; Guyau and Kropotkin referred to them, respectively, as 'schools' or 'universities of crime' (see Testa, Chapter 8 in this volume; Weide, Chapter 9 in this volume). Goldman saw prisons themselves as criminal (see Weiss, Chapter 15 in this volume). St John and Carpenter (see Cox and Taylor, Chapter 5 in this volume; Baldwin, Chapter 6 in this volume) also believed that prisons manufactured criminals, while Tolstoy worried about the moral depravity created by executions (see Zorin, Chapter 4 in this volume).

This critique is as true today as it was in the past. Prisons are profoundly dehumanizing institutions, filled with socially disadvantaged people who have experienced multiple forms of social exclusion. Despite the best intentions of those hoping to find some virtue in the current incarceration binge, the punitive rationale, which underscores the very existence of prisons, inevitably undermines humanitarian attempts to bring about desired personal transformations or tackle social exclusion (Scott, 2008).

Just as for libertarian socialists, for contemporary penal abolitionists, the prison place is a toxic environment, for all humans placed in such a degrading and damaging situational context are vulnerable to harm. Prisons are inherently problematic institutions; they are places of interpersonal and institutional violence, and legal, social and corporeal death – and these terrible outcomes are embedded in the very fabric of penal institutions (Scott and Codd, 2010; Scott, 2015). Berkman notably expressed concern about the prison's tendency to exacerbate mental health problems (see Hough, Chapter 16 in this volume). It is possible for prisons to offer a place of reflection and refuge for a few people when all other options have failed, but, given the deprivations, pains and iatrogenic harms that underscore daily prison regimes, the prison is generally indefensible. Many early anarchists and early socialists experienced the prison firsthand (such as Debs, Gori, Kropotkin, Goldman and Berkman, who are the focus of chapters in this volume), either leading them to reject or confirm their rejection of these institutions as places that could serve no other goal than the delivery of pain and suffering. Together with abolitionists today, they recognized that the criminal law cannot provide safety and protection, and that we cannot achieve human liberation and emancipation through punitive means.

Criminal processes always fail as they are about domination and, as such, are incapable of successfully responding to the terrible events and losses that human beings sometimes have to face. Undoubtedly, one pain cannot be compensated by another. As Guyau eloquently put it, the harms of an evil act are irreversible – they cannot be reversed by penal sanctions (see Testa, Chapter 8 in this volume). Given its futility and counterproductivity, it can never, as Tolstoy also noted, be moral to perform deliberate acts of pain infliction on another human – indeed, he regarded the judge sending a man to the gallows as worse that the murderer himself (see Zorin, Chapter 4 in this volume). Similarly, Goldman considered the state to be the real offender (see Weiss, Chapter 15 in this volume). The death penalty was regarded by Darrow and Gori as a pure act of revenge (see Manfredi, Chapter 12 in this volume; Kersten, Chapter 14 in this volume). Kropotkin and Darrow also worried about the pains that coercive forms of punishment inflicted on the innocent families of the hanged and incarcerated (see Weide, Chapter 9 in this volume; Kersten, Chapter 14 in this volume).

What is required are visions of freedom and justice that reach across the divide between anarchists, Marxists and democratic socialists. Advancing what we term here as 'libertarian socialism' is something which reflects the dreams and aspirations of the early socialists – a united socialism that can provide a sustained challenge to capitalism and the coercive institutions of the capitalist state. The shared commitment to penal abolitionism can help bring the disparate non-authoritarian streams of socialism back into dialogue with each other and to recognize that socialist diversity is something which is present in theory as well as in the lived experience of ordinary people. By looking backwards to socialisms past, we may also be able to start to look forwards and work collectively in a concerted challenge against criminal injustice.

Looking forward: socialist inspirations in red and black

The early anarchist and socialist thinkers explored in the following chapters of this book were all committed to radical social transformations. They all question the right of the state to punish. Indeed, there is often recognition that once a harm or wrong has been perpetrated, it can never really be taken back. What socialists and abolitionists maintain is that harm can be, to at least some extent, mitigated through therapy or other pro-social environments. The response is more cooperation, greater solidarity and moral education. Our responsibilities to others cannot be neutralized, even if those people are acting in ways that are problematic.

To be a penal abolitionist means 'bearing witness to the violence of incarceration and being prepared "to stand up against it"' (Bernat de Celis, 2014: 22). Penal incarceration should be rejected for three fundamental reasons: first, the prison is counterintuitive to *socialist values and ethics*; second, the prison reflects an abstraction of humanity and its continued existence can lead only to further *dehumanization*; and, third, the prison has a clear political function in *maintaining social inequalities* (Bernat de Celis, 2014). We find these ideas in the works of Malatesta, Kropotkin and Spanish anarchists such as Anselmo Lorenzo, Martínez Ruiz and Ricardo Mella, among many others. The absolutist argument advanced by Tolstoy (see Zorin, Chapter 4 in this volume) that all violence is morally reprehensible is profoundly significant in the context that the harms of imprisonment are often conceived by penal abolitionists as a form of state violence. The dehumanization of the prison place is central to the writings of anarchists and socialists imprisoned such as Debs, Goldman, Berkman (see Phillips, Chapter 13 in this volume; Weiss, Chapter 15 in this volume; and Hough, Chapter 16 in this volume). The prison cannot be humanized and therefore a further key theme of penal abolitionists is the demand for nonpenal forms of intervention. This requires radical transformation of the social system which perpetuates penal incarceration alongside pragmatic interventions for handling human conflict and problematic conduct that respect human diversity. Guyau's critique of sanction is particularly relevant in this respect, marked as it is by an ethical orientation that seeks to render happiness accessible to all, by affirming the dignity of every human being's desire for happiness (see Testa, Chapter 8 in this volume). Fulfilling this aim begins with accepting the key tenets of libertarian socialism and the abolition of state coercion.

Libertarian socialism privileges freedom and voluntary associations outside of the orbit of the state. A genuinely free and democratic society nurtures the development of community-based interstitial initiatives that bring about positive change in our everyday lives. Commitment to pro-social behaviour can only emerge from freedom rather than from fear and threat of coercion. For anarchists (such as Kropotkin and Malatesta), the capitalist state is inherently immoral, hierarchical and coercive. It is characterized by what Poulantzas (1978) calls the 'mechanism of fear' and is indifferent to the wellbeing of the powerless. However, while libertarian socialists share this analysis, they do not always follow the anarchists in advocating the abolition of the state. For many libertarian socialists (see, for example, Scott, 2012), it is possible to both question the legitimacy of the coercive state and highlight the impossibility of achieving real justice under capitalism, while recognizing that the state can play a positive role. Indeed, the neo-Gramscian conception of the capitalist state – as developed and elaborated on in the writings of Gramsci (1971), Poulantzas (1978), Hall (1988), and Jessop (1990), among others – provides a nuanced understanding of the nature and constitution of the state. Instead of conceiving of the state as a single monolithic authoritarian entity, it is understood as being constituted by multiple alliances and power blocs that cut across political and civil society. While the capitalist state remains inherently problematic, the constitution of the state is on a much more contradictory terrain, with potential for socialists to exploit these contradictions (Scott, 2013; Scott and Sim, 2023).

Without dismissing the considerable disagreements among those committed to a non-authoritarian socialist transformation with regards to whether there can be such a thing as a 'non-coercive state' (see, for example, Turcato, Chapter 11 in this volume), transcending this debate is a common commitment to abolish the penal apparatus of the capitalist state and reject the power to punish. This shared commitment to penal abolition offers hope for building cooperation and alliances among different socialist/anarchist movements. It is the potential for unity and collective struggle against the authoritarian state that we wish to emphasize in this volume.

To achieve socialist transformation, it is essential that non-authoritarian socialists and anarchists stand together against the dehumanizing and deadly ravages of neoliberal capitalism and the state intuitions facilitating its domination and exploitation. Penal abolitionism needs to proudly don the colours of both *red and black*. At a time when social and economic insecurities are encouraging scapegoating, it is ever more important to foster a more reflective understanding of the causes of social problems. Indeed, the darker the times, the greater the need for enlightened thinking. Libertarian socialist alternatives can reach beyond the hegemonic neoliberal and penal logics that currently inform penal policy and offer a new way of responding to troubled and troublesome individuals.

Notes

1. This chapter's title is inspired by this subheading of Prichard et al (2012): *Libertarian Socialism: Politics in Black and Red*. We also use this phrase in the book *Emancipatory Politics and Praxis* (see Scott, 2016: 8).
2. We do explore some writings in the early 20th century too, but these authors were all born in the 19th century.
3. That being said, Nocella, Seis and Shantz (2020) have recently provided a valuable reader of anarchist reflections on crime and punishment.
4. Alongside this, there have been more radical calls to defund the police (Cunneen, 2023).
5. See https://abolition.nu/
6. On a global level, the 'World Without Prisons' global prison abolitionist coalition was formed in 2020 and brought together socialist organizations from across the globe to connect national and international struggles and political and social prisoners 'who are mostly working-class victims of poverty, racism, marginalization and neglect' (World Without Prisons, 2020). There is also the 'International Conference of Penal Abolition' (ICOPA), which was formed in the early 1980s and works towards transformative justice.
7. Anarchist and Marxist abolitionist texts have been championed by a number of smaller or independent publishers – see, for example, EG Press, Haymarket, Waterside Press and AK Press.
8. Movimento NO PRISON, see noprison.eu
9. We note that not all of the authors of this volume would perhaps agree with our approach here. The authors were chosen for their knowledge and understanding of a given thinker rather than their commitment to an abolitionism in red and black.
10. The writings of Henri de Saint-Simon and Charles Fourier are also relevant here.
11. See, however, reflections on the 'abolitionist rhizome' and the diverse roots of abolitionisms.
12. The work of Guyau and Darrow are very closely associated with socialist and anarchist thought.

References

ACLU (2020) 'The Democratic platform heads in right direction on criminal justice, but still misses the moment', 18 August. Available from: https://www.aclu.org/news/racial-justice/the-democratic-platform-heads-in-right-direction-on-criminal-justice-but-still-misses-the-moment [Accessed 15 February 2024].

Bantigny, L. (2019) 'Un Événement', in Collectif, *Le Fond de l'Air est Jaune: Comprendre une Révolte Inédite*, Paris: Seuil, pp 45–56.

Bell, E. (2011) *Criminal Justice and Neoliberalism*, Basingstoke: Palgrave Macmillan.

Berlin, I. (1958) *Two Concepts of Liberty: An Inaugural lecture delivered before the University of Oxford on 31 October 1058*, Oxford: Clarendon Press.

Bernat de Celis, J. (2014) 'Whither abolitionism?', in J. Moore et al (eds) *Beyond Criminal Justice*, London: EG Press, pp 17–24.

Bevir, M. (2011) *The Making of British Socialism*, Princeton: Princeton University Press.

Bianchi, H. (1994) *Justice as Sanctuary: Toward a New System of Crime Control*, Eugene: Wipf and Stock Publishers.

Blair, T. (1993) 'From the 1997 election archive: Tony Blair on why crime is a socialist issue', *New Statesman* (29 April 2017). Available from: https://www.newstatesman.com/archive/2017/04/1997-election-archive-tony-blair-why-crime-socialist-issue [Accessed 15 February 2024].

Boone, M. and van Swaaningen, R. (2013) 'Regression to the mean: punishment in the Netherlands', in V. Ruggiero and M. Ryan (eds) *Punishment in Europe: A Critical Anatomy of Penal Systems*, Basingstoke: Palgrave Macmillan, pp 9–32.

Burns, M. (2024) 'What happened to Biden's promises on criminal justice reform?', *The Hill* (17 January). Available from: https://thehill.com/opinion/campaign/4413082-what-happened-to-bidens-promises-on-criminal-justice-reform/ [Accessed 15 February 2024].

Christie, N. (1977) 'Conflicts as property', *British Journal of Criminology*, 17(1): 1–15.

Christie, N. (1981) *The Limits to Pain: The Role of Punishment in Penal Society*, Oslo: Universitetsforlaget.

Cohen, S. (1988) *Against Criminology*, Cambridge: Polity Press.

Coyle, M.J. and Scott, D. (eds) (2021) *International Handbook on Penal Abolition*, Abingdon: Routledge.

Cunneen, C. (2023) *Defund the Police: An International Insurrection*, Bristol: Policy Press

CURB (2024) 'Prison closures'. Available from: https://curbprisonspending.org/advocacy/prison-closures/ [Accessed 15 January 2024].

Davis, A.Y. (2003) *Are Prisons Obsolete?*, New York: Seven Stories Press.

Dupond-Moretti, E. (2023) RTL France on X. Available from: https://twitter.com/RTLFrance/status/1681546093039964162?s=20 [Accessed 15 February 2024].

EELV (2021) 'Projet pour 2021'. Available from: https://www.eelv.fr/files/2021/10/VI.-En-France-en-Europe-et-dans-le-monde-vivre-libres-en-su%CC%82rete%CC%81.pdf [Accessed 15 February 2024].

European Prison Observatory (2016) *Manifesto for a New Penal Culture*. Available from: http://www.prisonobservatory.org/upload/Manifesto%20English%20variation%202.pdf [Accessed 15 February 2024].

Ferrell, J. (1998) 'Against the law: anarchist criminology', *Social Anarchism*, 25. Available from: https://theanarchistlibrary.org/library/jeff-ferrell-against-the-law-anarchist-criminology [Accessed 15 February 2024].

Ferrell, J. (2021) 'An anarchist criminology for uncertain times', *Journal of Criminology*, 54(1): 93–106.

Ferrari, L. and Pavarini, M. (2018) *No Prison*, London: EG Press.

Fitzgerald, M. and Sim, J. (1979) *British Prisons*, Oxford: Basil Blackwell.

France Info (2023) 'Emeutes après la mort de Nahel: les mesures sécuritaires présentées par le gouvernement', 27 October. Available from: https://www.francetvinfo.fr/replay-jt/franceinfo/21h-minuit/23-heures/emeutes-apres-la-mort-de-nahel-les-mesures-securitaires-presentees-par-le-gouvernement_6147792.html [Accessed 15 February 2024].

Gaarder, E. (2009) 'Addressing violence against women: alternatives to state-based law and punishment', in A. Randall, A. de Leon, L. Fernandez, A.J. Nocella and D. Shannon (eds) *Contemporary Anarchist Studies*, Abingdon: Routledge, pp 62–72.

Garland, D. (2001) *The Culture of Control: Crime and Social Order in Contemporary Society*, Oxford: Oxford University Press.

Gilmartin (2023) 'To change Spain, the left needs to rein in a reactionary judicial establishment', *Jacobin* (16 November). Available from: https://jacobin.com/2023/11/spain-right-left-judiciary-catalonia-psoe-sanchez [Accessed 15 February 2024].

Gramsci, A. (1971) *Selections from the Prison Notebooks*, London: Lawrence & Wishart.

Grawert, A. and Richmond, P. (2022) 'The First Step Act's prison peforms', *Brennan Centre for Justice* (23 September). Available from: https://www.brennancenter.org/our-work/research-reports/first-step-acts-prison-reforms [Accessed 15 February 2024].

Green Party US (2021) '#NoNewJails Nationwide, say Greens', 26 July. Available from: https://www.gp.org/nonewjails_nationwide_say_greens [Accessed 15 February 2024].

Guenther, L. (2016) *Solitary Confinement: Social Death and Its Afterlives*, Minnesota: University of Minnesota.

Hall, S. (1988) *The Hard Road to Renewal*, London: Verso

Hamilton, C. (2022) 'Radical right populism and the sociology of punishment: Towards a research agenda', *Punishment & Society*, 25(4): 888–908.

Hillyard, P., Pantazis, C., Tombs, S. and Gordon, D. (eds) (2004) *Beyond Criminology: Taking Harm Seriously*, London: Pluto Press.

Hulsman, L.H.C. (1986) 'Critical criminology and the concept of crime', *Contemporary Crises*, 10: 63–80.

Hyman, G. (1979) *A Theory of Criminal Justice*, Oxford: Oxford University Press.

James, J. (2021) 'Foreword: the alchemy of abolitions', in M.J. Coyle and D. Scott (eds) *International Handbook on Penal Abolition*, Abingdon: Routledge.

James, J. (2025) 'Angela Davis and contributions and contradictions of abolition', in D. Scott (ed.) *Abolitionist Voices*, Bristol: Bristol University Press.

Jessop, B. (1990) *State Theory*, University Park: Pennsylvania State University Press.

Kropotkin, P. (1905) *Mutual Aid*, New York: McClure Phillips & Co.
Kropotkin, P. (1924) *Ethics*, London: George Harrap and Co Ltd.
Lea, J. and Young, J. (1993) *What Is To Be Done about Law and Order? Crisis in the Eighties*, London: Penguin.
Marshall, P. (2008) *Demanding the Impossible: A History of Anarchism*, London: Harper Perennial.
Mathiesen (1974) *The Politics of Abolition*, Oxford: Martin Robertson.
Mélenchon, J.-L. (2022) 'Les livrets thématiques de l'avenir en commun'. Available from: https://melenchon2022.fr/livrets-thematiques/justice/ [Accessed 15 February 2024].
Ministère de la justice (2023) 'Statistiques mensuelles de la population détenue et écrouée', 28 March. Available from: https://www.justice.gouv.fr/documentation/etudes-et-statistiques/statistiques-mensuelles-population-detenue-ecrouee [Accessed 15 February 2024].
Moore, J., Rolston, W., Scott, D. and Tomlinson, M. (eds) (2014) *Beyond Criminal Justice*, Bristol: EG Press.
Newman, M. (2005) *Socialism: A Very Short Introduction*, Oxford: Oxford University Press.
Newsom, G. (2023) 'Governor Newsom announces historic transformation of San Quentin state prison', 17 March. Available from: https://www.gov.ca.gov/2023/03/17/san-quentin-transformation/ [Accessed 15 February 2024].
Nocella, A.J, Seis, M. and Shantz, J. (eds) (2020) *Classical Writings in Anarchist Criminology*, London: AK Press.
Ocasio-Cortez, A. (2024) 'Instead of investing in mass incarceration, we need to invest in the most vulnerable members of our society'. Available from: https://www.ocasiocortez.com/issues#real-public-safety [Accessed 15 February 2024].
Ocasio-Cortez, A. (2019) https://twitter.com/AOC/status/1181207065072676864 [Accessed 15 February 2024].
OHCHR (2019) 'France: UN experts denounce severe rights restrictions on *gilets jaunes* protesters', 14 February. Available from: https://www.ohchr.org/EN/NewsEvents/Pages/DisplayNews.aspx?NewsID=24166&LangID=E [Accessed 15 February 2024].
OIP (2024) 'Comment expliquer la surpopulation des prisons françaises?', 18 February. Available from: https://oip.org/en-bref/comment-expliquer-la-surpopulation-des-prisons-francaises/ [Accessed 15 February 2024].
Orwell, G. (2002[1938]) *Homage to Catalonia*, London: Penguin.
Pepinsky, H.E. (1978) 'Communist anarchism as an alternative to the rule of criminal law', *Contemporary Crises*, 2: 315–327.
Pinta, S. and Berry, D. (2012) 'Conclusion: towards a libertarian socialism for the Twenty-first century?', in A. Prichard, R. Kinna, S. Pinta and D. Berry (eds) *Libertarian Socialism: Politics in Black and Red*, Basingstoke: Palgrave Macmillan, pp 294–303.

Poulantzas, N. (1978) *State, Power, Socialism*, London: Verso

Pratt, J., Brown, D., Brown, M., Hallsworth, S. and Morrison, W. (eds) (2005) *The New Punitiveness: Trends, Theories and Perspectives*, Cullompton: Willan Publishing.

Proudhon, P.J. (1989) *General Idea of Revolution in the Nineteenth Century*, London: Pluto Press.

Ruggiero, V. (2013) 'Conclusion', in V. Ruggiero and M. Ryan (eds) *Punishment in Europe: A Critical Anatomy of Penal Systems*, Basingstoke: Palgrave Macmillan, pp 287–296.

Soctt, D. (2008) *Penology*, London: Sage.

Scott, D. (2013) 'Visualising an abolitionist real utopia', in M. Malloch and W. Munro (eds) *Crime, Critique and Utopia*, Basingstoke: Palgrave Macmillan: 90–113.

Scott, D. (ed.) (2013b) *Why Prison?*, Cambridge: Cambridge University Press.

Scott, D. (2015) 'Eating your insides out', *Prison Service Journal*, 221: 58–62.

Scott, D. (2016) *Emancipatory Politics and Praxis*, Bristol: EG Press.

Scott, D. (2018) *Against Imprisonment*, Hook: Waterside Press.

Scott, D. (2020) *For Abolition*, Hook: Waterside Press.

Scott, D. (ed.) (2025) *Abolitionist Voices*, Bristol: Bristol University Press.

Scott, D. and Codd, H. (2010) *Controversial Issues in Prisons*, Milton Keynes: Open University Press.

Scott, D. and Sim, J. (eds) (2023) *Demystifying Power, Crime and Social Harm*, London: Palgrave Macmillan.

Scott, J. (2012) *Two Cheers for Anarchism*, Princeton: Princeton University Press

Shantz, J. (2014) 'Radical criminology lives'. Available from: http://journal.radicalcriminology.org/index.php/rc/article/view/1/html [Accessed 17 February 2024].

Skirda, A. (1982) *Nestor Makhno: Anarchy's Cossack: The Struggle for Free Soviets in Ukraine 1917–1921*, Chico, CA: AK Press.

Spade, D. (2020) *Mutual Aid: Building Solidarity through This Crisis (and the Next)*, London: Verso.

Starmer, K. (2023) 'Starmer unveils mission to halve serious violent crime and raise confidence in the police and criminal justice system to its highest levels', *Labour Party* (23 May). Available from: https://labour.org.uk/updates/press-releases/keir-starmer-unveils-mission-to-halve-serious-violent-crime-and-raise-confidence-in-the-police-and-criminal-justice-system-to-its-highest-levels/ [Accessed 15 February 2024].

Tifft, L. and Sullivan, D. (1980) *The Struggle to Be Human: Crime, Criminology and Anarchism*, Orkney: Cienfuegos Press.

Todd-Kvam, J. (2019) 'Bordered penal populism: when populism and Scandinavian exceptionalism meet', *Punishment & Society*, 21(3): 295–314.

World Prison Brief (2024) 'Changing patterns of imprisonment'. Available from: https://www.prisonstudies.org/ten-country-prisons-project/changing-patterns-imprisonment [Accessed 15 February 2024].

World Without Prisons (2020) https://www.worldwithoutprisons.org/ [Accessed 15 February 2024].

Wright, A. (1987) *Socialisms: Theories and Practices*, Oxford: Oxford University Press.

2

The Embryonic Abolitionist Ideas of William Godwin in the Late 18th Century

Ruby Tuke

Introduction

The author William Godwin, proponent of political justice, radical philosopher and proto-anarchist, was one of the most famous political theorists of the late 18th century. Writing at a unique period in which the outbreak of the French Revolution (1789) had unsettled existing ideas about rights and entitlements in Britain, Godwin's political works, as well as his numerous novels, explore different models of penal justice. He wrote his celebrated work *An Enquiry Concerning Political Justice* (1793) – revised and republished a number of times – at a crucial period in the history of penal reform in England (Godwin, 1993). In the first quarter of the 18th century, 'no more than one-tenth of convicts received prison sentences' (McGowen, 1995: 76). By the end of the century, however, imprisonment accounted for 'at least two-thirds of criminal sentences' (McGowen, 1995: 76). Over the course of the 18th century, the public spectacle of violence, which had formerly characterized punitive justice, waned in usage while imprisonment as punishment *in itself* gained widespread adoption.

The contribution of some of his contemporaries to the prison debate in Britain – namely Jeremy Bentham and John Howard – has been well documented (Ignatieff, 1978; Morris and Rothman, 1995). However, Godwin's ideas present a radical departure from both punitive and reformative justice models that were emerging at the turn of the 19th century and would come to dominate criminal justice policy for the next hundred years and more. For the radical philosopher, any given action should necessarily provide some kind of social benefit, and 'whatever is not attended with any beneficial purpose, is not just' (Godwin, 1993: 369). Punishment of any kind is unjust because it does not benefit the criminal, the victim or society. Similarly, Godwin sought 'to correct larger social disparities and define justice beyond retribution or punishment in order to repair harm to offender, victim, and the community' (Fenno, 2009: 16–17). These restorative methods ultimately sought the happiness and improvement of all members of society: victim and offender alike.

Crucially, Godwin's model dissects the justifications for punishment from what would today be considered an 'abolitionist perspective' (see Chapter 1 in this volume for a further discussion of penal abolition). Although by no means a uniform, uncontested position, there are some points upon which its proponents would broadly agree. Most penal abolitionists would regard imprisonment as immoral because it causes pain and suffering to other humans. Prisoners tend disproportionately to be poor and/or come from other marginalized groups of society. Abolitionists would also point out that locking people up does not get rid of 'crime' or criminals, but reinforces the existing criminal (in)justice system. In the place of imprisonment, penal abolitionists call for the related concepts of transformative, generative, liberative and/or restorative justice. Supporters of restorative justice propose a form of conflict resolution which removes the state and the law from human disagreements. Issues between people can be dealt with from within a community by those who are directly affected, not handed over to impersonal bodies with no knowledge of the situation or of those involved.

In spite of the fact that Godwin's views about crime and punishment clearly anticipate a penal abolitionist approach and ideas associated with the restorative justice movement, the political philosopher's ideas have been largely absent from any critical discussion of the history of these related movements.[1] In this chapter, I demonstrate how his radical critique of the penal justice system in the 1790s corresponds with the principles of the present-day penal abolitionist movement. By understanding Godwin's abolitionist sentiments, we can see how his writings might inform, even strengthen, the penal abolitionist movement in the present day.

Criminals are not born but made

Godwin's view of human nature departs from a theological conception of original sin, as well as from later positivist conceptions of the criminal in the field of criminology. Regarding people's character as a *tabula rasa*, early on in *Political Justice* he comments that we are born with 'no innate principles: consequently we are neither virtuous nor vicious as we first come into existence' (Godwin, 1993: 10). If people do not come into the world with a fixed nature but are a blank canvas, then crimes cannot be the product of innately bad or criminal individuals. Instead, Godwin is convinced that crimes tend to originate from the effects that legal institutions – especially their support for private wealth and property – have on the organization of society and human affairs: 'The original sin of the worst men, is in the perverseness of these institutions, the opposition they produce between public and private good, the monopoly they create of the advantages which reason directs to be left in common' (Godwin, 1993: 381).

According to the political philosopher, crimes exist because society is currently structured so that individual gain tends to be at odds with what would be good for society in general: sharing resources fairly, treating people equitably and exercising our moral form of private judgement. Godwin appears certain that an unjust society, one that is divided into different classes of people, does nothing to encourage human progress. In fact, he says that 'oppression stimulates them to mischief and piracy and superior force of mind often displays itself only in deeper treachery or more daring injustice' (Godwin, 1993: 389). Rather than crime being a result of criminals, Godwin claims that material inequality actually drives a large amount of crime.

Strikingly, Godwin does not believe that there is an essential difference between criminals and noncriminals; they are simply 'the offspring of their different circumstances' (Godwin, 1993: 402). In case any ambiguity remains, he makes the radical implications of his point crystal clear: 'the [criminal] man whom they [the non-criminals] now so much despise, would have been as accomplished and susceptible as they, if they had only changed situations' (Godwin, 1993: 402). Such conclusions would have been alarming to anyone with even vaguely reactionary sentiments in the 1790s. To claim that *anyone* could become a criminal or, conversely, thrive given the right circumstances is to unsettle not just assumptions about the criminal justice system but also the entire distribution of wealth and resources in society. Godwin surmises that such an unsettling prospect probably accounts for why the rich do not protest against the fact that the vast majority of convicted criminals are poor: 'proud of their fancied eminence', the political philosopher muses, they are able to 'behold with total unconcern the destruction of the destitute and the wretched' (Godwin, 1993: 401–402). To brand large swathes of the poor as delinquents is to see their whole class as essentially different from the rich minority, which justifies the continued reproduction of inequality in society.

What Godwin emphatically does not claim, then, is that crime exists in some kind of objective, definable form. In order to dispel this convenient myth, he provides a range of examples that would all be categorized as murder according to the law. The scenarios he cites include killing someone to prevent a very serious harm being committed; killing a person to save one's father; killing to stop one's daughter being raped; killing someone who is a witness to one's crime; killing a person for telling the truth; and killing out of envy (Godwin, 1993: 78). The variety of the examples highlights the numerous circumstances, motives and feelings that cause someone to take the life of another. Godwin makes this clear when he asks the reader: 'can you pretend in each instance to ascertain the exact quantity of wrong and to invent a species of corporal punishment or restraint, equivalent to each?' (Godwin, 1993: 78). It is not that he denies the harm that has been inflicted in some of the cases, or the severity of the action of ending someone's life in all of them; rather, he seeks to illustrate the law's reductive view of human interactions.

Godwin's rejection of 'crime' as an objective state and his emphasis on understanding the circumstances leading up to each crime is remarkably similar to the views of later penal abolitionists. In his seminal paper, Louk Hulsman pointed out that 'within the concept of criminality a broad range of situations are linked together', but the majority of them 'have separate properties and no common denominator' (Hulsman, 1986: 65). This led to his famous claim that crime does not have an 'ontological reality' (Hulsman, 1986: 66). Hulsman, like Godwin before him, questioned the very idea that crimes could be measured against one another and be labelled, to produce 'types' or 'standards' of delinquency.

Penal abolitionist scholars have also shown how the labels 'crime' and 'criminals' engender dangerous effects. They tend to reproduce the perceived objective differences to which they are referring. As Michael J. Coyle notes, 'justice (language) paradigms, such as the retributive/punitive one that is based on the distinctions "offenders", "victims", "crimes", and the like, become deeply accepted obvious interpretations of social situations' (Coyle, 2016: 5). This point is key. Instead of regarding the multifaceted scenarios that end in harmful action, the criminal justice system brands individuals as criminals. This label becomes difficult for offenders to lose, which can impact familial relations, job prospects and the ability to make money lawfully. In other words, the labels contribute to a vicious punitive cycle of crime and punishment (Becker, 1963).

The fact that crimes arise from specific circumstances accounts for one of the reasons why, according to Godwin, the punitive justice system does not deter others from committing offences. He states that 'no two crimes were ever alike; and therefore the [sic] reducing them explicitly or implicitly to general classes, which the very idea of example implies, is absurd' (Godwin, 1993: 376–377). Godwin's reasons for opposing the policy of making an example out of an offender correspond with findings in abolitionist scholarship. Thomas Mathiesen has pointed out that punishing criminals does not serve as a deterrent to other would-be offenders. Rather, 'most people who refrain from problematic conducts do so for reasons unconnected to the penal law' (Mathiesen 1990: 12). Expanding on the research of Mathiesen, Vincenzo Ruggiero adds that 'social conditions, reputation, moral choice and social commitment have a far stronger deterrent efficacy' – factors with which Godwin would agree (Ruggiero, 2015: para 37).

Yet, Godwin does not simply reject the policy of punishing an individual to serve as an example to others because of adverse outcomes, but from a moral standpoint: 'What then could be more shameless than for society to make an example of those whom she has goaded to the breach of order, instead of amending her own institutions, which, by straining order into tyranny, produced the mischief?' (Godwin, 1993: 381)

Godwin challenges the ethical legitimacy of punishing certain crimes which society at large has caused. Controversially for his time, his comment indicates that the real shame falls upon a society that has created those harmful conditions. He writes that 'when I am made to suffer as an example to others, I am treated myself with supercilious neglect, as if I were totally incapable of feeling and morality' (Godwin, 1993: 381). To punish someone in order to deter others is to completely ignore the pain and suffering that the individual must endure. As well as being unlikely to generate the desired outcome for society, Godwin is convinced that it is morally abhorrent to treat a fellow human in such an abject and senseless manner.

However, the main issue with defining criminal acts is that such classifications tend to be very much biased against the poor, lowly and disregarded members of society. The relatively minor actions of many poor people are considered criminal, yet the wealthy and privileged are often allowed to get away with significant moral, and indeed criminal, wrongs. For example, in *Political Justice*, Godwin states that robbery and theft are considered serious offences, yet they are often carried out as a result of dire necessity (Godwin, 1993). By contrast, systemic crimes that hurt the poor are left largely unchallenged and, often, so are individual ones. Actions carried out by rich people against the poor and most vulnerable members of society are frequently not considered crimes, and those that are rarely prosecuted (Scott and Sim, 2023). The inadequacy of the criminal justice system to deal with significant harm is a topic that he focuses on in his first novel and to which we now turn.

Harmful versus criminal behaviour

Godwin's novel *Things as They Are; or, The Adventures of Caleb Williams* (1794) provides numerous examples of the ways in which the penal system inflicts injustices against the poor and marginalized in society (Godwin, 1992). The gothic-inspired tale is littered with descriptions of prisons and the miserable experiences of prisoners, a flawed legal system, and includes a range of harmful behaviour directed at the vulnerable members of society – some of which is criminal, but most of which is not. In doing so, the text 'reveals and undercuts the fiction of a just criminal system or a stable definition of crime' (Fenno, 2009: 29). The eponymous narrator of the tale, an intelligent and curious boy from a peasant family, recalls the devastating events that occur to him as a result of becoming the servant of Mr Falkland, 'a country squire' and social recluse with a dark past (Godwin, 1992: 5). Detecting something amiss in his employer's character, Caleb discovers Falkland's awful secret: that he has committed the murder of his antagonist, Mr Tyrrel, another landowning squire, and allowed Tyrrel's tenants, the Hawkins father and son, to be hanged for the crime. As a result of Caleb's discovery, Falkland utilizes the law and his henchman to pursue his servant and throw him in jail. The published ending of the novel features a courtroom scene in which a sickly Falkland is eventually found guilty of Tyrrel's murder and dies a few days later.

However, even before they are wrongly convicted and hanged for murder, the Hawkins father and son are persecuted mercilessly by their landlord because the elder man will not accede to placing his beloved son in servitude to Tyrrel. The squire becomes 'bent' on destroying them and employs a variety of legal and criminal means of doing so (Godwin, 1992: 40). Tyrrel strips the father of his job and establishes a dam on his own land to flood the family's corn and ruin their crop. Even though the latter action is clearly carried out with malicious intent, Tyrrel is not breaking the law because it is on his own property. The tyrannical landlord also prevents Hawkins from being able to access his own farm by getting another of his tenants to block a private road that leads up to it. Once again, there is little that the simple tenant farmer can do in the face of such cruel and oppressive (yet legal) action. Tyrrel's aim in blocking his access is to make the elder 'Hawkins a sort of prisoner in his own domains', which conveys the sense that the removal of freedoms is not always carried out in literal prisons, but is often abetted by the law (Godwin, 1992: 41).

When Hawkins finally takes legal action against the squire, Tyrrel is not afraid, as might be expected, but welcomes it with relish. He knows he can employ a variety of costly legal instruments to deliberately slow down the process in a way that would make the charge prohibitively expensive for the plaintiff and so work in his favour (Godwin, 1992: 41). Although Godwin imagines, as he states in *Political Justice*, that the law is generally 'administered with tolerable impartiality', in property cases, he claims that 'the practice of law is arrived at such a pitch as to render all justice ineffectual' (Godwin, 1993: 26). This inadequacy arises from 'the length of our chancery suits, the multiplied appeals from court to court, the enormous fees of the counsel, attorneys, secretaries, clerks, the drawing of briefs, bills, replications and rejoinders', all of which 'render it often more advisable to resign a property than to contest it, and particularly exclude the impoverished claimant from the faintest hope of redress' (Godwin, 1993: 26). The rich can simply use the law to grind the poor into submission.

The bleak irony of the tale is that when, out of desperation, the younger Hawkins eventually stands up to the bullying and coercive tactics of the landowner by removing the obstructions to their farm, he is the one who is arrested for burglary and placed in a county jail (Godwin, 1992: 41). This action leads to the family's loss of the farm and ultimate ruin. The suggestion is that the criminal justice system is not fit for purpose and allows some harms to be inflicted, while those with access to money can act with impunity.

But even if the case of the real wrongdoer were somehow guaranteed to go to trial, Godwin suggests that serious problems in that system prevail. Pamela Clemit notes that 'the prominence of trial scenes in the novel further highlights Godwin's critique of institutional justice' (Clemit 1993: 56). For Godwin, the trial system in Britain was deeply flawed and often led to what might be considered unjust outcomes. In the case of Falkland's first trial for the murder of Tyrrel, his chivalrous reputation convinces the gentlemen of the court of his innocence from the outset: 'nobody entertained the shadow of a doubt upon the subject' (Godwin, 1992: 90). The jury ignores the fact that Falkland had a strong motive for killing Tyrrel and that the benevolent landowner nevertheless places an inordinate value on honour and his own reputation – to the detriment of his otherwise impeccable judgement.

It is not just the jury who are influenced by the status of the defendant. The witnesses in the Tyrrel murder trials are also swayed by the fact that Falkland is a wealthy gentleman and the Hawkins family are simple peasant farmers. In Falkland's first trial, witnesses 'who had been accidentally on the spot, remembered to have seen Hawkins and his son in the town that very evening, and to have called after them, and received no answer, though they were sure of their persons' (Godwin, 1992: 91–92). The implication is that the witnesses probably had not seen the Hawkins men, but convinced themselves afterwards that they had. As Godwin writes in *Political Justice*, witnesses may be 'ignorant and prejudiced' against a defendant for reasons which are not altogether rational, but are based on class and privilege (Godwin, 1993: 380). In the novel, the consequences of such prejudice prove fatal. The Hawkins father and son are both hanged because the jury is blindsided by the wealth and status of the first defendant.

Problems in the interpretation of events by witnesses occur again when Caleb is falsely accused of stealing from his master. In Caleb's case, the members of Falkland's household and Forrester, his master's brother, are outraged by the crime he has apparently committed because it has violated the generosity of his benevolent landlord. What is intimated in the novel is that their excessive repugnance towards the theft really derives from the fact that Caleb has breached the laws of private property, which is held in such veneration under British law. Thus, the witnesses interpret his prior behaviour through the prism of his perceived guilt, and he is sent to jail for a crime he did not commit. Godwin is not of course suggesting that the testimony of all witnesses should be discounted in criminal cases. Nor is he saying that trials should aim to only use impartial witnesses. In spite of his desire for a perfect form of communion between fellow humans, in which they exercise their rational judgement to determine the best course of action, in *Political Justice* he readily attests that 'absolute impartiality it would be absurd to expect from them [witnesses]' (Godwin, 1993: 387). Rather, he wishes to acknowledge that the story or version of events in trials about crimes and people who are deemed potential 'criminals' is constructed and subject to errors in interpretation, recollection and judgement.

In the original courtroom scene that Godwin wrote but did not publish, Falkland is cleared of any wrongdoing by the court. The truth of Caleb's story is only discovered in the final pages of the novel. In the revised published version of the courtroom scene in which Falkland is found guilty, the ending still fails to provide the reader with a satisfactory sense that justice has been delivered. It is evident that the murder of Tyrrel, the wrongful conviction and hanging of the Hawkins family, and even the relentless pursuit of Caleb have taken a severe toll on Falkland. In volume III he is visibly altered by the events and shows signs of illness and pain (Godwin, 1992: 247, 250). Caleb's revelations appear to hasten his former master's death and he is left feeling immensely guilty at the novel's end (Godwin, 1993: 276). As Jon Mee writes, 'the final encounter with the law in *Caleb Williams* provides only testimony to its inadequacy as a tribunal to judge personal relations' (Mee, 2015: 207). Existing criminal justice institutions have not adequately dealt with the systemic and interpersonal harms that have been explored in the novel. In fact, there is nothing to stop them from happening again to some other poor, unwitting victim.

Godwin impresses upon the reader that women are very likely to be the victims of male harm. In the novel, Tyrrel does not just terrorize his tenants; he also persecutes his cousin, Emily Melvile. Emily is the squire's charge who has been brought up in his household (though not as an equal family member) and is dependent on Tyrell's goodwill. When she falls in love with his nemesis, Falkland, her former benefactor is outraged and decides to make her life torture. Tyrrel finds Grimes, a hideous suitor, for her to marry as punishment. But Emily refuses to marry someone she does not love and so her cousin holds her prisoner. He suggests to Grimes that he rape Emily in the woods, which he likely would have done – except that she is saved by Falkland (Godwin, 1993: 67). Godwin's novel indicates that violence against women is often overlooked, especially when the woman has little social standing or wealth of her own. This situation persists in the present day. As David Scott points out, 'some criminal harms, like rape and violence against women, are still not taken as seriously as they should be' (Scott, 2020: 26). There are notoriously low conviction rates for these criminal harms. Even if offenders are caught, they would simply be thrown in jail, which does not actually reform their characters – a point to which Godwin attends in some detail.

Jails: 'seminaries of vice'

In the decades preceding the start of the 19th century, 'public imprisonment' became 'more firmly established as a criminal sanction, replacing other forms of bondage' (McGowen, 1995: 73). Yet, for Godwin, the public jail created exactly the unsavoury conditions that would lead to further criminal activity. He writes in *Political Justice* that 'jails are to a proverb seminaries of vice' (Godwin, 1993: 403). The reason is that 'offenders of every description are thrust together, and left to form among themselves what species of society they can' (Godwin, 1993: 403). It is apparent that he views the 'society' formed in prison as the dark shadow of the free, rational and benevolent one that he imagines is possible and necessary outside. So great is the negative influence of the prison place that Godwin makes the radical claim that almost anyone who found themselves in the same situation – exposed to the prison environment – would fare just as badly. It would take someone 'of sublime virtue, to 'not come out of them [prison] a much worse man than [when] he entered' (Godwin, 1993: 396). His bold assertions indicate that prisons do not contain harmful behaviour so much as nurture it.

Reformers during the period attempted to tackle what was widely considered to be the problem of the public jail providing a breeding ground for illness and criminal activity. Appalled by what he had observed on his trips to numerous prisons across the country, John Howard recommended the creation of a more humane, sanitary and progressive form of jail, which separated prisoners from one another in solitary confinement (cited in Scott, 2008). Howard argued that such measures would provide prisoners with the space for religious and moral introspection. His stark suggestions evidently arose from a genuine sense of horror at both the chaos and filth of the public jail system and the continuing use of physical punishment. This desire to find a solution to the public prison's woes explains how, as Randall McGowen notes, almost every writer who publicly supported penal reform during the late 18th century 'had favourable words for some kind of solitary confinement' (McGowen, 1995: 85).

Yet Godwin goes entirely against the grain of reformist thinking by deploring solitary confinement and Howard's recommendations. In *Political Justice* he writes that although the prison reformer likely had 'the purest intentions' when devising this model, he regards a prison comprising solitary confinement as no improvement on the public jail (Godwin, 1993: 403). It separates individuals not just from harmful influences but also, crucially, from the social relations that Godwin regards as essential to their improvement. Humans are, according to him, 'social animal[s]'; they need to be around each another to learn and to have occasions to demonstrate their virtuous character. People cannot be regarded in isolation but must always be considered in 'relation to each other' (Godwin, 1993: 404). He finds it almost impossible to imagine how offenders could be improved by removing the care and positive influence of others. The fundamentally social and loving nature of people leads him to ask if solitary confinement 'is not ... the bitterest torment that human ingenuity can inflict?' (Godwin, 1993: 404).

In identifying the torment that separation from constructive and virtuous relations provokes in the prisoners, Godwin appears to identify the psychological distress that later penal abolitionists also observe. David Scott similarly emphasizes the importance of positive relationships in nurturing the offender. Like Godwin, he notes that 'humans are intersubjective beings where self is formed within a social world; shared with other people and dependent upon the love, fellowship and support of others' (Scott, 2020: 42). Scott refers to the litany of mental health issues that a large number of prisoners face, which are either created or exacerbated by the state of isolation, loneliness, fear and monotony that they experience in prison (see Scott, 2020: 38–39). Contrary to the idea that the prison can ever provide an opportune space for serious reflection, both Scott and Godwin suggest that solitary confinement is likely to weaken bonds of friendship and sociability, and send the prisoner into a morose state – just the kind that lends itself to further criminal behaviour.

In *Caleb Williams*, Godwin describes the misery of being a prisoner in affecting terms:

> We talk of instruments of torture; Englishmen take credit to themselves for having banished the use of them from their happy shore! Alas! he that has observed the secrets of prison, well knows that there is more torture in the lingering existence of a criminal, in the silent intolerable minutes he spends, than in the tangible misery of whips and racks. (Godwin, 1992: 160)

For Caleb, the psychological pain of being imprisoned is worse than any physical harm. In making this comparison between physical violence and mental torture, the text anticipates the critique of a humanization thesis: a model of a prison that moved away from corporal punishment and towards a supposedly more humane and progressive form of punishment in which time in prison is an end in itself.[2]

But for Caleb, it is specifically the experience of time, of 'the silent intolerable minutes he spends' alone in prison, that is worse than physical 'instruments of torture'. Godwin's description of the temporal experience of the prisoner anticipates scholars and proponents of present-day penal abolitionists. Scott refers to Henri Lefebvre's (1991) concept of 'prison time' to explain how time spent in prison 'can be excruciatingly painful and [can] open a window to re-experiencing past trauma' (Scott, 2020: 32). This is because it leads to an 'increased sense of time consciousness' (Scott, 2018: 14). The prisoner becomes conscious of the waste of time – time which they will never get back – and that exacerbates their suffering even further.

Significantly, the prison experience as it is described in *Caleb Williams* is not eased but worsened by the people who are employed to contain the prisoners. Godwin's novel attests to the fact that prisoners endure violence and humiliation at the hands of those who are meant to uphold the law. The guards, turnkeys and other informal jailors who feature in the novel are not virtuous individuals, but are immoral, debased beings who exploit their positions of power to inflict cruelty. The guards who catch Caleb attempting to escape from jail put his legs in 'fetters' – even though his ankle is severely damaged – in order to deliberately cause 'intolerable' pain (Godwin, 1992: 175). The turnkey exacerbates Caleb's already grim situation by hurling abuse at him instead of fetching the surgeon as requested. It is only through bribing the turnkey that Caleb gets access to urgent medical attention, which indicates that offenders must participate in unscrupulous behaviour if they are to survive the prison environment (Godwin, 1992: 176).

Caleb realizes that there is nowhere for him to turn for help: 'to whom shall the unfortunate felon appeal?' (Godwin, 1992: 187). Referring to this episode, Colleen Fenno astutely notes that 'the disproportionate balance of power within the punitive system puts prisoners in an extremely vulnerable position, without recourse to protection' (Fenno, 2009: 30). There is little point in complaining since the accusations will not be taken seriously and will only make Caleb's situation worse. It is clear that Godwin believes that prisoners often endure both physical and psychological pain at the hands of those who are meant to be upholders of the law. The cruel and inhumane behaviour of some prison guards is something that contemporary penal abolitionists stress. Scott fittingly describes prison guards and wardens as 'caretakers of punishment' (Scott, 2006). Rather than protecting society from these criminals, the prison staff seem to reproduce the punitive conditions that make their jobs necessary in the first place. Bad behaviour becomes much more likely within the penal (in)justice system, which encourages the prisoner to be viewed as entirely bad, deserving of punishment and separate from the prison guards and indeed the rest of society.

Certainly, Godwin is keen to emphasize that such prison guards are not simply examples of 'bad apples'. To dismiss them as such would be reductive and avoids the more difficult task of acknowledging the larger structural issues in society. Guards are both products and reproducers of what we might term today 'institutional violence'. *Caleb Williams* does not so much draw attention to individual cases of wrongdoing as reveal the violent tendencies inherent in the criminal justice system. Nevertheless, it is evident that, in the novel, those worst afflicted by this violent system remain those who are imprisoned by the state. This unwavering focus on the pain of the prisoner forces the reader to engage and empathize with those who are not typically seen. Similarly, the research of contemporary penal abolitionists aims to draw attention to what is often ignored: 'the unnecessary suffering and impact of institutionally-structured violence on the everyday life of those imprisoned' (Scott, 2018: 14). This focus is important since 'acknowledgement of human suffering' is crucial to considering the existing justice system and that the suffering is primarily the prisoner's (Scott, 2018: 42).

The alternative to coercion and punishment

If Godwin repudiates traditional forms of corporal and capital punishment, as well as the views associated with the emerging modern prison, then how does he actually envision tackling crime and punishment? He is confident that if people's human needs were met, the vast majority of crimes would disappear and, crucially, there would be little need for imprisonment. He claims that although born neither good nor bad, humans are naturally inclined to value the principles of benevolence and equity – when these inclinations have not been ruined by the imposing powers of the state and its support for the unequal distribution of wealth and resources within society. As such, in his philosophy, the abolition of prisons is not conceived in isolation, but is part of a wider social project of benevolence and improvement for all. A project for universal happiness and improvement would place great emphasis on community and localized forms of debate and mediation.

Instead of justice being something that is imposed on people by centralized forms of power, communities would settle any issues arising between individuals for the good of the group. Godwin claims that 'general justice and mutual interest are found more capable of binding men than signatures and seals' (Godwin, 1993: 304). Engagement within the community would consist of individuals with shared interests and firsthand knowledge of events and particular contexts. This direct knowledge would provide much greater insight into the causes of events – as opposed to some arbitrary and ill-fitting application of a law. This kind of civic life would deter people from committing harm to others in the vicinity. According to Godwin, humans overwhelmingly seek the positive regard of others and, in a community-based society, would have every means available of effecting it. By contrast, the incentive to harm an individual within the community would be almost non-existent when weighed against the disapproval that one would face from the rest of the members. He writes that 'no individual would hardly be enough in the cause of vice, to defy the general consent of sober judgment that would surround him' (Godwin: 1993: 300). For any harms that did occur, Godwin argues that community-based justice would consist of regarding the action in terms of its effects on the community as well as on individuals (Godwin, 1993: 378). Justice would then be a question of considering 'the intention of the offender' and the 'future likelihood of injury' (Godwin, 1993: 278). But it would also involve the offender understanding and acknowledging the consequences of their actions on the victim, their community and themselves.

As well as often being driven by necessity, Godwin argues that it is the uncertainty of being arrested, charged and then found guilty in court which makes crimes more tempting to commit (Godwin, 1993: 394). In contrast, in such a localized form of authority, the restorative process would inevitably follow any harmful behaviour. As he writes in *Political Justice*, by removing the doubt about whether or not one might get caught, 'it would be as reasonable to expect that a man would wilfully break his leg, for the sake of being cured by a skilled surgeon' as he would willingly commit a crime that he knew would be addressed by the community. It would inevitably lead to a long and painful process (Godwin, 1993: 394). It is important to stress here that the considerable pain that Godwin anticipates is not caused by deliberate punishment, but would emerge as part of the process of getting the offender to understand the effects of their actions on the victim and the community – what we would today call 'restorative justice' (Godwin, 1993: 394).

Critics of restorative justice, or even those who are broadly sympathetic towards its aims, may object along the following lines. It is all very well to talk about using reason to abolish law courts and prisons, but the present state of society is full of vice. The world is not yet ready to change the criminal justice system because criminals would take advantage of the situation. Though there may be a time in the future when society can manage without prisons and punishment, 'at present they would be found deaf to her mandates, and eager to commit every species of injustice' (Godwin, 1993: 383). Yet, Godwin deftly rebuts these anticipated charges: 'coercion', he asserts, 'has no proper tendency to prepare men for a state in which coercion shall cease' (Godwin, 1993: 383). This is certainly true. The use of imprisonment as punishment has not led to fewer criminals or prison sentences. On the contrary, we are now approaching record numbers of people imprisoned in England and Wales, and this figure is expected to rise in the coming years.[3] Even the staunchest supporter of prisons has to accept that they do not seem to have reduced crime in any meaningful sense.

If we do accept that we live in an imperfect world, then when, exactly, will these changes begin? Godwin argues that 'the moment in which they [citizens] can be persuaded to adopt any rational plan for this abolition, is the moment in which the abolition ought to be effected' (Godwin, 1993: 391). In essence, the point at which ideas of justice have infiltrated society – as a result of education and free and open debate – is the precise moment for change. He rejects the view that because people and society are currently imperfect, no amendments to the current system can take place. If that were the case, then nothing would ever improve. But nor is Godwin suggesting that society should simply do away with all forms of imprisonment immediately. Doing so would lead to (temporary) violence and social disorder. Rather, voluntary participation in debate and the propagation of the ideas of social justice and equality will provide the framework with which these forms of state oppression will reveal themselves as immoral and unnecessary and, ultimately, lose all legitimacy.

Godwin's theory of perfectibility, much like the present-day penal abolitionist cause, was not actually end goal-oriented, as many of his critics supposed (Godwin, 1993: 22). He anticipated that a certain degree of knowledge, education, debate and literature would be necessary prior to improving society, but was clear that this this cannot be used as an excuse for infinite deferral. When most people in society have become 'convinced of the flagrant absurdity of its institutions, the whole will soon be prepared for tranquilly and by a sort of common consent to supersede them' (Godwin, 1993: 16). Apart from anything else, he pointed to the fact that society itself is not fixed, but develops and improves (Godwin, 1993: 22). This point is comparable to Coyle's comments regarding the supposedly utopian elements of the penal abolitionist discourse. Coyle, like Godwin, highlights the fact that abolition is an incomplete, unfinished project (see also Coyle and Scott, 2021). Doing so helps to prevent paralysis, which would stifle any progress because it could not achieve all.

Conclusions

Strikingly for the period in which he was writing, Godwin claimed that the existence of prisons did not justify their use. Rather, he was convinced that their existence indicated that society had been structured in opposition to our natural human instincts. Prisons counteract feelings of love, the desire to look after those in need, a freedom and independence of mind, and an ability to exercise reason to think through unique and complex ethical problems. As he puts it in *Political Justice*, 'the more the institutions of society contradict the genuine sentiments of the human mind, the more severely it is necessary to avenge their violation.' (Godwin, 1993: 394)

By emphasizing the miserable outcomes that are generated and reproduced under the criminal justice system, Godwin clearly anticipates penal abolitionists who tend to see the present justice model as antithetical to 'the intrinsic human good' (Scott, 2018: 42). To point out these similarities is to illuminate a rich, and perhaps longer, history of abolitionist thought in Britain than is generally acknowledged. But how might learning about this history prove useful to ongoing abolitionist debates today? Godwin's inclusion in this field adds legitimacy to what is already a rapidly ascending and diverse cause. Reading his writing from the tumultuous, fertile decade of the 1790s underscores the fact that the present criminal justice system is not reflective of a fixed natural state, but, much like female disenfranchisement and the existence of slavery – opposition to which occurred during the same period – is the result of historical processes and therefore able to change.

Given the totalizing nature of Godwin's vision, it is perhaps unsurprising that, having enjoyed a brief period of success in certain progressive and intellectual circles in the early 1790s, his ideas were then criticized by those seeking to maintain the status quo (Tuke, 2021: 142–144). His philosophy was regarded as fantastical when faced with the supposed reality of a vice-ridden society. The apparent proliferation of crimes and criminals at the start of the new century prompted calls for an overhaul of the existing prison system. As the 19th century progressed, elements of Howard's and Bentham's policy ideas were adopted into the reformed prison system. Godwin's astute observations – about the origin of crimes and the nature of criminality, his complete refutation of punishment, his comments about the unjust legal system, the horrendous mental and physical experience of prisoners and his support for what we can be called a restorative form of justice – were largely forgotten.

The anarchist Peter Kropotkin (see Weide, Chapter 9 in this volume) admired and was influenced by Godwin's writings: 'Justice', declared Kropotkin, following his political antecedent, 'is nothing but the recognition of equity for all the members of a given society' (Kropotkin, 1992: 234). It is not a set of rules and laws that are arbitrarily imposed on people by the state. For Kropotkin, the problem with Bentham, the late 18th-century figure most influential in the reformation of the penal system, was that he regarded morals and law as the same thing. In a similar vein, perhaps the greatest lesson that Godwin's writing can impart to us is that the application of justice is as much a question of ethics as it is jurisprudence. The continuing task of proponents of the abolitionist cause is to demonstrate that the current criminal justice system is not just ineffective but also ethically abhorrent. That remains as important now as it was over two centuries ago.

Notes

[1] Colleen Fenno and Philip Jenkins (1984) are notable exceptions.
[2] Louk Hulsman notably critiqued the humanization thesis (Hulsman, 1986: 64–65).
[3] At the time of writing, the total number of people imprisoned in England and Wales is 87,864 (Ministry of Justice, 2023). The Ministry of Justice expects the prison population to exceed 100,000 by 2026, although predictions of prison numbers in the past have proved unreliable.

References

Becker, H. (1963) *Outsiders*, New York: Free Press.
Clemit, P. (1993) *The Godwinian Novel: The Rational Fictions of Godwin, Brockden Brown, Mary Shelley*, Oxford: Clarendon Press.

Coyle, M.J. (2016) 'Penal abolition as the end of criminal behavior', *Journal of Social Justice*, 6: 1–23.

Coyle, M.J. and Scott, D. (eds) (2021) *International Handbook of Penal Abolition*, Abingdon: Routledge.

Fenno, C.M. (2009) 'On trial: restorative justice in the Godwin Wollstonecraft-Shelley family fictions', PhD thesis, Marquette University. Available from: https://epublications.marquette.edu/cgi/viewcontent.cgi?article=1068&context=dissertations_mu [Accessed 10 June 2023].

Godwin, W. (1992) *Collected Novels and Memoirs of William Godwin, Caleb Williams*, vol. 3, London: William Pickering.

Godwin, W. (1993) *Political and Philosophical Writings of William Godwin: An Enquiry Concerning Political Justice*, vol. 3, London: William Pickering.

Hulsman, L.H.C. (1986) 'Critical criminology and the concept of crime', *Contemporary Crises*, 10(1): 63–80.

Ignatieff, M. (1978) *A Just Measure of Pain: The Penitentiary in the Industrial Revolution 1750–1850*, New York: Pantheon.

Jenkins, P. (1984) 'Varieties of enlightenment criminology', *British Journal of Criminology, Delinquency, and Social Behaviour*, 24(2): 112–130.

Kropotkin, P. (1992) *Ethics: Origin and Development*, Montreal: Black Rose Books.

Lefebvre, H. (1992) *The Production of Space*, Oxford: Blackwell.

Mathiesen, T. (1990) *Prison on Trial: A Critical Assessment*, London: Sage.

McGowen, R. (1995) 'The well-ordered prison: England, 1780–1865', in N. Morris and D.J. Rothman (eds) *The Oxford History of the Prison: The Practice of Punishment in Western Society*, Oxford: Oxford University Press, pp 79–109.

Mee, J. (2015) 'The novel wars of 1790–1804', in P. Garside and K. O'Brien (eds) *English and British Fiction 1750–1820*, vol. 2, Oxford: Oxford University Press, pp 199–215.

Ministry of Justice (2023) 'Population bulletin: weekly 1 December 2023'. Available from: https://assets.publishing.service.gov.uk/media/6569a9a2cc1ec500138ef01b/prison-pop-1-dec-2023.ods [Accessed 14 December 2023].

Morris, N. and Rothman, D.J. (eds) (1995) *The Oxford History of the Prison: The Practice of Punishment in Western Society*, Oxford: Oxford University Press.

Ruggiero, V. (2015) 'The legacy of abolitionism', *Champ Pénal/Penal Field*, 12. DOI: https://doi.org/10.4000/champpenal.9080

Scott, D. (2006) 'The caretakers of punishment: prison officers and the rule of law', *Prison Service Journal*, 168: 14–19.

Scott, D. (2008) *Penology*, London: Sage.

Scott, D. (2018) *Against Imprisonment: An Anthology of Abolitionist Essays*, Hook: Waterside Press.

Scott, D. (2020) *For Abolition: Essays on Prisons and Socialist Ethics*, Hook: Waterside Press.

Scott, D. and Sim, J. (eds) (2023) *Demystifying Power, Crime and Social Harm*, London: Palgrave Macmillan.

Tuke, R. (2021) 'Gifts, giving, gratitude: the development of William Godwin's radical critique of charity in the 1790s', in O. O'Brien, H. Stark and B. Turner (eds) *New Approaches to William Godwin: Forms, Fears, Futures*, Basingstoke: Palgrave Macmillan, pp 127–154.

3

Robert Owen and the Owenites: Abolitionist Ideas in the Early British Socialist Movement

Ophélie Siméon

Introduction

Penal abolitionism has a very long history in socialist thought. Indeed, with its focus on community and the collective, this political strand has traditionally attempted to 'procure social peace without a punitive corrections apparatus' (Nagel, 2007: 325). This chapter shines a light on abolitionist ideas in Britain from the 1810s to the 1840s through a critical consideration of the writings of Robert Owen and his followers, the 'Owenites'. Abolitionist sentiments pervade Owen's first major work, *A New View of Society* (1813–1816), and while he was not the first to fundamentally dispute the judicial system and prisons in Britain (William Godwin, for instance, precedes him by a number of decades – see Tuke, Chapter 2 in this volume; Geiser, 2021), he placed great emphasis on the punishment question and the necessity of developing alternative forms of social control in his vision of the ideal society.

This chapter details the key ethical and political dilemmas that Owen attempted to overcome in the context of rising mass industrialization and the subsequent pauperization and perceived moral decline of British society. It also examines how these quandaries shaped the formation of his abolitionist ideas. For Owen, in line with the tenets of philosophical necessitarianism,[1] human nature arises in conjunction with prevailing social conditions and thus it is society, not the individual, that ultimately bears responsibility for the generation of social evils. Alongside his moral critique of capitalist, individualistic societies and the call for a more cooperative approach to social organization, Owen argued that as much as crime was the result of poverty, state punishment was an unjust, patently absurd and evil institution, merely content with curing symptoms of social distress while failing to address its root causes. Consequently, in place of punishment, Owen called for alternative forms of social control grounded in rational persuasion, shaming and broader forms of moral education.

The chapter also considers the immediate influence of Robert Owen's thought on the development of abolitionist ideas and sentiments among the early British socialists – or Owenites – who included William Thompson, John Minter Morgan and many others. The chapter concludes with critical reflections on the historical significance of the Owenite tradition for penal abolitionism and its continued relevance for modern-day abolitionist social movements and activists.

The making of Robert Owen's abolitionist thought

Unlike his educational theories or his role as the 'father of British socialism', Robert Owen's abolitionist views have received very little scholarly scrutiny (Garrán Martínez, 2016). Though he never wrote standalone treatises on the topic, the overlapping issues of crime, punishment and the law remained an underlying preoccupation from the start of his public career in the early 1810s throughout his years at the helm of Britain's first socialist movement (1825–1845). Indeed, Owen's interest in social reform was spurred by a desire – which he shared with other early socialists like Charles Fourier and Henri de Saint-Simon – to right the wrongs of the new industrial age, particularly the threat of rising distress and social turmoil in the midst of unprecedented wealth (see also Scott and Bell, Preface, this volume). As a successful mill owner at New Lanark, Scotland, Owen was certain that industrialization and technical advance held tremendous economic promise, but at the expense of the health, morals and general wellbeing of the labouring classes. The prevention of crime, poverty and ignorance was thus a matter of national urgency, and he believed that men of ample means and influence like himself had a moral duty to engage in such reform campaigns. Interestingly, Owen was appointed Justice of the Peace for Lanarkshire in around 1810 and it was under this title that he published anonymously the first edition of his first major political treatise, *A New View of Society* (1813–1816). Owen's proposed solution essentially applied the principles of philosophical necessitarianism to the field of social reform and originated as a philanthropic 'Plan' for the relief of distress and crime. A religious sceptic, he argued that individual character was not moulded by the stain of original sin, but was shaped by environmental factors, which he called 'circumstances'. Consequently, to eradicate the vices of modern society, putting the blame on individuals was nothing but a preposterous endeavour. The poor and/or the criminal were merely the victims of unfortunate circumstances, often passed on through generations. Society alone was thus responsible, for it had foregone its ancestral sense of community in favour of greed, individualism and competition, thus widening social divisions, themselves a breeding ground for ignorance, poverty and crime. By the same token, any negative disciplinary measure – such as corporal punishments or imprisonment for petty crime – was bound to reinforce these same divisions, as coercion would only foster a negative association in people's minds between discipline and pain, thus hindering any prospect of successful reform.

Consequently, and in the context of the economic crisis that arose in Britain following the end of the Napoleonic Wars, Owen increasingly advocated the creation of a rational environment – namely, one that would foster bonds of solidarity, equality and cooperation through benevolent employment and education – as the only viable solution for the British poor. Published in four instalments between 1813 and 1816, *A New View of Society* identified the pillars of Owen's abolitionism: the creation of a system of national schooling for the poor; an overhaul of the penal system with a focus on prevention as opposed to repression; and the curtailing of crime-inducing habits, such as gambling and alcohol consumption. In around 1815, Owen refined these plans with a new project, known as the 'Villages of Cooperation'. Devised as an improvement upon the Old Poor Law system, the scheme aimed to relocate Britain's poor into a network of self-sufficient communities on the land, where they would be provided with employment and education (One of His Majesty's Justices of Peace for the County of Lanark [Robert Owen], 1813–1817, Third Essay; Owen, 1817a, 1817b, 1817c).

Much like the rest of Owen's system in general, the intellectual roots of his abolitionist ideas are difficult to identify. He most probably borrowed from Locke's theory of rational policing through positive association. More generally, his deterministic system of character formation and his identification of general happiness as the goal and yardstick of all reform do seem to be indebted to William Godwin and Jeremy Bentham, both of whom were close personal acquaintances of Owen's (Harrison, 1969: 84–85; O'Hagan, 2011: 71–90; Siméon, 2017: 23–24; Tuke, Chapter 2 in this volume).

It is thus safe to say that Owen's abolitionist thought was imbued with the reformist spirit of his age – a movement which he himself amply contributed to, from his praise for Elizabeth Fry's work at Newgate Prison to his proposals for factory and Poor Law reform (Owen, 1817d; Cooper, 1979; Matheuszik, 2013: 214–215). Many of the measures he championed – and especially his refusal of corporal and capital punishment – were a direct transposition of the management principles he had been implementing at New Lanark since the early 1800s. As Owen's public profile was growing in the 1810s, he was adamant that 'the result of daily experience among the poor and working classes, on an extensive scale' would legitimize his forays into the fields of poor relief and general social reform (Owen, 1991: 51). On the New Lanark factory floor, Owen's necessitarian ideals shaped a management style based on the transparency of rules, scientific management and positive enforcement. Corporal punishment was banned and negative disciplinary measures such as fines and dismissals were only to be used as a last resort, and only considered necessary in cases of deliberate insubordination, such as repeated pilfering, intoxication at work or absence without leave (Factory Inquiry Commission, 1833: 73–75; Owen, 1858: 35). These principles coalesced into a much-documented surveillance device, the 'silent monitor'. Each factory worker was given a wooden cube whose sides were each painted in a different colour showing both their economic performance and conduct: black (mediocre), blue (pass), yellow (satisfactory) and white (excellent). By putting the behaviour of each in the open for all to see, the device provided an alternative to purely disciplinary methods, such as corporal punishment, while enforcing a constant degree of control and surveillance (Owen, 1857–1858: 81; Siméon, 2017: 63). Many of the reformers who visited New Lanark at Owen's bequest marvelled at the efficiency and rationality of the 'monitors'. During his tour of the mills in 1823, the French journalist and author Marc-Antoine Jullien noticed that the monitors were mostly yellow and white, and was astonished to see that 'there were so few complaints in these factories where so many are gathered together, and where discipline is so laxly enforced' (Jullien, 1823: 22).

As Owen himself put it, all arrangements at New Lanark were 'so formed as to place the conduct of the people at all times before the eye of the community' (House of Commons, 1823), thus fostering habits of self-regulation. Of course, as discussed in Michel Foucault's *Discipline and Punish* (1977[1975]), the inculcation of habits of order among the labouring classes was an objective of capitalist society. Contrary to most of his contemporaries, who did not challenge the punishment logic, Owen argued that well-balanced surveillance and self-regulation was by no means a form of coercion, but the vehicle of individual and collective emancipation. Again, just why Owen was ready to depart from the discourse of traditional management and discipline remains a mystery, as evidence of his formative readings remains virtually non-existent. This was part of a self-publicizing strategy, whereby Owen presented himself as self-made, his ideas stemming entirely from his own life experience. This, in turn, served to differentiate him from classical political thinkers, whom he disparagingly called 'mere closet theorists' (Owen, 1991[1820]: 271; Siméon, 2017: 21). Given Owen's involvement in various philanthropic associations as early as the 1790s, including the Manchester Board of Health, which campaigned in favour of better living and working conditions for the city's factory labourers, one can simply remark that his ideas, interests and methods built upon late Enlightenment ideals of human perfectibility, which he applied to the factory system, thus refusing to see his workers as mere 'hands'(Harrison, 1969: 7–33; Siméon, 2017: 21–22).

Owen's self-regulation ideals were also extended to the arena of local governance. The village was split into 12 'neighbourhood divisions', each with its own elected representatives, or 'principals' who acted as local judiciaries, settling disputes and enforcing order – a model directly inspired by the Kirk Session, the traditional governing body within Scottish Presbyterian parishes. The principals liaised between Owen and the population, and dealt with cases covering public intoxication, debt, failure to pay rent, adultery and illegitimate pregnancies. Criminal offences would then be referred to the local courts, in accordance with the law of the land (Owen, 1855[1800]: 1–3; Siméon, 2017: 59–60).

This system, according to Owen, showed that the New Lanark population had to a great extent acquired the ability of self-regulation, thus producing a superior character in the local population, with very low crime and reoffending rates. Before Owen's time, these cases were brought forward to the Lanark magistrates, who examined the villagers' complaints once a week – an arrangement which in his view did not resolve disputes satisfactorily since the justices did not belong to the factory community. In contrast, he claimed that under his system, the village had only known three instances of serious misconduct in seven years (House of Commons, 1823: 94, 99). These claims cannot be verified in the absence of archival evidence, but they are nonetheless key to understanding Owen's abolitionist thought. By the 1820s, the focus on community as a source of harmony would not merely serve as the foundation of penal reform. Following a process of political radicalization, it would become part of a complete reorganization of society, in which the higher degree of civilization first tried out at New Lanark would be extended to humankind as a whole (Owen, 1857–1858: 191; Siméon, 2017: 102).

Socialism and abolitionism: the role of community

In August 1817, during a meeting at the City of London Tavern, Owen first publicly stated his wish to turn the 'Villages of Cooperation', originally a scheme for poor relief, into a blueprint for the regeneration of society along communitarian lines. In his eyes, all institutions, including established religions, the system of private property and the judiciary, encouraged unnecessary and harmful divisions between the classes, thus hindering general improvement (Owen, 1820). The whole of humanity, not just the poor, would now have to relocate to Villages of Cooperation: it was time to forgo piecemeal reform to embrace a 'social system' or 'science of society', as Owen now called his philosophies, later shortened to 'socialism' (Owen, 1826–1827; Claeys, 1986).

This watershed moment in Owen's political formation also marked a shift in his ideas on penal reform. While his earlier writings had called for a general reform of the judiciary and prison system – including but not limited to the abolition of capital punishment – he now predicted the general disappearance of the corrections apparatus as a whole. This amounted to a form of natural abolitionism, whereby a rational environment – that is, one that would foster bonds of solidarity, equality and cooperation – would gradually eliminate not only crime, but all forms of conflict and aggression, thus rendering obsolete all traditional organs of power, including the police, prisons, and courts. While maintaining his support for the prison reform movement, Owen increasingly came to think that such philanthropic endeavours offered useful but ultimately piecemeal guidelines to alleviate crime. The full effect of these reforms could only be enjoyed in intentional communities inspired by his 'Villages of Cooperation' scheme. In the long run, following a process of general, voluntary re-education, Owen was adamant that the state and government apparatus would naturally wither away, to be superseded by a worldwide network of harmonious communities (Owen, 1857–1858: 191). Within those, the coercive policing of old would be superseded by rational self-government, based on self-restraint and the force of public opinion.

This system of natural abolitionism, as opposed to that enshrined into a legal code (and thus resting, in Owen's eyes, on a form of artificial authority, since it entailed obedience to an external set of rules, as opposed to a reliance on the goodwill of individuals) was refined in various publications throughout Owen's political career, most notably in a series of articles published between 1826 and 1827 in the *New Harmony Gazette*, and detailing the minutiae of socialist life in the new communities. Power and management would be vested in elected representative committees who would exert their authority over all areas of community life, including police and justice. Ultimately, when 'all shall have been equally well-educated', each community would be placed under the jurisdiction of its elders (Owen, 1826–1827: art. ix–xi; Siméon, 2017: 100–101). In Owen's eyes, gerontocracy was the only regime rational enough to quell social divisions, limit the existence of crime and bring about social harmony while easing the natural abolition of coercive law enforcement. Taking cues from both the Kirk Session and New Lanark's 'principals', this system of government led by elders would provide an alternative to the perceived flaws of democracy and aristocracy alike. Owen deemed the former violent and selfish, as it served the interests of the people at the expense of all other classes, thus providing a breeding ground for revolution, social chaos and unchecked criminality. Aristocracy was no better, as power granted by birth negated Owen's deterministic outlook and also fostered social inequalities – another source of crime. In contrast,

Figure 3.1: Frontispiece of *The Crisis*, 7 September 1833

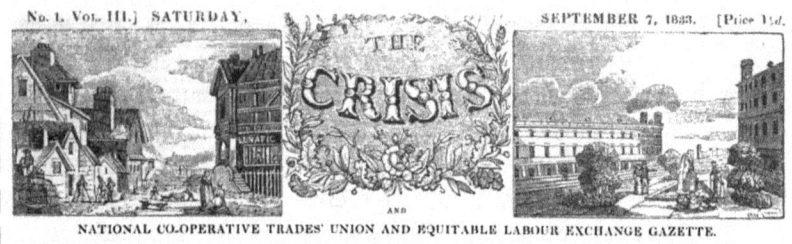

Source: Courtesy of HathiTrust

government within the community would allow everyone, regardless of class,[2] to take power in turn, once they reached the right age. Gerontocratic rule would thus establish a natural aristocracy of wisdom and experience, one which would foster harmonious policing and social relations – and ultimately eliminate all crime – and therefore the need for a penal system.

Penal abolitionism and the Owenite movement

In 1824, Robert Owen embarked on a full-time career as political leader and social reformer. Over the next 20 years, he succeeded in federating the first socialist movement in Britain, also known as 'Owenism'. As his general communitarian schemes began to make inroads into British radical circles, his abolitionist stance also gained prominence among his disciples. The movement was not devoid of ideological faultlines when it came to envisioning the ideal society of the future – what the Owenites called the 'New Moral World'. Many early socialists, most notably William Thompson and the future Chartist founders William Lovett and Henry Hetherington, dismissed Owen's gerontocratic regime in favour of democratic representation. There was nevertheless a consensus regarding the ability of a communitarian system to discourage crime and thus obviate the very need for a punishment apparatus.

The contrast between the old and new systems was made even more apparent when *The Crisis*, which became the official Owenite periodical in the period 1832–1834, unveiled its new frontispiece in September 1833 (Figure 3.1). The present society was depicted as a collection of negative symbols – the inn, the lunatic asylum and the gallows (Gregory, 2021: 103). As shown in the editor's statement, the artist had

> intended to represent the irrational and the rational arrangements of society ... In the old or present condition of mankind, we see the drunken, the criminal, the idle, and the crippled (each the victim of

injustice and mal-arrangement, jostling against and mutually irritating, the proud and the wealthy; while in the new, all are elevated to the same noble equality, alike instructed from birth in the best habits, manners, and acquirements, and … enabled … to live in perpetual competency, and generally to progress towards the highest degree of refinement, physical and mental, which the human mind can rationally imagine or desire. (*The Crisis*, vol. 3, 7 September 1833)

Many Owenite writers thus offered visions of the ideal community and the abolitionist ideals that lay therein. William Thompson, for instance, supported Owen's broad call for natural abolitionism. Though there was no mention of penal reform in his *Inquiry into the Principles of the Distribution of Wealth* (1824), Thompson was adamant that the advent of a communistic society based on the elimination of private property would erase economic inequalities and thus considerably reduce crime (Kaswan, 2014: 12). Indeed, punishments that only served to maintain inequalities under the current system were deemed irrational and counter-productive in essence, as the temptation to break such unjust laws was simply too strong. Additionally, he examined how public opinion and the inculcation of individual and collective responsibility would also work to deter crime in the communities of the future (Thompson, 1824: 230–231). To that end, and in line with Owen, Thompson recommended that only the 'gentlest punishments' focusing on rehabilitation rather than repression would be used, so that:

The terror of the punishment to others – and even shame would then be terrible – would be always joined with a process of reform towards the offender. Thus would the laws execute themselves, and the public force, in this most important branch of government, might be almost dispensed with, and justice would no longer be sarcastically reproached with relying on violence and cruelty as the means of ultimate benevolence. (Thompson, 1824: 213)[3]

In preparation for the advent of the 'New Moral World', the Owenites also supported an array of interim reform measures, such as the abolition of the death penalty (Siméon, 2017: 100; Gregory, 2021: 10). Commenting on Owen's *A New View of Society*, John Minter Morgan suggested that some of the proposed 'Villages of Cooperation' might serve as an asylum 'to those whose loss of character has rendered them outcasts of society' with a view to preventing reoffending, mitigating physical punishment and offering a remedy to overcrowding, especially for young offenders. These alternative bridewells rested firmly on the Owenite principle according to which crime did not originate with innate individual flaws, but was a product of social irrationality. Under the present capitalist system, the depreciation of manual labour in the context of excessive mechanization was chiefly to blame (Morgan [Philanthropos], 1819: 11, 27). Taking cues from both Owen and Elizabeth Fry, whose 'humane exertions' he highly praised, Minter Morgan was confident that the development of penal reform along communitarian lines would help prevent crime through education and useful employment (1819: 76). These ideas were taken up in a later treatise, *Religion and Crime* (1840), which attempted to fuse Owen's abolitionist theories with Minter Morgan's own religious beliefs. Other socialists, like F.D. Maurice and J.M. Ludlow, shared similar views (Maurice, 1843; Ludlow, 1893; Harrison, 1969: 28; Robert, 1979: 52). Though they were all in various ways critical of Owen's scepticism, they shared his will to establish 'a new society, one in which cooperation, not competition, would be the rule' (Robert, 1979: 51). The parish – not the state or the intentional community – would have to become the heart of relief and the prevention of crime, thus offering a revised take on the Old Poor Law system. Men of means and influence were therefore encouraged to act in unison with parish authorities to employ, feed and educate the jobless. The advent of such a system of parochial aid would serve as an antidote to both the workhouse and the prison (Harrison, 1969: 27).

In addition to the abolition of violent punishment and the focus on preventative policing measures, the Owenites also denounced the absurdity of prison sentences for petty crime. The issue certainly hit close to home, as the majority of early British socialists were working-class labourers for whom unemployment and debt were a constant source of anguish. Many Owenites, including Henry Hetherington, were involved in the unstamped press movement[4] and were regularly sent to jail for bankruptcy and seditious activities. But the most notorious penal *cause célèbre* within early socialist circles was undoubtedly the Tolpuddle Martyrs, whose affiliation to the Owenite Grand National Consolidated Trades' Union resulted in their unlawful imprisonment and ultimate deportation to Australia. The Owenites overwhelmingly supported their brethren and denounced the miscarriage of justice, going as far as to organize a mass demonstration from Copenhagen Fields to Whitehall in April 1834 to ask for the sentence to be overturned (Home Office, 1834; *Morning Star*, 22 April 1834, cited in Siméon, 2018: 29). As pardon was denied, the Tolpuddle case fed into the Owenite critique of the British judiciary and penal system. Many of the attacks also drew from the writings of the radical John Gray, who, though not an Owenite himself – he opposed the community of property that formed the bedrock of the 'Villages of Cooperation' – had a tremendous influence among early British socialists. Gray's *Lecture on Human Happiness* (1826) called for the abolition of debtors' prisons, arguing that such institutions overwhelmingly targeted the productive classes, thus hindering the wealth of the nation while exacerbating social and economic divisions – precisely as personal bankruptcy was the product of these divisions. The paradox was summarized thus: 'Persons confined in prison for debt. Here is a glorious specimen of the present system. We first put it into the power of 17,500 individuals to get *into* debt; and then put them in prison, to prevent the possibility of getting *out of it!*' (Gray, 2005[1826]: 62).

Conclusion: Penal abolitionism and the Owenite tradition

The Owenite dream of a society without prisons or punishment did not come to pass. From the 1820s to the mid-1840s, a small network of communities based on the 'Villages of Cooperation' model were established on both sides of the Atlantic. Yet none survived long, due to a combination of financial strife and infighting. With the rise of Chartism, Owen's top-down, paternalistic blueprint of gerontocratic rule found ever little favour among his disciples. In 1845, the flagship community of Queenwood (Hampshire) filed for bankruptcy, effectively putting an end to Owenism as an organized political movement. Despite this, Owen and most of his followers remained politically active, including in the field of penal reform. Established one year after the Queenwood debacle, the Society for the Abolition of Capital Punishment (SACP) found many Owenites among its ranks and also attracted radical Unitarians like Douglas Jerrold Sarjeant, Henry Ashurst and Mary Howitt, who, though not affiliated to Owenism, did nurture links with socialist circles (Gleadle, 1995; Gregory, 2021: 162).

The Owenite impact on the wider abolitionist movement is nevertheless difficult to assess. After 1845, Owen's followers embraced the cause of Chartism, secularism and cooperation based on the Rochdale model, thus cementing their former leader's status as the 'Father of British socialism'. Owen's pioneering views on penal reform were widely celebrated in that context. In May 1851, the *Northern Star* published the proceedings of a 'tea party and *soiree*' in the honour of Owen's eighty-first birthday. One of the attendees, Robert Cooper, deplored that his friend had been 'derided as a visionary', even when he was 'the first to advocate the doctrines of Secular Education, Sanitary Reform, Abolition of Death Punishments, &c., and illustrated by their Bulwers, Jerrolds, and Dickens, who were only disciples of Owen, advocating separate portions of his complete system of society' ('Celebration of the Birthday of Robert Owen', *Northern Star*, 24 May 1851; Gregory, 2021: 103).

This sentiment echoes Owen's ambivalent reputation within the British reform movement. Throughout his public career, he had sought support and financial backing from 'those who have influence in the affairs of men' (Owen, 1991, 1: 10). But his shift from paternalism to socialism following the publication of the *Report to the County of Lanark* (1820) made him a *persona non grata* among the reform-minded upper and middle classes. Even those who respected Owen's philanthropic endeavours, like Henry Brougham and William de Crespigny, were reluctant to align with his more 'utopian' notions (Siméon, 2017: 134–135). Many among the abolitionist movement felt the same. For instance, the radical minister William Joseph Fox – a prominent member of the SACP – welcomed a congregation of progressives at his Finsbury Chapel, including William Lovett and the feminist pioneer Anna Doyle Wheeler (1830). Yet he was keen to distance himself from Owen's communitarian socialism and general religious scepticism, though he did respect his reform work (Fox to Owen, 1840).

Despite their association with various institutions, the Owenite impact on the abolitionist movement was not a dominant one, due to the socialists' perceived radicalism, and due to the coexistence, within abolitionist circles, of discourses and intellectual influences as varied as 'evangelicalism, Benthamism, phrenology … and modern theories on insanity' (Gregory, 2021: 174). Moreover, the ultimate failure of Owenite communities seemed to validate such misgivings, even within radical circles. After 1845, even the cooperative movement – itself the most direct outgrowth of Owenism – abandoned the intentional community as its prime locus of reform in favour of the democratic nation state. With the notable exception of William Morris, 'the principal focus of socialist activity in Britain would never again be the small-scale community' (Claeys, 1986: 291, see also Holland, Chapter 7 in this volume).

The issue of control and personal surveillance within the Owenite communities in lieu of a state-sanctioned punishment apparatus proved another bone of contention. John Stuart Mill, for instance, denounced the power of unchecked public opinion as a serious threat to civil liberties. Likewise, the radical William Cobbett dismissed the 'Villages of Cooperation' as 'parallelogram of paupers', no better than a workhouse, and denounced the loss of individual freedom that these institutions would entail. The Owenites retorted that the community's watchful eye offered a much subtler and fairer form of control than the one exerted by the police, the judiciary and the prison system, insofar as communal government would operate following a process of voluntary, natural re-education towards the greater good. As all would have the community's interest at heart, William Thompson argued, prying and judgement would vanish, while freedom of expression would prevail (Thompson, 1830: 33–34; Claeys, 1986: 123).

Such faith in a natural conversion to an abolitionist regime, guided by the power of a just public opinion, may sound idealistic. Nor does the extent of public surveillance sit well with modern notions of democracy (Foucault, 1977; Christie, 1982: 86). The potential corollary of a world without prisons – that is, 'a disciplinary society in which the Panopticon gaze is omnipresent' (Nagel, 2007) – which would pose a threat to civil liberties in the name of security may explain why full abolition is generally a less popular option than calls for an overhaul of penal codes and institutions along more humanitarian lines.

However, this does not mean that the Owenite take on abolitionism is entirely devoid of relevance. Even though its concrete impact on later penal reform movements appears negligible, many of the ideas first put forward by Robert Owen and his disciples have retained their bite. Though it makes no reference to this strand of early socialism, modern abolitionist thought still insists on finding 'alternatives to punishment, not only alternative punishments' (Christie, 1982: 11). That includes a focus on community-based, not individual accountability and a critique of the capitalistic undertones of the current prison system, especially in the context of mass incarceration and the development of private, for-profit carceral facilities. This is fully in line with abolitionist ideals, which insisted on avoiding recidivism, reconciliation through education and the reintroduction of offenders – with the exception of violent criminals – into society. Distant echoes of Owenism may, for instance, be found in the abolitionist handbook *Instead of Prisons*, which hoped that 'gradual reductions in the degree and type of punishments can, in the long range, lead towards the total elimination of sanctions' (Knopp et al, 1976: 11). Moreover, the Owenites' focus on community-based governance and policing is also reminiscent of restitution practices and restorative justice overall, with its insistence on group discussion, healing and community service (Morris, 1995; Sullivan and Tift, 2001: 11).

In view of these similarities, the Owenite take on penal abolitionism cannot be entirely dismissed as a misguided vision of the good society. Owenism may have been 'utopian', but only because it established the right to a better life as a condition of general progress, even for those labelled as criminal. To that end, they designed practical solutions to the coercive penal apparatus of their day that firmly opposed the dominant discourses on crime and punishment – namely, the idea that the poor and the working classes were innately predisposed to a life of idleness and misdeed. If imagination is indeed an instrument of critique, then the Owenite vision of a future without crime and prisons was firmly embedded in the empirical realities of modern capitalist society (Ricœur, 1985; Claeys, 2011; Levitas, 2013; Siméon, 2021: 160).

Notes

[1] Necessitarianism is a philosophical concept, most famously defended by Spinoza, which argues in favour of a deterministic view of human nature. This strand of thought focuses on the inevitability of external circumstances in shaping both human character and social institutions, and denies the prevalence of free will over human actions and existence.

[2] Owen was rather nonspecific regarding gender, while other early socialists like William Thompson explicitly stated that power would be shared among men and women in

the communities of the future. See Thompson, 1830; and Thompson and Wheeler, 1994[1825].

[3] My sincere thanks to Mark J. Kaswan for his enlightening remarks on William Thompson's communitarian ideals.

[4] The term refers to the cheap, radical publications that refused (out of limited means and/or political conviction) to pay a government-imposed tax on newspapers under the Stamp Act 1712. Following widespread outrage at what amounted to anti-radical censorship, the Act was repealed in 1855 (Hollis, 1970).

References

Primary sources

Archives and manuscripts

Factory Inquiry Commission (1833) *First Report: Employment of Children in Factories*, Parliamentary Papers 1833 (XX).

Fox, W.J. to Robert Owen, 2 March 1840. Robert Owen Collection, Manchester: National Co-operative Archive ROC/6/30/2.

Home Office Papers (1834) HO 52/54, London: National Archives.

House of Commons (1823) *Report from the Select Committee on the Employment of the Poor in Ireland*.

Books, pamphlets and periodicals

'Celebration of the Birthday of Robert Owen' (1851) *Northern Star and Leeds General Advertiser*, 24 May.

Gray, J. (2005[1826]) *A Lecture on Human Happiness*, in G. Claeys (ed.) *Owenite Socialism: 1823–1831*, London: Routledge, pp 44–93.

Jullien, M.-A. (1823) 'Notice sur la colonie industrielle de New Lanark en Écosse, fondée par M. Robert Owen', *Revue encyclopédique*, 18.

Ludlow, J.M. (1893) 'Some of the Christian Socialists of 1848 and the following years', *Economic Review*, pp 486–500.

Maurice, F.D. (1843) *The Kingdom of Christ: Or, Hints Respecting the Principles, Constitution, and Ordinances of the Catholic Church*, New York: D. Appleton & Company.

Morgan, J.M. [Philanthropos] (1819) *Remarks on the Practibility of Mr. Robert Owen's Plan to Improve the Condition of the Lower Classes*, London: S. Leigh.

Morgan, J.M. (1840) *Religion and Crime; Or, The Condition of the People*, London: Henry Hooper.

One of His Majesty's Justices of Peace for the County of Lanark [Robert Owen] (1813–1816) *New View of Society: or, Essays on the Principle of the Formation of the Human Character, and the Application of the Principle to Practice*, London: R. Taylor.

Owen, R. (1855[1800]) 'Regulations and rules for the inhabitants of New Lanark', in R. Owen, *The New Existence of Man upon the Earth: Containing a Proposed Treaty of a Holy Alliance of Government for the People of the Civilised World*, London: J. Clayton.

Owen, R. (1817a) *Address, dated September 19th 1817; on Measures for the Immediate Relief of the Poor*, in R. Owen, *A New View of Society and Other Writings*, G. Claeys (ed.), London: Penguin Classics, pp 227–231.

Owen, R. (1817b) *Report to the Committee of the Association for the Relief of the Manufacturing and Labouring Poor, Laid before the Committee of the House of Commons on the Poor Laws*, London: printed by the author.

Owen, R. (1817c) *A Further Development of the Plan for the Relief of Mankind*, in R. Owen, *A New View of Society and Other Writings*, G. Claeys (ed.), London: Penguin Classics, pp 204–226.

Owen, R. (1817d) 'A Further Development of the Plan Contained in the Report to the Committee of the Association for the Relief of the Manufacturing Poor; with Answers to Objections. And an Account of the Effects Produced on Female Prisoners in Newgate by the Application in Practice of These Principles, Carried into Execution by Mrs. Fry and other benevolent Individuals of the Society of Friends', *The Times*, 30 July: 3–4.

Owen, R. (1820) *Report to the County of Lanark*, in R. Owen, *A New View of Society and Other Writings*, G. Claeys (ed.), London: Penguin Classics, pp 250–308.

Owen, R. (1826–1827) 'The Social System', *New Harmony Gazette*.

Owen, R. (1857–1858) *The Life of Robert Owen, Written by Himself*, London: Effingham Wilson.

Owen, R. (1858) *Threading My Way: Twenty-Seven Years of Autobiography*, London: Trübner & Co.

Owen, R. (1991) *A New View of Society and Other Writings*, G. Claeys (ed.), London: Penguin Classics.

Thompson, W. (1824) *An Inquiry into the Principles of the Distribution of Wealth Most Conducive to Human Happiness*, London: Longman, Hurst, Rees, Orme, Brown & Green.

Thompson, W. (1830) *Practical Directions for the Speedy and Economical Establishment of Communities: On the Principles of Mutual Co-operation, United Possessions and Equality of Exertions and of the Means of Enjoyment*, London: Strange.

Thompson, W. and Wheeler, A.D. (1994[1825]) *Appeal of One Half of the Human Race, Women, Against the Pretensions of the Other Half, Men, to Retain Them in Political, and Thence in Civil and Domestic, Slavery*, M. Foot and M. Mulvey Roberts (eds), Bristol: Thoemmes.

Wheeler, A.D. (1830) 'Rights of Women. A Lecture Delivered by Mrs. Wheeler, Last Year, in a Chapel near Finsbury Square'. *British Co-operator*, pp 12–15.

Secondary sources

Christie, N. (1982) *Limits to Pain*, Oxford: Martin Robertson.

Claeys, G. (1986) *Citizens and Saints: Politics and Anti-politics in the Early Socialist Movement*, Cambridge: Cambridge University Press.

Claeys, G. (2011) *Searching for Utopia: The History of an Idea*, London: Thames & Hudson.

Cooper, R.A. (1979) 'The English Quakers and prison reform 1809–23', *Quaker History*, 68(1): 3–19.

Foucault, M. (1977[1975]) *Discipline and Punish: The Birth of the Prison*, New York: Random House.

Garrán Martínez, J.M. (2016) 'El Mundo jurídico en la filosofía utópica de Robert Owen', *Bajo Palabra. Revista de Filosofía*, 12: 127–140.

Geiser, S. (2021) 'Punitive injustice in Caleb Williams: Godwin's veiled call for penal reform', in J. Lynch and J.T. Scanlan (eds) *The Age of Johnson: A Scholarly Annual*, vol. 24, New Brunswick, NJ: Rutgers University Press, pp 139–159.

Gleadle, K. (1995) *The Early Feminists. Radical Unitarians and the Emergence of the Women's Rights Movement, 1831–51*, Basingstoke: Palgrave Macmillan.

Gregory, J. (2021) *Victorians against the Gallows. Capital Punishment and the Abolitionist Movement in Nineteenth-Century Britain*, London: Bloomsbury Academic.

Harrison, J.F.C. (1969) *Owen and the Owenites in Britain and America: The Quest for the New Moral World*, New York: Routledge.

Hollis, P. (1970) *The Pauper Press: A Study in Working-Class Radicalism of the 1830s*, Oxford: Oxford University Press.

Kaswan, M.J. (2014) *Happiness, Democracy, and the Cooperative Movement: The Radical Utilitarianism of William Thompson*, Syracuse, NY: SUNY Press.

Knopp, F. et al (1976) *Instead of Prisons: A Handbook for Abolitionists*, Syracuse, NY: Prison Research Education Action Project.

Levitas, R. (2013) *Utopia as Method*, London: Palgrave Macmillan.

Matheuszik, D.L. (2013) 'The angel paradox: Elizabeth Fry and the role of gender and religion in nineteenth-century Britain', DPhil thesis, Vanderbilt University.

Morris, R. (1995) *A Practical Path to Restorative Justice*, Toronto: Rittenhouse.

Nagel, M. (2007) 'The role of prisons in a socialist future or: the incorrigible ethos of incarceration', in A. Anton and R. Schmitt (eds) *Toward a New Socialism*, Lanham, MD: Lexington Books, pp 325–245.

O'Hagan, F. (2011) 'Robert Owen and education', in C. Williams and N. Thompson (eds) *Robert Owen and His Legacy*, Cardiff: University of Wales Press, pp 71–90.

Ricœur, P. (1985) *Lectures on Ideology and Utopia*, G.H. Taylor (trans.), New York: Columbia University Press.

Robert, D. (1979) *Paternalism in Victorian England*, London: Croom Helm.

Siméon, O. (2017) *Robert Owen's Experiment at New Lanark: From Paternalism to Socialism*, London: Palgrave Macmillan.

Siméon, O. (2018) 'The Grand National Consolidated Trades' Union, 1833–1834: class and conflict in the early British labour movement', in E. Avril and Y. Béliard (eds) *Labour United and Divided from the 1830s to the Present*, Manchester: Manchester University Press, pp 21–32.

Siméon, O. (2021) *Contemporary Thought on Nineteenth Century Socialism*, vol. 1, Abingdon: Routledge.

Sullivan, D. and Tifft, L. (2001) *Restorative Justice: Healing the Foundations of Our Everyday Lives*, Monsey, NY: Willow Tree Press.

4

'Do What Is Right, and Let Come What May': Tolstoy and Penal Abolition

Andrei Zorin

The Resurrection

In the whole history of the abolitionist movement, Tolstoy's position was arguably one of the most radical. He did not bother too much about the question of how to replace, humanize or reform the existing system of legal punishment, clearly believing it to be beyond humanization or reform, but insisted that incarcerating human beings, let alone murdering them in the name of so-called 'law', was an abomination that could not be justified by any plausible arguments and should be stopped immediately and unconditionally.

This chapter will discuss Tolstoy's criticism of the system of legal violence based on his belief that the divinely ordained equality of human beings meant that no form of coercion could ever be legitimate. The first section of the chapter starts by describing his personal experience of dealing with violence and the ways it shaped his moral and social philosophy. Of course, the concept of nonviolence is one of the most well-known and widely discussed elements of Tolstoy's philosophy. However, the absolute character of the nonviolence principle somehow obscures Tolstoy's lifetime passion in analysing the phenomenon of violence, reconstructing its inner logic and establishing the complex hierarchy of its forms. This hierarchy will constitute the subject of the next section. The final section will discuss Tolstoy's perception of prison and penal institutions, as most clearly expressed in his last major novel *Resurrection*.

Why do people kill each other?

The question of the nature and legitimacy of violence worried Tolstoy throughout his life. In one of his earliest stories, *The Raid*, written in 1852 when he was 23 and participated in the war in the Caucuses, an old officer asks an autobiographical narrator: 'Do you simply wish to see how people are killed?' In the final text, the question is left unanswered, but in the drafts, the unhesitant author answers in the affirmative: 'Yes that is exactly what I wanted to see – a man who has no resentment against other person kills him and why' (Tolstoy, 1928–1964, III: 16, 227)

On 6 April 1857 in Paris, Tolstoy for the first time in his life witnessed an execution. In Russia, where public executions had been outlawed before his birth, he did not have such an opportunity. Murderer Francis Richeux was guillotined in the presence of a crowd of up to 15,000 people. The same day, Tolstoy recorded his impression in his diary and wrote about it in a letter to his Moscow friend Vasily Botkin. As it was usual for his diary and letter writing, he immediately passed from recording his immediate experience to philosophizing about the main questions of human existence:

> I have seen many horrible things in war and in the Caucasus, but if a man were torn to pieces before my eyes it would not have been so revolting as this ingenious and elegant machine by means of which a strong, hale and hearty man was killed in an instant ... The insolent, arrogant desire to carry out justice and the law of God. – justice, which is determined by lawyers taking their stand on honour, religion, and all contradicting each other ... Then the repulsive crowd, the father explaining to his daughter what a convenient and ingenious mechanism that does it etc. The law of man – what nonsense! The truth is that the state is a conspiracy designed not only to exploit, but above all to corrupt its citizens ... I will certainly never go and see such a thing again, and I will never serve *any* government anywhere. (Tolstoy 1978, I: 96–97)

This moment was one of the most decisive in Tolstoy's life. He returned to it many times, finding in this particular experience the roots of his attitude to institutionalized violence. Nearly 30 years later in his treatise *What Then Must We Do?*, he recalled the day when he saw:

> how, in the presence of thousands of spectators, they cut a man's head off with a guillotine. I knew that the man was a dreadful criminal; I knew all the arguments that have been written in defence of that kind of action, and I knew it was done deliberately and intentionally, but at the moment the head and body separated and fell into the box

I gasped, and realized not with my mind nor with my heart but with my whole being, that all the arguments in defence of capital punishment are wicked nonsense, and that however many people may combine to commit murder – the worst of all crime – and whatever they may call themselves, murder remains murder, and that this crime had been committed before my eyes, and I by my presence and non-intervention had approved and shared in it. (Tolstoy, 1991: 8)

Mortals, according to Tolstoy, were not entitled to make laws; all they had to do was to obey the eternal rules of God, but even those could not be enforced, as church hierarchy and coercion in the sphere of religious beliefs were especially repulsive. But the worst abomination in the history of humanity was the state itself with its monarchs, parliaments, politicians, laws, courts, prisons, soldiers, judges, bureaucrats, tax collectors and so on that presupposed the existence of hierarchy and the exercise of power by some over others.

In spite of his aversion to all legal procedures, Tolstoy once decided to participate in a trial in a military tribunal. In 1866, he took upon himself the defence of Private Vasily Shabunin, who had assaulted an officer and was facing capital punishment. In spite of all Tolstoy's efforts, Shabunin was sentenced to death by the tribunal. Tolstoy tried to use his connections at the court and petitioned Emperor Alexander II, but his letter was not delivered to the Emperor for procedural reasons. This failed intervention tortured Tolstoy for years to come. He reproached himself that in spite of his wish to speak to the judges about the eternal truths of human and Christian morality, he had based his defence upon the paragraphs of military statutes trying to prove that Shabunin's crime should not be punished so severely (see Kerr, 1982).

Forty years later, when his disciple Pavel Biriukov wrote in Tolstoy's biography about this case, Tolstoy confessed to him bitterness and shame that the recollections of this episode still arose in him:

Yes, it was terribly revolting to me now to reread my pitiful, disgusting speech for the defence ... Speaking of the most obvious offence against the laws of God or men, that some men were preparing to commit against their brother, I did nothing better than to cite some stupid words written by somebody else called laws. (Kerr, 1982: 176)

Tolstoy's self-accusations were only partially caused by the failure of his petition. Rather, he reproached himself that in trying to help the unfortunate soldier, he had not listened to the voice of his own conscience and used arguments devoid of any moral sense and still could not achieve anything. From the point of view of mature Tolstoy, death was not the worst outcome for Shabunin and, in any case, the vain hopes of rescuing the victim should not have made the writer take part in a shameful show that inevitably constitutes the essence of any court proceedings. That aversion became one of the main cornerstones of his social and moral philosophy.

In his essay *What Do I Believe*, written after he had undergone a spiritual crisis and a religious conversion, Tolstoy formulated the five main commandments of Jesus deducted from his study of the Gospels that constituted, from his point of view, the only foundation not only of true Christianity, but also of any valid religion and moral code (Tolstoy, 1933: 74–78). The third of these commandments was based on Jesus' rule 'never to swear oaths' (Matthew 5:34) that, according to Tolstoy, meant absolute prohibition to pledge loyalty to earthly governments and to participate in legal proceedings.[1] Tolstoy believed that humans should free themselves from the obligation to judge others and to subjugate their personal conscience to the authority of the state and the law.

This moral autonomy of any person implied the principle of not resisting evil with violence that constituted, according to Tolstoy, the fourth and the most important of Christ's commandments. Neither the restoration of justice, nor life-threatening circumstances, nor even the danger to one's close relatives or other fully innocent people could serve as a justification for violence – one should never resort to force, but instead one should accept one's fate with humility and prayer. Violence was especially abhorrent because it constituted the most powerful tool and the ultimate expression of coercion.

Finally, the fifth commandment was not to regard other human beings as enemies or aliens, thus abolishing the division of humankind into nations and making war all but impossible. Tolstoy insisted on the literal interpretation of these commandments: 'It is impossible to admit a slightest compromise over an idea. Compromise will inevitably come in practice (as you rightly say) and therefore it is even less possible to admit compromise in theory', he wrote to his American follower Chaim-Wolf Kantor in 1890 (Tolstoy, 1978, vol. II: 456).

Divine essence and the moral dignity of human existence was hugely more important for Tolstoy that any practical considerations. In his preface to the book written by his disciple Vladimir Chertkov about William Lloyd Garrison, one of the most famous American slavery abolitionists, Tolstoy brought forward the strongest argument that Garrison made against slavery:

> Garrison understood that which the most advanced among the fighters against slavery did not understand; that the only irrefutable argument against slavery is the denial of the right of any man over the liberty of another under any conditions whatsoever.
>
> The Abolitionists endeavoured to prove that slavery was unlawful, disadvantageous, cruel; that it depraved men, and so on; but the

defenders of slavery in their turn proved the untimeliness and danger of emancipation, and the evil results liable to follow it. Neither the one nor the other could convince his opponent. Whereas Garrison, understood that the slavery of the negroes was only a particular instance of universal coercion, put forward a general principle with which it was impossible not to agree – the principle that under no pretext has any man the right to dominate, i.e., to use coercion over his fellows …

For the purpose of combating slavery, he advanced the principle of struggle against all the evil of the world. (Tchertkoff and Holah, 1904: vii)

This argument made all violence inconceivable and indefensible. No crime, regardless of its horror and brutality, could be punished by incarceration, let alone capital punishment, which is the utmost manifestation of coercive power of one human being over another, and thus can and should never be legitimized or rationalized. In the same essay on Garrison, Tolstoy recalled his conversation with 'remarkably intelligent and progressive' American thinker and politician William Jennings Brown, who:

> with the evident intention of gently and courteously showing me my delusion, asked me how I explained my strange principle of non-resistance to evil by violence, and as usual, he brought forward the argument, which seems to everyone irrefutable, of the brigand who kills or violates a child. I told him that I recognize non-resistance to evil by violence because, having lived seventy-five years, I have never, except in discussions, encountered that fantastic brigand, who, before my eyes, desired to kill or violate a child, but that perpetually I did and do see not one, but millions of brigands using violence towards children and women and men and old people and all the laborers in the name of the recognized right of violence over one's fellows. When I said this, my kind interlocutor, with his naturally quick perception, not giving me time to finish, laughed and recognized that my argument was satisfactory. (Tchertkoff and Holah, 1905: vii)

The robber attacking his victim and the judge sending the robber to the gallows both violated the eternal rules of religion and morality. However, their relative culpability was not the same. In his artistic and philosophical works, Tolstoy analysed and described the multiple forms that coercion and violence could take in human history and human society and the relations between these.

Tolstoy's theory of violence

As discussed in the previous section, Tolstoy's encounter with state violence happened very early on in his life and his interest in these problems was already evident in his early fiction, diaries and essays. However, his focus on the dialectics of 'crime and punishment' became obsessive in the later period of his life and works when he formulated his religious, moral and philosophical doctrine based on the principle of nonviolence, and especially after Dostoevsky's death, when he took upon his shoulders the responsibility for the representation of this topic in his artistic works that in this period constantly deal with murders, executions, incarcerations and other forms of criminal or institutionalized violence. Very often using Dostoevsky's model, he based his narratives on criminal chronicle. Trials, arrests, prisons and executions are at the centre of such works as *God Sees the Truth But Is Slow to Tell* (1872), *The Power of Darkness* (1886), *Kreutzer Sonata* (1889), *Resurrection* (1898), *The Light Shines Even in the Darkness* (1900), *After the Ball* (1903), *Forged Coupon* (1904), *Divine and Human* (1905). The same motives figure even more prominently in his unfinished works and his drafts.

Passionately rejecting any kind of violence and above all murder, Tolstoy did not consider death as something bad in itself. On the contrary, he was sure that a person should be constantly ready for death and regarded it as a necessary transition to a different state or unification of the animal existence locked in the confines of material body to what he called general life. Thus, there is no reason for a human being to be afraid of her own death, or even that of loved ones. In the previously quoted letter to Chaim-Wolf Kantor, Tolstoy strongly objected to his correspondent's statement that mad people should be forcefully isolated for their own good to preserve them from committing crimes:

> If I admit that a madman can be locked up, I ought to admit too that he ought to be killed. Why should he go on suffering? … If people may be locked up, the result will be the violence from which world now suffers – there are 100,000 prisoners in Russia … The fact [is] that a madman might kill me or you, or my daughter or your mother. But what is so terrible about that? We all can and we all have to die. But we don't all have to do evil. But in the first place, madmen rarely kill; and if they do, surely the object which needs to be pitied and helped is not me – a madman can only kill me – but the madman himself – most likely deformed and suffering; he needs to be helped, he needs to be thought about. (Tolstoy, 1978, II: 157)

The evil committed by violence, and first of all by murder of the living creature is not caused by the harm done to the victim, but by that done to the soul of the murderer which is poisoned and ruined by this act. As is the case with any other human being, the murderer's soul belongs to the 'general life', some unified universal soul which is inevitably contaminated by the evil we commit. But even the cruellest crime might be partially redeemed by sincere repentance – the evildoer has to see his sin from the perspective of an ideal of rational and moral life, be horrified by it, repent and correct his earthly ways. Thus, the assessment of all historically existent forms of violence could be based on the chance of repentance they provide to the perpetrator and the possibility for the criminal to realize the sinfulness of his actions.

The main criterion for the distribution of the different types of violence on the different layers of the comparative scale of evil is the possibility – or rather probability – of repentance. The sin becomes more terrible when the sinner is convinced of the legitimacy of his actions: so outright criminal violence, including most horrifying murders, leaves a better chance for salvation then that committed under the pretext of legality. Robbers and murderers acting at their own risk deserve more compassion than executioners or judges who send people to the gallows protected by the law and the repressive apparatus of the state. Tolstoy considered Schiller's *Robbers* to be the best tragedy ever written because the German author has shown that:

> the man who deprives another one of the fruits of his labour by stealth or robbery knows that what he did is evil, while the one who does the same by the methods that society believes to be legal does not see his life as evil, and thus this honest citizen is morally incomparably worse than the robber. (Tolstoy 1928–1964, LXIII: 24)

According to Tolstoy, even most hardened murderers always know deep in their hearts that their actions break God's eternal rules and have to suppress the voice of conscience within them, but in some circumstances their conscience may be reawakened.

Tolstoy's belief in the human potential for moral redemption was radical and did not have any limits or exemptions. In his tragedy *The Power of Darkness* (1886), he includes a character who first helps his adulterous lover to poison her husband, then seduces the husband's daughter from the first marriage and finally commits the vilest imaginable crime of murdering his own newborn son. However, this monstrous act finally leads him to the understanding of the basic moral maxims and thus to repentance:

NIKÍTA.	I smothered the baby in the cellar with a board! I sat on it and smothered it—and its bones crunched! (*Weeps*) And I buried it! I did it, all alone!
AKOULÍNA.[2]	He raves! I told him to!
NIKÍTA.	Don't shield me! I fear no one now! Forgive me, Christian Commune! (*Bows to the ground*). *Silence.*
POLICE OFFICER.	Bind him! The marriage is evidently off! *Men come up with their belts.*

NIKÍTA.	Wait, there's plenty of time! (*Bows to the ground before his father*) Father, dear father, forgive me too – fiend that I am! You told me from the first, when I took to bad ways, you said then, 'If a claw is caught, the bird is lost!' I would not listen to your words, dog that I was, and it has turned out as you said! Forgive me, for Christ's sake!
AKÍM.	(*rapturously*) God will forgive you, my own son! (*Embraces him*) You have had no mercy on yourself, He will show mercy on you! God – God! It is He! (Tolstoy, 1904: 95)

Akim, the father of the murderer, serves in the play as the embodiment of Christian morality. Before Nikita's confession, he was not aware of his crimes, though he clearly knew that his son had ruined his soul. He reacts to Nikita's confession not with horror and dismay, but with rapture because he knows that the way to redemption is open even for the most terrible criminal.

In the story *The Forged Coupon* (1904) that Tolstoy was drafting and editing for 15 years, he speaks about the infectiousness of evil that keeps spreading and growing from the financial document forged by two schoolboys to the cruellest murders. However, this chain of crime is broken when the murderer Stepan Pelageyushkin kills and robs the old woman who, seeing the knife in his hands, does not even try to defend herself, but says: 'Oh, that is a terrible sin. What are you doing? Take pity on yourself. Destroying other people's souls and what's worse your own too' (Tolstoy, 2015, 76). Stepan still murders the virtuous woman, but is never able to get away from the consciousness of his crime and after terrible pangs of conscience finds the path to redemption and moral resurrection. At the end of the story, the governor of the region where Pelageyushkin serves his sentence says about him: 'He murdered six people; but he's a saintly man. I'll vouch for him' (Tolstoy, 2015, 100).

In the process of his moral regeneration, Pelageyushkin helps to mend the souls of other hardened sinners – most notably of the murderer, convict and executioner Makhorkin, who refuses to perform his duties of an executioner that allowed him to earn some money in prison and serve his sentence comfortably. According to Tolstoy, the executioners are morally inferior to murderers: first, because they can justify their actions claiming that they were just following orders; and, second, because killing the people they do not subject themselves to any risk. Still, even the most stupid and ignorant among them can't help knowing that their trade is contemptible and thus could be to some degree open to repentance.

In *The Divine and the Human* (1905), the last story Tolstoy published in his lifetime, we encounter the same situation. Svetlogub, the revolutionary, on being sentenced to death, had experienced the epiphany of all-forgiving love. During the execution, he addresses the executioner about to hang him with a simple question: 'Don't you pity me?' As Tolstoy writes, Svetlogub 'looked with astonishment at the executioner, hastily and deftly carrying out his terrible duty. The executioner's face was the simple face of a Russian working person – not evil, but concentrated on performing a necessary and complicated task as well as he could' (Tolstoy, 2000: 147–148). The concentration on the technical side allows the executioner to believe his job is necessary; thus, being faced with the question so obviously alien to the mechanistic routine of the legal murder, the executioner at first becomes angry at his victim. However:

> Svetlogub's words, 'Don't you pity me?' would not leave his head. A former murderer, he was still a prisoner; becoming the executioner had provided him with some measure of freedom and more comfort. But from this day on, he refused to perform his job. Within a week he drank away not only all the money he had received from Svetlogub's execution, but all of his rather expensive wardrobe. Soon he was reduced to such a state that he was put in 'the hole' in the prison. From 'the hole' he was moved to the prison hospital. (Tolstoy, 2000: 148–149)

To a significant extent, Tolstoy's vision of the mentality of executioners can also refer to soldiers who take to arms and kill according to their oath and orders of their commanders. Moreover, while executioners have some vague understanding that their craft is vile, soldiers tend to take pride in their mission. Tolstoy regarded military service as the most terrible of social evils and believed that the universal rejection of it would cause the destruction of the unjust world order and herald the beginning of the moral regeneration of humankind. This problem became central in one of the most important of Tolstoy's social-philosophical works, *The Kingdom of God Is within You*, where Tolstoy refuted the idea that institutionalized violence can be justified by religious, political, moral or scientific arguments.

In general, Tolstoy's attitude to war, conscription and military violence is beyond the scope of this chapter. However, this very treaty ends with the description of his meeting with a regiment of soldiers preparing do the executioners' job – to suppress peasant rebellion:

> smart young fellows in their clean new uniforms, were standing about in groups or sitting swinging their legs in the wide-open doorways of the luggage vans. Some were smoking, nudging each other, joking, grinning, and laughing, others were munching sunflower seeds and

spitting out the husks with an air of dignity. Some of them ran along the platform to drink some water from a tub there, and when they met the officers they slackened their pace, made their stupid gesture of salutation, raising their hands to their heads with serious faces as though they were doing something of the greatest importance. They kept their eyes on them till they had passed by them, and then set off running still more merrily, stamping their heels on the platform, laughing and chattering after the manner of healthy, good-natured young fellows, traveling in lively company.

They were going to murder of their fathers or grandfathers just as if they were going on a party of pleasure, or at any rate on some quite ordinary business. (Tolstoy, 1894: 292–293)

Thirty-three years earlier, Tolstoy had been shocked by the mechanical soullessness of the guillotine execution. This time he witnessed with his own eyes the transformation of young people, who were not cruel by nature, into the mechanical tools of murder – living guillotines. According to him, this horrifying transformation was enabled by the division of violence, allowing the perpetrators to feel they are not guilty of the evil they commit. Those who had to kill physically acquired the possibility to discharge themselves of any responsibility for their actions because they were following orders, while those who gave them these inhumane orders could avoid the unpleasant necessity of killing with their own hands.

In his famous novel *War and Peace* written in the 1860s, Tolstoy glorified popular resistance to invasion. After his religious conversion in the late 1870s and early 1880s, he regarded military service as one of the worst abominations in human history. Native government was no more legitimate than any foreign one: living under the rule of the French, the Turks or whoever else would be a lesser evil for his compatriots than going to war and killing people. By the same token, prosecutors, judges, ministers and generals sending people to death could also reassure themselves by claiming they were only obeying their monarch or the abstract laws they had to implement. This game of transferring responsibility to the shoulders of others, be it the person of the head of state or the anonymous laws, reveals the essence of the state whose only goal is to sustain the impeccable functioning of the mechanism of violence that seemingly functions independently of the personal actions and the responsibility of the evildoers.

In *The Divine and the Human* (1905), the general who signed the death sentence of Svetlogub which he knew to be unjust says to himself: 'I am just following orders and I should be above these considerations ... trying to inspire an attitude of alienated cruelty that didn't exist in his heart.' He recalls his last meeting with the Tsar and experiencing again 'the feeling of servile affection that he derived from his unconditional devotion to his

Tsar, he drove away his momentary hesitation, signed the rest of the papers' (Tolstoy, 2000: 125).

The high-ranking statesmen who had never had the unpleasant feeling of a person dealing with the physiologically disgusting experience of actual murder can more easily convince themselves that their actions are just and rightful, and because of that, they are further removed from the possibility of repentance than actual murderers. The pianist Alexander Goldenveizer, who often visited the Tolstoy family, recorded in his diaries the conversation about executions:

> Sofia Andreevna [Tolstoy's wife] tried to prove that all the murders are no less an evil than executions, but no one talks about them. Elizaveta Valerianovna [Tolstoy's favourite niece] objected that the execution is the murder that is considered just and here is the main horror. Lev Nikolaevich said: – If you ask who is worse, the miserable executioner who is bribed and made drunk or the prosecutors and judges who bribe him and condemn people to death – there can be no doubt, I think. (Goldenveizer, 1959: 223)

The special role in this pyramid of violence belongs to those who are located at its summit – the bearers of supreme power. On the one hand, the tsars do not have anyone to whom they can pass on the responsibility for their decisions; on the other hand, they usually tend to believe they are beyond moral and religious criteria considered mandatory for ordinary people, and are not prone to listening to the voice of conscience. Tolstoy continued to think for many decades about the people endowed with supreme power.

In *The Forged Coupon* (1904), the Tsar, the only person in the whole state endowed with the right to pardon criminals, receives the plea from the widow of the owner of the large landed estate who in the outburst of Christian forgiveness begs him to spare the lives of the peasants who were responsible for her husband's death:

> The Sovereign sighed, shrugged his shoulders under his epaulettes and said: 'The law...' and set down his wine-glass for the footman to fill it with sparkling Moselle. Everyone pretended to be amazed by the wisdom of the word pronounced by the Sovereign. And nothing further was said about the telegram. The two peasants, the old man and the young one, were hanged by a Tartar hangman specially sent out from Kazan, a cruel murderer given to bestiality ...
>
> As usual, the Tsar fell asleep as soon as this head touched the pillow. That night he was awoken by a terrible dream. There were gibbets standing in a field and corpses dangling on them; and the corpses had their tongues hanging out, and the tongues grew longer and longer.

And someone was crying out, 'Your doing, your doing'. The Tsar awoke in a sweat bathed in perspiration and began thinking. For the first time he began to think about the responsibility he carried …

But he saw the human being in himself only from a distance, and he could not do those simple things that were demanded of him as a human being, because of the demands assailing him from all sides as Tsar. And he hadn't the strength to recognize that the human requirements were more important that the demands on him as Tsar. (Tolstoy, 2015: 95–97)

Obviously, referring to the authority of the law was the Tsar's last resort to deny responsibility for his cruelty, but in this case this ruse was only partially successful. Around the time he was trying to complete this story, Tolstoy, recalling his failed effort to help private Shabunin, condemned himself for petitioning the Tsar to pardon the unfortunate soldier. As he wrote:

If I had been free from the universal stupor, I should have done one thing with respect to Alexander II and Shabunin. I should have asked him not to pardon Shabunin, but to pardon himself that he get away from the terrible shameful position in which he found himself, involuntarily having a part in all crimes (according 'to law') because being in the position to stop them he did not stop them. (Kerr, 1982: 177–178)[3]

Tolstoy writes here that in defending Shabunin, he did not yet understand many truths that he discovered later. However, right at that time he was writing *War and Peace*, in which he had fully expressed the same perceptions. In burning Moscow, protagonist Pierre Bezukhov is captured by the French and becomes the witness of the shooting of the prisoners. The monstrosity of the ritual that transforms humans into the soulless instruments of murder crushes Pierre's belief in the preordained divine order of the world and in humanity and plunges him into despair. He only manages to overcome this despair with the help of another captive, peasant-soldier Platon Karataev, who serves as the hero. Karataev is usually unable to repeat his own words and when Pierre, stunned by the depth of his remarks, asks him to repeat what he said, he utters something completely different. Still, he has the favourite story that he knows by heart and keeps telling it to the same listeners verbatim. Pierre heard it six times – the seventh and last recital takes place on the eve of Platon's death.

This is the story about a merchant convicted for a murder he did not commit – the real culprit put the bloody axe under his pillow. The slandered merchant spent ten years, 'as appropriate' as Karataev puts it, doing hard labour. Once by chance does he recite the story of his sufferings to his co-prisoners in presence of the villain who suddenly repents and begs forgiveness:

> And the old man said, 'God will forgive you, we are all sinners in His sight. I suffer for my own sins,' and he wept bitter tears. Well, and what do you think, dear friends?' Karatáev continued, his face brightening more and more with a rapturous smile as if what he now had to tell contained the chief charm and the whole meaning of his story: 'What do you think, dear fellows? That murderer confessed to the authorities. 'I have taken six lives,' he says (he was a great sinner), 'but what I am most sorry for is this old man. Don't let him suffer because of me'. So he confessed and it was all written down and the papers sent off in due form. The place was a long way off, and while they were judging, what with one thing and another, filling in the papers all in due form – the authorities I mean – time passed. The affair reached the Tsar. After a while the Tsar's decree came: to set the merchant free and give him a compensation that had been awarded. The paper arrived and they began to look for the old man. 'Where is the old man who has been suffering innocently and in vain? A paper has come from the Tsar!', so they began looking for him; here Karatáev's lower jaw trembled, 'but God had already forgiven him – he was dead! That's how it was, dear fellows!' Karatáev concluded and sat for a long time silent, gazing before him with a smile.
> And Pierre's soul was dimly but joyfully filled not by the story itself but by its mysterious significance: by the rapturous joy that lit up Karatáev's face as he told it, and the mystic significance of that joy. (Tolstoy, 1966: 939–940)

Later, Tolstoy returned to this episode and expanded it into a separate story, *God Sees the Truth But Waits* (1872). The story is written from the point of view of an omniscient author and contains many expressive details – the characters acquire names and biographies. However, the smile of Karatáev who is looking forward to his own demise and shares his most sacred wisdom with his peers is irrevocably lost (see the important discussion of the story in Jahn [2004] and McLean [2004]).

According to Karatáev, earthly justice can only diminish the meaning of divine providence that manifested itself in the fate of the accused merchant. Platon on the eve of his death feels mystical joy thinking about the Christian self-sacrifice of the person who accepted suffering and death for the sins of the others, and hopes for the same divine forgiveness and absolution experienced by the innocent merchant who fully accepted his punishment without having committed a crime. However, the salvation open to the avowed murderer who killed six people is unavailable for the state bureaucrats and the Tsar who act according to the existing legal order. God does not allow them to mend the evil that they have done and to join the world of eternal justice. They would have to live their lives as murderers who not only have not repented, but even do not understand they need repentance. The next section of the novel starts with the exclamation 'À vos places' uttered by French soldiers escorting Napoleon's carriage that passes the places where the prisoners of war await their fate.

This episode, written long before Tolstoy started formulating his social philosophy, shows his remarkable consistency in his basic perceptions of violence, crime, punishment and the legal system. Juxtaposing hardened criminals and state bureaucrats running the distribution of justice, Tolstoy clearly sees the former as the lesser evil. Their way of life, however abominable it is, is not so hopelessly removed from Christianity and morality, and leaves more chance for redemption and salvation than the everyday practices of those who persecute them.

Tolstoy and the penal system

Unlike Dostoevsky, Tolstoy did not have personal experience of incarceration, though on many times occasions he expressed his desire to be arrested and dismay to be left at large while his followers were persecuted. For many years he kept visiting prisons, but mostly to alleviate the suffering of the prisoners or to explore some details necessary for his own descriptions of crimes and criminals. In 1886 he met George Kennan, an American traveller who for two years studied the life of prisoners and eastern Siberia, and later published a book *Siberia and the Exile System* (Kennan, 1891) that later became for Tolstoy one of the main sources of his information about the life of the convicts. Still, until late the 1890s, he did not venture into the direct description of prison life.

Tolstoy's prolonged silence on the topic that deeply interested him could have been caused by his reluctance to compete with Dostoevsky. He considered *Crime and Punishment* that tells the story of the fall and repentance of a murderer to be Dostoevsky's best novel, but especially praised his *Notes from the House of the Dead* based on Dostoevsky's experience of serving his hard-labour sentence in Siberia among hardened criminals and villains. Tolstoy was deeply touched by Dostoevsky's attitude to convicts, including those who committed the most abominable crimes, whom he considered to be creatures endowed with living souls and capable of moral regeneration. He called the *Notes* 'the best book in all modern literature, Pushkin included ... sincere, natural and Christian' (Tolstoy 1978, II: 338) – a compliment that scandalized Dostoevsky, who was prone to a traditional Russian idolization of Pushkin (Tolstoy 1928–1964, LXIII: 24).

Tolstoy could also have avoided this topic as for decades he was specifically focused on capital punishment, or legalized murder as he saw it – the most horrible dramatic manifestation of the evils of the so-called legal system and the belief that the state as an institution has a moral right to send people to the gallows. However, in his last major novel *The Resurrection*, he had to deal with this subject at length. His work on the novel was long and tortuous. In 1887 he had been impressed by a story told to him by the lawyer Anatoly Koni about a man who, sitting as a member of a jury, suddenly recognized a prostitute accused of theft as a woman he had seduced many years earlier. Distraught and repentant, he decided to marry her, but the woman died before the wedding from typhus acquired in prison. At first Tolstoy insisted that Koni, himself a man of letters, should write about this case. Then, changing his mind, he asked Koni if he could borrow the plot. Permission was readily granted.

The first draft of *Resurrection* was finished in mid-1895. It was a rather short story focused on the themes of seduction and repentance. It starts in the courtroom, where Nekhlydov sees Katyusha Maslova, the girl he had once seduced, falsely accused of murder. The draft had a happy ending: the protagonist marries his newly rediscovered old love, emigrates to England and becomes a peasant in a commune. As in all early versions of Tolstoy's major works, this draft was supposed to be revised and expanded, but Tolstoy could not bring himself to do this. In 1897, however, he found a good reason to forge ahead.

The most radical of the many Russian sects that were receptive to Tolstoy's beliefs were the so-called Spirit-wrestlers ('Doukhobor Sectarians'), who rejected the institutionalized church and had been exiled by Nicholas I to the Caucasus. In the 1890s, one of their leaders was struck by the deep affinities between his beliefs and the ideas of the famous count, and urged his followers to burn their weapons, denounce military service and refuse to take the oath of loyalty to Tsar Nicholas II. As a result of this, some Spirit-wrestlers were beaten to death, while others were arrested or deprived of the means to survive in the severe mountain climate where they lived. Tolstoy and his associates issued an appeal on their behalf. Once again, Tolstoy himself was spared any repression, but other signatories were arrested and sent into exile.

Due to Tolstoy's intervention, the persecution of the Spirit-wrestlers began to attract international attention and the government felt compelled to grant them permission to emigrate to Canada. The resettlement of thousands of people was an expensive operation. Tolstoy decided to donate the income from his new novel to help the sectarians. In the summer of 1898, he started reworking and expanding *The Resurrection*.

Tolstoy turned the short story of a penitent intellectual and a good-hearted prostitute saving each other into a full-scale novel that became the most elaborate artistic representation of his philosophy, and the broadest panorama of Russian life not only in his own fiction, but, arguably, in the whole of Russian literature. In a way, he offered the reader his own version of *Crime and Punishment*. A significant part of the action takes place in Siberia, a place Tolstoy had never visited, but which had intrigued him for a long time. Nekhlyudov follows Katyusha there after her arrest and meets different sorts of convicts, including a number of revolutionaries. Inevitably prison life in all its horrifying and minute details not only takes up a significant part of the novel but also becomes one of its main philosophical problems. The penal system serves here as an embodiment of social evil.

At the very end of the novel, Nekhlyudov comes home having found out that Katyusha plans to marry another man. However:

> unexpected and important as his conversation with Simonson and Katusha that evening had been, he did not dwell on it. His position in that matter was so complicated and indefinite that he drove the thought of it from his mind. But the picture of those unfortunate beings, inhaling the noisome air, and lying in liquid oozing from the foul tub, especially the innocent face of the boy asleep on the leg of a criminal, recurred all the more vividly to his mind, and he could not get rid of it …
>
> 'It is just as if a problem had been set: to find the best, the surest means of depraving the greatest number of people!', thought Nekhlyudov, while getting an insight into the deeds that were being done in the prisons and halting-stations. Every year hundreds of thousands were brought to the pitch of depravity, and when completely depraved they were liberated to spread the moral disease they had caught in prison.
>
> In the prisons of Tumen, Ekaterinburg, Tomsk, and at the halting-stations, Nekhlyudov saw how successfully the object society seemed to have set itself was attained. Ordinary simple men holding the social and Christian morality of the ordinary Russian peasant, lost this conception, and formed a new prison-bred one, founded chiefly on the idea that any outrage to or violation of human beings is justifiable if it seems profitable. After living in prison those people became conscious with the whole of their being that, judging by what was happening to themselves, all those moral laws of respect and sympathy for others preached by the Church and by the moral teachers, were set aside in real life, and that therefore they, too, need not keep these laws. (Tolstoy, 2020: 450)

Tolstoy allows his character to come to this conclusion not at the early stages of his acquaintance with the penitentiary system, but at the end of it when he is not just shocked by the cruelty and bestiality of prison life, but also understands its inner mechanisms – and this realization tends to be more important for him than his own future. He has seen enough of the system to reject any attempts and any logic that would legitimize or rationalize it:

The only explanation for what was being done was that it aimed at the prevention of crime, at inspiring awe, at correcting offenders, and at dealing out to them 'lawful vengeance' as the books said. But in reality, nothing in the least resembling these results came to pass. Instead of vice being put a stop to, it only spread farther; instead of being frightened, the criminals were encouraged (many a tramp returned to prison of his own free will); instead of correction, every kind of vice was systematically instilled; while the desire for vengeance, far from being weakened by the measures of the Government, was instilled into the people, to whom it was not natural. (Tolstoy, 2020: 450)

Equally indefensible from Nekhlyudov's or Tolstoy's point of view were efforts to improve or humanize the existing system as the horrors he had witnessed were:

not being done accidentally, nor by mistake, nor only once, but had been done continuously for centuries, with only this difference, that at first people's nostrils used to be slit and their ears cropped; then a time came when they were branded and fastened to iron bars; and now they were manacled, and transported by steam instead of on carts.

The arguments brought forward by those in Government service who said that the things which aroused his indignation were simply due to the imperfect arrangements of the places of confinement, and that they would all be put to rights if prisons of a modern type were built, did not satisfy Nekhlyudov, because he knew that what revolted him was not a consequence of a better or worse arrangement of prisons. He had read of model prisons with electric bells, of executions by electricity as recommended by Tarde, and this refined violence revolted him yet more. (Tolstoy, 2020: 450)

According to Tolstoy, this universal derangement comes from not from the 'degeneration' or depravity of the prisoners, but is 'an inevitable consequence of the inconceivable delusion that men may punish one another' (Tolstoy, 2020, 450). In the final chapter of the novel, totally exhausted by his personal and social experience, Nekhlyudov reads the Gospel and finds there an answer to the questions that torture him. He understands the five commandments of Christ Tolstoy described in *What Do I Believe*; they explain to him not only the origins of evil but also the only way to deal with it:

It became clear to him that all the dreadful evil he had been witnessing in prisons and jails, and the quiet self-assurance of the perpetrators of this evil, resulted from men attempting what was impossible: to correct evil while themselves evil. Vicious men were trying to reform other vicious men, and thought they could do it by using mechanical means. And the result of all this was that needy and covetous men, having made a profession of this pretended punishment and reformation of others themselves became utterly corrupt, and unceasingly corrupt also those whom they torment ...

'But surely it cannot be so simple', thought Nekhlyudov; and yet he saw with certainty, strange as it had seemed at first that it was not only a theoretical but also a practical solution to the question. The usual objection, 'What is one to do with the evil-doers? Surely not let them go unpunished?' no longer confused him. This objection might have a meaning if it were proved that punishment lessened crime or improved the criminal; but since just the contrary is proved, and it is evident that it is not in the power of some to reform others; the only reasonable thing to do is to cease doing what is not only useless, but harmful, immoral, and cruel. For many centuries people considered to be criminals have been executed. Well, and have they been exterminated? Far from being exterminated, their numbers have been increased, both by criminals corrupted by punishments, and also by those lawful criminals – judges, prosecutors, magistrates, and jailers – who judge and punish men. Nekhlyudov now understood that society, and order in general, exist, not thanks to these lawful criminals who judge and punish others, but because notwithstanding their depraving influence men still pity and love one another. (Tolstoy, 2020: 480–481)

Conclusion

In the article 'Speaking the language of state violence: an abolitionist perspective', David Scott summarizes the differences between reformist and abolitionist approaches to prisons based on different understandings of conceptualization, causes and the nature of prison violence, and assumptions behind anti-violence strategies (Scott, 2016: 8–9). According to these criteria, Tolstoy firmly shares the abolitionist position. Penal institutions represented to him the worst and also the most visible manifestation of the vicious order they help to preserve. He saw no reason to try to reform and improve them – such efforts could only shift individual and public attention from the fundamental immorality of coercion to its excesses and perpetuate the evil by making it more tolerable. Tolstoy was certain that the whole penal system should be abolished in its entirety and without any exceptions.

However, Tolstoy's very philosophy that rejected the state as such and postulated that no one can have a right to legislate for anyone else made the project of abolition he envisaged incredibly difficult, if not outright impossible, to achieve. Nor did he believe in political or legal reforms or in revolutionary change, and actually did not seem to be interested in practical measures that could be taken on the path to an abolitionist project. Tolstoy never doubted that the only way to resist the unjust social order is to not participate in it – to abstain from military service, reject legal procedures and refuse to pay taxes. In order to liberate society, one had to first liberate oneself from evil. Moreover, Tolstoy was less concerned about the consequences of abolition – which he assumed would be positive – than about the need to do what was right in the present. In his 1896 *Letter to an American on Non-resistance*,[4] he wrote, 'Fais ce que doit, advienne que pourra' – 'do what is right, and let come what may' (Tolstoy, 2018: 325). This is an expression of profound wisdom – it was the last entry he made in his diary shortly before his death.

Tolstoy had huge respect for the ideas and personality of his fellow anarchist Pyotr Kropotkin (see Weide, Chapter 9 in this volume). Still, he was deeply sceptical about Kropotkin's hopes for revolutionary liberation. He was convinced that violent revolution would lead to the regeneration of an even more coercive and repressive state (see Perumova [1995] and Medzhibovskaya [2008] on the evolution of Tolstoy's general attitude towards revolutionary violence). Once, when Tolstoy's eldest son Sergey was accompanying Russian sectarians moving to Canada, Tolstoy implored him to visit Kropotkin on the way back and ask why he believed that the revolution could improve anything at all. Sergey dutifully fulfilled this request. Kropotkin replied that as humans are better than 'forms' (most likely meaning social institutions), one needs to destroy existing 'forms' to allow humanity to create better ones. When Sergei brought this reply home, his father remained completely unconvinced (see Tolstoy, 1962).

Tolstoy understood that this type of passive resistance implies even greater personal courage than can be expected from a soldier or a revolutionary. On the battlefield or in the conspiratorial cell, one is usually supported by peers, while a pacifist rejecting conscription or a citizen openly refusing to obey the laws of the land, including mandatory taxation, has to face the overwhelming force of the state alone. Moreover, Tolstoy understood that in the present moment such a level of heroism was not to be expected from the majority. However, he tried to convince his readers at the very least not to deceive themselves:

> I do not say that if you are a landowner you are bound to give up your lands immediately to the poor; if a capitalist or manufacturer, your money to your workpeople; or that if you are tsar, minister, official, judge, or general, you are bound to renounce immediately the advantages of your position; or if a soldier, on whom all the system of violence is based, to refuse immediately to obey, in spite of all the dangers of insubordination.

If you do so, you will be doing the best thing possible. But it may happen, and it is most likely that you will not have the strength to do so. You have relations, a family, subordinates and superiors; you are under an influence so powerful that you cannot shake it off; but you can always recognize the truth and refuse to tell a lie about it. (Tolstoy, 1984: 366–367)

The world of prisons, executions and mass killings is terrible, but, according to Tolstoy, not as terrible as the willingness to accept it as a social norm. Once, he replied to his son, who said to him that Christ's teaching is 'difficult' that he 'would not say it's difficult to run out of a blazing room through the only door' (Tolstoy, 1994: 175). He saw sincerity with oneself as the only door that can allow humanity to avoid imminent disaster, something which remains equally as relevant today.

Notes

[1] The first commandment, according to Tolstoy, was to be at peace with everyone and to consider none as foolish or unworthy, while the second was never to commit adultery.
[2] Akoulina is the mother of the murdered baby.
[3] On Tolstoy's attitude to revolutionary terror, see Medzhibovskaya (2008).
[4] Ernst Crosby, Tolstoy's follower in US and the author of the book *Tolstoy and his Message* (1903). See Whittaker, 1997.

References

Tolstoy's works
Tolstoy, L. (1904) *Plays: The Power of Darkness, The First Distiller, Fruits of Culture*, L. Maude and A. Maude (trans.), New York: Funk & Wagnalls Company.
Tolstoy, L. (1905) 'Introduction', in V.G. Tchertkoff and F. Holah (eds), *Short Biography of William Lloyd Garrison*, London: Free Age Press, pp v–xiii.
Tolstoy, L. (1928–1964) *Polnoe Sobranie Sochinenii v 90 tomakh* (complete works in 90 volumes), Moscow: GIKhl.
Tolstoy, L. (1933) *A Confession, A Gospel in Brief and What I Believe*, A. Maude (trans.), Oxford: Oxford University Press.
Tolstoy, L. (1966) *War and Peace*, a Norton critical edition, L. Maude and A. Maude (trans.), G. Gibian (ed.), New York, London: Norton.
Tolstoy, L. (1978) *Tolstoy's Letters*, vols I–II, R.F. Christians (ed. and trans.), New York: Charles Scribner & Sons.
Tolstoy, L. (1984) *'The Kingdom of God Is Within You': Christianity Not as a Mystic Religion But as a New Theory of Life*, C. Garnett (trans.), New York: Cassell.
Tolstoy, L. (1991) *What Then Must We Do?*, A. Maude (trans.), Bideford: Green Books.
Tolstoy, L. (1994) *Diaries*, R.F. Christian (ed. and trans.), London: Flamingo.

Tolstoy, L. (2000) *Divine and Human and Other Stories*, P. Sekirin (trans.), New York: HarperCollins.

Tolstoy, L. (2015) *The Death of Ivan Ilyich and Other Stories*, N. Pasternak-Slater (trans.), Oxford: Oxford University Press.

Tolstoy, L. (2018) 'Miscellanies' in *The Kingdom of God Is Within You: Christianity and Patriotism*, Frankfurt am Main: Verlag GmbH.

Tolstoy, L. (2020) *The Resurrection*, L. Maude (trans.), Oxford: Oxford University Press.

Literature

Goldenveizer, A. (1959) *Vblisi Tolstogo*, Moscow: GIKhl.

Jahn, G. (2004) 'Was the master well-served? Further comment on "God Sees the Truth, But Waits"', *Tolstoy Studies*, XVI: 82–86.

Kennan, G. (1891) *Siberia and the Exile System*, New York: The Century Co. I-II.

Kerr, W. (1982) *The Shabunin Affair: An Episode in the Life of Leo Tolstoy*, Ithaca, NY: Cornell University Press.

McLean, H. (2004) 'Could the master err? A Note on *God Sees the Truth But Waits*', *Tolstoy Studies*, XVI: 77–81.

Medzhibovskaya, I. (2008) 'Tolstoy's response to terror and revolutionary violence', *Kritika: Explorations in Russian and Eurasian History*, 9(3): 505–531.

Pirumova, N.M. (1995) *Trudy Mezhunarodnoi konferentsii, posviaschennye 150-letiu co dnia rozhdenia P.A. Kropotkina*, Moscow: Institut Economiki RAN. I, 145–156.

Scott, D. (2016) 'Speaking the language of state violence: an abolitionist perspective', *European Group for the Study of Deviance and Social Control. Newsletter*, N°2.

Tchertkov, V.G. and Holah, F. (1904) *A Short Biography of William Lloyd Garrison*, London: Free Age Press.

Tolstoy, S. (1962) *Tolstoy Remembered by His Son*, New York: Atheneum.

Whittaker, R. (1997) 'Tolstoy's American disciple: letters to Earnest Howard Crosby, 1894–1906', *Triquarterly*, 98: 210–250.

5

Arthur St John: Tolstoyan Abolitionism in Practice

Peter Cox and Paul Taylor

Introduction

In the posthumously published utopian novel *Why Not Now? A British Islander's Dream*, the author as lead character Arthur is introduced by his guide to features of the world he recognizes in its physical features, but that has been transformed entirely in its social relations:

> 'You are interested in prisons in your world, Arthur; perhaps I should say, in abolishing prisons?'
> I assented, wondering what was coming.
> 'Well, I suggest your going to one of our prisons until Sunday.'
> 'What', I exclaimed, 'Do you mean to say you have prisons still? Whatever for?' '... Yes, we have prisons still. And they are counted among our holiest places ... Some of us are quite fond of going there to fast and meditate – perhaps to rest- and to be refreshed ... In our prisons now the prisoners are, at any rate, all there of their own free will. They are places of holy freedom, of withdrawing and retreat.' (St John, 1939: 234)

Its writer, Arthur St John (1862–1938), was no stranger to arguments on penal abolition. He had been working on the themes for more than 30 years when this was written, exploring in word and action a very different vision of prisons than we might understand today. They should not be based on coercion or the deliberate infliction of pain. Nor are they designed for enforced estrangement and deprivation of liberty (Scott, 2013). In the novel, there are buildings referred to as prisons, but they are places of spiritual retreat rather than penal confinement. St John co-founded the Penal Reform League (PRL) in 1907 and served as its Honourable Secretary for almost 11 years – almost all its existence until its 1921 merger with the Howard Association to form the Howard League for Penal Reform. Nor were these explicit abolitionist sympathies a product of wistful reflection in retirement. In 1912 he addressed the four-day National Conference on the Prevention of Destitution, presided over by the Bishop of Oxford and attended by delegates from public authorities across the country, representatives from Poor Law Unions, school boards and over 90 different voluntary associations, in the capacity of Honourable Secretary to the Crime and Inebriety Section. He opened his presentation with the following challenge:

> The tendency of imprisonment is to make the prisoner less fit to live a useful, self-supporting life. I will assume that this has been demonstrated and agreed upon by the time this paper comes up for consideration. We now have to inquire how the tendency can be avoided or mitigated.
>
> The easiest answer to the question, and perhaps the wisest, would be: Pull down the prisons.
>
> It would, however, be unsafe to presume on the immediate prevalence of such wisdom in the community, and a great deal more water is likely to flow under London Bridge before we cease to imprison people. Therefore, I propose for the present to inquire whether certain modifications are feasible in our prison regime and system of conditional release which might tend to lessen the mischief – tend, that is, to turn prisoners out perhaps rather less of a burden, instead of more of a burden, on the community. (St John, 1912a: 538)

Between them, these two short excerpts provide a valuable insight into a set of contributions to emergent debates on crime and punishment, which were profoundly important in their time but have become largely overlooked and forgotten. There is a clear utopian imagination at work in St John's desire to reconstitute the prison as a place of nonpenal confinement, but this is paired with his realism and appreciation of the societal conditions that need to change for such a penal transformation. In this sense, St John's vision is a pioneering contribution to what has later been referred to as an 'abolitionist real utopia' (Scott, 2013), something we will remark upon throughout the chapter. Moreover, this real utopian imaginary extended to a range of projects and visions, from managing what we might now call a Fair-Trade wholefood cooperative to volunteering in pioneering projects for the treatment of shellshocked war veterans.

Until very recently, the PRL and its work rarely gained more than a passing mention in histories of the Howard League (Howard League, n.d.). Rose's studies of 1955 and 1961 had been little developed until more recent work by Logan (2016) and her insightful biography of Margery Fry (2018), who took over from St John as Honorary Secretary of the PRL and engineered the merger between the organizations. By contrast, Huws Jones' (1966) biography of Fry is almost entirely silent about the ideas and work of the PRL. Similarly, St John has had relatively little exposure in abolitionist and critical criminological writings to this point, and few will be familiar with his name or writings. Where they are discussed, it is in the context of diverse literatures, each of which often speaks to only one aspect of his work separated from others.[1]

To understand and contextualize St John's arguments and pioneering work on abolitionist real utopias, we need first to examine his background and the formation of his ideas, and then chart how these shaped a generation of discussions on prisons and imprisonment. Biographical detail contextualizes St John's intellectual development and is followed by a discussion of the PRL and its contribution to promulgating an abolitionist vision. The final section draws out some implications of the pioneering approach that his life and work demonstrate, and what continued relevance they may have.

The making of an abolitionist

Arthur St John was born in 1862 in Jullunder (now Jalandhar) in Punjab. Three previous generations of the family had served in the military, and after returning to England, he was schooled at the United Services College at Westward Ho!, 'a recent foundation intended to attract the sons of naval and military officers who could not afford the fees of the great public schools', where he was three years above Rudyard Kipling (Gilmour, 2002: 11). Enlisted in the Royal Inniskilling Fusiliers (1882), he was stationed successively across the British Empire, including in Ireland, Malta and India (Semple, 1939). Heading back on furlough to the Great Britain from Burma in 1888, he was apparently so affected by the writing of works by Tolstoy and Kropotkin (see Zorin, Chapter 4 in this volume, and Weide, Chapter 9 in this volume) that he retired from military service: life as an adjutant was incompatible with the demands of radical politics focussed on the transformation of society. Nevertheless, he continued to use his rank title as Captain St John to ensure his credibility in future ventures whenever necessary. Tolstoy's impact on radical politics in England in the late 1880s was considerable (Hardy, 2000) and gave further impetus to existing forms of ethical anarchism and ethical socialism. This ethical radical politics 'concentrated on personal experience, moral transformation, and utopian experiments' (Bevir, 2011: 234) and was influenced by American transcendentalist and idealist thought, particularly that of Henry David Throreau and Thomas Davidson. The Tolstoyan influence provided greater impetus to finding ways to transform political idealism into experimental actions for their realization (Linehan, 2012; for the ideas of Tolstoy, see Zorin, Chapter 4 in this volume). For example, the discussion meetings of the Fellowship of New Life which resulted in the formation of the Fabian Society also gave rise to the formation of a series of Brotherhood projects: a 'church' for meeting and discussions, together with various ethically run businesses (Armytage, 1957).

Radical politics at the time was fluid. Boundaries between groups and ideas were far from fixed or rigid, and memberships and affiliations overlapped. Edward Carpenter (see Baldwin, Chapter 6 in this volume), member of the Fellowship of New Life, was typical of someone whose ideas were readily taken up and shared among a variety of groups (Rowbotham, 2008). St John's skills and experience as an adjutant ideally suited him to practical organization and by 1893, he had become involved with the Brotherhood Church in Croydon. The area was at the time a centre of radicalism and host to a number of prominent Russian exiles, including Vladimir Tchertkov (Hardy, 1979), a leading associate of Tolstoy.

When the Brotherhood opened a 'Grocery and Provision Store' in what is now Hackney, selling goods purchased from cooperatives and land colonies (settlements experimenting with new forms of land ownership and cooperative living), St John became its manager (Holman, 1978). Activists in England were in regular correspondence with (and were sometimes visitors to) Tolstoy, and by 1896, St John's dedication and expertise were sufficiently recognized for Tolstoy to recommend him to the German Hungarian anarchist philosopher Jenő Henrik (Eugen Heinrich) Schmitt as a relevant correspondent (Alston, 2013: 98).

At the end of that year, St John was one of the first settlers at the Brotherhood's Tolstoyan settlement in Purleigh, Essex (Gray, 2019), after having previously been tasked with investigating the practical issues of community creation through visiting the colony founded by the Unitarian minister Herbert Mills at Starnthwaite, Westmoreland. The colony only lasted a few years into the new century. While all these events were unfolding, Tolstoy had been agitating since mid-1895 on behalf of the 'Doukhobor Sectarians' (Spirit-wrestlers), pacifist dissenters who were persecuted for their refusal of military service and were sentenced to mass exile (Biryukov, 1895; Tolstoy, 1895). St John was consequently appointed to travel with Tolstoy's own envoy, Pavel Biryukov, to convey in person to Tolstoy monies raised to support the migration of the Doukhobors (Alston, 2014). The bulk of these funds were from the Society of Friends (prior providers of famine relief to the Doukhobors). Though not a Quaker himself, St John was of good enough standing to be entrusted with this considerable responsibility. After meeting Tolstoy, the pair travelled on to negotiate with the Doukhobors directly, but were arrested: Biryukov was sent to Siberia and St John was deported (St John, 1899). With many complications, he continued to organize on behalf of the large refugee community and eventually sailed with them to their resettlement in Saskatchewan, where he stayed until early 1900 (Tarasoff and Ewashen, 1994). He was clearly well trusted and capable as an envoy and diplomat, and was one to stand fast by his principles, as well as being committed to financial transparency.[2] He earned the ire of the Manitoba and Northwestern Railway Company when acting as representative for Doukhobor rail workers' complaints about pay and conditions: the Company described him as a useless troublemaker (Buyniak, 1999).

That an entire community of around 7,500 people should be rendered illegal and exiled on government decree clearly provoked St John to a deeper consideration of issues of crime and incarceration. Leaving Canada, he appears to have travelled south through the US, visiting progressive reform institutes and involving himself in a number of discussions on the nature of crime and punishment and penal reform (*The Friend*, 1900). Examples which he was later to mention in writings include the provincial reformatory farm in Guelph, Canada, and a similar one in Warrensville, Ohio, together with the Elmira reformatory programme (St John, 1912a, 1912d). He continued to follow the fortunes of American programmes for assessment and probation (including the Children's Court at Columbus, Ohio, the Juvenile Psychopathic Institute of Chicago and the New Jersey Training School for Feeble-minded Girls and Boys at Vineland, New Jersey) and to publicize their work in Britain (St John, 1911b). Similarly, experimental educational institutions such as the George Junior Republic near Freeville, New York, were highlighted as examples of the means through which transformations of moral values might be developed (St John, 1911a).

St John stayed briefly in Britain before going once more to visit Tolstoy, but was again arrested and then deported. While working as editor of the radical newspaper *The Midland Herald* (from 1902 to 1905) in 1903, St John married Leonora Maxwell-Müller (1862–1953), former Lady Superintendent of the Indian Army Nursing Service. They had first met in India in the 1880s, and Leonora continued to serve as a member of the Indian Office Nursing Board, which interviewed and selected candidates for the Indian Nursing Service. She took the name of Leonora Maxwell St John and her concern over both care and carers clearly influenced the form of Arthur's approach to abolitionism and wider social reform. She also used the pages of the *British Journal of Nursing* to publicize the PRL's work and to campaign for nurses in prisons (Maxwell St John, 1914). Over the next few years, St John continued correspondence with Tolstoy and wrote and published pamphlets on a range of issues of social, political and economic reform. A life member of the newly established Sociological Society, he was also active in the Humanitarian League, serving alongside Edward Carpenter on the Indian Humanitarian Committee (from 1906) and on its Law and Prisons Committee (from 1908).

Established by Henry Salt in 1891, the Humanitarian League can easily be read as a clearinghouse for a range of radical concerns, each identifiable as a single-issue campaign (Weinbren, 1994). However, a more faithful reading of participants' own accounts, elaborated by biographical studies, argues that these multiple concerns were not and should not be understood as disparate issues (see Carpenter, 1916; Salt, 1921; Rowbotham, 2008). Rather, all these concerns derive from a fundamental reorientation towards the world (and human societies as part of that) that prioritizes the sanctity and dignity of life. From that premise, concerns for the humane treatment of people and animals, for the right to autonomy and self-determination, for good work, justly rewarded, and the equal distribution of profit all logically follow. Which issues need to or can be addressed at any given time depends on circumstance and opportunity. Tolstoy's writings, particularly *A Confession* (1882), *What Is to Be Done?* (1886) and *The Kingdom of God Is Within You* (1894) provided a powerful trigger for many towards such a reorientation and for enthusiastic action to put these principles into practice (Alston, 2013). Others reached similar conclusions by other paths and account for the complex of ideas and actions often clustered together under the banner of ethical socialism (Bongiorno, 2001; Manton, 2003) Mark Bevir (2011: 20) highlights the distinctiveness of ethical socialism (and anarchism) in 'the place it gave to personal transformation and communal utopianism', which were also features of St John's abolitionism. What is important about these various groups was that they could simultaneously embrace idealist and utopian visions of future society and social relations (see, for example, William Morris' *News from Nowhere*; see also Holland, Chapter 7 in this volume), experiments in personal lifestyle and relations intended to prefigure the kinds of futures desired, and also work on practical reforms grounded in the reality of existing politics and social structures. They collectively start to envision abolition. In this sense, they are an embryonic formulation of what today would be referred to as an 'abolitionist real utopia'. It should be no surprise that it was through Brotherhood-supported meetings that Ebenezer Howard's ideas for Garden Cities were first provided with a public platform (Beevers, 1988). The Garden City, as originally envisaged, was a utopian project that sought to alleviate social problems through planning (Hardy, 1991).

The multiple connections made by St John suggest, together with his marriage, a movement from active participation to more conventional writing and lobbying as he entered his forties, but the political implications of the ideas he proposed remained as radical as they had done at the outset.

The Prison Reform League

Direct action agitation for women's suffrage was taking a decisive turn in 1906. Sylvia Pankhurst was first arrested and sentenced to 14 days in prison in October and, four months later, was arrested and sentenced again. In Holloway, she wrote of the unsanitary conditions and 'casual humiliations and the misery of her fellow prisoners' – sketches she then sold to the press (Connelly, 2013: 31). Among the other activists to be arrested at this time was Annie Cobden-Sanderson, daughter of Richard Cobden and a close friend of Jane Morris (married to William). Annie was well integrated into both society and radical circles.

Most accounts credit the formation of the PRL to a joint initiative of Arthur St John and Annie Cobden-Sanderson at a celebratory breakfast for her release in February 1907 (Crawford, 2000: 568). Gardner (1930) modifies this account somewhat by noting their prior correspondence. Cobden Sanderson had been speaking of her two months spent in Holloway Prison in 1906 alongside Charlotte Despard, Emmeline Pankhurst and Mary Gawthorpe (Richardson, 2006; Cook, 2015), leading voices among those who defected from constitutional to militant tactics. St John had already been speaking and writing on imprisonment, no doubt inspired by his own experiences of Russian jails, conditions highlighted by Tolstoy in later writings, particularly in *Resurrection* (for more on this, see Zorin, Chapter 4 in this volume). What direct connections were made between St John and the suffrage campaigners (other than a mutual concern with imprisonment) remain to be definitively established, but Leonora's social networks and Arthur's mutual friendships with, for example, Peter Kropotkin bring together a number of networks of radical politics. Kropotkin was close enough to Annie and Richard Cobden to be a welcome holiday guest (see Cobden-Sanderson, 1926). Gardner (1930: 39–40) notes that the list of vice-presidents of the PRL at its foundation under the chair of Dr Wm. Geikie Cobb, the Rector of St Ethelburga's-Bishopsgate, was 'quite a formidable list ... including a K.C., the late Judge Atherley Jones, then an M.P., the Earl of Lytton, the Hon. Sir John Cockburn, K.C.M.G., and Archdeacon Wilberforce'.[3] This accounts for the PRL's appearance on national committees and conferences, despite it remaining, throughout its existence, a very small organization with few members and most of the work being done by its Honorary Secretary.

Cobden-Sanderson's experience of imprisonment was profoundly affecting and damaging, and she was soon to split from the Pankhursts and Women's Social and Political Union (WSPU) to co-found the Women's Freedom League (WFL) in 1907, refusing to separate suffrage issues from broader platforms of social reform (Cobden-Sanderson, 1926; Tidcombe, 2017). However, with her work for the WFL, establishing the Tax Resistance League ('No Vote No Tax') and continuing contributions to the Independent Labour Party (ILP), she appears to have played little public role in the future work of the PRL.

Whereas Carpenter (see Baldwin, Chapter 6 in this volume) backed away from considering prisons unnecessary, a position maintained by Tolstoy and

Kropotkin (Rowbotham 2008: 309), these concepts remained at the core of Arthur St John's vision for the PRL. The publicly declared object of the PRL was:

> so to change men's minds and alter the attitude of society towards crime and criminals, that, instead of brutalizing ourselves and our criminals by irrelevant punishment, we shall really protect society by reclaiming criminals to useful activities, or, if irreclaimable, by keeping them out of mischief in permanent kindly care, and, in the meantime, leave off making criminals out of defective, weak-willed, or high-spirited youngsters. (Women's Franchise, 5 December 1907)

That these aims were reported in the jointly published journal of the WFL and the Men's League for Women's Suffrage (the two militant organizations formed following the split in the WSPU) should come as no surprise.

Operating from St John's home address in Highgate, the PRL listing in the 1908 *Reformer's Year Book* (Pethick, Lawrence and Edwards, 1908) names Sime Seruya as the Honorary Treasurer and St John as the Honorary Secretary, a position he was to hold until 1918. Seruya was a Lisbon-born actress, one of those imprisoned in February 1907 for the demonstration outside the House of Commons, and, with fellow inmate Cobden Sanderson, one of the founders of the WFL. She had smuggled letters written on toilet paper out of the prison to describe the conditions she encountered. Additionally, she was a founder of the Actresses' Franchise League and ran the International Suffrage Shop (Cockin, 2017), and was well connected in suffrage and in wider radical circles. In the 1930s, she supported Republican Spain through her International Sound Films Ltd. and was arrested for anti-fascist leafletting (Clark, 2008; López-Martín, 2019), demonstrating continuity with Sylvia Pankhurst's political trajectory.

So what were the kind of reforms that the PRL proposed? We can get a feeling for the PRL's work not only from the pamphlets and statements produced but also through papers presented by St John to a range of conferences in the prewar years and in his contributions to the *Sociological Review* and the *Eugenics Review*.[4] A characteristic of all his writing is this notion of a 'real utopia', with a core commitment to abolition, typified by the title of his 1912 review paper 'The futility of prison'.

Coupling a utopian vision with practical measures designed to alleviate current problems that can also be read as gradualist steps towards future transformative action allowed St John to hold fast to his central point, while gaining a broad audience as a practical ally in various efforts to deal with perceived social problems. While specific topics may appear to range widely, the analysis presented forms a coherent whole.

One of St John's early forays came in a contribution to the newly founded *Sociological Review*, in which he argued that the purpose of sentencing 'shall be reformative or hospitable (of the nature of asylum, with necessary check, stimulation or support)' (St John, 1908: 377). Neither punishment nor retribution do anything to improve either person or wider society and therefore should not be part of criminological analysis. However, caring programmes of social rehabilitation require indeterminate sentences, although he is careful to note that *only* programmes of 'reformative treatment' should be allowed to be indeterminate. Deterrence based on fear is ultimately self-defeating, he argues elsewhere, since it only increases the social acceptability of terror and violence: 'Until we have learned that this "terror" defeats its own supposed end (even if it were just to make one man suffer for crimes which others might commit) we can, I submit, make little headway with effective measures for dealing with crime' (St John, 1929: 234).

Notably, St John connects the problematic use of deterrence in both prisons and international relations: '[J]ust as in penal matters progress is barred by the habit of trusting to terror and violence, so in international affairs the same delusion stands in the way of security and peace' (St John, 1929: 234).

St John's arguments, which remained constant throughout his life and work on penal reform and in the many other social projects in which he was engaged, are rooted in an ethic of care, not punishment: 'an offender should, if possible, be treated according to his individual needs in society, and only confined if all other means are hopeless' (St John, 1912b: 66). That which dehumanizes or degrades either those classed as offenders or those in charge of them is an outrage to humanity. The PRL's vociferous campaigning against forcible feeding of suffragette prisoners throughout the period of the militant campaign bears witness to this. The campaign cost the support of some influential supporters (and financial backers, leading to severe financial problems by 1914), but six women were elected to the executive board of the PRL at the end of 1911, of whom the majority had experience of incarceration for suffragette militancy (*London Evening Standard*, 1912).

Reform requires rethinking the whole construction of crime. Rejecting punishment as a justification for imprisonment, St John argued strongly that current relations of inequality prevented any deeper understanding of wrongdoing: 'Until we have removed the social conditions that make for crime and degeneracy we cannot tell what will remain to be done when they are removed' (St John, 1929: 236). However, as noted earlier, his idealism is also tempered with a deeply pragmatic approach – his is a real utopian abolitionism. The ideal cannot be realized immediately, so in the meantime, one needs to work on the reform of those institutions and regulations that currently exist until such time as they can be abolished.

A significant step in this was St John's championing of probation, a subject that was undergoing considerable transformation at that point in time. In the manner envisaged at the time and promoted by St John, the role of probation was to befriend and assist lawbreakers in the community so that they might be better and more comprehensively rehabilitated and enabled to make any restitution required (see St John, 1912a). It was most definitely not a role to be associated with surveillance or punishment.

Multiple examples of rehabilitation and practical employment schemes are given throughout St John's works, as described earlier. Many of these had been inspired by visits to Canada and the US during his travels in 1899 and as a delegate to international conferences. Collectively, they can be characterized as experiments to embody the ideals of an ethical society – what Erik Olin Wright (2010) termed 'real utopias'. St John had been an inaugural resident of the Brotherhood farm colony at Purleigh but soon left, and the project was always wrought with difficulty. Not doubt this experience contributed to a lesser enthusiasm for labour colonies than was exhibited by Edward Carpenter. (Gray, 2019). Rather, St John, recognizing the need for some form of residential rehabilitation and relearning, wanted to dissociate such schemes from the institutions of prisons as they are commonly understood. Consequently, he took a complex position on indeterminate sentencing, a topic that was the subject of much debate at the time. If the purpose of a sentence is to ensure care for those who cannot exist elsewhere, then support should be available for as long as required. The argument is that such persons as are now incarcerated should be provided with asylum, a place of safety and support where proper and appropriate care can be given. In other words, these are nonpenal forms of detention. Therefore, any period of intervention needs to be as long as necessary for rehabilitation and supported by a proper process of probation. His position here is entirely consistent with that taken 30 years later in the extract that opens this chapter.

A precondition of such a dramatic challenge to existing practice is the need for adequate education from an early age that develops autonomy and collective responsibility in order to integrate persons into society with adequate industrial training for prisoners as part of their rehabilitation. To address the former, St John commended Montessori education as an important component of social progress (St John, 1927). Indeed, his comments on finding new ways of handling and addressing human conflicts and wrongdoing consistently depend on rethinking the role and purpose of education (St John, 1904, 1911a, 1911b). His emphasis on practical solutions and opportunities, even while advancing a politically radical agenda (St John, 1906), is notable. He was gently scathing in his review of Lombroso:

> One gains the impression that the 'criminal anthropologist', though he has, rather indirectly, done excellent pioneer work, has never quite thought out the practical part of the subject, the true principles and best methods of dealing with criminals. He almost seems to have been too busy looking for stigmata and examining shapes and dimensions of skulls to attend to the more weighty and practical matters of how

and why individuals come to commit crimes, and how they may be prevented and induced to do better things. (St John, 1912b: 66)

By way of contrast, St John commends the common-sense approach of HM Prison Commissioner James Devon, author of *The Criminal and the Community* (Devon, 1912b), reflecting that the degree of reform advocated lies 'some way beyond what one has faith enough to hope for in this generation' (St John, 1912c: 211). Indeed, 'until we have removed the social conditions that make for crime and degeneracy we cannot tell what will remain to be done when they are removed' (St John, 1929: 236).

A major campaign theme for the PRL was protesting against the treatment of prisoners (especially the force-feeding of hunger strikers). Forcible feeding was both physically damaging and mentally traumatizing, as accounts related in Holmes (2020), Tidcombe (2017) and Hobhouse and Brockway (1922) make clear. Moreover, St John argued that 'acquiescence in such a moral outrage' effected 'the deterioration of the moral sense of the community' (St John, 1913: 149). The society that tolerated such treatment was collectively complicit.

Alongside this, St John engaged with conferences and meetings established in response to the social unease of the time. Attending the 1912 National Conference on the Prevention of Destitution, he deputized for James Devon, presenting his paper explaining the harmful effects of imprisonment: 'Punishment not only degrades, but is meant to degrade. All its advocates admit it, but not always consciously. They are not content with any proposal unless it hurts the offender, and then they deplore his degradation' (Devon, 1912a: 500).

St John's own paper followed on from Devon's position. The quotation at the outset of his paper succinctly summarizes its argument and, judging by the transcript of the following discussion, was very well received. Specifically, his proposals were met with approval precisely because of their practical content. Yet, as his remarks to the national conference on destitution (cited earlier in this chapter) demonstrate, the abolitionist basis for his interventionist work remained. Balancing an ideal of abolition with immediate reforms to reduce incarceration again led him to advocate a 'sentence whose term was not predetermined because it involved a course of training, and one could not tell beforehand how soon it would achieve its object' (St John, 1912d: 533). He was well aware of the radicalism of his proposals, recognizing that his proposals might be viewed as 'a utopian aspiration no doubt' while insisting that should the case be logically argued and the facts made clear, the case for abolition would have 'a large response' (St John, 1911b: 130). Once again, it is clear that the ideas and aspirations of St John envision what is now referred to as an 'abolitionist real utopia' (Scott, 2013).

In July 1912, St John attended the First International Eugenics Conference. Eugenic views were intertwined with much sociological discussion of the time (Renwick, 2011), but at the conference he and Peter Kropotkin focused their contributions on the need to tackle existing social and economic inequalities. Unless all have access to the same level of housing, nutrition and education, they jointly argued, consideration of heredity was rendered moot (Eugenics Education Society, 1912). Speaking alongside Kropotkin once more at the annual meeting of the British Medical Association on the Treatment of Crime and Criminals in the following year, St John's contribution was noted as:

> 'Directly contrary to conventional ideas of criminology' ... 'All the harm done to society by all the burglars and all the thieves is a mere bagatelle compared to the harm done by the law courts of England', he declared. 'Everybody knows the law courts are making criminals day by day', said Captain St John. 'We have to protect ourselves not only from criminals but also from people who deal with criminals.' (*Vulcan Advocate*, 1913: 6; see also 'An Old Gaol Bird', 1913)

St John's analysis was supported by firsthand testimony of experience as a prisoner and by Kropotkin's assertion that:

> imprisonment is not an effective force in deterring crime. Twenty-four hours of bread and water and a plank bed might be a deterrent to people accustomed to good food, he said, but it is no deterrent to those who sleep under bridges or by the shores of the Thames. Prisons are the universities of crime. We must do something to change our system. (*Vulcan Advocate*, 1913: 6)

A practical outlet for implementation of these approaches was found through St John's involvement in the Committee for Social Investigation and Reform (founded in 1913) and its Women's Training Colony, partly inspired by St John's 1912 paper, 'A Reformatory for Girls and Young Women', presented at the Conference of the Ladies' National Association (Shrubsole, 2010). Supported and funded by a number of those involved in suffrage campaigns, the WTC provided a rehabilitation opportunity for women charged with soliciting. St John joined its Executive Committee in 1917.

The early years of the PRL are dominated by two factors. First, abolition remains the underlying goal. Despite constant advocacy of practical reforms, all the proposals made are consistent with a central abolitionist aim. Its grounds are in Tolstoyan nonviolence and anarchist politics, coupled with a deeply pragmatic sensitivity. It is also clear that the PRL's work remained steadfastly connected with a feminist analysis contributed by continued close connections with radical suffrage perspectives and campaigns. The PRL's position is that there should always be substitutes for imprisonment in dealing with offences against the law. The position of the PRL was thus philosophically sophisticated, grounded in strategies looking to exploit contradictions and promote historically immanent alternatives, just like those of abolitionists today (Scott 2013; Scott and Gosling, 2016).

The First World War saw the PRL reportedly go into 'a hibernation of three and a half years' (*British Journal of Inebriety*, 1919: 83). After a brief service in Belgium, Leonora Maxwell St John took a post as matron of the Hôpital Militaire Auxiliaire N°. 307 at Neuilly (near Paris), a French Red Cross hospital 'under homeopathic auspices' in 1914, and it appears likely that Arthur's service as an ambulance driver reported by Semple was in connection with her work (*The War Hospital at Neuilly*, n.d.; Semple, 1939). Following its closure, Leonora served with the Serbian Relief Fund as matron of its hospitals in Serbia and Macedonia (*British Journal of Nursing* 1916: 92; 1917: 149).

Because the homeopathic approach of the time was concerned with treatment of the whole person, the homeopathic treated mental health problems arising among ordinary soldiers due to battlefield conditions alongside surgical cases. Back in England, by March 1917, Arthur St John followed this up by getting involved as a committee member for the establishment of a 'Recuperative Hostel for Sailors and Soldiers, invalided from HM services with Nerve Strain' (*British Journal of Nursing*, 1917: 176). Presided over by Frederic Milner, this project took over premises close to St John's home in Hampstead and became the prototype for the later work of the Ex-Services Welfare Society provisions for shellshock victims (Reid, 2007). Both this and the Women's Training Colony represent practical implementations of the PRL's principles of individual care, training and rehabilitation for those who might otherwise be incarcerated, whether in jails or asylums.

The PRL's circle of supporters and adherents reflected a melding of various strands of idealist or *utopian* politics with practical and *realistic* project work, and many were closely connected with peace initiatives, holding fast to an internationalist perspective (see Holmes [2020] for an overview). Arthur St John brought influences from his direct contacts and friendships with Tolstoy and Kropotkin (see Zorin, Chapter 4 in this volume, and Weide, Chapter 9 in this volume), together with a clear legacy of internationalism from his earlier dealings as an envoy for the Quakers. His proximity to Quaker activism is also visible in his later involvement in a Friends'-led project for a (clearly Kropotkin-influenced) New Town (1919) to explore ways to bring together fields, factories and workshops (Hardy, 2000). The close links to militant suffrage activism have already been noted. Logan (2016) importantly notes that 'Rose's (1961) account of the PRL's early work almost totally neglects the feminist input'. She meticulously redresses the balance, showing PRL collaboration with other groups arising from broader feminist campaigning and the role of the PRL executive of activists such as Gertrude Eaton of the Women's Tax Resistance League. Eaton was still lecturing in the name of the PRL on the need for abolition of the death penalty in the 1920s, after the amalgamation with the Howard Association. Further connections are clearly visible through the links between PRL supporters and conscientious objection and feminist pacifist and anti-war work. Examining the activities of fellow project supporters and committee members, there is a clear bridge between those holding absolutist positions and those engaged in humanitarian relief work for victims of war, including understanding soldiers as potential victims, as demonstrated by the concern with shellshock rehabilitation.

The tensions between absolutist stances and contingent responses to the war that were prominent in discussion and action in relation to conscientious objection and war relief work had previously been played out in the discussions on prison reform. The two often combined as the PRL's work connected those imprisoned for objection. Particularly important for the PRL in early 1918 was the input of Stephen Hobhouse (nephew of Sidney Webb), who urged that Margery Fry, a friend since childhood, should take over as St John sought to retire as Secretary.

Margery Fry, like both Arthur and Leonora St John, had been involved with humanitarian relief work during the war. Despite her personal antipathy to St John, 'a ginger and pepper little sentimentalist', as she reportedly wrote, Fry took over the PRL and was to steer its amalgamation with the Howard Association (Logan, 2018: 92). If Fry had no time for Tolstoyan idealism, the same could not be said for Stephen Hobhouse. Deeply affected by his cousin Emily Hobhouse's investigations into and campaigning against concentration camps in the Anglo-Boer War (Brits, 2016), Stephen Hobhouse underwent what he termed an 'Enlightenment' or 'Revolution' as a result of reading Tolstoy (Hobhouse, 1951: 57). Consequently, he devoted his following years to a series of humanitarian concerns, especially those connected with the Society of Friends. Refusing to take up what he termed 'semi-military service' in the Quaker ambulance unit (Hobhouse, 1951: 154), he was imprisoned as an 'absolutist' conscientious objector and served 14 months until his release in December 1917, writing an account of his experiences in *An English Prison from within* (1919).

When the newly formed Labour Research Department turned its attention to a Prison System Enquiry in 1918, it invited Hobhouse to be secretary and editor of the projected report (Fry was a member of the executive committee of the enquiry). There was clearly a strong element of class and privilege in operation since, as Hobhouse (1951: 174) notes, the joint experiences of suffrage and conscientious objectors over the previous decade 'had made prisoners of a large body of men and women of education and veracity, and in some cases of literary ability ... [providing] a golden opportunity to describe in detail and assess carefully the results of imprisonment, physical, mental and moral, on the various types of prisoners'.

Hobhouse found himself unable to finish the large volume of work required (728 pages or a quarter of a million words), and the final report was finished by fellow conscientious objector, socialist and co-founder of the No-Conscription Fellowship, Fenner Brockway (Hobhouse and Brockway: 1922; Bailey, 1997). Though largely severed of its idealistic foundations, *English Prisons To-Day* presented a sharp indictment of the existing system. Its conclusion is bold:

> The whole existing treatment of crime and of criminals rests upon a theory, or theories, which modern thought and experience are showing to be both confused and erroneous. Punishment is commonly justified on some or all of various grounds. These may be distinguished as revenge, retribution, prevention, and deterrence. Of these, the two former imply necessarily guilt in the criminal; the two latter do not. But it is commonly assumed both that criminals are guilty, and that their punishment tends to prevent future crime. This assumption requires reconsideration in the light of facts … imprisonment cannot and does not cure … It must be recognised as an established fact that our principal punishment actually creates or perpetuates rather than abates crime in those upon whom it is inflicted. (Hobhouse and Brockway, 1922: 590, 593)

The fundamental abolitionist real utopian arguments envisioned and pioneered by St John are clearly still visible, though the reforms proposed tend towards being an end in themselves rather than a prelude to abolition.

St John was consistent beyond his direct involvement with the PRL, as we saw in the opening quotation. In 1929 another review essay for the *Sociological Review* on three recent publications, including Brockway's *A New Way with Crime*, saw him conclude:

> these excellent books are calculated to help to clear from our path the old delusions which stand in the way – 'retribution', 'deterrence', 'the vindication of justice', and the like – so that we may be the more free to set about the real task of 'protecting society' by converting criminals into good citizens and caring properly for those who need permanent care. (St John, 1929: 240)

In St John's posthumously published novel *Why Not Now?* (1939), there is little explicit discussion of prison abolition outside of the conversation quoted at the outset of this chapter. Rather, the whole discussion of abolitionism to which he had devoted much of his adult life (he was still giving public lectures on the topic in his sixties) is subsumed within a wider framework of social relations. As mentioned previously, these can best be summed up in terms of relations of care. What are the proper relations of persons to one another, he asks his readers, through the lives and actions he describes? What are the impulses that we allow to govern our interactions? What steps might we as individuals and societies be able to undertake in order to commence a journey of social transformation? The novel's literary shortcomings are obvious and limit its appeal, but one theme is recurrent in his depiction of a society transformed – namely, that institutions that we take for granted today, including prisons and universities, address issues that are products of social structures and arrangements. Changing the underlying conditions of society renders them redundant in the forms in which we know them today. The lobbying and propaganda of the PRL responded to the immediate conditions of its time. Beneath the issues for reform that it presented, and proposing possible solutions for implantation, ran a more profoundly radical political vision: to establish a society in which deterrence and retribution were unnecessary.

Looking to the past in scripting future goals for abolitionism

The ethical socialism of St John was inspired by the ideas of hugely influential thinkers like Tolstoy, Kropotkin, Carpenter and Morris (all of whom are the subject of chapters in this volume) and also forged through the practical connections with activists in the women's suffrage movement. His ethical socialism also placed the failings of the philosophical justifications of punishment in the spotlight, as well as questioning the illegitimacy of penal confinement. St John clearly recognized that penal change and social change are intimately connected, and that the former will not arise without the latter. His work, ideas and interventions should then be of considerable interest to penal abolitionists today, not only as a means of inspiration, but also because his writings and proposed interventions envision an embryonic version of an 'abolitionist real utopia' (Scott, 2013). There are of course tensions here when comparing with abolitionist theory and praxis today – St John does not seem to call for 'negative reforms' that can undermine the logic of the prison from within, nor does he seem to focus on the harms and wrongdoing of the powerful, both of which are central to an abolitionist real utopia – but the similarities are clearly there nonetheless.

Today the prison system's presence in our social landscape is almost taken for granted. Many shy away from the realities within prisons, and while some advocate for prison reform, they may hesitate to support abolition. Given the surge in incarceration policies, the role of penal abolitionists becomes paramount. Can the past guide us in understanding penal abolitionism and negative reforms today? For instance, in what ways can St John's life and actions inform today's abolitionist principles? Gaining widespread support for a shift in punishment approaches is challenging and, historically, both penal reform and penal abolitionism have faced significant hurdles.

Influences in any movement vary, often shaped by organizational needs or impactful leaders. St John's approach fused values from various social struggles, and the values and principles of an ethical socialism, emphasizing message clarity and effective dissemination platforms. He merged insights from diverse domains, including religion, literature, arts and civil rights, which enriched the PRL's strategies. Drawing on successful tactics in other social areas also proved advantageous.

St John recognized his mission's enormity and potential setbacks. He maintained a dual strategy: pushing for political activism and suggesting tangible interventions to alleviate prisoners' sufferings. For him, clear messaging was crucial, emphasizing factual representation over exaggeration, and ensuring the abolitionist message remained undiluted in both political and public spheres. This is clearly something that is relevant for penal abolitionists today.

St John also understood the importance of selecting the right medium for message dissemination. His critique of Lombroso showcases his confidence in challenging prevailing scientific views. Formal channels, like scholarly debates, were instrumental for him and, as seen in the works of Scott (2013) and Scott and Gosling (2016) on an 'abolitionist real utopia', remain a critical asset in the challenge to existing political discourse on punishment.

In conclusion, in order to make meaningful progress, it is essential to acknowledge the past. The strategies and direction of organizations addressing societal issues should be rooted in their historical context. While St John's contributions to prison reform and abolitionism might be underdiscussed, this chapter hopes to shed light on the importance of such early abolitionist voices and how St John envisioned a nonpenal future.

Notes

1. Victor Gray's (2019) half-page sketch does connect St. John's work in the Tolstoyan communities, the Doukhobor migration, the PRL, the Women's Training Colony and his pacifism and vegetarianism, but in a work primarily concerned with local history.
2. Minute books of the Friends' Doukhobor Relief Committee (MS Box 02/4). These minutes contradict a number of later published accounts of the organization of the exile.
3. A KC or King's Council is a senior trial lawyer recognized for their excellence in advocacy. KCMG stands for Knight Commander of the Most Distinguished Order of St. Michael and St George, and Honour given for services in relation to the British Empire
4. A list of known essays, speeches and reviews is provided in the reference list and referenced in-text. Having no personal archive surviving, some of his addresses are known only through excerpts printed in news reports. St John was scathing of the eugenicist approach and was not afraid to say so at the Eugenicist Society's own meetings.

References

Alston, C. (2013) *Tolstoy and His Disciples: The History of a Radical International Movement*, London: I.B. Tauris.

Alston, C. (2014) 'A great host of sympathisers: the Doukhobor emigration and its international supporters, 1895–1905', *Journal of Modern European History*, 12(2): 200–215.

'An Old Gaol Bird' (1913) *London Evening News*, 24 July.

Armytage, W.H.G. (1957) 'Kenworthy and the Tolstoyan communities in England', *American Journal of Economics and Sociology*, 16(4): 391–405.

Bailey, V. (1997) 'English prisons, penal culture, and the abatement of imprisonment, 1895–1922', *Journal of British Studies*, 36(3): 285–324.

Beevers, R. (1988) *The Garden City Utopia: A Critical Biography of Ebenezer Howard*, London: Macmillan.

Bevir, M. (2011) *The Making of British Socialism*, Princeton: Princeton University Press.

Biryukov, P. (1895) 'The persecution of Christians in Russia (with a preface by Tolstoy)', *The Times*, 23 October.

Bongiorno, F. (2001) 'Love and friendship: ethical socialism in Britain and Australia', *Australian Historical Studies*, 32: 1–19.

British Journal of Inebriety (1919) 16(3): 83.

British Journal of Nursing (1916) 57: 92.

British Journal of Nursing (1917) 58(3): 149.

British Journal of Nursing (1917) 58: 176.

Brockway, F. (1928) *A New Way With Crime*, London: Williams and Norgate.

Brits, E. (2016) *Emily Hobhouse. Feminist, Pacifist, Traitor?* Cape Town: Tafelberg.

Buyniak, V.O. (1999) 'The Manitoba and North Western Railway dispute with the Doukhobors', *Saskatchewan History*. Available from: https://doukhobor.org/the-1899-manitoba-and-northwestern-railway-dispute-with-the-doukhobors/ [Accessed 23 February 2024].

Carpenter, E. (1916) *My Days and Dreams*, London: George Allen & Unwin.

Clark, J. (2008) 'Striving to preserve the peace! The National Council for Civil Liberties, the Metropolitan Police and the dynamics of disorder in inter-war Britain', PhD thesis, Open University.

Cobden-Sanderson, T.J. (1926) *The Journals of Thomas James Cobden-Sanderson*, London: Richard Cobden-Sanderson.

Cockin, K. (2017) *Edith Craig and the Theatres of Art*, London: Bloomsbury.

Cook, C.M. (2015) '(Julia Sarah) Anne Cobden-Sanderson 1853–1926'. Available from: https://wilpf.org.uk/wp-content/uploads/2015/03/Anne-Cobden-Sandersonv1.pdf [Accessed 23 February 2024].

Crawford, E. (2000) *The Women's Suffrage Movement: A Reference Guide 1866–1928*, London: Routledge.

Devon, J. (1912a) 'The relation between crime and destitution and the effects of imprisonment', *Report of the Proceedings of the National Conference on Destitution, June 11–14, 1912*, London: P.S. King & Son.

Devon, J. (1912b) *The Criminal and the Community*, London: John Lane.

Edwards, J. and Pethick Lawrence, F.W. (eds) (1908) *The Reformers Year Book*, London: Harvester Press.

Eugenics Education Society (1912) *Problems in Eugenics Vol. II. Report of Proceedings of the First International Eugenics Congress held at The University of London, July 24th to 30th, 1912*, London: Eugenics Education Society.

The Friend (1900) LXXIII: 319.

Gardner, A.R. (1930) 'The Howard Association after 1901 and the Penal Reform League', *Howard Journal*, 3(1): 36–42.

Gilmour, D. (2002) *The Long Recessional: The Imperial Life of Rudyard Kipling*, London: David Gilmore.

Gray, V. (2019) *A New World in Essex: The Rise and Fall of the Purleigh Brotherhood Colony, 1896–1903*, Colchester: Campanula Books.

Hardy, D. (1979) *Alternative Communities in Nineteenth Century England*, London: Longman.

Hardy, D. (1991) *From Garden Cities to New Towns*, London: E & FN Spon.

Hardy, D. (2000) *Utopian England: Community Experiments 1900–1945*, London: Routledge.

Hobhouse, S. (1919) *An English Prison from within*, London: George Allen & Unwin.

Hobhouse, S. (1951) *Forty Years and an Epilogue: The Autobiography of Stephen Hobhouse*, London: James Clarke & Co.

Hobhouse, S. and Brockway, F. (eds) (1922) *English Prisons To-day: Being the Report of the Prison System Enquiry Committee*, London: Longmans, Green & Co.

Holman, M.J. de K. (1978) 'The Purleigh Colony: Tolstoyan togetherness in the late 1890s', in M. Jones, (ed.) *New Essays on Tolstoy*, Cambridge: Cambridge University Press, pp 194–222.

Holmes, R. (2020) *Sylvia Pankhurst: Natural Born Rebel*, London: Bloomsbury.

Howard League (n.d.) Available from: https://howardleague.org/100-years-as-the-howard-league-for-penal-reform/ [Accessed 28 October 2021].

Huws Jones, E. (1966) *Margery Fry: The Essential Amateur*, Oxford: Oxford University Press.

Linehan, T. (2012) *Modernism and British Socialism*, Basingstoke: Palgrave Macmillan.

Logan, A. (2016) 'The Penal Reform League and its feminist roots', *Howard League ECAN Bulletin*, 28 (February).

Logan, A. (2018) *The Politics of Penal Reform. Margery Fry and the Howard League*, Abingdon: Routledge.

London Evening Standard (1912) 29 April: 12.

López-Martín, L. (2019) 'Help Spain by showing films: British film production for humanitarian aid during the Spanish Civil War', *Culture and History Digital Journal*, 8(2). DOI: https://doi.org/10.3989/chdj.2019.019.

Manton, K. (2003) 'The fellowship of the new life: English ethical socialism reconsidered', *History of Political Thought*, 24(2): 282–304.

Maxwell St John, L. (1914) 'Nursing in prisons'. Paper presented to the Nursing and Midwifery Conference, 10–12 June.

Penal Reform League (n.d.) *The Penal Reform League* (handbill), London: PRL.

Reid, F. (2007) 'Distinguishing between shell-shocked veterans and pauper lunatics: the ex-services' welfare society and mentally wounded veterans after the Great War', *War in History*, 14(3): 347–371.

Renwick, C. (2011) 'From political economy to sociology: Francis Galton and the social-scientific origins of eugenics', *British Journal for the History of Science*, 44(3): 343–369.

Richardson, S. (2006) '"You know your father's heart": the Cobden sisterhood and the legacy of Richard Cobden', in A. Howe and S. Morgan (eds) *Rethinking Nineteenth-Century Liberalism: Richard Cobden Bicentenary Essays*, Farnham: Ashgate, pp 229–246.

Rose, G. (1955) 'Some influences on English penal reform, 1895–1921', *Sociological Review*, 3(1): 25–46.

Rose, G. (1961) *The Struggle for Penal Reform*, London: Stevens.

Rowbotham, S. (2008) *Edward Carpenter: A Life of Liberty and Love*, London: Verso.

Salt, H.S. (1921) *Seventy Years among Savages*, London: George Allen & Unwin.

Scott, D. (2013) 'Visualising an abolitionist real utopia: principles, policy and praxis', in M. Malloch (ed.) *Crime, Critique and Utopia*, Basingstoke: Palgrave Macmillan, pp 90–113.

Scott, D. and Gosling, H. (2016) 'Before prison, instead of prison, better than prison: therapeutic communities as abolitionist real utopia?', *International Journal for Crime, Justice and Social Democracy*, 5(1): 52–66.

Semple, D. (1939) 'Introductory Note' in A. St John, *Why Not Now? A British Islander's Dream*, London: C.W. Daniel Co., pp 7–12.

Shrubsole, G. (2010) '"To re-enter the temple by means of the gate called beautiful": new approaches to prostitution, criminality and rehabilitation? The work of the Committee for Social Investigation and Reform, c.1913–1921', unpublished thesis. Available from: https://guyshrubsole.wordpress.com/2010/12/27/arts-crafts-and-prostitution/ [Accessed 23 February 2024].

St John, A. (1899) 'An inconvenient visit to the Caucasus [published in 6 parts]', *New Order*, January–June.

St John, A. (1904) *Education: A Depreciation of Cramming and a Plea for Natural Education*, London: Simple Life Press.

St John, A. (1906) 'A practical policy', *The Humane Review*, 5: 103–114.

St John, A. (1908) 'Discussions: the indeterminate sentence and the need for reformative treatment', *Sociological Review*, 1(4): 377–382.

St John, A. (1911a) 'The community and its children: their co-operation in their own training', *Sociological Review*, 4(2): 125–139.

St John, A. (1911b) 'Crime and eugenics in America', *Eugenics Review*, 3(2): 118–130.

St John, A. (1912a) 'Modifications in prison regime and conditional release', in *National Conference on the Prevention of Destitution 1912. Report of the Proceedings*, London: P.S. King & Son, pp 517–522.

St John, A. (1912b) 'Criminal anthropology and common sense', *Sociological Review*, 5(1): 65–67.

St John, A. (1912c) 'The futility of prison', *Eugenics Review*, 4(2): 210–211.

St John, A. (1912d) 'Discussion on Captain St John's paper', in *National Conference on the Prevention of Destitution 1912. Report of the Proceedings*. London: P.S. King & Son, pp 528–535.

St John, A. (1913) 'Forcible feeding and the Penal Reform League', *The Hospital*, 8 November.

St John, A. (1927) 'Montessori and social progress', *Sociological Review*, 19(3): 197–207.

St John, A. (1929) 'A new way with criminals', *Sociological Review*, 21(3): 233–240.

St John, A. (1939) *Why Not Now? A British Islander's Dream*, London: C.W. Daniel Co.

Tarasoff, K.J. and Ewashen, L. (1994) *In Search of Utopia: The Doukhobors*. Ottowa: Ottawa: Spirit Wrestler Publishers.

The War Hospital at Neuilly (n.d., probably 1916) The Anglo-French-American Hospital. An account of the work carried on under homeopathic auspices during 1915–1916 at the Hôpital Militaire Auxiliaire, No. 307, Neuilly-Sur-Seine in conjunction with the French Red Cross Society, by the British Committee sitting at The London Homeopathic Hospital.

Tidcombe, M. (2017) *The Prison Diary of Annie Cobden-Sanderson with a Facsimile of the Original*, London: Libanus Press.

Tolstoy, L. (1882) *A Confession* [first English translation 1884, Geneva] Edition used A. Maude and L. Maude (trans.) *A Confession and What I Believe*, London: Oxford University Press, 1921.

Tolstoy, L. (1886) *What Is to Be Done?* [first English translation 1887] Edition used A. Maude (trans.) *What Then Must We Do?*, London: Green Classics, 1991.

Tolstoy, L. (1894) *The Kingdom of God Is Within You*, W. Delano (trans.), London: Water Scott.

Tolstoy, L. (1895) 'Dukhobortay Sectarians', *The Times*, 23 October.

Vulcan Advocate (1913) 15 October: 6.

Weinbren, D. (1994) 'Against all cruelty: the Humanitarian League, 1891–1919', *History Workshop*, 38: 86–105.

Women's Franchise [newspaper] (1907) 05 December: 11

Wright, E.O. (2010) *Envisioning Real Utopias*, London: Verso.

6

Edward Carpenter's Realist Utopian and Contingent Abolitionism

Jonathan Baldwin

Introduction

Edward Carpenter (1844–1929) is perhaps most well known as an early gay rights activist, a philosopher and poet heavily influenced by Walt Whitman (1819–1892), and a revolutionary socialist, founder of the Sheffield Socialist Society. He wrote and rallied against the codes and customs of Victorian Britain, particularly on the subjects of sex and sexuality, he himself being an openly gay man who lived with his partner, George Merrill (1867–1928), at a time when homosexual acts between men were illegal. The subject of crime and punishment was a deeply concerning matter for Carpenter, and his observations on it were clearly illustrated in his scathing assessment of the Victorian prison system. In *Prisons, Police and Punishment* (Carpenter, 1905), he reprimanded the British state for its arcane laws and penal institutions in three ways: together they manufactured criminals and were responsible for the repeat offender; as branches of capitalist corruption they enslaved the working classes; and they held humanity in a stranglehold that prevented the path to true freedom and selfhood. Although the penal system of Carpenter's day had advanced from its most primitive stage, which he defined by the notion of 'Revenge', it continued to bear the atavistic features of the second phase, 'Punishment', with its irrational and unreasonable enforcement, and had not yet passed the third stage of 'Deterrence', with its failed methods of preventing crime. He believed that this process would reach its resolution in the stage of 'Reclamation', when in a society without fear and without the desire to punish, the criminal offender is educated, reformed, and returns as a fellow citizen. However, unlike a number of his contemporaries within Britain's anarchist circles, Carpenter did not see absolute penal abolition as a reasonable action. In fact, his anarchist utopian projections of the Common Life still held a place for incarceration, even corporal and capital punishment.

In this chapter I consider Carpenter's views on prisons and punishment in light of what David Scott calls an 'abolitionist real utopia', where rather than unambiguously calling for the destruction of the system of incarceration, he laid out his critique of prisons, his ideas of immediately changing the legal system, and a road map for radical social change that could lead to an (anti-)penal utopia (Scott, 2013). Furthermore, I argue that Carpenter's anarchist penological thought fits into the frames of 'contingent abolitionism' whereby prisons cannot be a form of justice in a society that is wholly unjust, but could have a role to play in a fair and liberal community where they are considered as the last resort in a radical penology with a 'politics of bad conscience'. Lastly, I will take into account how the newly emerging but everywhere-permeating discourses of degeneration at the turn of the 20th century – in particular that of the 'born criminal' – affected Carpenter's views on how to deal with the individual who threatened social harmony and the lives and liberty of others.

Carpenter's writings on prisons

In a foreword to an excellent and very overdue collection of anarchist writings on penological issues, distinguished historian of socialist and anarchist thought Ruth Kinna sums up why so much of anarchist thought is focused on penological enquiry. The ideology and doctrines that anarchists espouse are by and large effectively criminalized by the social order they seek to dismantle, often resulting in them being exposed to firsthand knowledge of the penal system. Many of them often wrote about prisons because they had been incarcerated themselves (Kinna, 2020: 7).

The collection rightly includes the writings of such late 19th-century anarchists as Peter Kropotkin (1841–1921), Errico Malatesta (1853–1932), Alexander Berkman (1870–1936) and Emma Goldman (1869–1940), whose penological thought is relatively well documented. Each believed in the abolition of prisons in some way or another. Malatesta (see also Turcato, Chapter 11 in this volume) saw the abolition of prisons as a necessity not only because it was an unjust form of state violence, but also because they did not work:

> It [the failure of penological reform as a means to reduce crime] is true of the past and the present, and we think it will apply in the future too, if the whole concept of crime is not changed, and all the organisms which live on the prevention and repression of delinquency are not abolished. (Malatesta, 2015[1920]: 105)

With his humanitarian ethics and extensive experiences of prisons in Russia and France, Peter Kropotkin (see also Weide, Chapter 9 in this volume) was rather unequivocal in his calls to abolish the penal system: 'Burn the guillotines; demolish the prisons; drive away the judges, policemen and informers ... No more laws! No more judges! Liberty, equality, and practical human sympathy are the only effectual barriers we can oppose to the anti-social instincts of certain among us' (Kropotkin, 1886: 23).

That Carpenter's *Prisons, Police and Punishment* was not included in the collection is not particularly surprising – I would argue that Carpenter is not as prominent a figure in the history of anarchist thought as those listed. Indeed, purists could question whether or not his sociopolitical views are 'anarchist enough' – a charge that was also levied at him in his day – for him to feature among such nobility.[1] His politics of course were undoubtedly anarchist, and both he and many of his friends and peers described them as such (Goodway, 2006: 53–57). And yet I consider the omission of Carpenter a missed opportunity, not only because he published a full text on the subject, but also because his oscillating and somewhat 'complicated' anarchism itself complicates the history of anarchist penological writings.

I have previously scrutinized Carpenter's approaches to criminology and penology (specifically in light of his utopian politics), and some of that analysis from my doctoral thesis is included in this chapter (Baldwin, 2016). Prior to that, the academic treatment of his views on crime and prisons had placed them as belonging to a narrative whereby a positivist, radical secularism informing a socialist ideal favoured forced labour and medicinal cure for the criminal. Philip Jenkins rhetorically asks how Carpenter as a socialist *and* homosexual could 'possibly favour the discretion and medical imperialism inherent in the new penology' (Jenkins, 1982: 361).[2] Other writers have given Carpenter's criminological thought little more credit. In Sheila Rowbotham's thoroughly researched and detailed biography, Carpenter's texts concerning crime, though grounded in their historical and political settings, are not treated to any critical engagement (Rowbotham, 2008: 146, 251, 308–309). Tony Brown's collection of essays is an excellent example of writing a history of Carpenter's ideas, and his work is placed among that of his fellow radicals, actively participating in the contemporary dialogues concerning feminism, sex and sexuality, socialism and science (Brown: 1990). Again, however, Carpenter is not found to be occupying the debate on crime, criminals or prison reform. Although Victor Bailey justly allocates space to Carpenter in his paper on the 'abatement of imprisonment', there is little expansion, the libertarian socialist being seen as only repeating positivist calls for treating crime as disease (Bailey, 1997: 306–307). The best analysis of Carpenter's penological views is Ian Taylor's 1991 article in which he considers how Carpenter's critique of Victorian prisons and, necessarily, Victorian society could potentially be of use in Thatcher's Britain 'in the development of a "left realist" crime policy' (Taylor, 1991: 19). The most important conclusions from Taylor on what we can learn from Carpenter are, first, that the penal system sits within a social and economic system that does not discourage crime:

> The *fundamental* reason for the 'inadequacy and ineffectuality' [quoting Carpenter] of the penal system of the time is that it is pursuing its aims in the context of social and economic relations – of a free market dominated by Business and Commerce – that do not produce the pre-conditions of a *generalised moral order*. The critical emphasis here, as in many other utopian socialist critiques of 'Industrial Society' in the Victorian period, is on the fundamental contradiction that exists between the unregulated market relations of a capitalist economy, and the dominant, bourgeois or aristocratic, conceptions of a moral life which authority was attempting to defend or to institutionalise through the reactive and/or 'deterrent' imposition of punishment on offenders. (Taylor, 1991: 18)

Second, Carpenter's 'practicality' and 'utopianism' were foundational values for any effective penal policy (Taylor, 1991: 20–24). To a certain degree, this chapter picks up where Taylor left off and further analyses Carpenter's practical and utopian penological views.

Just as Kinna notes, Carpenter was deeply affected by the penal system of his day. Three events can help to illustrate this. He personally felt the full force of the law on 13 November 1887 in the Metropolitan Police's violent clampdown of demonstrators taking part in the socialist-led march on Trafalgar Square, later writing of the blows he and his friend received (Carpenter, 1887: 6). On 4 April 1892, severe sentences passed on the Walsall Anarchist bomb plotters, who had been conspired against by a police agent provocateur, saw Carpenter's contemporaries including one-time fellow Sheffield Socialist, Fred Charles (c. 1860–c. 1934), condemned to long periods of incarceration – Carpenter was called as a character witness for Charles. And on 6 April 1895, three months after Carpenter's *Homogenic Love, and Its Place in a Free Society* was circulated to a reception of 'no little fluttering and agitation', Oscar Wilde (1854–1900) was arrested for homosexual intercourse under the charge of 'gross indecency' (Carpenter, 1916: 196). Indeed, Carpenter references in *Prisons* Wilde's experiences of incarceration, opening the text with an epigraph taken from *The Ballad of Reading Gaol* and including in the appendix a discussion of Wilde's accounts of the cruel and dehumanizing effects of imprisonment. In the first of these three events, Carpenter experienced firsthand not only the possible brutalities of law enforcement, but also on a wider scale the oppressive nature of the state as it cracked down on its constituents demanding an alternative to socioeconomic iniquity. The second was an example of how the name of anarchism was being perverted into a violent, chaotic, anti-social doctrine, reinforced by a corrupt legal system to mete out excessive punishment of those it deemed a threat. And in the third, Carpenter saw how anybody who deviated from 'traditional' norms and practices could be 'made' a criminal by the state and punished with incarceration. Underlying these three sites is Carpenter's belief in the necessary twin roles of the wider socialist movement: first, its 'searching criticism of the old society'; and, second, its 'vital enthusiasm towards the realization of a new society' (Carpenter, 1916: 126). Carpenter's penological views were always part of his transformative ideal.

Carpenter's real abolitionist utopia

In taking up Stanley Cohen's tripartite challenge for penal abolitionists to make a diagnostic, prognostic and transcendental case for abolition (Cohen, 1998), and considering Anthony Giddens' utopian realism (Giddens, 1990, 1994) and Ian Loader's criminological application of it (Loader, 1998), Scott looks to Erik Olin Wright's portrait of practical utopianism (Wright, 2010) and develops what he terms an 'abolitionist real utopia' (Scott, 2013). Such a framework necessarily seeks first to diagnose and critique the power to punish, second to advocate radical but possible alternatives, and third to present a coherent strategy of emancipatory change. In the following section of this chapter I aim to show how Carpenter's writing on crime fits into such a framework and arguably makes him a utopian realist abolitionist.

Scott presents ten theses that outline abolitionists' diagnosis and critique of the criminal system – Cohen's first task (Scott, 2013: 92–97). While Scott by no means considers that an abolitionist real utopia would have to meet each and every thesis, I can see Carpenter doing just that. The first three can be considered as charges against the social ambiguity of crime: crime has no ontological reality; conflict and antagonism exist everywhere, but the state is selective on what constitutes crime, making it immeasurable; and everyone breaks laws, but only some are criminalized, and this is largely down to them coming from a specific social background (Scott, 2013: 93–94). Carpenter first wrote about such ambiguity long before *Prisons* in an article he wrote in 1889 called 'Defence of criminals': 'As a matter of fact society keeps changing its opinion. How then are we to know when it is right and when it is wrong? The Outcast of one age is the Hero of another ... the Accepted of one age is the Criminal of the next' (Carpenter, 1889: 31).

Carpenter goes on to clarify society's selective criminalization: with property and possession the ruling code of what can be referred to as the 'Commercial age', the common thief is made to be the foremost social threat: 'when, as to-day, Society rests on private property in land, its counter-ideal is the poacher' (Carpenter, 1889: 32). Reiterating this argument in

Prisons, Carpenter details the inherent unfairness of having an ethical and legal system based on protecting those who have acquired – at the initial expense and exploitation of the worker – material gain. With assistance from Kropotkin's 1882 article 'Law and authority', he makes the case that crimes against property are 'but a kind of fringe and spray of reaction and protest against the central and monumental inequity of our social arrangements' (Carpenter, 1905: 51). Carpenter's justification follows a traditional anarchist line. Perhaps first posited by William Godwin (1756–1836) in 1793 (see Tuke, Chapter 2 in this volume) – 'the first offence must have been his who began a monopoly, and took advantage of the weakness of his neighbours' (Godwin, 1793: 808) – it was Pierre-Joseph Proudhon (1809–1865) who voiced it most famously in his exclamation, 'property ... is theft' (Proudhon, 1994[1840]: 13). A Proudhonian criminology posits that social organization with the rights of property at its base would lead to social dissonance: '[M]oral evil, or, in this case, disorder in society, is naturally explained by our power of reflection. The mother of poverty, crime, insurrection, and war was inequality of conditions; which was the daughter of property' (Proudhon, 1994[1840]: 191).

Writing at the dawn of the following century, Carpenter's stance in *Prisons* stepped in the footprints of the father of anarchism: the seed of crime was born from the property system. The poor, the unemployed and the homeless are irrevocably drawn to crime, pushed by the deleterious social conditions of life, and Carpenter could only but wonder why the number of those criminals generated from such conditions was not higher (Carpenter, 1905: 52–53). With the balance of the law skewed unfairly against the poor and propertyless, Carpenter sarcastically criticizes its leniency towards those at the other end of society: upper-class shoplifters were seen by the law not as lowly thieves, but as kleptomaniacs in need of treatment; and financial speculating on markets was not a matter for the police, contrary to betting coins in the streets (Carpenter, 1905: 32). As such, Carpenter meets the first three theses of the abolitionist real utopia's critique of the criminal system.

Another critique outlined by Scott includes the grounding of criminal law in allocating culpability and blame to individuals, punishing them for complex transgressions of social norms (Scott, 2013: 94). A constant backdrop in *Prisons*, and a referential point to which Carpenter explicitly turns, was the 1895 'Gladstone Report' of the Home Office Departmental Committee on Prisons. Carpenter's inquiry should largely be interpreted as his rejection of the basic premise on which the Blue Book's penological perspective was founded: 'that prison treatment should have as its primary and concurrent objects deterrence and reformation' (Home Office, 1895). The harmony of these objectives was entirely unpalatable for Carpenter. It becomes apparent that his position in *Prisons* is that the convention of punitive incarceration can only be used for *either* deterring criminals *or* reforming them. The need for society to protect itself from social disharmony caused by conflict is clear, he says, but that is a different attitude altogether from society punishing its constituents. The fear of punishment 'may make a man conform to the respectabilities', he admitted, echoing Kropotkin, 'but it never yet made him a good citizen' (Carpenter, 1905: 13). Fear of culpability, of being individually punished for transgressing the prescribed values of society, did not for him encourage a more moral existence.

The damaging and dehumanizing effect of the prison on the individual and society, it being ineffectual and inapplicable in solving most human (mis)conduct, and the fact that it does nothing to stop the influences of the criminal's powerless social environment are three more of Scott's interrelated diagnostic theses (Scott, 2013: 94–96). Carpenter points out the fact that not only do prisons have little impact on 'bettering' individuals or even reducing crime, but they also encourage recidivism. Using damning statistics from the government's own prison reports over a period of several years that showed an increasing proportion of prisoners were repeat offenders, he concludes that the prison system 'does not create citizens, but rather habitual criminals' (Carpenter, 1905: 14–15, 68–69). One of the reasons for this, he says, is that very little is done to improve the social and cultural capital of prisoners when they are serving their sentence – who are often in prison for the very reason that their social position and lack of opportunities render them relatively powerless (Carpenter, 1905: 70–72). Their disadvantages concerning access to education, employment, health and housing are not changed by serving time in prison, and such cultural impoverishment remains when they return.

Lastly, Scott states that punishment itself is morally illegitimate and so must be done with a bad conscience, prison populations are out of control, and punishment harms not only the prisoner but also everyone in society at large (Scott, 2013: 96–97). Carpenter is very clear that the system of prison and punishment not only fails at what it attempts to do, but is also morally illegitimate: 'Nor is it merely a question of the absurdity and inadequacy of Law, but also, as I have just hinted, of its absolute wickedness' (Carpenter, 1905: 38). He also quotes Kropotkin's harsh words that the system of incarceration shows the depravity of society:

> But has anyone ever really tried to hold the balance between the benefits thus attributed to Law and Punishment, and the degrading effect of the punishment on humanity? Let a man only consider the total mass of evil passions roused among the spectators by the atrocious punishments that used to be inflicted in the public streets. Who indeed has nursed and developed the instincts of cruelty in man (instincts unknown among animals – man having become the cruellest animal on earth) if not the king, the judge and the priest, armed with the Law, and causing men's flesh to be torn off in rags, burning pitch to

be poured in their wounds, their limbs to be dislocated, their bones broken, their bodies sawn asunder, in order to maintain their authority? (Carpenter, 1905: 38–39)

Carpenter reiterates:

The prison, as it has hitherto existed, is simply a hardening institution, which inures folk to crime and the criminal life, and deliberately renders them unfit to become decent and useful members of society. It is an epitome of folly and wickedness. In the prison, the State is seen, like an evil stepmother, beating its own children – whom it has reared in poverty and ignorance, and among conditions which must inevitably lead to crime – beating them for its own sins and neglect, and confirming them in their hatred of itself and each other. (Carpenter, 1905: 40)

Society as a whole is degraded by the penal system as it is. While Carpenter never explicitly expresses concern about the prison population or overcrowding, he does express concern that tens of thousands of criminals are incarcerated because they could not pay a fine, and a huge proportion of those who are imprisoned are in need of psychiatric treatment and should never have been sentenced to incarceration in the first place.

Carpenter's critique of the penal system of his day largely covers what Scott outlines as the utopian realist abolitionist's necessary diagnosis of the power to punish and the criminal system. Scott then moves on to outline the radical alternatives that abolitionists must provide once they have given their critiques. These alternatives need to be grounded in the principles of the 'abolitionist compass' that satisfies Cohen's insistence for immediate humanitarian aid, but does not perpetuate injustice nor legitimate the existing penal system. Scott's abolitionist compass has six principles that, like the ten theses of critique, can be shown to be held in Carpenter's utopian realist abolitionism (Scott, 2013: 97–100).

The first is that human dignity must be protected and human suffering minimized (Scott, 2013: 98). Carpenter's penological views can be seen in the light of a humanitarian rehabilitative ideal, where prisoners are to be cared for and 'reclaimed' by society, which is at fault for losing them in the first place. The penological system of his day is one he labelled as 'wicked' and in one of several appendices in *Prisons*, focusing on corporal punishment, he declares 'it is obvious ... that from a moral point of view the appeal to physical pain is the lowest that can be made' and must only ever be done from a curative perspective by one 'the patient' trusts and respects (Carpenter, 1905: 139). Carpenter was optimistic that the Common Life – a utopia of 'voluntary' collectivism and socialism (Carpenter, 1905: 111) – was emerging, which would bring 'a far-reaching sense of human dignity and equality' and 'a freer, more fluid, more swiftly sensitive and responsive state of the social organism, in which Law if still retained, will assimilate itself rather to Custom, and will relax the rigid, harsh and senseless grip with which to-day it strangulates humanity' (Carpenter, 1905: 62–63).

The next two principles of the compass require abolitionism to be politically emancipatory and directed towards social justice, and therefore actively compete with current institutions and their policies and practices that are unaligned to such an ideal (Scott, 2013: 98–99). While *Prisons* is markedly different from, for instance, *Towards Democracy* (1883–1902) or *England's Ideal* (1884–1887) – two texts unmistakably utopian in form and function – Carpenter would always hold on to his utopian vision of a self-governing, communal society, and it can be found in his most pragmatic of texts. He concluded *Prisons* with the essay 'Non-governmental society', a revised version of his 1897 'Transitions to freedom'. In this essay, he calls for society to provide suitable employment for all individuals that is both 'useful' and 'pleasurable', and for private property to be in the hands of and benefit for the community, and certainly not supported by the armed forces. At the same time, he states, 'it is getting time to be practical', and he makes serious recommendations to nationalize industries and reduce unemployment, as well as to improve the security of the working classes by encouraging the growth and spread of trade unions and cooperative societies (Carpenter, 1905: 105–108). The eventual consequences of this would see universal affluence or at least the absence of poverty, the system of property and capitalism gradually eroding, and the disappearance of the system of law that props them up (Carpenter, 1905: 110–113).

Another principle is that any alternative to the current criminal system must be grounded in transparency and accountability (Scott, 2013: 99). Carpenter was clearly concerned about this and devotes a chapter to 'The police system' with Juvenal's famous question 'Who shall watch the watchmen?' as the subheading. In this chapter, Carpenter makes the argument for the abolition of the police, who for him exist solely to uphold the egregious system of property, and their replacement with individuals whose duties are focused on health and decent living conditions (Carpenter, 1905: 89). He also makes recommendations to make heads of police immediately accountable to the public and voted in for fixed terms just like government officials of a democracy (Carpenter, 1905: 85–87).

Lastly, the abolitionist compass should include the principles that recommendations are *genuine* alternatives to prison and are meaningful interventions that are participatory (Scott, 2013: 99–100). Carpenter makes a number of suggestions in his chapter 'Prison reform' (Carpenter, 1905: 64–79), and a number of these not only serve these principles but also make for an 'abolitionist praxis', marking Cohen's final task – presenting a coherent strategy of emancipatory change (Scott, 2013: 106–110). Carpenter summarizes his recommendations at the end of the chapter. He calls for the immediate conversion of all prisons into industrial reformatories which would focus on rehabilitating the prisoner through medical assistance, education, training and 'healthy', paid labour. In emphasizing the connection between reformatories and good labour, he also argues for individuals to have employment opportunities on release, including work in which they had already developed skills while incarcerated. Another recommendation of Carpenter's is for the immediate abolition of short sentences and the replacement of these with warnings or fines – sentences of incarceration at the reformatories would only be suitable for repeat offenders. Furthermore, he calls for the adoption of the 'indeterminate sentence' whereby individuals need not be incarcerated for a specific length of time, but could be reintroduced to society as soon as they had proven their rehabilitation.[3] Two other emancipatory recommendations which Carpenter called for was the immediate abolition of capital punishment and the establishment of a Criminal Court of Appeal (Carpenter, 1905: 78–79). His damning indictment of the criminal system, radical recommendations for reform and transcendental alternatives to the way in which society approached the problem of crime make his *Prisons* an early example of Scott's real abolitionist utopia.

Carpenter's contingent abolitionism

Antony Duff distinguishes contingent abolitionism from absolute abolitionism:

> Furthermore, the most radical abolitionists are what we may call 'absolute', rather than 'contingent', abolitionists. A 'contingent' abolitionist argues that while some system of state punishment (very different from our own) would in principle be justifiable in some kind of society (very different from our own), punishment as practiced in our own society cannot be justified, since it cannot, in those societies, be what it would need to be to be justified … [whereas] 'absolute' abolitionists argue that no system of state punishment could ever be justified in any kind of society. (Duff, 2003: 31)

One could be forgiven for presuming that an anarchist abolitionism would be 'absolute' – the belief that society should not have structures of hierarchy would hold the concept of the prisons anathema. And yet the radical, somewhat utopian image of the modern benevolent reformatory appealed even to anarchists. Indeed, a young Kropotkin, as a Lieutenant of the Amúr Cossacks posted in the Transbaikal region of Siberia and tasked with helping the local government draw up a manifesto for the improvement of

Russia's penal system, would recommend that prisons should be remodelled as modern reformatories. Years later, writing *In Russian and French Prisons*, Kropotkin would come to realize that such an approach made radical reform impossible. No system of incarceration, no matter how it looked, could improve moral faculties and make society more cohesive: 'I must confess that at that time I still believed that prisons could be reformatories, and that the privation of liberty is compatible with moral amelioration ... but I was only twenty years old' (Kropotkin, 1887: 18).

The answer to the issue of crime and criminality in Russia would emerge only through the fundamental reorganization of society, Kropotkin believed that 'to see a new departure in the Russian penal institutions we must wait for some new departure in Russian life as a whole' (Kropotkin, 1887: 23). Here flows the undercurrent of Kropotkin's anarchist criminological tract. No humanitarian reform of the criminal justice system would come to the good of both the individual and society alike as long as there remained practices within it that subjected those who were deemed to have acted immorally to harm or loss (particularly, with regard to the latter, loss of their freedom). Modern reformatories would be built on rotten foundations; the two pillars of the institution of criminal law, discipline and punishment, had to be felled altogether.

However, although he regarded Kropotkin and his thought highly, Carpenter saw such absolute abolition as 'quite impracticable' (Carpenter, 1905: 46). He was certainly an abolitionist, and his recommendations for radical prison reform were always surrounded by suggestions that absolute abolition may be possible in his future utopian 'Non-governmental society'.[4] But his abolitionist real utopia did not have time for such fanciful musings, and he made the suggestions for radical reform to the criminal system as part of a wider social transformation, as previously outlined. The 'impracticable' calls for absolute abolition to the more reasoned suggestions for radical reform highlights a variation in the approaches found in his 1889 article 'Defence of criminals' and the 1905 *Prisons*. The latter was largely a response to texts and developments emerging from within the confines of governmental enquiry. A shape similar to that of 'Defence of criminals' would not fit well in such a frame. But it may also reflect a development in his political outlook, a participant in the thick of a transforming political landscape. The utopianism emanating from the socialist movements in the 1880s had dissipated in the succeeding decade. Rowbotham follows Carpenter's directional shift at the beginning of the 1890s that saw him, swimming with the tides of change, moving away from the anarchist-communist idealized future and instead starting to focus on the collectivist-socialist transitional phase (Rowbotham, 2008: 140, 170–178). He saw, like others, the need for the socialist movement to embrace a pragmatic radical political programme rather than merely living a life of liberty. The birth of the Independent Labour Party in 1893 represented 'an impulse towards a wider-reaching socialism' (Rowbotham, 2008: 171). The aspirations of radical party politics were perhaps wider, with real opportunities for change apparently within reach, but it was certainly a shorter-sighted perspective. The utopia of the future faded into the distance, overshadowed by the reform of tomorrow. As Carpenter said in 1897 in 'Transitions to freedom', reprinted in *Prisons*, 'it is getting time to be practical' (Carpenter, 1897: 187).

The salient point is that *Prisons* was a piece of work constructed in a climate consumed by ideas of practical reform in criminal law. A critical site had been reached, a result of the incompatibility of newly emergent concerns and epistemologies and the space set out by the 'classical' apparatus born in the 18th century. It was a specific point that insisted on intervention rather than speculation, practical action rather than far-removed apotheosis: 'There will necessarily be a long and difficult period of transition. That, however, is no reason why we should not begin at once to make the transition. Indeed, it is clear that if we are to save ourselves from destruction we *must* do so' (Carpenter, 1905: 46–47).

Carpenter was writing *Prisons* within a framework that required alternative measures grounded in the real world of crime and its prevention. A diagnosis of the criminal and of the deficiencies of the existing structure of the moral and legal constitution had been introduced in 'Defence of criminals' and developed in *Prisons*. However, the latter, composed within the centre of a perceived critical point, was to prescribe remedial action. The question then emerges: what becomes of Carpenter's abolitionist real utopia once the radical reforms of the penal system and wider social transformations had been achieved? It is in this space that we can define his abolitionism as contingent, whereby punishment can be justifiable in his 'ideal' future. Certainly one of the reasons that allows for this somewhat surprising position is Carpenter's criminological belief in degeneration.

The close relationship between crime and social disadvantage is a relatively unexceptional observation made by Carpenter. However, the assumed essential qualities of such a relationship shape a specific approach in his criminological enquiry. In *Prisons*, Carpenter quoted Dr Robert Gover's testimony from the 1895 Home Office Report, whereby it is stated that the criminals in England and Wales' prisons 'are recruited from strata or classes of society not far removed from paupers' and that of these many were found to be insane. Carpenter continues to excerpt from Gover's testimony:

> A ratio higher than that [of prisoners who are insane] prevailing among the population in general is only what might be expected, when regard is paid to hereditary influences, and to influences of a degrading, demoralizing and morbid character surrounding, from infancy onwards,

the children of the classes from whom criminals are chiefly recruited. (Carpenter, 1905: 74–75)

A subtle disparity materializes from the doctor's words. It is made clear that a causal relationship is presumed to exist between both one's heredity and debased environment and the resulting insanity (one should note that to attest insanity is influenced by surroundings of a 'degrading', 'demoralizing' and 'morbid' nature is, in this historical context, a form of *petitio principii*, for the signification of such terms and the uncertain object of insanity would have allowed for a rephrasing of the argument to 'Things that can upset one's mental faculties might disturb one's mind'). But the idea of pauperism being an influence on criminal behaviour is not presented in such terms. Here, Gover merely *located* an abundance of crime and criminals within the poorest parts of society. For him, the slums were where depraved influences were *found*. Carpenter, however, consistently traced the causative lines of crime straight back to the condition of poverty itself, a condition from which depraved influences were *made*.

As already mentioned, Carpenter argued that impoverishment pushes one to steal by 'the sheer necessity of getting some kind of living in a world where every avenue of so called honest livelihood is closed' (Carpenter, 1905: 61). But he also saw that such social conditions change the very constitution of all those who reside therein: '[M]oral lunatics', he tells us, are not recruited from, but 'are the products of our slums and other diseased social conditions' (Carpenter, 1905: 61). The slum is not specified as that which merely houses degrading influences. Diseased social conditions do not only contain demoralizing contagion; they are *causes* of crime themselves. The social conditions that arose from the property system not only provided the stage on which criminal acts could be performed, but influenced the very characters of those waiting in the wings. The subtle contrast between the reach of his and Gover's reasoning is that for Carpenter, the imbalanced moral minds of criminals that the doctor condemned are themselves a 'consequent' of poverty (Carpenter, 1905: 75). Carpenter's approach can be found to have occupied the scientific domain that had emerged from Cesare Lombroso's (1835–1909) biological positivist school, as he encountered the criminal as a physiological object shaped by phenomenal conditions. Of course, by locating the pathogen of crime in the environment, his affinities stayed close to the Italian school's French rivals, headed by Alexandre Lacassagne (1843–1924). Carpenter, too, saw a middle ground in the nature-nurture debate. But despite viewing criminal behaviour from both the environmental and physiological positions, he would visualize its sources far more clearly in the former – the conditions of life in its entirety largely shaped the condition of the individual. The influence of the social environment on the individual's bearing was to form the foundations of his criminological enquiry. This is precisely how Carpenter justifies his contingent abolitionism – how could punishment be justifiable in a society which literally breeds and fosters criminal minds and their bodies? Yet in a utopian future, such individuals would be far less tolerated.

Corporal punishment as sentenced by corrupt judges and carried out by wicked wardens was abhorrent to Carpenter. Yet, as a form of benevolent remedial treatment, under the charge of medical heads of reformatories, it was acceptable (Carpenter, 1905: 37–38, 138–139). The epistemological framework adopted by Carpenter legitimized such methods by positioning criminality inside the individual's body. If it was not something that originated or was fostered in a squalid environment, it could be treated as an affliction that could be cured or removed by physical means so as to make one a social creature once again. It is on such a ground that Carpenter could advocate capital punishment, although quite unwillingly. In the case of 'hopeless recidivists' and those whose 'criminal propensities ... have been proved to be entirely ineradicable', death would be the only means to prevent them from harming society (Carpenter, 1905: 145). Whereas corporal punishment was acceptable if it removed the criminal affliction from the individual body, capital punishment would have to be used to remove the criminal affliction from the social body – a form of social surgery. On this subject, Carpenter again distinguished himself from the absolute abolitionists of the anarchist tradition:

> Personally, I am not a non-resister, like Tolstoy. I do not think that society is saved by non-violence, and I think there *are* cases in which a good hiding may considerably benefit a man. I do not believe that society will be saved by the rule of nonviolence, nor by any hard and fast rule – *certainly not by the rule of Violence*. But I believe in good sense. (Carpenter, 1905: 37–38)

'Sensible' violence, then, in Carpenter's view could be applied by those professionals, medical or otherwise, who were safeguarding society from the object of the criminal as it was defined by science, particularly the branches of psychiatry and medical psychology. The epistemological grounds on which Carpenter could justify such measures of coercion and force as a means to protect society from dangerous individuals would also, as seen in the thought of a number of his socialist contemporaries, be used to legitimize the discussion of sterilization in the practice of negative eugenics (Baldwin, 2016; see also Forero Cuellar, Chapter 10 in this volume). The rehabilitative ideal, particularly when assimilated by an ideological approach that would, to varying degrees, elevate the wellbeing of the social over the liberty of the individual, could be a method of violence, even in the gentle hands of Carpenter.

Carpenter's writing on prisons makes for an interesting if not somewhat puzzling read, particularly for those who are interested in the complex history of penological ideas among socialists and anarchists. We find both in *Prisons* itself and in his overall body of work Carpenter oscillating between utopian dreams of a society without laws, police or prisons, and practical recommendations for penal reform where incarceration was a means of social defence, but with a 'politics of bad conscience'. As I have alluded to in this chapter, the abolitionist praxis found in Carpenter's *Prisons* is quite distinct from his earlier utopian *Towards Democracy* and *England's Ideal*, and his statement that 'it is getting time to be practical' underlies his real abolitionist utopia. I have already queried why he may have considered it such a time when writing *Prisons*, but one could also muse on the fact that the subject of crime and punishment was so personal to Carpenter as a homosexual man in the Victorian age. It deeply affected him, just as it did Oscar Wilde and others who transgressed the repressive sexual codes of the time, in a similar way to how the subject deeply affected Kropotkin and other anarchists. When they wrote about prisons, police and punishment, they had something to say.

Notes

[1] Contemporary anarchist John Creaghe was scathing in his criticism of Carpenter's 'soft' anarchism (Rowbotham, 2008: 164–165).

[2] Jenkins' approach reduces the complex biosocial discourse found in socialist criminology to mere deterministic social Darwinism: 'Many [radicals] were driven to socialist conclusions by Darwinian views, reminding us that social Darwinism was not a conservative preserve ... This broad philosophical approach was reflected in socialist attitudes to criminology. English-speaking radicals wholeheartedly espoused the various theories of determinism in competition in these years' (Jenkins, 1982: 364). Such a history ignores Carpenter's criticism of Darwin's 'survival of the fittest', his devotion to Jean-Baptiste Lamarck's (1744–1829) theory of a living being's will or desire as a driving factor in evolution, and his belief in various theories of cooperation and mutual aid (see, for instance, Carpenter, 1889: 129–147).

[3] Of course, one could call Carpenter naïve to back a system so clearly open to abuse, and Taylor (1991: 25) and Radzinowicz and Hood (1986: 273) do just that. However, Carpenter did state in *Prisons, Police and Punishment* that on this specific recommendation of reform it would have to be the case that a maximum sentence time would be set (Carpenter, 1905: 25). The point he is making here is that once an individual has proven their rehabilitation, they should rightly be reintroduced to society.

[4] See, for instance, Carpenter's ending of the chapter 'The police system', where he makes clear his hopes for a future that has dispensed of police, and his closing thoughts on 'Non-governmental society', where he romantically muses on the demise of law and 'brute authority' (Carpenter, 1905: 89, 112–113).

References

Bailey, V. (1997) 'English prisons, penal culture, and the abatement of imprisonment, 1895–1922', *Journal of British Studies*, 36(3): 285–324.

Baldwin, J. (2016) 'Crime and utopia: socialist and anarchist projections in Britain, 1870–1914', PhD thesis, Royal Holloway, University of London.

Brown, T. (ed.) (1990) *Edward Carpenter and Late Victorian Radicalism*, London: Frank Cass.

Carpenter, E. (1887) 'How the police provoked violence', *Pall Mall Gazette*, 14 November: 6.

Carpenter, E. (1889) 'Defence of criminals: criticism of immorality', *Today*, 2(63): 31–41.

Carpenter, E. (1889) 'Exfoliation: Lamarck versus Darwin', in E. Carpenter (ed.) *Civilisation: Its Cause and Cure, and Other Essays*, London: Swan Sonnenschein, Lowrey & Co., pp 129–147.

Carpenter, E. (1897) 'Transitions to freedom' in E. Carpenter (ed.) *Forecasts of the Coming Century. By a Decade of Writers*, Manchester: The Labour Press, pp 174–192.

Carpenter, E. (1905) *Prisons, Police and Punishment: An Inquiry into the Causes and Treatment of Crime and Criminals*, London: Arthur C. Fifield.

Carpenter, E. (1916) *My Days and Dreams: Being Autobiographical Notes by Edward Carpenter*, London: George Allen & Unwin.

Cohen, S. (1998) 'Intellectual scepticism and political commitment: the case of radical criminology', in P. Walton and J. Young (eds) *The New Criminology Revisited*, London: Macmillan, pp 98–129.

Duff, R. A. (2003) *Punishment, Communication, and Community*, Oxford: Oxford University Press.

Giddens, A. (1990) *The Consequences of Modernity*, Cambridge: Polity Press.

Giddens, A. (1994) *Beyond Left and Right*, Cambridge: Polity Press.

Godwin, W. (1793) *Enquiry Concerning Political Justice and its Influence on Morals and Happiness*, 2. London: G. G. J. and J. Robinson.

Goodway, D. (2006) *Anarchist Seeds beneath the Snow: Left-Libertarian Thought and British Writers from William Morris to Colin Ward*, Liverpool: Liverpool University Press.

Home Office (1895) *Report of the Departmental Committee on Prisons*, London: HMSO, C 7702, para 25.

Jenkins, P. (1982) 'The radicals and the rehabilitative ideal, 1890–1930', *Criminology*, 20: 347–372.

Kinna, R. (2020) 'Foreword' in A.J. Nocella II, M. Seis and J. Shantz (eds) *Classic Writings in Anarchist Criminology: A Historical Dismantling of Punishment and Domination*, Chicago: AK Press, pp 7–8.

Kropotkin, P. (1886) *Law and Authority: An Anarchist Essay*, London: International Publishing Co.

Kropotkin, P. (1887) *In Russian and French Prisons*, London: Ward and Downey.

Loader, I. (1998) 'Criminology and the public sphere: arguments for utopian realism', in P. Walton and J. Young (eds) *The New Criminology Revisited*, London: Macmillan, pp 190–212.

Malatesta, E. (2015[1920]) *Umanità Nova*, 2 September in V. Richards (ed. and trans.) *Errico Malatesta: His Life & Ideas*, Oakland, CA: PM Press, pp 104–105.

Proudhon, P.J. (1994[1840]) *What Is Property?*, in D.R. Kelley and B.G. Smith (eds and trans.) *What Is Property?* Cambridge: Cambridge University Press.

Radzinowicz, L. and Hood, R. (1986) *A History of English Criminal Law: Vol. 5: The Emergence of Penal Policy*, London: Stevens.

Rowbotham, S. (2008) *Edward Carpenter: A Life of Liberty and Love*, London: Verso.

Scott, D. (2013) 'Visualising an abolitionist real utopia: principles, policy and praxis', in M. Malloch and B. Munro (eds) *Crime, Critique and Utopia*, Basingstoke: Palgrave Macmillan, pp 90–113.

Taylor, I. (1991) 'A social role for the prison: Edward Carpenter's *Prisons, Police and Punishment* (1905)', *International Journal of the Sociology of Law*, 19: 1–26.

Wright, E.O. (2010) *Envisioning Real Utopias*, London: Verso.

7

William Morris' Utopian Case for Prison Abolition

Owen Holland

Bloody Sunday and its aftermath

Early on the morning of 18 February 1888, William Morris set off with Moncure Douglas and Louisa Susan Kaufman to greet two prisoners who had been released from Pentonville prison during the small hours of the day (Morris, 1984–1996, vol. 2: 742). Morris records his experience of arriving at the prison in a letter to his daughter Jenny:

> I walked down the street to look at the miserable place and it made my blood boil to think that men should elaborate such a monument of folly, and thought how I should like to live to pull it down or turn it into a floor-cloth factory or something of that sort. (Morris, 1984–1996, vol. 2: 744)

Morris' moral indignation at the social fact of incarceration is clear enough, but his desire to pull down the prison was no mere tilt at some bourgeois windmill. The political writings which he produced during his socialist period in the 1880s and 1890s elaborate a much fuller and incipiently abolitionist critique of the prison system, formulated largely on the hoof as he propagandized in regular articles against the state's increasingly punitive response to the nascent socialist movement. This penal abolitionist argument finds its fullest expression in Morris' utopian romance *News from Nowhere* (1890), where he imagines a future society in which prisons will have been abolished as part of a more thoroughgoing transition towards 'the present rest and happiness of complete Communism' (Morris, 1910–1915, vol. 16: 186). But the utopian vision he adumbrates in *Nowhere* was also intimately bound up with, and responsive to, the more immediate experiences of the movement.

The two prisoners whom Morris had travelled to greet on 18 February were the Scottish Radical Member of Parliament R.B. Cunninghame Graham and the trade unionist John Burns. Both men had been imprisoned for a period of six weeks as a consequence of their participation in the so-called 'Bloody Sunday' demonstration of 13 November 1887, in which hundreds of socialists, Irish nationalists and Radicals had been violently assaulted by the Metropolitan Police under the command of General Charles Warren (Thompson, 1977: 482–503).[1] Despite their relatively short period of incarceration, Morris observes the mental and physical toll that imprisonment had taken on his two comrades, writing that '[Graham's] voice as well as Burns' was certainly weaker when they spoke in the evening'; Morris was similarly dismayed when Burns 'showed [him] the bit of bread that the poor men have for their breakfast and supper – just two mouthfuls – no more' (Morris, 1984–1996, vol. 2: 744).[2] Burns, he notes, 'looked a good deal pulled down' (Morris, 1984–1996, vol. 2: 744). Two weeks later, on 3 March, Morris reported in the Socialist League's *Commonweal* journal that Burns 'spoke the other day so heartily, and wisely also, about pulling down Pentonville', the 'hideous den' in which he had 'recently suffered' (Morris, 1996: 375). Recovering quickly from his period of incarceration, Burns attended two public meetings on Saturday 18 and Monday 20 February organized by the Law and Liberty League to celebrate his release, and, as H.A. Barker records, he 'had courage enough to acknowledge that his month's imprisonment was as nothing to the "ten years" imprisonment of Michael Davitt, the two years of Ernest Jones, the fifty years of [Auguste] Blanqui, or the sufferings of Kropotkin' (Barker, 1888a: 58). Setting aside his own incarceration, Burns invokes a radical martyrology of well-known political prisoners, encompassing proponents of Irish nationalism, Chartism and anarchism. Meanwhile, Morris' report confirms that Burns also gave voice to abolitionist sentiments, echoing Morris' own instinctive view that the Benthamite panopticon of Pentonville in particular, and prisons in general, ought to be demolished, or otherwise repurposed to more socially useful ends.

Among Morris' extensive network of political contacts within the late Victorian socialist movement, Graham and Burns were two of the more prominent activists to receive a custodial sentence as a result of their political work. However, in writing publicly about their imprisonment, Morris does not accentuate the heroism or endurance of these two men. Instead, he emphasizes that 'Burns and Graham went to jail on behalf of the unemployed', for whom the series of demonstrations in Trafalgar Square had initially been organized, 'and for the matter of that for the employed also; those who are employed to produce wealth which their employers and not themselves enjoy' (Morris, 1994: 351).[3] Taking note of Burns' public speeches in *Commonweal*, Morris pushed the point by appealing to the supporters of Irish Home Rule and the Radicals with whom socialists had cooperated on Bloody Sunday, formulating questions that identify the role of the prison system in propping up an economic order based on exploitation and stark inequality:

> Will people never understand then, not even Home Rulers and extreme Radicals, what our prison system means? Must we Socialists teach them even this? Pentonville must not compete with the slums, or its terror will be gone ... Therefore its diet and discipline must be on such a scale as is torture to a gentleman like Graham, or even an artisan like Burns. If only Pentonville could be pulled down before revenge overtakes us for this folly and cruelty! (Morris, 1996: 375)

Characteristically, Morris frames his appeal to political allies by way of an attempt to radicalize their thinking on a particular question of immediate concern, and he does so in a way that implicitly recognizes what Bettina Aptheker would describe, in a different and much later context, as 'the *class* nature of the prison system' (Aptheker, 2016: 59). In this instance, Morris clearly establishes the relationship between the prison system and the extreme poverty of London's slums as one of mutual reinforcement, reminding his readers that prison conditions are deliberately designed to be worse than slum conditions, in order to ensure that slum dwellers are not inadvertently incentivized to seek imprisonment as a form of temporary respite from the depredations of slum life.[4]

There are other resonances between Morris and 20th-century abolitionist thinkers as well. Writing in the same volume as Aptheker, Angela Y. Davis comments that the modern prison:

> [cloaks] itself with the bourgeois aura of universality – imprisonment was supposed to cut across all class lines, as crimes were to be defined by the act, not the perpetrator – [but] has actually operated as an instrument of class domination, a means of prohibiting the have-nots from encroaching upon the haves. (Davis, 2016: 34)

Albeit differently located and facing markedly divergent historical conditions than Davis and her co-thinkers, Morris wrote from within a roughly comparable milieu of revolutionary communist political organization, and he formulated a remarkably similar critique of the prison system. In response to the emergent socialist movement's early skirmishes with the carceral institutions of the bourgeois state, Morris' journalism becomes peppered with brief but insightful critiques of the prison system, which accentuate its place in a larger structure of class oppression. For instance, when three participants in an open-air socialist meeting at Hyde Park were sentenced in May 1887 to 'six months' hard labour' after a police-instigated fracas, Morris observed that the convicted prisoners would struggle to appeal the sentence because 'the bail *must be liable to the expenses of the appeal if it is rejected*, which in plain terms means that if an ordinary working man is arbitrarily convicted … no matter how preposterous the behaviour of the magistrate may be, the working-man *cannot* appeal' (Morris, 1994: 241–242).

Skewering the false universality of bourgeois law in terms that echo Marx and anticipate Davis, Morris proceeds to comment, with caustic acerbity, that: 'This is the meaning of there being the same law for rich and poor, of justice never being sold in this country, and the like damned hypocritical twaddle. Justice is *always* sold in this country' (Morris, 1994: 242). The more that Morris and his comrades came into direct contact with the carceral institutions of the Victorian state, the fiercer these comments would become. Yet Morris did not campaign for penal change as a single issue, to be treated as discrete from the larger project of socialist education and agitation; instead, he envisaged prison abolition as part of a more durable and totalizing effort towards revolutionary social transformation, in which *all* the institutions of the bourgeois state would wither away. Exposing 'the boasted equality before the law' as a 'gross sham' was important to Morris chiefly because it aided a 'speedy education towards revolution' (Morris, 1994: 328). Similarly, when the liberal *Daily News* published an exposé of prison conditions in August 1886 entitled 'School in prison', Morris observed in *Commonweal* that it 'draws up a very small corner of the curtain' and 'shows a picture of petty tyranny and torture' (Morris, 1996: 120). However, he went on to add that 'in this matter of prison life, as with work-a-day life, the society of to-day has become hopeless of any real progress' and 'is becoming conscious that it is but waiting till the Revolution shall sweep it away' (Morris, 1996: 120). In keeping with his general rejection of palliative measures for social reform, Morris' journalistic reflections on the prison system did not pursue improvement in the *conditions* of life within prison, even though he was mindful of just how bad those conditions were (Morris, 1994: 367–368). He argued instead to end the *practice* of incarceration which underpinned the bourgeois state's monopoly on the use of force, and, in his view, this could only be achieved as part of a postrevolutionary reorganization of society.

Morris' anti-carceral utopia

One of Morris' most powerful arguments for prison abolition is to be found in his 1890 utopian romance *News from Nowhere*, in which he imagines the everyday life of a fully communist society projected into the late 21st century. Early in William Guest's journey into Nowhere, Morris' utopian protagonist innocently inquires of his hosts whether there are any prisons in the future society, only to be met with a confused response: 'Dick flushed red and frowned, and the old man looked surprised and pained' (Morris, 1910–1915, vol. 16: 44). Readers might suspect they have something to hide, but Dick is not accompanying Guest on a tour of a confabulated Potemkin village; on the contrary, Dick expands upon his evident embarrassment with the following exclamation:

> Man alive! how can you ask such a question? Have I not told you that we know what a prison means by the undoubted evidence of really trustworthy books, helped out by our own imaginations? ... And if there were people in prison, you couldn't hide it from folk, like you may an occasional man-slaying; because that isn't done of set purpose, with a lot of people backing up the slayer in cold blood, as this prison business is. Prisons, indeed! O no, no, no! (Morris, 1910–1915, vol. 16: 44)

Dick's response confirms Guest's inkling that there are, in fact, 'no prisons at all' in Nowhere (Morris, 1910–1915, vol. 16: 44). Likewise, the heated tone of Dick's reply helps to establish the moral texture of the society's opposition to the practice of forcible incarceration, recalling Morris' own incandescence on seeing Pentonville.[5] For 19th-century readers of Morris' utopian romance, the dialogue between Guest and Dick enacts a moment of utopian defamiliarization, at least insofar as it invites such readers to imagine a society so wholly different from their own that the very thought of its existence contains the potential to shock them into a new conceptualization of present horizons of possibility. In this respect, Dick's response to Guest – along with many other moments in Morris' text – embodies what E.P. Thompson (following Miguel Abensour) characterizes as the 'open, exploratory character of Utopianism: its leap out of the kingdom of necessity into an imagined kingdom of freedom in which desire may actually indicate choices or impose itself as need' (Thompson, 1977: 798–799). The work of estrangement or defamiliarization begins to take place, in Thompson's influential account, when 'habitual values ... are thrown into disarray', thereby opening a passage into 'Utopia's proper and new-found space: *the education of desire*' (Thompson, 1977: 790–791). In this chapter of *Nowhere*, then, Morris takes aim, through the generic medium of utopian romance, at what he elsewhere describes as the smug complacency and 'optimism' of the 'ordinary middle-class person, who ... is not more sure of anything than of the perfection of our prison system', securely regarded as 'the culmination of all reason' (Morris, 1996: 119–120). In Nowhere, by contrast, Dick expresses a countervailing set of 'habitual values', offering a direct challenge to bourgeois common sense that draws upon positions Morris had articulated elsewhere in *Commonweal*; rather than taking the existence of prisons as a given and immutable fact, Dick instead reminds Morris' 19th-century readers that at least *some* of their contemporaries 'couldn't fail to know what a disgrace a prison is to the Commonwealth at the best' (Morris, 1910–1915, vol. 16: 44).

It is no coincidence that Guest's inquiry about Nowhere's system for punishing criminals (or, rather, the absence of such a system) arises out of a prior conversation about the history of Trafalgar Square. On arriving in the Square, which Guest is delighted to see that the Nowhereans have transformed into an orchard, he is momentarily and disconcertingly transported back in his mind's eye to the scene of the 1887 Bloody Sunday demonstration, which had led to the arrest and imprisonment of Burns and Graham. At this point in their journey, Guest and Dick are travelling with an old man who claims to have read a 'muddled account' of Bloody Sunday, including a discussion of the police violence meted out to the demonstrators, 'in a book ... called James' Social Democratic History', from which he has gleaned that the 'Government of London ... or what not other barbarous half-hatched body of fools, fell upon these citizens (as they were then called) with the armed hand' (Morris, 1910–1915, vol. 16: 42). When Guest informs the old man that a 'good many people were sent to prison because of it', the old man instinctively assumes that Guest must be referring to 'the bludgeoners', and both the old man and Dick are surprised when Guest corrects the assumption, telling them that 'the bludgeoned' were the ones sent to prison (Morris, 1910–1915, vol. 16: 43). The idea appears so ridiculous to the old man that he imagines Guest must have been 'reading some rotten collection of lies', leaving Guest sheepishly to pursue further inquiries about how such matters are handled in Nowhere (Morris, 1910–1915, vol. 16: 43).

Morris again mobilizes the device of utopian defamiliarization in Guest's dialogue with the old man, reimagining an episode of contemporary history viewed *as if* from the perspective of a communist future, and thereby casting into stark relief what Morris described in 'Coercion for London' (1887) as the political credulity of 'the unsuspecting "cultivated" person, rejoicing in the security of property and person in this civilized and "free" country', who fails to see 'what law means under our present system – a cunning instrument for the oppression of the poor by the rich' (Morris, 1994: 241–243). Readers of *Commonweal* would have been familiar with Morris' various condemnations of the state's punitive response to the Bloody Sunday demonstration, and some might have encountered his article 'London in a State of Siege' (1887), in which he analysed Bloody Sunday as a deliberate ruling-class escalation of the class war, during which the 'police struck right and left like what they were, soldiers attacking an enemy ... nominally for behoof of a party, but really on behoof of a class' (Morris, 1994: 303–305).

In *Nowhere*, by contrast, readers are invited to imagine a society in which the oppositional and counterhegemonic impetus of Morris' journalism has become normalized and habitual, so much so that it now constitutes the common sense of the proverbial man in the street. In this respect, these defamiliarizing narrative episodes of Morris' utopian text complement and expand the propagandistic polemic of his journalism, appealing to a readership that would have encountered these different strands of Morris' socialist agitation in the columns of the same *Commonweal* journal.

Yet the terms in which Dick formulates the reason for the absence of prisons in Nowhere also deserve further comment. According to Dick, 'if there were people in prison, you couldn't hide it from folk'. This has the appearance of being an unobtrusive and apparently passing remark on Dick's part. However, on closer inspection, it conveys much about the moral and philosophical basis of the Nowhereans' collective decision not to incarcerate any of their fellow citizens – or, to use Morris' preferred nomenclature, their neighbours. Implied in Dick's formulation is an ideal of transparency, with roots in the political philosophy of Jean-Jacques Rousseau, which presupposes that an individual's relationship to the social collective (or general will) will be translucently, wholly knowable and desirable as such (Starobinski, 1988). In Martin Jay's account, Rousseau's ideal of 'total transparency' relied upon the dream of 'a new social order in which humans would be utterly open to each other's gazes, a utopia of mutually beneficial surveillance without reprobation or repression' (Jay, 1993: 92–93).

In keeping with this logic, it would be impossible to 'hide' the existence of prisons in Nowhere because social life is organized in the form of decentralized, federated communes, such that, as Morris put it in his 1889 review of Edward Bellamy's *Looking Backward*, 'the unit of administration [is] small enough for every citizen to feel himself responsible for its details' (Morris, 1994: 425). One effect of these social arrangements is to ensure that individuals 'cannot shuffle off the business of life on to the shoulders of an abstraction called the State, but must deal with it in conscious association with each other' (Morris, 1994: 425). Such localized forms of 'conscious association', in turn, act as a check against the reintroduction of inhumane or coercive practices from the capitalist past; the social relations of Nowhere are sufficiently transparent, or visible, that 'you couldn't hide it from folk'.

Visual discourse has been prominent in the generic history of narrative utopia as well. In Morris' Foreword to the 1893 Kelmscott Press edition of Thomas More's *Utopia* (1516), he praises the book as 'a link between the surviving Communism of the Middle Ages ... and the hopeful and practical progressive movement of to-day' (Morris, 1936: vol. 1: 289). Yet readers of More's *Utopia* will recall that he depicts Utopian society as a place of panoptic surveillance: all More's Utopians are said to be 'in the present sight and under the eyes of every man' (Bruce, 1999: 68). In More's text, unlike Morris', this regime of transparency appears to be motivated by the need to regulate (or pre-empt) crime, as well as the possibility of political dissent, since the Utopians' ocular severity goes together with a ban on loitering and a prohibition of 'wine-taverns', 'ale-houses' and 'stews', allegedly because such places might give 'occasion of vice or wickedness', providing 'lurking corners' or 'places of wicked councils and unlawful assemblies' (Bruce, 1999: 68). These spaces represent a threat in More's *Utopia* because they contain the potential for dissent, and consequently pose a risk of contagion. If this visual economy of surveillance quickly evokes darker possibilities, such as the glass-world of Yevgeny Zamyatin's *We* (1921) and the ubiquitous telescreens of George Orwell's *Nineteen Eighty-Four* (1948), then the inextricability or otherwise of the link between means and ends, as well as the nature of the political will which animates the seat of vision, surely ought to be of some concern.

For some commentators, utopia, in whatever guise it may appear, is only ever a short step away from the gulag or the concentration camp.[6] Yet it would be hard to see how such authoritarian techniques of repression might emerge in Nowhere, given the lack of any centralized state authority along with the general recognition, or social consensus, that 'the absence of artificial coercion' is a necessary precondition for individual self-realization and flourishing (Morris, 1910–1915, vol. 16: 92). This is not to suggest that Morris' utopia has abolished the right to *privacy*, but, unlike the dystopian satires of Zamyatin and Orwell, Morris imagines a mode of collective and solidaristic watchfulness which is compatible with, and even necessary to ensure, individual liberty, at least insofar as he posits a social form in which 'people about the roads and streets' could not 'look happy if they knew that their neighbours were shut up in prison, while they bore such things quietly' (Morris, 1910–1915, vol. 16: 44). The logic of Dick's position, here, appears to be that no utopian denizen of Nowhere could ever countenance the existence of prisons because s/he would experience the fact of another's incarceration as a curtailment of her or his own freedom. In a curious revision of John Stuart Mill's ideal of negative liberty, whereby one is free to act according to one's will provided that one's action does not impede the liberty of another, Morris' Nowhereans instead experience any forcible deprivation of liberty, even when imposed upon another person, as a threat to their own freedom, thus bringing them closer to Marx's view that 'the free development of each is the condition for the free development of all' (Marx and Engels, 1998: 26).[7] Morris imagines a form of *substantive* freedom in Nowhere, informed by his conviction that a transformation of 'moral consciousness' would accompany the communist reorganization of society, and that a 'new ethic' would gradually emerge after the revolutionary supersession of capital and private property (Morris, 1994: 621).

In a series of *Commonweal* articles, co-authored with Ernest Belfort Bax, Morris argues that:

> we may safely predict that [the future form of moral consciousness] will be in a sense a return on a higher level to the ethics of the older [pre-capitalist] society ... and the identification of individual with social interests will be so complete that any divorce between the two will be inconceivable to the average man. (Morris, 1994: 621)

Morris and Bax detect the 'first great popular manifestation' of this 'new ethic' in 'the heroic devotion of the working-classes of Paris in the Commune of 1871 to the idea of true and universal freedom' (Morris, 1994: 621). Bax, who was more philosophically inclined (and trained) than Morris, expands upon this idea in the concluding paragraphs of his essay 'Universal History from a Socialist Standpoint' (1886), writing that 'the society of the future ... [will] be a society in which all interests are again united, since they will have a definite social aim; in other words, since the interest of the individual will be once more identified, and this time *consciously*, with the interest of the community' (Bax, 1891b: 36). In his lecture 'Liberalism v. Socialism' (1890), Bax similarly contends that a socialist society would cease to be 'a mere aggregate of classes and class interests' and would instead become 'a connected system or *social* (instead of merely *political*) synthesis', preserving both 'the essential truth at the basis of primitive Communism' and the 'essential truth at the basis of modern Individualism' (Bax, 1891a: 88–89).[8] Morris accentuates the same desired synthesis in his review of Bellamy's *Looking Backward*, writing that 'variety of life' must go together with 'equality of condition' in order to achieve 'true Communism' (which he thought Bellamy's statist utopia had failed to express), since 'nothing but an union of these two will bring about real freedom' (Morris, 1994: 425). And for Bax, in particular, the projected transformation in ethics that would accompany the abolition of private property led him to envisage an associated obsolescence of the legal system that codifies the outmoded ethical presuppositions of class society.

As Bax explains in 'The Curse of Law' (1889), 'the legal method of settling disputes between individuals is a necessary bulwark of the system of individual property-holding, and of a class society, on which civilisation reposes', but 'ultimately civil law must disappear with the last vestiges of modern civilisation' (Bax, 1891a: 103). Bax outlines a similar argument in an earlier essay, 'Civil Law under Socialism', which first appeared in *Commonweal* on 24 July 1886, where he argues that a transition to socialism would mean that 'the whole department of law will become an anachronism', not least because civil action in the law courts 'almost always turns directly or indirectly on a question of property' (Bax, 1891b: 146–147). Morris' utopian vision drew deeply on the fervent atmosphere of intellectual debate that informed the political culture of the *fin-de-siècle* socialist movement, and Bax's ruminations on the future of law in a socialist society clearly influenced Morris' thinking at various points. There are no prisons in Nowhere, as William Guest learns somewhat after his discussion with Dick, because there is 'no civil law, and no criminal law' (Morris, 1910–1915, vol. 16: 84). As becomes evident, the institutional apparatus for administering punishment to those found to be in breach of these legal codes has passed into oblivion as part of a much more thoroughgoing reorientation of the society's collective ethical life, which Guest learns about at the British Museum in conversation with Old Hammond in Chapter XI, 'Concerning Government', and Chapter XII, 'Concerning the Arrangement of Life'. As Old Hammond explains, a 'tradition or habit of life has been growing on us; and that has become a habit of acting on the whole for the best' (Morris, 1910–1915, vol. 16: 80). With clear echoes of Bax, he goes on to clarify that, as part of this process, civil law 'abolished itself' in Nowhere because 'the civil law-courts were upheld for the defence of private property', and Nowhere's abolition of private property meant that 'all the laws and all the legal "crimes" which it had manufactured of course came to an end' (Morris, 1910–1915, vol. 16: 80–81). Lacking a concept of crime, Nowhere can clearly have no need for an institution designed to punish and correct the behaviour of the criminal.[9] Meanwhile, more fundamentally, it should also be clear that Morris' commitment to *prison* abolition was thus entirely dependent on the prior *abolition of private property* as part of a much wider revolutionary transformation – or abolition – of *class society*. Morris' abolitionism was thoroughly maximalist in this sense, insofar as it cannot be divorced from his communist politics.

'Keeping things dark is the necessary rule in a prison': reading Morris with Foucault

Morris' *News from Nowhere* offers the fullest statement of his political and philosophical rationale for supporting the idea of prison abolition, figured forth in the form of an imagined utopian alternative to 19th-century bourgeois society. Morris' utopian attempt to think *beyond* the coercive apparatus of the bourgeois state was also accompanied by other forms of creative response to the socialist movement's direct experience of confronting state power. In the pages of the *Commonweal* journal, where *Nowhere* was first serialized, regular readers would have encountered numerous reports on the arrest and imprisonment of Morris' fellow activists. Morris himself appeared before a magistrate at Marylebone Police Court on 24 July 1886 on charges of obstruction, only to be acquitted (with a fine of one shilling plus costs) because of his privileged class position (MacCarthy, 1994: 535–537).

As the climate of legal persecution intensified, Morris adopted the habit of referring in his *Commonweal* journalism to the various trial judges who presided over these cases as 'Nupkins'. Morris graces Judges Grantham, Newton, Mansfield and Saunders with this moniker for assorted instances of judicial despotism and incompetence (Morris, 1996: 185, 252, 303, 461). The name probably alludes to the character of George Nupkins, Esq., an irritable magistrate and justice of the peace in Charles Dickens' *The Pickwick Papers* (1837), and Morris exacts a peculiar kind of parodic retribution on such judges in his only stage-play, *The Tables Turned; or, Nupkins Awakened*, written in 1887 and first performed at the Socialist League Hall in Farringdon Road, London on 15 October of the same year. The first part of the play is comprised of a courtroom farce in which the eponymous Judge Nupkins (based on the real-life Judge Peter Edlin) hears a number of cases, including that of the socialist Jack Freeman, who is charged with 'obstructing the Queen's Highway', before the charges are preposterously elevated to include sedition and incitement to murder (Morris, 1936, vol. 2: 538). In the second part, the scene shifts to a postrevolutionary fête in the countryside, where Nupkins, now in hiding, encounters a group of communist revellers, including several previous occupants of his courtroom. Michel Foucault would recognize Nupkins as 'the figure of the judge obsessed by a desire for prison', and this desire clearly still preoccupies him in the postrevolutionary period (Foucault, 1987: 248). A victim of his own paranoid misapprehensions, Nupkins believes that the revolutionaries will hang him in revenge for his earlier actions, and begs to be incarcerated, or sentenced to 'hard labour for life', instead of executed, while longing for the 'happy days when [he] used to sentence people to be hanged' (Morris, 1936, vol. 2: 559, 556). He is surprised to learn at a hearing of the Council of the local Commune that, as in Nowhere, there are, in fact, no prisons in the future society. Far from exacting the 'terrible revenge' that Nupkins fears, Morris instead presents the revolutionaries' motivation in terms of forgiveness and neighbourly good fellowship; the former judge is acquitted with the injunction that he must simply 'learn to live decently' (Morris, 1936, vol. 2: 561, 565). The Communal Council has abandoned a punitive, or retributive, concept of justice because, as Jack Freeman patiently explains to Nupkins, '[p]eople punish others because they like to; and we don't like to' (Morris, 1936: 565). Insofar as Nupkins' neighbours pass any 'sentence' upon him, it is one of simple rustication, since he is expected to do no more or less than work alongside them in gathering the harvest and digging potatoes.

In *Nupkins Awakened*, then, Morris parodically turns the tables on the Victorian judiciary by imagining Nupkins' ultimate superfluity – and rehabilitation – in the postrevolutionary society of the future, anticipating the utopian and more fully abolitionist stance of *News from Nowhere*. Elsewhere in *Commonweal*, Morris also creatively reimagines the legal dilemma faced by a working-class socialist agitator in the seventh part of his long narrative poem *The Pilgrims of Hope*, which was serialized in 13 instalments in *Commonweal* between March 1885 and 3 July 1886. The working-class protagonist of *Pilgrims* joins 'the Communist folk', and soon volunteers to undertake propaganda work, speaking 'in street corners .../ To knots of men' (Morris, 1910–1915, vol. 24: 387). Richard loses his job in a carpenter's workshop as a consequence, and is subsequently arrested and sentenced to two months' imprisonment when some 'scum of the well-to-do, brutes void of pity or shame', provoke a conflict during one of his lecturing engagements (Morris, 1910–1915, vol. 24: 390). In an anticipation of Nupkins, the judge presumes to lecture Richard at the trial 'but not for the riot indeed/For which he was sent to prison, but for holding a dangerous creed', numbering him among those being 'punished by prison-torture for their political opinions' (Morris, 1910–1915, vol. 24: 391; Morris, 1996: 399). Narrated from the perspective of Richard's unnamed wife, his period of incarceration passes as an 'evil dream'; she apostrophizes her 'empty bed', and '[longs] for the dawning sorely', but remains steadfast in her determination to 'cherish a pleasure in pain', before ultimately travelling with Richard and her new lover Arthur to join the Communard revolution in Paris in 1871 (Morris, 1910–1915, vol. 24: 388–389). Much like *Nupkins Awakened*, albeit in a very different register, Morris responded in *The Pilgrims of Hope* to the ongoing campaign of police harassment against socialist speakers by narrativizing it. Through both the political parody of the stage-play (first performed as an entertainment for members of the League) and the hard-grained realism of the narrative poem serialized in *Commonweal*, Morris sought to stiffen the resolve of his fellow activists, strengthening their bonds of fellowship against the carceral apparatus of the state.

A week after the final instalment of *The Pilgrims of Hope* appeared in *Commonweal*, Sam Mainwaring (of the League) and John (or Jack) Williams (of the Social Democratic Federation) were arrested for obstruction in Bell Street, Marylebone, on 11 July, in circumstances uncannily similar to those which Morris had related in the poem. Williams, who was a painter and decorator by trade, would go on to offer a striking reminiscence of Victorian Britain's punitive regime, articulated by way of an interview with Harry Quelch, the editor of the Social Democratic Federation's journal *Justice*. Having grown up in a variety of workhouses (Edmonton, St Margaret's, St John's Westminster and Hornsey), Williams had firsthand experience of one of the most infamous carceral institutions of the Victorian state. As he explained to Quelch, this experience 'made [him] feel more bitter against the present system, and more earnest in [his] efforts towards changing it' (Hyndman et al, n.d.: 36). As part of his journey towards politicization, Williams also recalled witnessing the public hanging in Manchester of three

Irish Fenian agitators, William Allen, Michael Larkin and Michael O'Brien (the Manchester martyrs), on 23 November 1867:

> I shall never forget it. The sight I witnessed when, footsore and weary, I walked into Manchester on the morning of the execution, was one the like of which I have never seen. The streets were lined with troops and police. But what impressed me far more than the police and military were the solemn faces of the men and women, and even children, who were gathered in enormous crowds. Most of them were bareheaded. Some were on their knees praying, and many were crying. (Hyndman et al, n.d.: 36)

Williams attests to the spectacular display of state power, manifest in the ritualized ceremony of a public execution, designed, in this instance, to intimidate the anti-colonial movement in Ireland. He also offers up a recollection of what Foucault would recognize as the spectacle of the scaffold. In such 'ceremonies of public execution', Foucault writes, 'the main character was the people, whose real and immediate presence was required for the performance' (Foucault, 1987: 57). The anonymous crowd that lived on in Williams' memory was summoned to the role of spectatorship, but this role was ambiguous, as Foucault intimates, because spectatorship could produce solidarity, which could in turn invite protest. Public participation in such performances of state power could thus threaten to undermine the display, lending such occasions an air of 'carnival' or 'momentary saturnalia', which Foucault regards as one reason for the gradual transformation in the techniques of punishment that accompanied the long transition from feudalism to bourgeois modernity, and which helped to bring about the birth of the modern prison as a space of 'secrecy and autonomy in the exercise of the power to punish' (Foucault, 1987: 60–61, 129).

In Part One of *Discipline and Punish* (1975), Foucault observes a changing regime of penality over the course of the 18th and 19th centuries bound up with the 'disappearance of torture as a public spectacle' and the associated emergence of a different 'penal style', characterized by 'a bureaucratic concealment of the penalty itself' (Foucault, 1987: 7, 10). Over a period of around 80 years, Foucault writes, 'penal detention replaced public execution as a calculated technique for altering individual behaviour' (Foucault, 1987: 264). Yet even as this transformation was taking place, marking a shift from the public theatricality of punishment to the administrative and corrective rationality of bourgeois justice, it nonetheless proved 'difficult to dissociate punishment from additional physical pain', such that 'a trace of "torture"' remains present, according to Foucault, 'in the modern mechanisms of criminal justice' (Foucault, 1987: 16). By the late Victorian period, when the socialist movement emerged during the 1880s, the death penalty had not yet been abolished, but the last public hanging (of the Irish Fenian Michael Barrett) had taken place at Newgate on 2 May 1868.[10] The 19th-century criminal justice system was, *pace* Foucault, busily replacing 'the representative, scenic, signifying, public, collective model' of the 'power to punish' with 'the coercive, corporal, solitary, secret model', and Morris appears to have recognized the essential principle of this transformation in his comment that '[k]eeping things dark is the necessary rule in a prison' (Foucault, 1987: 131; Morris, 1996: 663).

In a piecemeal way, Morris was also sensitive to the traces of torture that animated the Victorian prison system, and this became a keynote of his political journalism. When Jack Williams was first imprisoned in November 1885 for his part in the socialist free speech agitation at Dod Street, London, Morris expressed his solidarity in *Commonweal*:

> It is clear that the idea of our English Prisons is to inflict torture on the prisoners: a man in for a month is treated worse than one in for two, and he again worse than if his sentence were six months: the meaning of which is that the shorter-termed prisoners can bear more torture than the longer, and therefore shall have it. (Morris, 1996: 40)[11]

Morris had helped to establish *Commonweal* earlier during 1885 and the first issue appeared in February; Williams' case was one of the first political trials of which Morris took public notice. Five years later in May 1890, as Morris was approaching the end of his time as the journal's editor, he can be found repeating largely the same point. In response to the publication of a report by a Commission established to investigate the ill-treatment of anarchist prisoners in Chatham prison (the so-called 'dynamiters'), Morris urges his readers to remember that:

> The prison system of this country is, and is meant to be, a system of torture applied by Society to those whom it considers its enemies; but this fact is kept in the dark as much as possible, lest ordinary good-natured people, who do not want to torture persons unless fear drives them to it, should be shocked, and the system should be swept away – or at least altered. (Morris, 1996: 663)

Morris appears to hesitate between abolition (sweeping away) and reform (alteration). However, he was sufficiently aware that a spurious programme of philanthropic reform already undergirded the Victorian prison system, but this had not made it any the less repugnant to him. On 14 January 1887, Charles Mowbray and Fred Henderson were arrested in Norwich after addressing a rally of unemployed workers, some of whom had gone on to smash windows. Mowbray and Henderson were both working-class members of the Socialist League, and when Morris read an account of their trial in a local Norwich paper, he commented in his private diary that 'the judge's summing up of the case was amusing and instructive, as showing a sort of survival of the old sort of bullying of the Castlereagh times mixed with a grotesque attempt at modernisation on philanthropic lines: it put me in a great rage' (Boos, 2018: 50–52).[12]

Spuriously philanthropic modernization also forms a topic of conversation between Dick and William Guest in Nowhere, when Guest briefly alludes to 'the Medieval period' and 'the ferocity of its criminal laws', of the kind that Foucault might identify with spectacular displays of public torture and execution (Morris, 1910–1915, vol. 16: 43). Dick responds with a slightly more measured iteration of the 'great rage' that Morris experienced in reading about the case of Mowbray and Henderson:

> As to the great improvement of the nineteenth century, I don't see it. After all, the Medieval folk acted after their conscience ... whereas the nineteenth century ones were hypocrites, and pretended to be humane, and yet went on tormenting those whom they dared to treat so by shutting them up in prison, for no reason at all, except that they were what they themselves, the prison-masters, had forced them to be. (Morris, 1910–1915, vol. 16: 43–44)

Dick has gleaned his knowledge of medieval penal practices from 'good books on that period' (Morris, 1910–1915, vol. 16: 44), and it is not too fanciful to imagine that there might be a Nowherean version of *Discipline and Punish*, since Dick appears to have adopted a broadly Foucauldian critique of the spuriously 'humane' basis of 19th-century prison reform, sharing Foucault's view that the various, repeated attempts at prison 'reform' are always 'isomorphic, despite [their] idealism, with the disciplinary functioning of the prison' (Foucault, 1987: 270–271).[13] The 19th-century prison system, Dick suggests (again *pace* Foucault), was a means of producing and typologizing forms of illegality which could then be all the more efficiently controlled and regulated. Yet where Foucault suggests that, by the middle of the 19th century, 'the penitentiary order had become sufficiently well established for there to be no question of dismantling it', Morris' Nowhereans have exceeded this imaginative horizon and opted for abolition instead (Foucault, 1987: 248).

Prison abolition and the withering of the bourgeois state

To complicate matters still further, prisons have disappeared along with schools in Nowhere, since Guest also learns that Dick only understands the meaning of the word 'school' with reference to 'a school of herring' or 'a school of painting', but he cannot parse its meaning 'in the sense of a system of education' because there is no formal education system (Morris, 1910–1915, vol. 16: 28). In Pierre Bourdieu's terms, both the right *and* left hands of the state appear to have vanished in Morris' vision of the communist future (Bourdieu, 1998: 1–10).[14] *News from Nowhere* might be read in this light as Morris' attempt speculatively to think through the possibility of a social revolution that has realized the communist endeavour to bring about the withering of the bourgeois state, with all the attendant consequences for really-existing institutions that such a revolution might entail over the *longue durée*. The apparent simplicity of the resulting social arrangements has led some critics to object that Morris' dream-vision was little more than a sophisticated form of wish fulfilment. Graham Hough, for instance, dismisses *News from Nowhere* as 'another Earthly Paradise, but one that is attached to the contemporary world by a slender thread of social analysis' (Hough, 1961: 111–112). Raymond Williams gives voice to a similar frustration, albeit in a more sympathetic register, when he writes of Morris' utopian romance that '[t]he air of late Victorian holiday is made to override the complexities, the divergences, the everyday materialities of any working society' (Williams, 1980: 205). One could reply, as William Empson might have been tempted to do, that Nowhere's ostensible simplicity is of a piece with the text's extended 'pastoral process of putting the complex into the simple' (Empson, 1974: 22). It is certainly the case, for example, that Morris' envisaged abolition of the prison system goes together with a serious (and difficult) meditation on the nature of freedom in the absence of the coercive authority of the state, and the social relations envisaged by Morris are surely not without complexity in this respect. This is perhaps why Old Hammond tells Guest that 'we have simplified our lives a great deal from what they were ... yet our life is too complex for me to tell you in detail by means of words how it is arranged; you must find that out by living amongst us' (Morris, 1910–1915, vol. 16: 79). Old Hammond's dialectic of the simple and complex appears to invest primacy in experiential rather than abstract or *a priori* modes of knowledge, and, as some of Guest's later encounters demonstrate, the experience of living in Nowhere entails various kinds of entanglement which evoke the self-evident depth, or messiness, of utopian emotional life.

In Dick's previously quoted dialogue with Guest, for instance, he makes it clear that although prisons no longer exist in Nowhere, an 'occasional man-slaying' may still take place. Far from depicting utopia as a hermetically sealed and harmonious (or flat) totality, free from contradiction and internal strife, Morris here acknowledges the continuing intricacy of the social relations and the complexity of emotional life that will animate the society of the future, in which negative emotions such as jealousy or anger will persist, and may even produce sporadic outbreaks of violence. During his river journey up the Thames in the final section of the narrative, Guest encounters a man named Walter Allen and learns that a Nowherean community in Maple-Durham has suffered a 'death by violence' (Morris, 1910–1915, vol. 16: 165). Walter explains that the death came about as a consequence of a love triangle, when the rejected suitor, who had been wallowing in his rejection for some weeks, exchanged 'some hot words with the successful lover' and then 'got hold of an axe and fell upon his rival when there was no one by; and in the struggle that followed the man attacked, hit him an unlucky blow and killed him' (Morris, 1910–1915, vol. 16: 166). Morris designs the episode carefully as a case of self-defence; it can be regarded (in legal terms) as an instance of involuntary manslaughter rather than wilful murder, since 'the slayer had no malice' and did not intend to kill his victim (Morris, 1910–1915, vol. 16: 166). Even so, the event has proven to be traumatic enough for the small community to which the surviving couple belong. Since manslaughter no longer exists as a legal category and incarceration is out of the question, Walter deliberates with Dick about the best course of action, and Walter explains 'we have advised him to go away – in fact, to cross the seas; but he is in such a state that I do not think he *can* go unless someone *takes* him, and I think it will fall to my lot to do so' (Morris, 1910–1915, vol. 16: 166). Walter admits that this is 'scarcely a cheerful outlook' for him, but he is also unconsciously expressing the new, communal ethic that animates Nowhere's social life, whereby collective deliberation about the best course of action to pursue in the face of a complex episode of wrongdoing has taken the place of punitive incarceration and punishment (Morris, 1910–1915, vol. 16: 166).

The episode in Maple-Durham, which appears in the third and final section of the narrative, returns to and concretizes (by way of a particular example) the conversation that has already taken place between Guest and Old Hammond in the British Library. Long before Guest encounters Walter Allen, Old Hammond informs him that 'crimes of violence' can still occur in Nowhere because '[h]ot blood will err sometimes' (Morris, 1910–1915, vol. 16: 81–82). While criminal law would have regulated such crimes in the prerevolutionary past, Old Hammond makes it clear that Nowhere has abolished criminal law along with civil law. Since he acknowledges that there are nonetheless occasional transgressions against the 'habit of good fellowship', the crucial question for Old Hammond does not revolve around the prevention of such behaviour, but instead concerns what forms of recompense the transgressor will be expected to make and what forms of punishment (if any) society will seek to impose (Morris, 1910–1915, vol. 16: 80). On the topic of punishment, Old Hammond explains that Nowhere does not seek to invest itself with what Foucault would describe as the power to punish, because this would be a futile exercise of collective self-harm:

> That *punishment* of which men used to talk so wisely and act so foolishly, what was it but the expression of their fear? And they had need to fear, since *they* — i.e., the rulers of society — were dwelling like an armed band in a hostile country. But we who live amongst our friends need neither fear nor punish. Surely if we, in dread of an occasional rare homicide, an occasional rough blow, were solemnly and legally to commit homicide and violence, we could only be a society of ferocious cowards. (Morris, 1910–1915, vol. 16: 82)

Since the social and economic causes of crime (private property, 'family tyranny' and so on) have disappeared in Nowhere, the sources of fear which Hammond describes have concomitantly dried up, obviating the need for punishment. Old Hammond's extended sociological explanation for the social fact of crime during the 19th century anticipates the argument that Edward Carpenter would articulate more fully in *Prisons, Police and Punishment* (1905), a book which 'challenged the cultural bias in how crime was defined and exposed the power relations embedded within the practice of the legal system' (Rowbotham, 2008: 309; see also Baldwin, Chapter 6 in this volume).

Carpenter's criminological interests reached back into the 1880s, motivated in no small part by the legal persecution of homosexuals, which reached a climax of sorts in the spectacular trial of Oscar Wilde on charges of gross indecency in 1895. Carpenter had argued in 'Defence of Criminals' (1889) that: 'In general we call a man a criminal, not because he violates any eternal code of morality — for there exists no such thing — but because he violates the ruling code of his time, and this depends largely on the ideal of the time' (Carpenter, 1889: 120).[15] In his autobiography, Carpenter praised *News from Nowhere* for giving expression to 'the emotional presentiment and ideal of a sensible free human brotherhood', and Morris' utopian vision certainly supports Carpenter's identification of 'true Democracy' with the absence of 'an external government' (Carpenter, 1916: 216; Carpenter, 1889: 128; see also Baldwin, Chapter 6 in this volume). Motivated by an ideal of 'free human brotherhood', Old Hammond is keen to inform Guest that Nowhere's means of regulating any sporadic outbreaks of violence appears to involve a form of restorative justice in which the responsibility to make recompense lies with the individual who is deemed to have transgressed against the society's ideal of free cooperation. As he puts it, 'when any violence is committed, we expect the transgressor to make any atonement possible, and he himself expects it' (Morris, 1910–1915, vol. 16: 82). Far from conceiving incarceration (or some comparable form of punishment) as a means by which a criminal might repay a debt to society, Old Hammond explains that such punishment would constitute an 'additional injury' to the commonwealth rather than a meaningful form of 'atonement' (Morris, 1910–1915, vol. 16: 83). If atonement for wrongdoing is a genuine aim, as many 19th-century prison reformers wished to argue, then Morris' utopian case for prison abolition suggests it can only truly be achieved in the absence of external coercive authority, and therefore in a society *without* prisons.

Notes

1. As Thompson points out, numerous '[s]entences of hard labour, ranging from one month to a year, were doled out on largely perjured evidence', while Burns and Graham received relatively mild sentences by contrast (Thompson, 1977: 492).
2. Ibid.
3. As Morris makes clear in this article, entitled 'A speech from the dock', Burns struck a similar note when he appeared in court charged with illegal assembly. For the printed version of the speech which Burns delivered in court on 18 January 1888, see Burns (1888). For Graham's account of the events, see Cunninghame Graham (1888). H.A. Barker commented that the trial conclusively demonstrated that 'whatsoever the authorities do *is* law' (see Barker, 1888b).
4. The principle of 'less eligibility' was first introduced as part of the 1834 Poor Law Amendment Act and was intended to preserve the deterrent effect of imprisonment (Sieh, 1989).
5. A keynote of Morris' journalism is his sheer rage at the very existence of 'Pentonville and its sister hells' (Morris, 1996: 504).
6. For discussion of this point, see Kateb (1972) and Jacoby (2005: 49–82).
7. For an alternative view of Morris' negotiation of Mill's liberalism, see Camarda (2015).
8. In Mark Bevir's helpful summary of Bax's political thought, he observes that, for Bax, 'liberty is not majority rule', but 'consists of the realization of one's relationship to society' and 'requires people to recognize that their interests are the same as those of the community' (Bevir, 2011: 60).
9. This absence of the concept of crime is later rehearsed in the writings of Dutch abolitionist Louk Hulsman (1986).
10. See Gattrell (1994) for more detailed reflections on public executions in England.
11. As Williams recalls in his interview with Quelch, he was imprisoned on two further occasions on a similar charge of obstruction in relation to meetings held at Bell Street.
12. Robert Stewart (1769–1822), Viscount Castlereagh, was Chief Secretary for Ireland between 1798 and 1801, during which time he presided over a vicious campaign of repression against the United Irishmen, earning him the nickname 'Bloody Castlereagh'. In February 1817, Castlereagh, in his capacity as leader of the House of Commons, introduced the Habeas Corpus Suspension Bill as part of a broader clampdown on free speech and public protest.
13. Foucault regarded the end of the 19th century as a particularly 'fruitful [period]' for such efforts (Foucault, 1987: 270–271).
14. Bourdieu identifies the left hand of the state with 'those who are called "social workers": family counsellors, youth leaders, rank-and-file magistrates, and also, increasingly, secondary and primary teachers', while the right hand is constituted by the 'technocrats of the Ministry of Finance', as well as 'the public and private banks' (Bourdieu, 1998: 2). I am modifying Bourdieu's conceptualization of the state's right hand to include its carceral institutions, even though Bourdieu would prefer to regard some of the professionals attached to these institutions ('rank-and-file magistrates') as being imbued with the (presumably social-democratic) ethos of the left hand.

15 The essay first appeared across two issues of *To-Day* in February and March 1889; as its title makes clear, Carpenter shared mid-century Fourierist ideas which '[place] a positive value on crime' (Foucault, 1987: 289).

References

Aptheker, B. (2016) 'The social function of prisons in the United States', in A.Y. Davis (ed.) *If They Come in the Morning: Voices of Resistance*, new edn, London: Verso, pp 51–59.

Barker, H.A. (1888a) 'Prisoners for liberty', *Commonweal*, 4(111): 57–58.

Barker, H.A. (1888b) 'The trial of Burns and Graham', *Commonweal*, 4(107): 28.

Bax, E.B. (1891a) *Outlooks from the New Standpoint*, London: Swan Sonnenschein.

Bax, E.B. (1891b) *The Religion of Socialism: Being Essays in Modern Socialist Criticism*, 3rd edn, London: Swan Sonnenschein.

Bevir, M. (2011) *The Making of British Socialism*, Princeton: Princeton University Press.

Boos, F.S. (2018) *William Morris' Socialist Diary*, 2nd edn, Nottingham: Five Leaves.

Bourdieu, P. (1998) *Acts of Resistance: Against the New Myths of Our Time*, R. Nice (trans.), Cambridge: Polity Press.

Bruce, S. (ed.) (1999) *Three Early Modern Utopias*, Oxford: Oxford University Press.

Burns, J. (1888) *Trafalgar Square: Speech for the Defence*, London: Kent and Matthews.

Camarda, J. (2015) 'Liberal possibilities in a communist utopia: minority voices and historical consciousness in Morris' *News from Nowhere*', *Nineteenth-Century Contexts*, 37(4): 301–320.

Carpenter, E. (1889) *Civilisation: Its Cause & Cure, and Other Essays*, London: Swan Sonnenschein.

Carpenter, E. (1905) *Prisons, Police and Punishment*, London: Arthur C. Fifield.

Carpenter, E. (1916) *My Days and Dreams, Being Autobiographical Notes*, New York: Charles Scribner's Sons.

Cunninghame Graham, R.B. (1888) 'Bloody Sunday', *Commonweal*, 4(148): 354–355.

Davis, A.Y. (2016) 'Political prisoners, prisons and Black liberation', in A.Y. Davis (ed.) *If They Come in the Morning: Voices of Resistance*, new edn, London: Verso, pp 27–43.

Empson, W. (1974) *Some Versions of Pastoral*, new edn, New York: New Directions.

Foucault, M. (1987) *Discipline and Punish: The Birth of the Prison*, A. Sheridan (trans.), London: Penguin.

Gattrell, V.A.C. (1994) *The Hanging Tree: Execution and the English People, 1770–1868*, Oxford: Oxford University Press.

Hough, G. (1961) *The Last Romantics*, 2nd edn, London: Methuen.

Hulsman, L. (1986) 'Critical criminology and the concept of crime', *Contemporary Crises*, 10(1): 63–80.

Hyndman, H.M. et al (n.d.) *How I Became a Socialist: A Series of Biographical Sketches*, London: Twentieth Century Press.

Jacoby, R. (2005) *Picture Imperfect: Utopian Thought for an Anti-utopian Age*, New York: Columbia University Press.

Jay, M. (1993) *Downcast Eyes: The Denigration of Vision in Twentieth-Century French Thought*, Berkeley: University of California Press.

Kateb, G. (1972) *Utopia and Its Enemies*, New York: Schocken.

MacCarthy, F. (1994) *William Morris: A Life for Our Time*, London: Faber & Faber.

Marx, K. and Engels, F. (1998) *The Communist Manifesto*, D. McLellan (ed.), Oxford: Oxford University Press.

Morris, W. (1910–1915) *The Collected Works of William Morris*, M. Morris (ed.), 24 vols, London: Longmans, Green and Co.

Morris, W. (1936) *William Morris: Artist, Writer, Socialist*, M. Morris (ed.), 2 vols, Oxford: Basil Blackwell.

Morris, W. (1984–1996) *The Collected Letters of William Morris*, N. Kelvin (ed.), 4 vols in 5, Princeton: Princeton University Press.

Morris, W. (1994) *Political Writings: Contributions to 'Justice' and 'Commonweal', 1883–1890*, N. Salmon (ed.), Bristol: Thoemmes Press.

Morris, W. (1996) *Journalism: Contributions to 'Commonweal', 1885–1890*, N. Salmon (ed.), Bristol: Thoemmes Press.

Rowbotham, S. (2008) *Edward Carpenter: A Life of Liberty and Love*, London: Verso.

Sieh, E.W. (1989) 'Less eligibility', *Criminal Justice Policy Review*, 3(2): 159–183.

Starobinski, J. (1988) *Jean-Jacques Rousseau: Transparency and Obstruction*, A. Goldhammer (trans.), Chicago: University of Chicago Press.

Thompson, E.P. (1977) *William Morris: Romantic to Revolutionary*, revised edn, London: Merlin.

Williams, R. (1980) *Problems in Materialism and Culture*, London: Verso.

8

Beyond Sanction: Jean-Marie Guyau between Penal Abolition and Social Defence

Federico Testa

Introduction

In 1883, Jean-Marie Guyau published a seminal article entitled 'Critique of the idea of sanction' in the *Revue philosophique de la France et de l'étranger*, later republished as the third book of his *Esquisse d'une morale sans obligation ni sanction*.[1] In this text, he challenges expiatory ideas of punishment, based on a critique of what he sees as a traditional association between moral merit and 'sensible states' – that is, between virtue and wellbeing on the one hand, and vice and suffering on the other.

This chapter seeks to offer a close reading of Guyau's critique of sanction, demonstrating how his analysis undermines the practice of penal justice and renders punishment based on moral demerit a philosophically impossible and morally condemnable endeavour. This reading reveals Guyau's pioneering contribution to the discussion of penal abolition. The chapter then moves on to discuss some of the philosophical presuppositions of Guyau's positive theses. First, it analyses his proposition of an ethics of *generosity*, and the insight that Gabriel Tarde qualified as one of universal amnesty, which provides an alternative way to confront moral vice beyond sanction by means of an attitude of pity and charity. Second, it revisits his pioneering sociological diagnosis of a mitigation and humanization of punishments, showing how he identifies the idea of 'social defence' as a defining trait and guiding value in the historical development of penal practices. Guyau's work effectively lays the foundations for an abolitionist critique of morality and penal justice. His eclectic philosophical presuppositions led him to formulate fertile ethical and sociological hypotheses. However, due to these very presuppositions and perhaps to the early interruption of his research by his premature death, he did not provide an unambiguous solution to the problem of punishment.

Critique of sanction

Guyau begins his analysis by noting our tendency to place the notion of *sanction* at the core of morality: we link physical affections or states of being to the moral quality of our conduct, believing these to occur as morally significant, proportionate or appropriate consequences of our deeds in the form of punishment or reward. There would be 'a sanction linked to every moral act' (Guyau, 2012: 184; 1898: 152). Sanction, we believe, is the true support of moral law and an expression of its intrinsic justice. Guyau sets out to examine this association, and his critical enterprise rests upon a distinction between the realm of moral volition and deliberation on the one hand, and the realm of sensibility, sensation and affective states on the other.[2] In Guyau's view, we are used to positing an immediate link between vice and pain or suffering, and, in the same manner, between moral merit and a good, happy, 'sensible' state. We tend to think and act as if virtue entailed an intrinsic 'right to happiness', and treat those who engage in vice as deserving of unhappiness (Guyau, 2012: 183; 1898: 152).

For Guyau, this association is held to be valid by divergent schools in moral thought. For example, according to Kant, Guyau argues, every rational being links *a priori* sadness and misfortune to vice, and happiness to virtue, by means of a synthetic judgement (Guyau, 2012: 183; 1898: 152). At the other end of the spectrum of the ethical debate, even those who Guyau calls 'determinists' – who logically deny the notion of 'merit' – see this common tendency to conceive of every action as being followed by sanction as legitimate, in such a way that an ethicist like Henry Sidgwick saw in the idea of a morality without sanction a contradiction in terms (Guyau, 2012: 183; 1898: 144, 148).[3]

In this association between sanction and moral law, Guyau identifies an underlying idea according to which there must exist 'proportionality between a good or bad state of the *will*, and a good or unhappy state of *sensibility*' (Guyau, 2012: 184; 1898: 152–153): a link between good and evil (or moral merit or demerit) and states of feelings and passions (pleasure or suffering). This, Guyau shows, is at the root of dominant ideas of judicial punishment. But where does this association come from? Is there any reason why 'the greatest criminal should receive, because of his crime, a simple pinprick, and the virtuous man a *prize* for his virtue?' (Guyau, 2012: 184; 1898: 153–154).

To answer these questions, Guyau sketches a critique of this 'idea of sanction' (Guyau, 2012: 184; 1898: 153). By doing this, 'the brave Guyau' – as Nietzsche once referred to him[4] – raises a sceptical question over the grounds of morality, challenging received ideas and prejudices (Guyau, 2012: 189;

1898: 159). One of the key consequences of this inquiry concerns the idea of judicial punishment. If there is no intrinsic link between moral conduct and states of feelings and sensations, why should one punish a misdeed by means of physical pain? Why should punishment be conceived of as 'an art of unbearable sensations' (Foucault, 1991: 11)?

Guyau invites us to investigate what '*moral* reason could there be for a being that is *morally* bad to receive sensible suffering, and for a good [or righteous] being to receive a surplus of enjoyment' (Guyau, 2012: 189; 1898: 159). He seeks to demonstrate that this apparently 'self-evident' proposition is, in fact, a rudimentary 'empirical and physical induction' (Guyau, 2012: 189; 1898: 159). For him, in addition to being philosophically problematic, the idea of sanction is also 'morally condemnable' (Guyau, 2012: 184; 1898: 154). As we will see, one of the consequences of Guyau's critique is an abolitionist position in penal reflection, which leads him to conclude that 'all penal justice' is 'unjust' (Guyau, 2012: 185; 1898: 154).

Guyau begins by challenging the most evidently problematic way to link sanction to human conduct, which is to say that this association – and therefore punishment – is grounded in the workings of nature; that no being can 'violate' the laws of nature with impunity. Human punishment and its application in society would merely extend this logic. After all, isn't it the case that if one tries to defy the law of gravity, for example, by 'bending too far over on the tower of St. Jacques', one necessarily finds this aspiration punished by a violent fall? Are not the 'indigestion of the glutton and the drunkenness of a tippler' also cases of sanction meted out by nature against human transgressions of its laws? (Guyau, 2012: 186; 1898: 155). Wouldn't the consequences of these actions be a form of *expiation* for their lack of measure?

As naïve as Guyau's examples might sound, they capture our *anthropomorphic* tendency to project human feelings, reasons and ethical notions onto the functioning of nature. However, what we evaluate as negative or immoral is *indifferent* from the point of view of nature itself. It is only in the encounter with our passionate bodies, to the suffering experienced in such courses of action, that the natural, necessary and in themselves neutral events of nature acquire ethical significance.[5]

We can illustrate Guyau's idea by means of his underlying distinction between natural and human laws. If human laws are contingent and can be violated, a natural law is conceived of under the sign of necessity, for this reason requiring no external or conventional mechanism to enforce it, being therefore independent of sanction. Commenting on these examples of alleged natural sanction, Guyau writes that 'nothing is more inexact', adding that 'nature *punishes* no one … for the reason that nobody is truly guilty with respect to it: one does not violate a natural law, or it would not be a natural law' (Guyau, 2012: 185; 1898: 155). What human beings often perceive as expiation is but a *verification* of a law, for 'the *natural consequences* of an action are never linked to the human intention that dictates the act', since they will take place necessarily (Guyau, 2012: 186; 1898: 156). The laws of nature, Guyau explains, are 'a-moral' because 'they are necessary' (Guyau, 2012: 186; 1898: 156). Sanction cannot exist where the law is 'inviolable'. Punishment therefore cannot have a 'natural' justification.

By clearly separating the realm of moral intention and action from that of the workings of nature, Guyau shows how the notion of sanction has no meaning when it comes to natural events. It must then be conceived as entirely belonging to the realm of morality. Let us now closely follow Guyau's reasoning and examine his analysis of three notions upon which the idea of sanction seems to rely, once we discard the idea of natural expiation, namely: (a) *merit*, (b) *order* and (c) *distributive justice*. We will then be able to understand his distinction of *will* (moral action properly speaking) and the *sensibility* (the realm of *pathos* and sensation), and more clearly grasp Guyau's contribution to the reflection on penal abolition.

On the impossibility of punishment: the gap between moral agency and sensibility

Merit

The first notion that allows Guyau to analyse the flawed relation between moral intention and the realm of affective states, is the notion of *merit*. According to him, 'the classic theory of merit' maintains that the ascertainment of demerit in action – 'I have forfeited the esteem [*j'ai démérité*]' should entail the conclusion 'I deserve punishment' (Guyau, 2012: 189; 1898: 159). The first statement designates the intrinsic quality of the moral will (*vouloir*), whereas the second ascribes a tangible or physical consequence to it. For Guyau, it is precisely this passage from the moral to the 'sensible' realm – 'from the deep to the superficial parts of our being' – that appears as unjustified.

Why should one attach empirical consequences at the level of sensations to the defining quality of one's moral deliberation? For Guyau, this idea, allegedly justifying all punishment, rests on a categorial mistake, which attributes qualities of an instance to another, incommensurable one. For the sake of argument, Guyau proposes to accept the idea of 'free will' (*libre arbitre*), which alone could ground the notion of moral merit.[6] I can only be considered as meritorious for a good deed if I have intentionally chosen this course of action – I can only be punished or rewarded on the basis of this capacity to freely determine a course of action. Now, within this framework, the link between moral will and sensibility lacks justification. This is because from the point of view of the free will hypothesis the different faculties of human beings are neither truly linked nor determined one by the other: 'the will is *not* the pure product of the intelligence, which stems from sensibility'. The latter 'is not the true centre of our being' (Guyau, 2012: 189; 1898: 160). Thus, it becomes difficult to understand how our physical body could be accountable for the movements and choices of the will. If sensibility is not the centre of our being or the source of moral agency, on what grounds can it be affected by punishment? How could it answer for the voluntary acts that ultimately do not find their origin in it?

In Guyau's view, 'if the will has freely willed [*voulu*] evil, this is not a fault of sensibility' – the latter 'has only played the role of mover [*mobile*], and not of cause' (Guyau, 2012: 190; 1898: 160). Sensibility is the *means* by which a moral decision is actualized, but not its originating principle. The notion of 'free will' presupposes the causal role of a spontaneous agency (the *will*) which cannot be mistaken by the material means through which this intention is put to practice. Still, sanction under the form of punishment affects only *sensibility* and *not* the will, the tangible motive and not the intangible source of action, the tool and not the real subject who employs it.[7] Once one understands that the will is nowhere to be found in the domain of sensibility and that punishment as the imposition of pain can only produce effects upon the latter, then one also comes to realize that punishment *never* reaches its target. If this is the case, punishment also constitutes a moral *evil,* since it inflicts gratuitous pain upon the tangible domain of the body and its passions, which is not accountable for the acts of the will – and is thus ultimately morally blameless. As Guyau explains: 'Join the tangible evil [*mal sensible*] of punishment to the moral evil of the fault, under pretext of expiation, and you will have doubled the sum of evils without mending anything' (Guyau, 2012: 190; 1898: 160). Sanction is never applied upon the domain it would have to reach in order to be efficacious. It is at best *symbolic* – but always inefficient since it cannot attain its goal.

Guyau uses a historical simile to clarify this reflection:

> During the *Terreur Blanche*, living eagles were burned in the place of him whom they symbolised. Human judges, in their hypothesis of an expiation to be inflicted on freewill, don't do anything different from this; their cruelty is equally vain and irrational. While the innocent body of the accused struggles in their hands, his will, which is the real eagle, the supreme eagle free in flight, soars out of their reach high above them. (Guyau, 2012: 192; 1898: 163)

As this passage shows, free will – conceived as the true agent of conduct – escapes all tangible sanction. By means of physical punishment operating over the body of the criminal, sanction does not efface the harm he has committed, but instead introduces new evil in the world. In Guyau's words, 'legislators and judges, by deliberately striking the guilty, become their fellows [*leurs égaux*]' (Guyau, 2012: 190; 1898: 160). Therefore, 'punishment would be as blameworthy as the crime, and the prison would be no better' (Guyau, 2012: 190; 1898: 160). The punitive application of justice becomes a true 'school of crime' and the murder committed in name of the law is even more absurd than the one that is committed illegally (for further discussion, see Bell and Scott, Chapter 1, this volume). In a striking abolitionist formulation, Guyau writes that 'it is impossible to see in "expiatory sanction" anything resembling a rational consequence of the fault; it is simply a mechanical sequence, a material repetition, and imitation [*copie*]' of 'the fault itself' (Guyau, 2012: 190; 1898: 160–161). The immorality of punishment is a consequence of the logical and practical impossibility of its true realization. This leads us to another aspect of Guyau's analysis of this impossibility, which appears in the second notion he identifies as one of the pillars of sanction and punishment: the notion of *order*.

Order

For Guyau, sanction is usually seen as the consequence of the violation of an established *order* by a rebellious will (Guyau, 2012: 190; 1898: 161). It appears as the expiatory suffering required for re-establishing or restoring this 'broken' or 'disrupted' order. In Paul Janet's view, for example, 'the order disrupted by a rebellious will is *re-established* by the suffering which is the consequence of the fault committed' (Janet: 1879: 707; Guyau, 2012: 188; 1898, 161).[8] Thus, punishment is both the threat that ensures the execution of the law and the expiation that repairs or corrects what has been violated.

There are, Guyau claims, two main problems with this view. First, it confuses the 'moral' and the 'social' question. The defence of the social body and the preservation of a social order against future offence is not per se linked to an idea of moral sanction – I will return to this shortly. The second problem concerns a series of philosophical confusions implicit in the idea of *expiation*, and a violent application of the law on the basis of actions that have already been accomplished.

From the point of view of morality, Guyau reveals an underlying fallacy in the idea of punitive expiation. How could one *pay* the price of an evil deed with physical suffering? Could this suffering ever efface the deed itself? The idea that punishment could fix the past or atone for a previously effected deed is prey to an erroneous description of the temporality of moral action. The unfolding of human action in time is irreversible. Hence there is also a fundamental *irreversibility of evil* – once an evil action has taken place, the harm it introduced in the world cannot be undone and effaced – pain cannot redeem crime. Guyau explains:

> It would be too convenient if a crime could be physically redeemed by punishment, and if it were possible to pay the penalty for a bad act by a certain amount of physical suffering ... No; that which is done remains done. Moral evil persists, notwithstanding all the physical evil which is added to it. (Guyau, 2012: 190; 1898: 161)

The discussion of the principle of 'order' as a justification for punishment, and of the fundamental irreversibility of human action, leads Guyau to further refine his distinction between the moral and the 'sensible'. Free will, he argues, if it exists, is unseizable or unreachable for us. Its resolutions are therefore 'irreparable, inexpiable'. Like flashes of lighting (*éclairs*), they 'dazzle us for a moment, and disappear' (Guyau, 2012: 191; 1898: 162). Similarly, good or evil acts 'mysteriously descend' from the heavens of 'the will to the sphere of the senses; but after that, it is impossible to reascend from this domain into that of free will in order to seize it and punish it'. Guyau concludes: 'The flash of lighting descends but cannot re-ascend [*l'éclair descend et ne remonte pas*]' (Guyau, 2012: 191; 1898: 162).

In Guyau's view, 'between free will and the objects of the sensible world there is no other link than the agent's willing [*le vouloir*]' (Guyau, 2012: 191; 1898: 161). Therefore, no action upon determined 'sensible' objects could produce any change in the agent's free immaterial will in such a way that punishment would only be possible if free will could *will* it. The only thing that could make moral sanction and punishment possible is the *will* of the criminal – the guarantee of their effects upon the will would have to be an act of the will itself. Yet, for this to be the case, the quality of this will would already have been transformed to the point of understanding the evil committed and manifesting willingness to be accountable and be punished for it. Having 'converted' to the good, the 'wrongdoer' would manifest a change of the intentional principle guiding his conduct. Consequently, the only possible justification for punishment (a transformation of the volitive qualities of the agent) would have already been rendered redundant. Either one punishes uselessly – since physical pain does not act upon the will or the nature of the agent's intention, but only upon the concrete medium of action, which is not the source of the action itself – *or* one no longer *needs* to punish (if the agent's will has moved away from its original evil intention). Moreover, given the irreversibility of evil and its focus on the *past*, punishment cannot act upon future developments of the agent's will, at most generating passions – such as fear – through its violent action upon sensibility (which can produce social effects, but not truly moral ones). In order for sanction to fulfil its alleged role, it would have to act upon the *future* developments of the agent's conduct rather than the unchangeable *past* accomplished deeds.

Distributive justice

The last justification of punishment Guyau tackles draws on the idea of 'distributive justice'. This is the principle that establishes a relation of proportionality in merit between one's labour and remuneration, expressed in the phrase 'to everyone according to their work' (Guyau, 2012: 192; 1898: 163). Sanction in this case is articulated as follows: '[1] he who does a lot must receive a lot; [2] he who does little must receive little; [3] he who does evil must receive evil' (Guyau, 2012: 192; 1898: 163). Guyau begins by noting that the last proposition does not follow from the previous ones: the fact that 'a smaller benefit seems to call for smaller recompense' does not entail that 'an offence should call for revenge' (Guyau, 2012: 193; 1898: 164). Additionally, the first two principles rest upon a confusion between social imperatives and moral rules. For Guyau, the principle 'to each according to their work' is a simple economic principle of fair social exchange, which synthesizes the ideal of 'reciprocity' – that is, the 'commutative justice' of 'social contracts'. This principle, however, can remain valid and operative independently of one's moral intention. It establishes only that 'independently of intention, the objects exchanged in society must be of the same value, and that an individual who produces a thing of considerable value must not receive in exchange an insignificant' counterpart (Guyau, 2012: 193; 1898: 164). By contrast, when one considers the nature, state and intention of the will, rather than material exchanges, this law loses its value.

Distributive justice is a fully social ideal, a utilitarian regulative principle for social exchange, addressing the *self-interested* aspect of labour and ensuring the individual's contribution to society. It is a 'mechanical' principle of social reciprocity, which instructs one to expect from others proportionally to what one gives them. For Guyau, this principle functions as 'an excellent form of encouragement' (Guyau, 2012: 194; 1898: 165), and operates as a practical rule drawing on the egoistic dimension of social actors. But it cannot ground moral sanction. Moreover, the moral deficit of this social principle when used as an ethical rule is clear: the risk is that, by following the logic of proportional remuneration, the work one accomplishes is no longer guided by intrinsic value. Agents could easily end up seeing remuneration itself as the end goal of their actions. A consequentialist approach could perhaps accept this presupposition, granting that the work accomplished brings about a greater good or a positive outcome for a greater number of people. However, in Guyau's view, when the reward becomes the final *aim* pursued, the good action becomes a means to an end, and one acts for the sake of sanction (remuneration). In this the properly moral merit of the action is lost. By contrast, he argues, a true and legitimate moral sanction should never 'become a fixed end or an aim in itself'.[9] It is clear that after his powerful critique of a morality of duty both in his 1878 *The Ethics of Epicurus* and in the chapters on the critique of transcendent duty in the *Esquisse*, Guyau is trying make place for a *deontological* principle of *disinterestedness*, the Stoic-inspired idea according to which virtuous action is its own reward – and that the *gaudium* it generates is but a corollary (a mere supplementary consequence rather than the end pursued). Following a similar logic, Guyau suggests that moral action concerns the realm of moral ends, which should be independent of the domain of sanction, whereas the latter only acquires meaning in the realm of the 'sensible' and empirical consequences of action. Therefore, a truly 'moral sanction' would have to 'be found entirely outside the regions of *finality*' and '*utility*'. To sum up, as we have seen, sanction would have to be able to reach the 'will as a *cause*, without wishing to direct it' by positing itself 'as an *aim*' so as not to jeopardize the moral merit of this will (Guyau, 2012: 194; 1898: 165).

Additionally, as in his reflection on the principle of order, Guyau introduces a reflection on the temporality of action in his consideration of distributive justice. If the principle of proportionality of exchange is seen as an encouragement for action in society, its focus lies on *future* activity; it seeks to direct one's course of action towards utility and fairness in society. However, when this notion is turned into the principle of the application of justice and punishment, it does not entail or foster any principle of action for the future. Rather, it seeks to attain a 'retroactive effect' and, as such, 'bears on the past, instead of modifying the future', being thus 'barren and morally empty' (Guyau, 2012: 194; 1898: 166). If one extrapolates the principle of distributive justice beyond the regulation of social exchanges, turning it into a 'metaphysical and absolute' justification for coercive and penal action, it becomes *immoral*. For Guyau, statements such as 'you are good; you are bad' should never become 'you must be made to enjoy or suffer' (Guyau, 2012: 194; 1898: 166). If suffering is not an internal corollary of the practice of evil, then an *external agency* must inflict it, afflicting the sensibility of he who has practised evil, which amounts only to adding further harm to the ineffaceable deed of the criminal. Guyau explains:

> The guilty should not be allowed the privilege of forcing the righteous to do him harm. Both vice and virtue are therefore responsible only with regard to themselves … After all, vice and virtue are only forms of the will, and under these forms the will itself continues to exist, and its *nature seems to aspire to happiness*. We do not see why this eternal desire should not, in all of us, find satisfaction. (Guyau, 2012: 194; 1898: 166, emphasis added)

One can see how, for Guyau, the three main alleged foundations of moral sanction rest on a series of philosophical misunderstandings and prejudices. The act of punishing appears to him to be a contradictory endeavour, increasing the evil and immorality it seeks to address, aiming at targets it can never attain or transform: the accomplished deed and the overall disposition of the agent's will and intention. By untying the knot binding sensibility and will, Guyau seeks to undermine the moral foundations of the social machines of sequestration and torture of deviant social actors.

Moreover, Guyau argues for the dignity of the human desire for happiness and defends the right of all to have their sensibility and affective states spared from systematic violence and afflictive punitive action. He understands the desire for happiness as inscribed in the very movement of human will, since 'every being susceptible of will spontaneously aspires to feel happy'. The differences in the quality of this *will* show themselves when there is a question of choosing the ways and means of attaining happiness: 'Some people believe their happiness to be incompatible with that of others, some try to find their happiness in that of others' (Guyau, 2012: 195; 1898: 167). If 'orthodox morality' sees this as a difference in *nature* between 'wills', this difference cannot 'do away with the permanent relation between will and happiness' (Guyau, 2012: 195; 1898: 167). It is a practical impossibility for the sentient being to negate this tendency to happiness – this would amount to a paradoxical movement where the will negates itself. Whenever there is will, there is also a movement towards happiness: 'In the same way that a man cannot sell himself as a slave, so he cannot remove from himself this kind of natural title to ultimate happiness which every sentient being believes himself to possess' (Guyau, 2012: 196; 1898: 168). In Guyau's reading, the claim that happiness should be reserved for the 'good person only' and the corresponding claim according to which 'all inferior individuals' would have a 'right to unhappiness' is 'the relic ... of ancient *aristocratic* prejudices' (Guyau, 2012: 195; 1898: 167). Against these, Guyau's critique of sanction is also marked by an ethical orientation that seeks to render happiness accessible to all, concerned with affirming the dignity of every human being's desire for happiness.

Finally, in his challenge to punitive rationalities, Guyau puts forward an idea of universal grace (*grâce*), which is one of the aspects of his project of a morality beyond obligation and sanction. This leads us to an important aspect of his approach, one of the positive facets of his critique of sanction: his defence of an idea of *charity* (*charité*) as an alternative to the practice of punitive justice. From the fact that 'all *penal* justice' worthy of the name is 'unjust' and that, as we have seen, 'all *distributive* justice has an exclusively social nature' and 'can be justified only from the point of view of society', Guyau concludes that 'generally speaking, that which we call *justice* is a completely human and relative notion'. He then adds that 'only *charity* and *pity* [*pitié*]' are a truly universal ideas 'which nothing can limit or restrict' (Guyau, 2012: 185; 1898: 154).

Beyond sanction: generosity and grace

The first positive development of Guyau's critique of punitive sanction is a notion of universal charity. He argues that even those who have practised evil or manifested an evil inclination must be 'treated with indulgence and pity ... It matters little if their ferocity be considered as fatal [or necessary] or free; they are morally always to be pitied'. By effecting punishment in the form of sensible pain upon a human being, one would create further *malheur*, and thus another reason – in addition to his moral insufficiency and weakness, and to his incapacity to fulfil his desire for happiness – for this being to be pitied, distancing him even more from the fulfilment of this natural aspiration. Guyau asks: 'Why should one want them to become physically pitiful also?' Why should one increase the misery of a morally miserable being by imposing physical misery upon him (Guyau, 2012: 195; 1898: 166)?

The reason one seeks to impose unhappiness and pain upon those who are 'bad' is not to make them better; rather, it is a will for revenge whose genealogy Guyau seeks to trace, and which is expressed in the notion of *expiation* – the imposition of 'unhappiness without *utility* and without object' (Guyau, 2012: 196; 1898: 168). He shows that the idea of a violent retribution has its origin in the tendency of living beings founded on a 'general law of life' and a 'primitive instinct' that lead them to respond to an exterior aggression by means of a defence that is often an attack (Guyau, 2012: 200–201; 1898: 173). Life itself, he claims, is a 'permanent revenge' (*revanche permanente*) against the obstacles it faces. It is here that he finds the 'physical point of emergence of the alleged moral need of sanction' (Guyau, 2012: 201–202; 1898: 174). We will go back to Guyau's attempt at differentiating *defence* and *revenge*. For situating Guyau's critique of penal justice, it is enough to stress that he sees this instinct being gradually limited in the evolution of the human species and the development of societies.[10] Moreover, he seeks to complement this description of the movement of life as one of reactive self-preservation (which is at the basis of his account of revenge), with the notion of a generous, sociable and altruistic drive of expansion towards others, which he calls *fecundity* – and is the foundation of an attitude of sympathy, pity and charity.[11]

Drawing on this notion of *fecundity*, Guyau's stance towards moral demerit relies on a view extending the right to happiness even to those who have 'forfeited the esteem'. As we have seen, their actions are ultimately mistaken routes taken in the effort to achieve happiness, a poor choice of means that damages the happiness of others. The truly moral attitude in the face of those who are at fault is an ethics of generosity and kindness: 'For the narrow and entirely human justice which refuses kindness to him who is already unhappy enough to be guilty, must be substituted another larger justice, which gives kindness [*le bien*] to all' (Guyau, 2012: 195; 1898: 167).

Within the framework of this universal idea of charity and the right of all beings to fulfil their natural tendency towards happiness, Guyau rehabilitates a theological idea of *grace*. He seeks to dissociate this notion of any idea of merit in action, as well as election and preference. As Guyau notes, that which is 'shocking in all morality that is more or less borrowed from Christianity, is the idea of … a choice, of favour' or a differential '*distribution* of grace' (Guyau, 2012: 196; 1898: 168). And he adds that 'the Christian idea of *grace* would … be acceptable on one condition – that of being universal, given to … all beings. In this way it would become … a kind of divine *debt*' (Guyau, 2012: 196; 1898: 168).

In this, we seem to find an instance of Nietzsche's critique of the 'brave Guyau', who in the philosophy of life expounded in the *Esquisse* demonstrates the immorality of life and its expansive force, but retreats in the face of his own conclusions by trying to argue for the existence of altruistic drives within life itself, reterritorializing the movement of life in the sphere of morality.[12] In Philippe Saltel's words, revisiting one of Nietzsche's 1884–1885 posthumous fragments, Guyau would thus appear as 'crypto-Christian' or a 'neo-Christian' (Saltel, 2008: 22).

Nonetheless, in Guyau's recourse to the idea of *grace*, universalized and generalized to all beings, we find an attempt to come to terms with what is one of the defining (and perhaps one of the earliest) philosophical questions in his own thinking: as Annamaria Contini puts it, the 'difficulty in reconciling the existence of evil and the idea of a universal reign of love postulated by Platonic optimism' (Contini, 1995: 77).[13] She highlights Alfred Fouillée's claim in his biographical note in *La morale, l'art et la religion d'après Guyau* that in order to solve this problem, Guyau elaborates an 'original' interpretation of the Neoplatonist doctrine of *procession,* 'conceiving of the universe as an infinite series of worlds in which the good is fully actualized or in the process of becoming so' (Contini, 1995: 77–78). According to Fouillée:

> [Guyau] proposed an ingenious interpretation of this theory [of *procession*]; he held that all possible degrees of goodness [*bien*] we dream of are already realized [somewhere] in an infinite series of worlds, and that the universe therefore consists of a hierarchy [literally, a ladder, *échelle*] of existences [organized] in decreasing degrees of perfection, which descends from absolute perfection to matter. Thus, all that is possible [*tout le possible*] is already actualized: we cannot conceive of any degree of being or goodness [*degré d'être ou de bien*], neither superior nor inferior, that wouldn't already exist somewhere, and which each being must attain one day, due to universal progress. (Fouillée, 1915: 3–4)

This Neoplatonist solution proposed by Guyau to the problem of evil becomes clearer when one situates it in the context of his early work of translation and commentary of the Early Church fathers (cf. Guyau, 1876). Indeed, we find an analogous development in the idea of *apokatastasis*, which argues for the restoration of fallen or corrupted beings to an original condition. This doctrine is at the basis of the idea of universal salvation, as is clear in the works of Early Christian Neoplatonists such as Origen of Alexandria. According to Ilaria Ramelli, Origen attempted to correct 'Plato's eschatological myths, in order to affirm the universality of the restoration of the souls' (Ramelli, 2009, 219).

For Origen, free will is the root of evil, but it is also the condition for individual salvation.[14] In a nutshell, he envisioned a cosmologico-theological system or process where, aided by *grace* and the incarnation of the *Logos* (commonly understood in Patristic philosophy as Christ),[15] fallen beings would use their free will to attain salvation in an indefinite sequence of worlds,[16] in which a finite number of intellects or souls would be placed by their Creator. The destruction and creation of this sequence of worlds is the occasion provided by God for beings to freely convert to the good, in such a way that no condemnation is eternal and no punishment final damnation.[17] Given these definite parameters – free will, a finite number of immortal souls created equal[18] – and God's capacity to produce an indefinite series of worlds, it follows that at some point in this process all souls will achieve salvation.[19] In this theological insight, one can clearly see a precedent of Guyau's critique of the idea of sanction, as well as his emphasis on the need for charity towards wrongdoers.[20]

French criminologist Gabriel Tarde engages with Guyau in his 1890 *Philosophie pénale* and notes the Neoplatonic and Christian undertones of Guyau's stance against sanction. Tarde qualifies Guyau's position as a 'spiritualist' response to the problem of evil and a solution to the problem of punishment:

> The conception of a penal law free from all vengeance and all hatred is a very old one in the history of spiritualism. As early as the third century, Gregory of Nazianzus affirms that God does not take vengeance by punishing the wicked, He calls them to Him and wakes them from the sleep of death. To Gregory of Nyssa, also, the thought of an eternal hell is intolerable. He dreams of a final and immense amnesty. (Tarde, 2001[1890]: 506–507)

Indeed, Guyau's reading of the doctrine of *procession* could be seen as an attempt to argue for universal salvation, and for the final disappearance of evil in the world. If the *will* of free beings cannot be changed from the exterior, their progress and conversion to the good can only take place internally by means of a choice stemming from *free will* itself. In the Early Christian Neoplatonists, we observe the junction of an idea of universal salvation and a theory of free will. However, even if one finds in the *Esquisse* the ethical echoes of this 'spiritualist' position, one does not find a metaphysical narrative maintaining that there is an infinite sequence of worlds, which would assure the universal restoration of free beings. Rather, Guyau points to a Platonic or Epicurean-inspired tendency towards happiness, which he supplements with an account of the autonomy of the will with regard to senses and sensibility.[21]

The different aspects of Guyau's thinking highlighted so far seem to function as the foundation for a fundamentally abolitionist view, according to which there is *no properly moral* justification for punishment and the application of penal justice. However, this is not the whole story. As Tarde highlighted, following Fouillée, Guyau also reflects on penal law sociologically, conceiving of it as a function of social association (Tarde, 2001[1890]: 40). Even in the most radical moments of his critique, Guyau claims that 'distributive justice has an exclusively *social* character' and that its exercise 'can only be justified from the point of view of society' (Guyau, 2012: 185; 1898: 154, emphasis added).[22] Guyau's position lays the groundwork for a radical abolitionist view of penal law; nevertheless, in his sociological considerations we will find a more reformist defence of a social need for punishment, freed from its violent and expiatory content, as well as passions of revenge and hatred, while ensuring maximal effects in terms of the preservation of social relations. This stance relies on his diagnosis of the transformations of penal justice in modernity.

Punishment and society: foresight and social defence

As we have seen, Guyau maintains that 'without reasons of social defence, punishment is as blameworthy as crime' (Guyau, 2012: 190; 1898: 160). The idea he bracketed in his critique of sanction was precisely that of 'social utility'. Rather than seeing moral merit or demerit as the ground of penal justice, Guyau shows that punishment in society can only be justified by a certain idea of *social defence* (Guyau, 2012: 197; 1898: 169). Even our mental habit of employing the notion of sanction in our judgement of human action has an origin that is ultimately *social* rather than moral (Aslan, 1906: 56).

The idea of sanction has a genealogy that ultimately goes back to the social aspect of human beings: Guyau claims that the idea of 'society' is deeply ingrained in our minds and is constitutive of our thinking (Guyau, 2012: 199; 1898: 171). It is thus on the grounds of our social instincts, socially oriented thinking, and effort to preserve society that we demand a response to an offence. Guyau argues that in earlier forms of social association, human beings demanded this response in the form of *vengeance*. Punishment could thus be more intense and violent than the crime itself (Guyau, 2012: 205; 1898: 179). The inflexible practice of distributive justice embodies this demand and sociologically expresses a physical instinct. Society here does not moderate the instinct that leads every animal to react to an attack by means of another, which takes place as a sort of reflex action (Guyau, 2012: 201; 1898: 176). It organizes means to exercise this instinctual response, which Guyau conceives of as the physical point of emergence of the notion of sanction (Guyau, 2012: 202; 1898: 175). Moreover, this 'physical' source is linked to an 'imaginary' one, which finds its expression in *sympathy*: our tendency as social beings to put ourselves in the place of someone in a more vulnerable position – we could easily be victims of the anti-social actions we see others suffer, while striving to fulfil our social duties (Guyau, 2012: 203; 1898: 176).

As social beings, we read the actions of others from the viewpoint of reciprocity and experience a psychological impossibility to accept the notion of unpunished evil. In the success of 'antisocial acts', human beings see an 'element of social destruction', so that crime appears as an exhortation to evil against which 'our highest instincts rebel' (Guyau, 2012: 198; 1898: 170). However, Guyau argues, with the further development of our social nature and the complexification of society, our psychological need for sanction and its instinctual origin begin to be restricted by the social order, and so punishment becomes less and less violent, more economic in its means, and efficient in the pursuit of its ultimate goal: the defence of the social body. In this sociological development, Guyau claims, human beings come to see *expiatory* forms of punishment as 'useless expenditure of social force' as soon as they go beyond 'the goal that justifies them scientifically: the defence of the individual and the social body against attacks' (Guyau, 2012: 205; 1898: 179). In this process, passions originally linked to the act of punishment, such as hate, gradually disappear in (allegedly) superior social states where the individual no longer has to defend herself alone against danger and offences (Guyau, 2012: 206; 1898: 179–180). In his analysis, Guyau links together the evolution of society and the transformation of punishment, its mitigation and restriction to utilitarian ends.[23]

In addition to this consideration of social defence, Guyau stresses the idea of *foresight*. As we have seen, sanction is always linked to the actualization of a certain moral action – already accomplished and positively or negatively qualified – deserving a certain distribution of tangible effects as a consequence. By contrast, social defence is not concerned with the past, but with the *future*. He explains that 'one cannot say that any past act *merits* a penalty, and punishment is only justified by the anticipation [*prévision*] of similar acts in the future. It does not concern *realities*, but rather mere *possibilities*, which it seeks to modify' (Guyau, 2012: 191n; 1898: 162n). Unlike *expiation* of past deeds, punishment must be concerned with future possibilities (that which the criminal is still capable of doing). In this emphasis on social defence and the punishment acting upon possibilities and future potential action, Guyau has captured what Michel Foucault calls the 'humanisation' of penalties,[24] and a certain notion of the power of society to act upon the *possible* rather than the *actual*, which is at the basis of Foucault's idea of 'dangerousness'.[25] Before Foucault, Guyau observed a modern imperative of reforming the criminal rather than inflicting pain and suffering. Indeed, Foucault shares this diagnosis regarding the new 'gentle ways' of punishing, which Guyau refers to as a gradual mitigation (*adoucissement*) of punishment. Before Foucault, Guyau showed how punishment – employed as a tool for defending society – came to be thought of not through the optics of dispendious retribution, but rather within the framework of an economy of forces. In Aslan's summary, 'the gradual mitigation [*adoucissement*] of penal sanction shows that the penalty has no moral reason and is only justified by its efficacy for social defence. The evolution of penalties is due to the law of the economy of force' (Aslan, 1906: 58). Thus, Guyau diagnoses an epochal tendency in the development of penal law and proposes a prognostic: the 'death penalty will either disappear, or be maintained as a preventive means' and 'even the rigour of prison-life has already been mitigated'. Thus, in 'our time', penalties are reduced to the minimum necessary (Guyau, 2012: 206; 1898: 180). Guyau seems to become an advocate of the advances in punishment towards the elimination of violence. In this, the social dimension of his work could be seen as defending a *reformism* that, in Foucault, appears as the occasion and condition for the establishment of a new form of power in society.[26]

Thus, in addition to a radical critique of sanction, Guyau's work is also marked by an acute perception of a historical transformation of punishment, a diagnosis regarding the transition of the violent spectacles of punishment to the calculated, economic and future-oriented forms of punitive intervention, aiming at the transformation of the 'dangerous' nature of the criminal and the fostering of social defence, which we will also find in a thinker like Foucault. However, unlike Foucault's genealogy of a new disciplinary and infinitesimal power that appears with the humanization of penalties, Guyau sees in this social and historical transformation a process guided by a legitimate ideal: that of achieving the 'maximum of social defence with the minimum of individual suffering' (Guyau, 2012, 207; 1898: 181; Aslan, 1906: 58). For him, this historical development reveals what could be seen as a *normative* principle. Punishment, where its application is necessary, should abdicate all aspects of excessive action upon the culprit's body (Guyau, 2012: 206; 1898: 180): 'Charity for all human beings, whatever may be their moral, intellectual, or physical value; this should be [*doit être*] the final aim pursued by public opinion' (Guyau, 2012: 211; 1898: 186). This ideal of *charity*, which underpins Guyau's radical critique of penal justice, also seems to be the one guiding a path of reforms. The 'deontological' aspect of

Guyau's thought is *abolitionist*, but its 'utilitarian' aspect leads him to support a reformist practice that he sees taking place in his own time, affirming and fostering the progressive content of this development.

Conclusion: Guyau's ambiguity

We have seen how Guyau's critical examination of sanction undermines all *moral* justification for legal punishment by challenging two key assumptions of punitive practice: the confusion between will and sensibility on the one hand, and between moral and social considerations on the other. When addressing the first, Guyau argues that if our 'sensible' being is not accountable for our will, it should be preserved from all forms of expiation and arbitrary physical pain. He seeks to supplement this negative critique by offering an account of a congenial tendency of living beings towards happiness and, consequently, their right to have their tangible being spared from violence. As a result, in his analysis, we find an early formulation of a penal abolitionist viewpoint according to which 'all penal justice' is fundamentally 'unjust'.

However, Guyau's stark distinction between the spheres of the will and sensibility generates a few philosophical tensions. On the one hand, he draws upon the main presupposition of the doctrines he seeks to dismantle: a 'transcendent' or 'transcendental' notion of free will. He shows the incompatibility between a view of moral action based on free will and the torture of the body by means of a *reductio ad absurdum*: if there is something like free will, nothing can act upon it by means of external tangible affects. On the other hand, in the course of his argumentation, Guyau seems to end up subscribing to this essentially dualistic conception of the moral agent. He considers the will in its autonomy, asserting the independent nature of moral intention with regard to empirical constraints and physical causes. This becomes particularly problematic if we consider Guyau's stance in the rest of the *Esquisse*: a naturalist and vitalist project which sees the movement of life itself as providing immanent moral grounds for an ethics without obligation or sanction, which seems to do away with the notion of free will. If Guyau is coherent with the principles he lays out in the rest of the book, then his exposition of the thesis of a *dual* nature of the moral agent presupposed by the doctrine of free will should be seen as an exercise revealing the inconsistencies and internal contradictions of any attempt to found a morality (and a juridical practice) of sanction upon the notion of free will. In this case, revealing the problematic confusion of sensibility and will appears as a negative path to argue for a morality beyond sanction based on life itself, which makes *no* recourse to the 'mysterious principle' of a transcendent free will. However, if Guyau in fact subscribes to the 'dual' conception of moral agency and the moral agent he lays out in his critique of sanction, this generates a position risking inconsistencies regarding the nature of human agency, which would demand more careful examination.

Furthermore, Guyau seeks to undermine the notion of sanction by positing a universal right to wellbeing – or a right not to be *caused* to suffer – independently of merit. This rests both upon the independence and innocence of sensibility with regard to moral volition and upon the intrinsic tendency of the will itself to pursue happiness. To these principles, he adds an ethical attitude of *generosity* and *kindness*, which, following Tarde, I linked to ideas of universal salvation in Christian Neoplatonism and the Early Church Fathers – a neglected but constitutive element in the formation of Guyau's approach to the problem of evil. Following this line, Guyau appealed to secularized notions of *charity* and *grace*, which he claimed should be extended to all beings, overcoming what he saw as the shortsightedness of human justice and the passionate aspects of its practice. Thus, to his negative critique of penal justice as unjust and violent, Guyau adds a positive ethical attitude, fully based on abolitionist principles and an idea of universal amnesty. If the outcome of this eclectic combination of theses is a radical critique of the grounds of punishment and the practical proposition of a nonpunitive ethics of generosity and charity towards all beings, Guyau also seems to preserve the possibility of a social response to offenders who threaten society and the cohesion of the social fabric.

Shedding light upon the confusion between moral sanction and social concerns, Guyau articulated a view conceiving of punishment independent of sanction and expiation – ultimately justified by social defence rather than the moral quality and merit of the offender. He preserves an insight that he seems to draw from his earlier discussion of the Epicurean view according to which the practice of justice derives from conventional collective agreements and is ultimately justified by the need to ensure the possibility of collective enjoyment and social utility.[27] In the *Esquisse,* he offers a justification of a reformed and progressive practice of justice aiming solely at social defence, attaining its maximum effectiveness with minimal suffering and expenditure of social force. Should one say that this ultimately leads Guyau to a defence of penal reform? Is there not a possibility that he is therefore a reformist rather than an abolitionist?

In order to answer this question, one must remember that this social justification of punishment is linked to Guyau's sociological diagnosis regarding the transformation of penalties, which he sees taking place in his own time. Like Durkheim and Foucault after him, Guyau notes an increasing mitigation of penalties. He claims that in this process, capital punishment is likely to disappear and that prisons and gallows – intrinsically 'places of perversion rather than conversion' – will 'probably be demolished' (Guyau, 2012: 206; 1898: 180).[28] Yet, unlike Foucault, who criticizes the new forms of power presupposed in this development, Guyau can be seen as *defending* what he sees as the progressive aspects of this historical process of migration, such as the reduction of pain and violence. Thus, within his diagnosis of a historical 'evolution' in the sphere of penal justice, Guyau finds some kind of positive content he can subscribe to.[29] In this sense, he could be seen as a reformist: by affirming the most advanced elements of the ongoing historical process, one would perhaps one day achieve the abolition of punishment. In other words, for Guyau, if there is a historical tendency towards the abolition of the prison, this tendency should be fostered and affirmed.

Nevertheless, and despite Guyau's reticence regarding positive alternatives to the problem of punishment and incarceration, it seems clear that he can only affirm processes of reform by making reference to other normative principles, which is what allows him to see this imperfect historical transformation as *positive*. These principles are to be found especially in his ethical notions of universal *grace* and *charity*, which embody the ideal of a universal amnesty. Guyau's approach thus seems to be twofold: drawing on utilitarian views, he seeks to affirm the most progressive reformist position possible within the current development of society while also subscribing to fundamentally abolitionist ethical principles. The achievement of this social 'evolution' would be the elimination of prisons and a gradual disappearance of punishment, which converges with his guiding ethical stance. In other words, we could say that Guyau can only be a reformist in terms of his sociology of punishment because his principles are abolitionist. If he remains ambiguous and doesn't give a final answer to the problem of punishment, he formulates what could be seen as an ethics of abolition.

Guyau can thus be seen as a neglected precursor of penal abolition, providing powerful tools to challenge the ethical and metaphysical grounds of punishment and incarceration. Nonetheless, in his pioneering analysis of the connection between types of social association and modalities of punishment, he underscores a principle of social defence, which he seems to conceive of as embodying a viable idea of social progress. Therefore, to the image of Guyau as a philosophical precursor of penal abolitionism, one should add that of an advocate of social utility and a practice of penal justice in constant evolution and reform, capable of ending all violent punishment. It remains to be seen whether the separation he proposes of the ethical and the social responses to 'wrongdoing', the former drawing on a secular, universalized, but nevertheless Christian-inspired 'theology' of abolition, and the latter on a pragmatic and utilitarian ideal of social defence and reform, constitutes a satisfactory response to the problem of punishment. Guyau's critical work on sanction leaves us in a space of ambiguity that remains to be explored.

Notes

[1] The first French edition is from 1885; Guyau (or his stepfather Alfred Fouillée) changed the structure of the book in the 1890 second edition (see Saltel in Guyau, 2008: 29). I provide references to this book in both the French original and in translation (Guyau,

2012 and 1898, respectively). I have modified Kapteyn's translation for greater precision when necessary.

2   'Sensibility' and 'sensible' in this context define the realm of sensorial, sensual or sensitive states, events and processes. Guyau does not define the concept, but uses it to refer to our bodily condition, feelings, affective states and to our capacity to be affected by means of physical causality. Guyau consistently associates these terms with the presence of sensations physical pain or pleasure in the body (in contrast with the intangible nature of the will).

3   In his 1878 *The Ethics of Epicurus* (2022), Guyau opposes Kant (a representative of a 'new Stoicism', incarnating an ethics of duty), to the Utilitarian school (embodying an 'Epicurean' pole of moral inquiry, privileging sensibility and pleasure). In the 1883/1885 text, both the classic moralities of duty and pleasure rely on the notion of sanction, and on a certain representation of moral action that ascribes sensorial and affective consequences (punishment or reward) to human conduct.

4   Cf. Nietzsche, 1987: 525 (NL 1885, 35 [34]).

5   'Nature, from her standing point is neutral – as unconscious of pleasure as of suffering, of good as of evil' (Guyau, 2012, 73; 1898, 38). The 'great whole, whose direction we are unable to change, has no moral direction – there is absence of aim, complete *non-morality* of nature, neutrality of the infinite mechanism' (Guyau, 2012: 75; 1898: 41).

6   His own position on the sources of action in the *Esquisse* is, however, more complex. He writes that action 'springs naturally from the working of life, which is, to a considerable extent, unconscious' (Guyau, 2012: 92; 1898: 79). The realm of ethics would be concerned with establishing some kind of equilibrium between unconscious and conscious spheres of activity, which can partly be done by finetuning human intentional conduct and the forces of life and their unfolding (Guyau, 2012: 245; 1898: 209).

7   Here we note what Contini referred to as the 'Epictetus-Plato-Kant' line of Guyau's thought, underscoring the existence of an autonomous moral sphere 'irreducible to the rigidly determined mechanism of physical causality' (Contini, 1995: 88). In Contini's view, Epictetus and Kant developed the idea of 'a self-legislating freedom, setting the grounds for a "morality of autonomous and self-moving will"' (Contini, 1995: 89). This 'will' is 'the sole true independent reality which nothing can affect from outside' (Contini, 1995: 85; cf. Guyau, 1875). Although the *Esquisse* tries to extract moral principles from the intrinsic movements and tendencies of life itself ('gravitation upon self' and extension to others expressing life's 'moral fecundity'), in Guyau's distinction between sensibility and will, one finds the use of the principle according to which the moral agent is defined by 'his capacity for judgement and self-determination' – the conception of a 'self-legislating freedom that dictates its law to itself, regulating ethical life from within' (Contini, 1995: 84). The tension between these two conceptions of moral agency is left unresolved in Guyau's text.

8   My translation.

9   His illustration is somewhat naïve: 'the child who recites his lesson correctly merely for the sake of afterwards receiving some sweets, no longer deserves these sweets from the moral point of view, exactly because he has made them his aim' (Guyau, 2012: 194; 1898: 165).

10 'At the beginning, punishment was much stronger than the fault committed. Because the means of social defence were rudimentary, it was necessary to punish the offence vigorously. Later, the excess of repression becomes useless, and one strives to reach proportionality between the social reaction to the attack ... Finally, present-day society has superior means of defence and is able to mitigate penalties' (Aslan, 1906: 58).

11 For Guyau, life 'cannot be entirely *selfish* ... This springs from the fundamental law which biology teaches us: *Life is not only nutrition; it is production and fecundity*' (Guyau,

2012: 235; 1898: 210), generous opening to others, sharing, giving and so on. Cf. Guyau, 2012: 114–119; 1898: 85–88; Ansell-Pearson and Testa, 2024.

12 See Nietzsche's comments in Guyau (2012: 245).
13 My translation.
14 Cf. Origen, 2019: 57 (1.5–6).
15 Cf. Justin Martyr, 2008: 83–84; Origen, 2019: 220.
16 Cf. Origen, 2019: 218 (3.5.7).
17 Cf. Origen, 2019: 127 (2.9.7–8). He also speaks of a 'perfect restoration of the whole of Creation' (221 [3.5.7]) and claims that 'nothing is beyond healing' (226 [3.6.5]).
18 'He created all whom he created equal and alike' (Origen, 2019: 125 [2.9.6]). On the creation of intellects as finite in number, changeable and equipped with free will and voluntary movement see Origen (2019: 121 [2.9.1]).
19 'In Origen's view, Christ-Logos, who is God, having created all creatures, will be able to heal all of them from the illness of evil … Origen, who inserts this declaration in the context of a discussion of the eventual conversion and salvation of the devil on the grounds that he is creature of God, is in fact arguing on the basis of God's omnipotence, which comes, not from Greek philosophy, but from Scripture (e.g., Matt. 19.25–26; Mark 10.26–27)' (Ramelli, 2009: 220). See Origen (2019: 190 [3.1.23]): 'Whence we are of opinion that, seeing the soul, as we have frequently said, is immortal and eternal, it is possible that, in the many and endless periods of duration in the immeasurable and different ages [worlds], it may descend from the highest good to the lowest evil, or be restored from the lowest evil to the highest good.'
20 In such a doctrine we find an alternative to a theological idea founded on *sanction*. Gabriel Aslan, one of Guyau's first commentators, wrote that 'if God is omnipotent, we cannot really offend Him, and He has no reason to punish us. If God is supreme intelligence, He must understand the cause of our sins, and all sanction of these sins becomes useless. Finally, if God is supreme goodness, He cannot inflict pain, even less so eternal pain' (Aslan, 1906: 56). Note, however, the inconsistency between Aslan's first and last propositions.
21 Guyau's positive ethical stance in the *Esquisse* does not rely on a discussion of the ultimate nature of the will. Instead, it grounds human agency in the drives and attributes of life itself.
22 Guyau also writes: 'When punishments do not find their justification in defence, it is precisely these punishments that are the real blows, no matter the euphemism used to refer to them' (Guyau, 2012: 197; 1898: 169).
23 We find a very similar diagnosis in the work of Émile Durkheim (1984); cf. Lukes and Scull (2013).
24 Cf. Foucault, 1991: 23, 101, 246, 269.
25 See Foucault, 1991, 2016, respectively.
26 From this perspective, Guyau's approach illustrates Foucault's critical discussion of social defence and of a power that functions on the basis of mechanisms of security (cf. Foucault, 2009, 2016). Guyau could be seen as a proponent of the discourses of social defence that had become dominant in the 19th century. A critique of Guyau's adherence to ideas of social defence on the basis of Foucault's analysis of their role in fostering forms of power over so-called dangerous individuals in modernity is an interesting theme I cannot develop here. Such a critique would have to be tempered by a careful consideration of Guyau's defence of divergence and what he calls moral *anomie* (cf. Ansell-Pearson and Testa, 2024), which clearly challenges the emphasis on *normalization* Foucault identifies in apparatuses of security and social defence.
27 See Guyau, 2022: 125–129.
28 Guyau remains vague about what an alternative to the prison would look like, only saying that they are likely to be replaced by 'transportation' (Guyau, 2012: 206; 1898: 180).

[29] From this perspective, we can read Guyau's comment stating that 'we must, therefore, approve of the new school of jurists, which is particularly numerous and brilliant in Italy, and which endeavours to place penal right outside all moral and metaphysical considerations' (Guyau, 2012: 206; 1898: 180).

References

Ansell-Pearson, K. and Testa, F. (2024) 'Jean-Marie Guyau on Life and Morality', in M. Sinclair and D. Whistler (eds) *Oxford Handbook of Modern French Philosophy*, Oxford: Oxford University Press, pp 138–150.

Aslan, G. (1906) *La morale selon Guyau et ses rapports avec les conceptions actuelles de la morale scientifique*, Paris: Félix Alcan.

Contini, A. (1995) *Jean-Marie Guyau: Una filosofia della vita e l'estetica*, Bologna: CLUEB.

Durkheim, É. (1984) *The Division of Labour in Society*, W.D. Halls (trans.), Basingstoke: Macmillan.

Foucault, M. (1991) *Discipline and Punish: The Birth of the Prison*, A. Sheridan (trans.), London: Penguin.

Foucault, M. (2009) *Security, Territory, Population: Lectures at the Collège de France 1977–1978*, G. Burchell (trans.), Basingstoke: Palgrave Macmillan.

Foucault, M. (2016) *Abnormal: Lectures at the Collège de France 1974–1975*, G. Burchell (trans.), London: Verso.

Fouillée, A. (1915) *La morale, l'art et la religion d'après Guyau*, Paris: Félix Alcan.

Guyau, J.-M. (ed.) (1875) *Manuel d'Épictète, traduction nouvelle, précédée d'une Étude sur la philosophie d'Épictète par J.-M. Guyau, suivie d'Extraits des Entretiens d'Épictète et des Pensées de Marc-Aurèle*, Paris: Delagrave.

Guyau, J.-M. (ed.) (1876) *La Littérature chrétienne du IIe au IVe siècle, extraits des Pères de l'Église latine, suivis d'extraits des poètes chrétiens, par M. Guyau*, Paris: Delagrave.

Guyau, J.-M. (1879) *La morale anglaise contemporaine: Morale de l'utilité et de l'évolution*, Paris: Germer Baillière.

Guyau, J.-M. (1898) *A Sketch of a Morality Independent of Obligation or Sanction*, G. Kapteyn (trans.), London: Watts & Co.

Guyau, J.-M. (2008[1885/1890]) *Esquisse d'une morale sans obligation ni sanction*, P. Saltel (ed.), Paris: Les Belles Lettres.

Guyau, J.-M. (2012[1890]) *Esquisse d'une morale sans obligation ni sanction, avec les textes de Nietzsche et Kropotkine*, J. Riba (ed.), Paris: Payot.

Guyau, J.-M. (2022[1878]) *The Ethics of Epicurus and Its Relation to Contemporary Doctrines*, K. Ansell-Pearson and F. Testa (ed.), F. Testa (trans.), London: Bloomsbury.

Janet, P. (1879) *Traité élémentaire de philosophie, à l'usage des classes*, Paris: Delagrave.

Justin Martyr (2008) *Writings of St Justin Martyr (The Fathers of the Church, Volume 6)*, T.B. Falls (ed. and trans.), Washington DC: Catholic University of America Press.

Lukes, S. and Scull, A. (2013) *Durkheim and the Law*, Basingstoke: Palgrave Macmillan.

Nietzsche, F. (1987) *Nietzsche Werke. Kritische Studienausgabe*, G. Colli and M. Montinari (eds), Berlin: Walter de Gruyter.

Origen of Alexandria (2019) *On First Principles. A Reader's Edition*, J. Behr (ed. and trans.), Oxford: Oxford University Press.

Ramelli, I. (2009) 'The Debate on Apokatastasis in Pagan and Christian Platonists: Martianus, Macrobius, Origen, Gregory of Nyssa, and Augustine', *Illinois Classical Studies*, 33–34: 201–234.

Saltel, P. (2008) *La puissance de la vie: Essai sur* l'Esquisse d'une morale sans obligation ni sanction *de Jean-Marie Guyau*, Paris: Les Belles Lettres.

Tarde, G. (2001[1890]) *Penal Philosophy*, P. Berne (trans.), New Brunswick, NJ: Transaction.

9

Pyotr Kropotkin: Foundations of Anarchist Prison Abolition

Robert D. Weide

Introduction

While prison abolition has become all the rage on the academic and activist left in recent years, many contemporary abolitionist scholars, particularly in the American context, omit the history of prison abolition in the anarchist tradition, and particularly its founder, Pyotr Kropotkin. This chapter seeks to rectify this glaring deficiency in much of the contemporary abolitionist literature to alleviate this mass historical amnesia and thereby return Kropotkin to prominence in the academic literature as perhaps the first abolitionist to draw on his own carceral experience in prisons and establish prison abolition as a core component of anarchist frameworks and praxis, connecting prison abolition to the abolition of the state entirely. The history and ideas of anarchist theorists and revolutionaries is important in that it is this anarchist tradition established by Kropotkin which created historical precedents for prison abolition in the course of anarchist revolutions in the early 20th century.

This modest chapter reviews, summarizes and analyses Kropotkin's life experiences, as well as the autoethnographic descriptions of prisons in which he was incarcerated, and abolitionist perspectives on penology and criminology that he helped pioneer. It concludes by examining some of the most celebrated works of the contemporary academic abolitionist literature in order to critique their failure to cite Kropotkin and the historical precedents of actual prison abolition he inspired, as well as speculate as to why they have excluded Kropotkin and his legacy from their scholarship, even though their work clearly rehearses the abolitionist perspectives published by Kropotkin over a century earlier.

Before embarking on this endeavour, it is important to offer some caveats as to sources cited and inconsistencies between them. This chapter relies primarily on four principal sources of Kropotkin's work on penology and criminology that have been published in print and/or online, as well as a number of secondary sources that provide a historical framing to the content of the four primary sources. Some of these secondary sources were published as an introduction or foreword to the printed sources of Kropotkin's work, while others were published as historical pieces addressing various aspects of Kropotkin's career and ideas.

The first primary source is Kropotkin's masterpiece of autoethnographic penology, published first as a series of articles in the English journal *Nineteenth Century* in the 1880s, and later assembled and published in 1887 (Kropotkin, 2017[1887]) as the book *In Russian and French Prisons*. The second is a slightly different version of the penultimate chapter of the book, published in an edited volume of Kropotkin's significant works by Roger N. Baldwin in 1970, and reprinted in 2002, entitled 'Prisons and their moral influence on prisoners'. It is not clear if this version of that chapter was taken from the original publication in *Nineteenth Century* or if it was a later revision published after or around the same time as the version of the chapter in the book *In Russian and French Prisons*. Based on the differences (and, in my view, improvements) to the content in the book, it can be surmised that it is the latter rather than the former. However, there is no source known to this author to justify that assumption. In any case, citations are taken from both sources interchangeably as they are so close to one another in terms of content and prose. There are also numerous online sources for the chapter, most of which seem to follow the content published in Baldwin's edited volume.

The third source cited in the chapter is from is Kropotkin's piece 'Law and authority', which was first published as a pamphlet/short book in 1886 (2002) and is still available as a pamphlet/short book from independent publishers, as well as from numerous sources online, although this is cited from the version published in Baldwin's edited volume. Finally, there are citations from a relatively short article entitled 'Prisons: universities of crime' published in 1913 by Kropotkin in volume 8, number 8 of Emma Goldman's periodical *Mother Earth*. This article is available from numerous sources online, and they all seem to publish the same version, although for reasons of fidelity, citations in this chapter are taken from the version published online by the anarchist collective TheAnarchistLibrary.org.

The incredible life of (ex-)prince Pyotr Kropotkin

Pyotr Alexeyevich Kropotkin was born a member of the Russian royal family. Thought to be a direct bloodline descendant of the Viking king Rurik who was invited by the Slavs of Novgorod to be their king in 862, Kropotkin had a better claim to the throne of the Russian Empire than did the Romanovs who had ruled it for three centuries at the time of his birth. However, at the tender age of 12, Kropotkin renounced his title of nobility out of a budding sense of social conscience. Some years later, after reading the work of the first self-proclaimed anarchist Pierre-Joseph Proudhon, and spending time with the Swiss anarchist collective the Jura Federation, Kropotkin embarked on the course that would be his life's work.

Kropotkin was brutally punished for his political ideas and spent half a dozen years in Russian and French prisons. However, his first observation of incarceration occurred as a result of his service in the Russian military as an army officer tasked with producing a geography of remote regions of the Siberian steppe, where he spent a period of five years. It was there in 1862 that he first observed the depravity of the Russian penal system firsthand, a topic he wrote about at great length in his book published a quarter of a century later, *In Russian and French Prisons* (2017[1887]). It was also in Siberia that he was introduced to the work of Pierre-Joseph Proudhon by the Russian poet and political dissident Mikhail Larionovitch Mikhailov, who was a prisoner of the penal colony where Kropotkin was stationed at the time (Avrich, 1988: 55; Woodcock, 2017[1991]).

Disillusioned with the failure to deliver reforms promised by Tsar Alexander II, Kropotkin resigned his commission in the army and returned to St Petersburg, where his political radicalization only continued to grow. However, he did not consciously become a fully fledged anarchist until he visited the Jura Federation in Switzerland in 1872. The Jura Federation was the epicentre of the international anarchist movement after the schism emerged in the First International Workingmen's Association between those aligned with the insurrectionary anarchism of Mikhail Bakunin and those aligned with the authoritarian communism associated with Karl Marx (Avrich, 2005; Eckhardt, 2016). While Kropotkin never met Bakunin, he was inspired by Bakunin's Swiss disciples, and returned to Russia with a zeal for revolution and a newfound courage to challenge the absolute autocracy of the Romanov dynasty (Avrich, 1988: 55–56; Woodcock, 2017[1991]).

However, with the assassination of Tsar Alexander II by anarchist revolutionaries in 1871, his successor, the reactionary Tsar Alexander III, had Kropotkin arrested and imprisoned for critiquing the authority of the Russian crown, beginning a series of incarceration experiences in Kropotkin's young adult life. Kept in draconian solitary confinement for two years at the Peter and Paul Fortress in St Petersburg, Kropotkin was then transferred to a newly constructed prison, the St Petersburg House of Detention, which was ostensibly more humane but so poorly designed that he almost died as a result of the lack of air circulation. An heir to the Russian throne dying in prison would have been embarrassing for even the ruthless autocrat Alexander III, so Kropotkin was transferred to the military hospital in St Petersburg, where he staged a daring escape, dashing across the prison yard and out the momentarily opened gates to a horse-drawn carriage driven by his comrades who spirited him away from a mob of sycophant Tsarists. Infamously, he spent the evening dining in disguise at one of the most opulent restaurants in St Petersburg, the only place the authorities wouldn't think to search for him, and eventually made his way out of the country and to England.

Finding the left in England devoid of any insurrectionary zeal, Kropotkin then made his way to his old comrades in Switzerland, but was ultimately expelled from the country at the request of Tsar Alexander III, who was still bitter that Kropotkin had escaped his clutches. Kropotkin then settled in France, but his misfortunes would continue when the French authorities arrested him along with dozens of other anarchists in 1882 and subjected him to a show trial, ultimately sentencing him to five years in prison. Fortunately, the physical conditions of confinement in France were far better than those he had suffered in his native Russia, but nonetheless only served to steel his resolve that prisons could not be reformed and must be abolished outright. He was ultimately released after four years of confinement in 1886 and expelled from the country, and, with little other option available to him, returned to England for the remainder of his life until he finally travelled to his native Russia at the end of his life, only to be disappointed with dashed hopes of a genuine revolution in the wake of the collapse of the floundering Romanov dynasty in 1917.

Kropotkin's abolitionist autoethnography of the prison

While Kropotkin was far from the first to expose the brutalities of the Russian prison system to the world, his first full-length book, *In Russian and French Prisons*, published in 1887, was the first truly autoethnographic account of incarceration ever published to outright call for the abolition of the institution of the prison. It was preceded and in partly inspired by the 17th-century Russian monk Avvakum Petrov and two other Russian literary giants of the 19th century: Fyodor Dostoevsky's fictional novel, *The House of the Dead*; and Anton Chekov's ethnographic account of the dire conditions suffered by prisoners in the even more remote penal colony on the barren hellscape of *Sakhalin Island* (Kropotkin, 2017[1887]; Chekhov, 2019[1883]; Dostoevsky, 2020[1860–1862]; see also the discussion in Zorin, Chapter 4 in this volume).

However, Kropotkin was perhaps the first to compose an actual autoethnography of prisons, using his own experience as one of a number of sources of data for his analysis and being the first to write from a prisoner's perspective outright advocating for the abolition of the prison and the state. He provided vivid authoethnographic descriptions of the carceral institutions in which he was confined, and ethnographic descriptions of the horrors of the prison colonies he witnessed in Siberia. These are complemented by a wide range of sources subjected to multiple methods of analysis, including an earnest treatment of the memoirs and letters of his contemporary prisoners and an absolute plethora of quantitative data drawn from a wide range of sources available at the time, documenting the vast numbers of poor souls subjected to such tortures over the centuries, the details of the legal cases and policies that governed such penal practices, contemporary and historical crime rates, the rates of recidivism that they produced and reproduced during and before Kropotkin's time, and countless other related topics (see Earle, 2017: 58–61). *In Russian and French Prisons* is not only the first anarchist autoethnography of the prison, but is also an incredible work of multiple methodology scholarship that would presumably be received with wide renown in academia were it to be published today.

Kropotkin mocked his own naïveté at his first engagement with incarceration in the opening pages: 'I must confess at that time I still believed that prisons could be reformatories, and that the privation of liberty is compatible with moral amelioration ... but I was only twenty years old' (Kropotkin, 2017[1887]: 18) At that young age, he still harboured the illusion that prisons could be reformed during his early experience with the prison colonies in Siberia in the early 1860s when he was appointed the secretary of the local committee for the reform of prisons in the region and set about that endeavour with all the credulous zeal of a neophyte reformist. His perspective would quickly change when he found himself incarcerated years later in solitary confinement in the Peter and Paul Fortress in St Petersburg.

Kropotkin dedicated an entire chapter to an autoethnographic description of the Peter and Paul Fortress prison in which he spent two years of his life in solitary confinement alongside such infamous rebels and revolutionaries as the enigma that was Sergei Nechaev (Kropotkin spells it Netchaieff) (Avrich, 1988: 48–49; Kropotkin, 2017[1887]: 108–114). His account is a harrowing firsthand thick description of the depravity of that notorious institution in such vivid detail that one can feel the cold in their bones of the perpetually damp concrete walls of that lethal tomb that claimed the lives of countless Russian dissidents over generations. His condemnation of the practice of solitary confinement that he himself experienced was as apt then as it is today:

> The want of fresh air, the lack of exercise for the body and mind, the habit of silence, the absence of those one thousand and one impressions, which, when at liberty, we daily and hourly receive, the fact that we are open to no impressions that are not imaginative – all these combine to make solitary confinement a sure and cruel form of murder. (Kropotkin, 2017[1887]: 74)

However, this somehow pales in comparison to the horrifying ethnographic description of not only those unfortunate souls exiled to prison labour camps in Siberia, but also their wives and children, who had little choice but to follow their husbands and fathers on a harrowing death march over the Ural Mountains and across the vast expanse of the Siberian steppe that spans over 5,000 miles (8,000 kilometres) of bleak wilderness, an arduous journey of two to three years – if they made it there alive. As Kropotkin recounts, the vast majority of children who attempted the journey did not survive – what he rightly called a 'Massacre of Innocents' (Kropotkin, 2017[1887]: 149). For those poor souls who survived the journey, Kropotkin described a hopeless circumstance of a lifetime of hard labour, often in gold mines deep in the ground, with inadequate nutrition and packed into decrepit quarters each night like captives on a slave ship, until they expired from sheer deprivation and hardship. Kropotkin estimated the yearly rate of attrition by death in one locale as high as 15 per cent (Kropotkin, 2017[1887]: 166). Based on data he was able to gather, he estimated that over half a million convicts and their families endured the hell of life and death in penal exile to Siberia over the course of the prior half century at the time of his writing.

The prisons in which Kropotkin was held in France during his internment as a political prisoner there would seem to have been a welcome relief compared to his experiences in Russia, but instead they only reaffirmed his steadfast conviction that the only solution to the institution of the prison is complete and total abolition of the prison as an institution. Prisoners of some means in France at the time could pay a fee of nine francs per month to have a larger, more comfortable space of confinement. In contrast, Kropotkin described conditions at one prison for those confined not so fortunate as follows: 'These cells are very dirty at Lyons, full of bugs, and never heated, notwithstanding the wetness of the climate and the fogs, which rival in density, if not in colour, those of London'. (Kropotkin, 2017[1887]: 259)

Even in the ostensibly benevolent prisons of France, Kropotkin found the prisoners fed a diet of guaranteed malnourishment, perhaps a modicum better than that of the poor souls in Siberia, only able to survive by purchasing supplemental foodstuffs at the canteen, if they were fortunate enough to have the means to do so. The primary diet consisted mostly of bread, supplemented with a soup consisting of rotten vegetables and rancid lard. While nowhere near the absolute isolation from all human contact of the Peter and Paul Fortress in St Petersburg, the prison at Clairvaux where Kropotkin was incarcerated practised a strict censorship of thought reminiscent of contemporary carceral institutions in the US:

> No socialist literature was admitted, and I could not introduce even a book of my own authorship dealing with socialist literature. As to

writing, the most severe control was exercised on the manuscripts I intended to send out of the prison. Nothing dealing with social questions, and still less with Russian affairs, was permitted to issue from the prison-walls. The common-law prisoners were only permitted to write letters only once a month, and only to their nearest relatives. (Kropotkin, 2017[1887]: 286)

Kropotkin also included heartbreaking ethnographic descriptions of other issues that are unfortunately germane to our own contemporary criminalization regime and of significant concern to contemporary abolitionists: juvenile detention and the effects of incarceration on their families. His account and prediction of the effects of juvenile incarceration in 19th-century France is as heartrending as it is analogous to our own draconian system of juvenile justice in the US:

The condemnations pronounced against children by the always condemning *Police Correctionnelle* Courts are, in fact, much more ferocious than those pronounced against adults … Brutalized as they are by the warders, and left without any honest and moralizing influence, they are foredoomed to become permanent inmates of prisons, and to die in a central prison, or in North Caledonia. (Kropotkin, 2017[1887]: 261–262)

Echoing William Godwin a century previously (Godwin, 1793[2013]; see also Tuke, Chapter 2 in this volume), Kropotkin reiterated another significant collateral casualty of punishment – the effect that incarceration has on the families of those incarcerated. Aside from the horrors of those whose fathers and husbands had been sentenced to exile in Siberia, this problem was even more pronounced in the deeply patriarchal 19th century, when a husband's absence doomed their wives and children to lives of destitution and deprivation:

The leading idea of our penal system is obviously to punish those who have been recognized as 'criminals'; while in reality the penalty of several years of imprisonment hurts much less the 'criminal' than people quite innocent – that is, his wife and children. However hard the conditions of prison-life, man is so made that he finally accommodates himself to these conditions, and considers them as an unavoidable evil, as soon as he cannot modify them. But there are people – the prisoner's wife and his children – who never can accommodate themselves to the imprisonment of the man who was their only support in life. (Kropotkin, 2017[1887]: 268–269)

Kropotkin's thoughts on this matter compelled him to suggest perhaps the only reform he was willing to entertain, allowing prisoners to work for a market wage to support their families on the outside, who, through no fault of their own, were cast into dire poverty as a result of their husbands' and fathers' incarceration (Kropotkin, 2017[1887]: 301).

In addition to the financial hardships imposed on the families of prisoners, Kropotkin also pointed to another topic of concern for contemporary families of the incarcerated – the impediments to meaningful and regular interaction with their loved ones:

> In French prisons – at least, in the Central prisons – the visits of relatives are not so severely limited, and the governor of the jail is even entitled in exceptional cases to allow visits in a common parlour without gratings. But the Central prisons are far from the great cities; and, as the great cities supply the largest number of convicts, and the condemned people chiefly belong to the poorest classes, only very few women have the means to make the journey to Clairvaux for a few interviews with their husbands ... And thus the best influence to which the prisoner might be submitted, the only one which might bring a ray of light, a softer element into his life – the intercourse with his relatives and children – is systematically secluded. (Kropotkin, 2017[1887]: 319–320)

These remain, of course, issues of significant concern not only to academics, activists and advocates, but especially to prisoners and their families in our own modern age of mass incarceration (Scott and Codd, 2010). For example, in my own State of California, what Ruth Wilson Gilmore famously dubbed the *Golden Gulag*, almost all of the prisons are located in remote rural areas, far from the population centres in the metropolitan regions where inmates' families live, making the infrequent pilgrimage to visit family members in prison an onerous undertaking, which Gilmore (2007) so eloquently described in intimate detail.

Theoretical principles of Kropotkin's abolitionist penology and criminology

It is noteworthy that when he was merely an outside observer as a young man, Kropotkin entertained the idea of prison reform, but after his own experiences in prisons at both ends of the reformist and punitive spectrum, he became convinced that there was absolutely no way to reform the prison as an institution and that the only solution to the depravity of incarceration was to abolish the institution of the prison entirely from society. His reasons for arriving at this conclusion were legion, but among the foremost was his resolute conviction that, rather than reforming prisoners and mitigating the possibility of recidivism, the conditions of confinement undermine the capability of prisoners to function in society upon their release. Kropotkin knew from firsthand experience the abject humiliation prisoners are subjected to during their incarceration. Furthermore, those confined are compelled by self-preservation to lie, cheat, steal and kill in order to guarantee their own survival in the perpetual insecurity of the prison, so that such behaviour becomes ingrained in them by the time they are released. As he put it: 'Before he entered the prison he may have felt reluctance to lie and deceive anybody; here he *will* learn to lie and deceive, until lying and deceit become his second nature' (Kropotkin, 2017[1887]: 330).

Thus, the prison invariably turns the prisoner into the enemy of society, virtually guaranteeing recidivism:

> The man who is shut up in a prison is far from being bettered by the change, that he comes out more resolutely the foe of society than he was when he went in. Subjection, on disgraceful terms, to humiliating work gives him an antipathy to all kinds of labour. After suffering every sort of humiliation at the instance of those whose lives are lived in immunity from the peculiar conditions which bring man to crime – or to such sorts of it as are punishable by the operations of the law – he learns to hate the section of society to which his humiliation belongs, and proves his hatred by new offenses against it. (Kropotkin, 2017[1887]: 24–25)

Kropotkin argued that taking revenge on criminals by sentencing them to prison only serves to teach them the principle of revenge:

> The prisoner's brain is thus working over and over again upon the idea of the injustice of a society which pardons and often respects such swindlers as so many company promoters are, and wickedly punishes him, simply because he was not cunning enough. And the moment he is out, he takes his revenge by some offense very often much graver than his first one. Revenge breeds revenge. The revenge that was exercised upon him, he exercises upon society. (Kropotkin, 1913)

Kropotkin was adamant throughout his work that prisons can only serve to exacerbate recidivism and never to mitigate it. In a subsequent article published a quarter of a century after *In Russian and French Prisons*, Kropotkin famously dubbed prisons the 'universities of crime' (Kropotkin, 1913). In the reprint of the last chapter of his book, he stated emphatically: 'So long as you deprive a man of his liberty, you will not make him better. You will cultivate habitual criminals' (Kropotkin, 2002[1887]: 222).

However, Kropotkin was ever the devout practitioner of rigorous scientific methodology and analysis, basing his arguments not merely on the anecdote of his own experience and the eloquence of his argument, but also on the data that were accessible at the time, which justified his perspective. Throughout his works, he regularly employed and cited descriptive statistics that prove the inefficacy of the institution of the prison at achieving the goals for which it ostensibly exists:

> Once a man has been in prison, he will return. It is inevitable, and statistics prove it. The annual reports of the administration of criminal justice in France show that one-half of all those tried by juries and two-fifths of all those who yearly get into the police courts for minor offenses received their education in prisons. Nearly half of all those tried for murder and three-fourths of those tried for burglary are repeaters. As for central prisons, more than one-third of the prisoners released from these supposed correctional institutions are reimprisoned in the course of twelve months after their liberation. (Kropotkin, 2002[1887]: 220–221)

Kropotkin cited statistical data to support his perspective that not only prison but also punishment itself is an utter failure at deterring crime:

> The severity of punishment does not diminish the amount of crime. Hang, and, if you like, quarter murderers, and the number of murders will not decrease by one. On the other hand, abolish the penalty of death, and there will not be one murder more; there will be fewer. Statistics prove it. But if the harvest is good, and bread cheap, and the weather fine, the number of murders immediately decreases. This again is proved by statistics. (Kropotkin, 2002[1886]: 215)

Another issue of significant concern to contemporary abolitionists is that of re-entry. Countless programmes in the US and abroad, from government offices, nonprofit organizations and on university campuses are dedicated to facilitating the successful re-entry of prisoners into society. However, from Kropotkin's perspective, the prison itself makes these innumerable efforts difficult to achieve by proscribing the development of qualities in the inmate that would facilitate their successful re-entry into society. Perhaps the most important quality required for successful re-entry is the aptitude for sound decision making, a skill that rarely has the opportunity for practice in a carceral environment where every aspect of an inmate's life is beyond their control, and which, like any other skill, degrades after an extended period of disuse:

> Now, in prisons, as in a monastery, the prisoner is secluded from all temptations of the outer world; and his intercourse with other men

is so limited and so regulated that he seldom fells the influence of strong passions. But, precisely in consequence of that he has almost no opportunity for exercising and reinforcing the firmness of his Will. He is a machine. He has no choice between two courses of action; the very few opportunities of free choice which he has, are of no moment. All his life has been regulated and ordered beforehand; he has only to follow the current, to obey under the fear of a cruel punishment. In these conditions such firmness of Will as he may have had before entering the prison, disappears. (Kropotkin, 2017[1887]: 323–324)

To Kropotkin, the prison is a totalizing institution in the way Michel Foucault (1995[1975]) imagined it nearly a century later. It not only confines the body but also penetrates the very essence of who someone is and how they regulate their own behaviour – or not.

While his concern rightly lay primarily with the prisoners and their families, Kropotkin even expressed concern for the effect of the prison on the character and conscience of those charged as the wards of the interred. Kropotkin recognized that like the prisoners, the guards and administration of the prison are likewise corrupted by the institution of the prison. However, their corruption is one that results from wielding authority rather than suffering the pains of confinement:

Men are men; and you cannot give so much authority to men over men without corrupting those to whom you give the authority. They will abuse it; and their abuses of it will be the more unscrupulous, and the more felt by the abused, the more limited and narrow is the world they live in. Compelled as they are to live in the midst of a hostile camp of prisoners, the warders cannot be models of kindness and humanity. To the league of prisoners, they are opposed by the league of the warders. And, as they hold the power, they abuse it like all those who hold power in their hands. The institution makes them what they are, petty and vexatious persecutors of prisoners. (Kropotkin, 2017[1887]: 333)

Such is the system of division that the ruling class employs to conquer both the prisoner and the prison guard, each cast in the role of the other's nemesis. And just as the prison corrupts the character of the prisoner by forcing them into circumstances that require deceit and violence, likewise it discards any among the warders who might be compelled by strength of character to conduct their duty with dignity and integrity. As Kropotkin (2017[1887]: 160) observed: 'An honest man, if he is occasionally nominated as the head of a hard-labour prison, will soon be dismissed, or expelled from an administration where honest men are a nuisance.'

As a result of these perspectives, Kropotkin was unequivocal in his insistence on the futility of reform. From his perspective, a prison cannot be improved or reformed, and any reforms that might correct some aspect of the prison, inevitably create unintended consequences that eclipse purported improvements: 'It is remarkable how so many improvements in the penitentiary system, although made with the excellent intention of doing away with some evils, always creates, in their turn, new evils, and become a new source of pain for the prisoners' (Kropotkin, 2017[1887]: 272).

This is a point that Kropotkin never wavered on throughout his life once he settled on it: 'I am often asked – what reforms I should propose; but now, as twenty-five years ago, I really do not see how prisons could be reformed. They must be pulled down' (1913).

As far as Kropotkin was concerned, the only solution to the institution of the prison was to abolish it outright and he was emphatic that this should be the first act of importance in any true revolution:

> The first duty of the revolution will be to abolish prisons – those monuments of human hypocrisy and cowardice. Anti-social acts need not be feared in a society of equals, in the midst of a free people, all of whom have acquired a healthy education and the habit of mutually aiding one another. The greater number of these acts will no longer have any *raison d'être*. The others will be nipped in the bud. (Kropotkin, 2002[1887]: 235)

However, Kropotkin did not stop at the abolition of the prison or the police, as do so many contemporary abolitionists. Rather, the abolition he advocated throughout his life was a full social revolution – the complete abolition of the state, private property and all sources of authority once and for all. From his perspective, only by deposing and dismantling all authority could true liberation be achieved. So long as the state exists, so would the prison.

Kropotkin steadfastly insisted that the law and all consecrated authority in the state exist for one purpose alone – to guarantee the pillage of society and the consecration of that plunder in the form of property. Therefore, the ultimate solution not only to the prison and the police, but also to all the ills of society must be the abolition of not just the prison and the police, but also of all laws and all authority wielded by the state. His views on law are unequivocal:

> The major portion have but one object – to protect private property, i.e., wealth acquired by the exploitation of man by man. Their aim is to open out to capital fresh fields for exploitation, and to sanction the new forms which that exploitation continually assumes, as capital swallows up another branch of human activity, railways, telegraphs, electric light, chemical industries, the expression of man's thought in literature and

science, etc. The object of the rest of these laws is fundamentally the same. They exist to keep up the machinery of government which serves to secure to capital the exploitation and monopoly of the wealth produced. Magistrature, police, army, public instruction, finance, all serve one God – capital; all have but one object – to facilitate the exploitation of the worker by the capitalist. Analyze all the laws passed and you will find nothing but this ... As for guaranteeing the product of his labour to the producer, there are no laws which even attempt such a thing. (Kropotkin, 2002[1886]: 210–211)

From Kropotkin's perspective, the sycophancy of statism and reverence for the law and authority is the result of the miseducation of the population, propagandized from infancy to revere all sources of authority imposed on them throughout their lives:

We are so perverted by an education which from infancy seeks to kill in us the spirit of revolt, and to develop that of submission to authority; we are so perverted by this existence under the ferrule of a law, which regulates every event in life – our birth, our education, our development, our love, our friendship – that, if this state of things continues, we shall lose all initiative, all habit of thinking for ourselves. Our society seems no longer able to understand that it is possible to exist otherwise than under the reign of law, elaborated by a representative government and administered by a handful of rulers. And even when it has gone so far as to emancipate itself from the thralldom, its first care has been to reconstitute it immediately. 'The Year I of Liberty' has never lasted more than a day, for after proclaiming it men put themselves the very next morning under the yoke of law and authority. (Kropotkin, 2002[1886]: 197)

It is important to recognize that, as the passages cited previously suggest, Kropotkin made an explicit differentiation between anti-social behaviour and crimes, which are an invention of the state by means of its laws – the former being a malady that would largely disappear in the wake of social revolution, and the latter an inevitable consequence of a society predicated on exploitation made possible by authority. The solution then to both, from an anarchist perspective, is the abolition of prisons, police, laws and the state, the concomitant redistribution of property and production, and the extension of common decency support, and solidarity to all members of society so that they have no impetus for anti-social behaviour in the first place:

Let us organize our society so as to assure to everybody the possibility of regular work for the benefit of the commonwealth – and that means of course a thorough transformation of the present relations between work and capital; let us assure to every child a sound education and instruction, both in manual labour and science, so as to permit him to acquire. During the first twenty years of his life, the knowledge and habits of earnest work – and we shall be in no more need of dungeons and jails, of judges and hangmen. (Kropotkin, 2017[1887]: 365–366)

Erasing the anarchism of prison abolition

Kropotkin never wavered from his position that only a social revolution, and not the political revolution advocated by Marxists, could bring about the abolition of the prison and the police. And truly, of all the Marxist political revolutions that have occurred since, not one has abolished the prison or the police as an institution – quite the opposite in fact. From the Cheka to the Gulag, Marxist states have always reconstituted the organs of oppression wielded by the state on the first day after the coup d'état that brought them to power. On the other hand, the only historical precedent for actual prison abolition has been the social revolutions executed by anarchist insurrections, however short-lived.

The first act of the anarchist revolutionaries of the Partido Liberal Mexicano who initiated the Mexican Revolution when they liberated a town, if only for a day, was to free the prisoners of the local jails (Blaisdell, 1962; Lytle Hernandez, 2022). Likewise, during the Russian Revolution, the Insurrectionary Army of the Ukraine immediately freed all prisoners of every town they liberated. During the war for liberation of the Ukraine, rather than take prisoners, they simply shot any who were guilty of atrocities against the communities they had liberated (Arshinov, 2005[1923]). However, the Spanish Revolution perhaps best reflects an explicit effort to put Kropotkin's abolitionist ideas into practice. Not only did the militias of the Confederación Nacional del Trabajo (CNT) free the prisoners of Spanish prisons by force of arms in the regions of Spain that they liberated during the Spanish Revolution, but, after freeing them, they offered them all rifles to join the CNT forces in their fight against General Francisco Franco's fascist coup d'état. A total of 90 per cent of the freed prisoners accepted the offer and an entire column of over 10,000 militiamen (and women) was created out of freed prisoners called the *Iron Column*, which played a pivotal role in the Spanish Civil War and only collapsed as a result of the betrayal of the revolution by the Soviet-backed Partido Communista de Espana and the Republican government, which caved in to Soviet demands that the CNT columns be disarmed and disbanded at the height of the war (Paz, 2011[1984]).

While notable libertarian socialist activists and scholars in the European context have continued to draw on Kropotkin's ideas and legacy (see, for example, Scott, 2016, 2018, 2020, 2025), indicating the continued importance of his work,[1] the historical precedents of actual prison abolition and the entire body of Kropotkin's work on prisons and legal abolition have unfortunately been ignored by some of the most prominent academic voices in the contemporary abolition movement, particularly in the American context, from Angela Davis to Ruth Wilson Gilmore (Davis, 2016[1971], 1997, 1998, 2003, 2005; Gilmore, 2022[1991], 2022[1993], 2022[1998], 2022[1999], 2022[2003], 2022[2005], 2007, 2022[2008], 2022[2009], 2022[2011], 2022[2016], 2022[2017], 2022[2018]). While the work of contemporary American abolitionists like Davis and Gilmore largely reflects Kropotkin's ideas, there is not even so much as an acknowledgement of his work or the actual historical precedents for prison and police abolition it inspired in any of theirs. That the prison is an instrument of labour management and social control is at the core of Kropotkin's analysis, and is likewise at the core of Davis and Gilmore's scholarship on prison abolition (Davis, 1971: 45–46; 2003: 16; 2005: 37–38, 113; Gilmore, 2022[2003]: 248; 2022[2005]: 331; 2022[2018]: 344–345).

However, the failure of reform that these contemporary authors express is limited largely to the police and prison, or at most capitalism, as if the state could continue without police and prisons. Davis is perhaps the most explicit in the sense that her abolitionist imagination is limited to 'radical transformations within the existing justice system'. (Davis, 2003: 113). Whereas anarchist revolutionaries of the 20th century abolished prisons and freed prisoners en masse by force of arms, Davis limits her imagination of a successful prison abolition campaign to 'academic research, public policy, and community organizing'. (Davis, 1997: 71). The fundamental quality that defines some of the most celebrated contemporary abolitionist scholars seems to be an abolitionist imagination that cannot imagine the abolition of the state entirely, much less the liquidation of the ruling classes – a sort of *anti-reform reformism* that seeks to abolish prisons in order to reform and therefore improve statist society, rather than abolish the present structure of human civilization entirely.

Kropotkin's concern for the families of prisoners has also been a topic of specific concern for Gilmore (2022[1999]; 2022[2007]), yet she completely ignores his foundational critique of the punishment inflicted on the families of those condemned to incarceration, as described previously. Likewise, Davis cites the 'inevitable part played by the punishment industry in the reproduction of crime' (Davis, 1997: 63), but fails to cite Kropotkin's analysis of how prisons virtually guarantee recidivism. Perhaps even more ironic, she dedicates a whole chapter to 'Abolitionist alternatives' in her 2003 book *Are Prisons Obsolete?*, but somehow ignores those suggested by Kropotkin over a century earlier.

Gilmore unmistakably echoes Kropotkin in his opening to 'Law and authority' when she suggests that obedience and acquiescence to the law is indoctrinated from childhood: 'One thing that's happened culturally over the last twenty years is that everyone is taught from childhood … to get as quickly as they can to someone in uniform. We're taught that doing so is the only safe way to deal with problems. And people believe it' (Gilmore, 2022[2005]: 328).

The irony, of course, is that Kropotkin decried the indoctrination of children over a century before Gilmore:

> Indeed, for some thousands of years, those who govern us have done nothing but ring the changes upon 'Respect for law, obedience to authority'. This is the moral atmosphere in which parents bring up their children, and school only serves to reinforce the impression. Cleverly assorted scraps of spurious science are inculcated upon the children to prove necessity of law; obedience to law is made a religion; moral goodness and the law of the masters are fused into one and the same divinity. (Kropotkin, 2002[1886]: 197)

Such glaring re-articulations of Kropotkin's ideas are quite common throughout the copious body of their work.

How could contemporary activists and academics who have made their careers as prison abolitionists have ignored, not only Kropotkin's foundational work on prison abolition, but also the only precedents for actual prison abolition in history that were inspired by his ideas? It is possible that some of the most celebrated contemporary abolitionist scholars are simply unaware of Kropotkin's work on prisons and criminal justice, as well as the actual historical precedents for prison abolition that he inspired. It is understandable that knowledge of Kropotkin's work could have been lost to contemporary abolitionist scholars in the wake of the pogroms unleashed against anarchists a century prior by Marxist icons Vladimir Lenin and Leon Trotsky in communist Russia, as well as their counterparts in the American context like A. Mitchell Palmer and J. Edgar Hoover (Dunn, 1948; Murray, 1964; Arshinov, 2005[1923]; Finan, 2007; Voline, 2019[1947]).

However, Gilmore, repeatedly uses the word 'anarchy' to describe racial capitalism, which betrays either an intentional misrepresentation or a lack of awareness of anarchist frameworks (Gilmore, 2022[2016]: 303; 2022[2017]: 481). Anarchy is the literal opposite of racial capitalism and anarchists have been dedicated to the abolition of racial capitalism from the publication of Bakunin's magnum opus *Statism and Anarchy* (1990[1873]) to the present. Thus, there is the possibility that contemporary Marxist abolitionist scholars intentionally exclude Kropotkin's work and any mention of actual historical precedents of prison abolition during the course of anarchist revolutions in the 20th century in order to cast anarchist frameworks into obscurity and to avoid acknowledging that no state established on allegedly Marxist principles has ever even attempted to abolish prisons (see also Turcato, Chapter 11 in this volume).[2]

The final conceivable reason for the exclusion of Kropotkin's work from the contemporary abolitionist literature, especially in American academia, is the myopia of the Anglo-American worldview that centres the institution of Black chattel slavery as the defining foundation of modern society. Many contemporary abolitionist scholars, particularly in the American context, trace their use of the word 'abolition' not to prison abolitionists of the 19th century, but to the 'abolition' of American slavery, which of course never occurred. The connection between slavery and abolition is at the core of W.E.B. Du Bois' (1998[1935]) magnum opus *Black Reconstruction in America*, which has seen a resurgence of interest since the publication of Cedric Robinson's magnum opus *Black Marxism* in 1983. Indeed, most contemporary abolitionist scholars explicitly link their perspectives to the legacy of the Anglo-American experience with Black chattel slavery and Du Bois' analysis of how it was reproduced through the mass criminalization of African Americans in the wake of the American Civil War (Davis, 1998. 80–81; 2016[1971]: 44–46; Gilmore 2022[2017]: 480–488). The penchant for ignoring and dismissing any scholarship that does not explicitly centre the African-American experience is quite pervasive in contemporary American academia, and so that seems to be a likely explanation for the exclusion of Kropotkin's work and the actual historical precedents of prison abolition he inspired from much of the contemporary American penal abolitionist literature.

The continuity between Kropotkin's work and contemporary abolitionist voices and the fact that the framework for prison abolition that he introduced has direct historical precedent for actual prison abolition by anarchists demonstrate how important his work on prisons is to the classical abolitionist literature and why it should be more faithfully included in the contemporary literature today. Much can be learned from his perspective, his methods, his experiences and his legacy for those who are dedicated to ending the abomination of the prison once and for all, and the state along with it.

Notes

[1] See also Earle (2017).
[2] For the case of Cuba and its attempts to reduce imprisonment and develop alternatives see de Haan (1990). However, as time has progressed, the Cuban state has increasingly used the prison as means of incarcerating political prisoner and prison populations have spiralled.

References

Arshinov, P. (2005[1923]) *History of the Makhnovist Movement, 1918–1921*, London: Freedom Press.
Avrich, P. (1988) *Anarchist Portraits*, Princeton: Princeton University Press.
Avrich, P. (2005) *The Russian Anarchists*, Chico, CA: AK Press.

Bakunin, M. (2009[1873]) *Statism and Anarchy*, Cambridge: Cambridge University Press.

Blaisdell, L.L. (1962) *The Desert Revolution: Baja California, 1911*, Madison: University of Wisconsin Press.

Chekhov, A. (2019[1883]) *Sakhalin Island*, London: Alma Classics.

Davis, A. (2016[1971]) 'Political prisoners, prisons, and Black liberation', in *If They Come in the Morning... Voices of Resistance*, New York: Verso, pp 27–43.

Davis, A. (1997) 'Race and criminalization: Black Americans and the punishment industry', in W. Lubiano (ed.) *The House That Race Built*, New York: Vintage Books, pp 264–279.

Davis, A. (1998) 'Racialized punishment and prison abolition', in J. James (ed.) *The Angela Y. Davis Reader*, Hoboken, NJ: Blackwell.

Davis, A. (2003) *Are Prisons Obsolete?*, New York: Seven Stories Press.

Davis, A. (2005) *Abolition Democracy: Beyond Empire, Prisons and Torture*, New York: Seven Stories Press.

de Haan, W. (1990) *The Politics of Redress*, London: Sage

Dostoevsky, F. (2020[1860–1862]) *The House of the Dead*, Overland Park, KS: Digireads.

Du Bois, W.E.B. (1998[1935]) *Black Reconstruction in America 1860–1880*, New York: The Free Press.

Dunn, R.W. (ed.) (1948) *The Palmer Raids*, New York: International Publishers.

Earle, R. (2017) *Convict Criminology: Inside and out*, Bristol: Policy Press.

Eckhardt, W. (2016) *The First Socialist Schism: Bakunin vs. Marx in the First International Working Men's Association*, Binghamton, NY: PM Press.

Finan, C.M. (2007) *From the Palmer Raids to the Patriot Act: A History of the Fight for Free Speech in America*, Boston: Beacon Press.

Foucault, M. (1995[1975]) *Discipline and Punish: The Birth of the Prison*, New York: Vintage Books.

Gilmore, R.W. (2007) *Golden Gulag: Prisons, Surplus, Crisis, and Opposition in Globalizing California*, Berkeley: University of California Press.

Gilmore, R.W. (2022[1991]) 'Decorative beasts: dogging the academy in the late 20th Century', in *Abolition Geography: Essays toward Liberation*, New York: Verso, pp 51–77.

Gilmore, R.W. (2022[1993]) 'Public enemies and private intellectuals: apartheid USA', in *Abolition Geography: Essays toward Liberation*, New York: Verso, pp 78–91.

Gilmore, R.W. (2022[1998]) 'Globalization and US prison growth: from military Keynesianism to post-Keynesian militarism', in *Abolition Geography: Essays toward Liberation*, New York: Verso, pp 199–223.

Gilmore, R.W. (2022[1999]) 'You have dislodged a boulder: mothers and prisoners in the post-Keynesian California landscape', in *Abolition Geography: Essays toward Liberation*, New York: Verso, pp 355–409.

Gilmore, R.W. (2022[2005]) 'From military-industrial complex to prison-industrial complex', in *Abolition Geography: Essays toward Liberation*, New York: Verso, pp 318–334.

Gilmore, R.W. (2022[2009]) 'Race, prisons, and war: scenes from the history of US violence', in *Abolition Geography: Essays toward Liberation*, New York: Verso, pp 176–195.

Gilmore, R.W. (2022[2011]) 'What is to be done?', in *Abolition Geography: Essays toward Liberation*, New York: Verso, pp 25–50.

Gilmore, R.W. (2022[2017]) 'Abolition geography and the problem of innocence', in *Abolition Geography: Essays toward Liberation*, New York: Verso, pp 471–495.

Gilmore, R.W. (2022[2018]) 'Prisons and class warfare', in *Abolition Geography: Essays toward Liberation*, New York: Verso, pp 335–352.

Gilmore, R.W. and Gilmore. C. (2022[2003]) 'The other California', in *Abolition Geography: Essays toward Liberation*, New York: Verso, pp 242–258.

Gilmore, R.W. and Gilmore, C. (2022[2008]) 'Restating the obvious', in *Abolition Geography: Essays toward Liberation*, New York: Verso, pp 259–287.

Gilmore, R.W. and Gilmore, C. (2022[2016]) 'Beyond Bratton', in *Abolition Geography: Essays toward Liberation*, New York: Verso, pp 288–317.

Godwin, W. (2013[1793]) *An Enquiry Concerning Political Justice*, Oxford: Oxford University Press.

Kropotkin, P. (2002[1886]) 'Law and authority', in R.N. Baldwin (ed.) *Anarchism: A Collection of Revolutionary Writings*, Mineola, NY: Dover Publications, pp 196–218.

Kropotkin, P. (2017[1887]) *In Russian and French Prisons*, Atlanta: Black Rose Books.

Kropotkin, P. (2002[1887]) 'Prisons and their moral influence on prisoners', in R.N. Baldwin (ed.) *Anarchism: A Collection of Revolutionary Writings*, Mineola, NY: Dover Publications, pp 220–235.

Kropotkin, P. (1913) 'Prisons: universities of crime', in E. Goldman (ed.) *Mother Earth* 8(8), TheAnarchistLibrary.org.

Lytle Hernandez, K. (2022) *Bad Mexicans: Race, Empire & Revolution in the Borderlands*, New York: W.W. Norton & Co.

Murray, R.K. (1964) *Red Scare: A Study in National Hysteria*, New York: McGraw-Hill.

Paz, A. ([2011[1984]) *The Story of the Iron Column: Militant Anarchism in the Spanish Civil War*, Chico, CA: AK Press.

Robertson, S. (1983) *Black Marxism: The Making of the Black Radical Tradition*, Chapel Hill, NC: UNC Press.

Scott, D. (ed.) (2016) *Emancipatory Politics and Praxis*, Bristol: EG Press.

Scott, D. (2018) *Against Imprisonment: An Anthology of Abolitionist Essays*, Hook: Waterside Press.

Scott, D. (2020) *For Abolition: Essays on Prison and Socialist Ethics*, Hook: Waterside Press.

Scott, D. (ed.) (2025) *Abolitionist Voices*, Bristol: Bristol University Press.

Scott, D. and Codd, H. (2010) *Controversial Issues in Prisons*, Milton Keynes: Open University Press.

Voline (2019[1947]) *The Unknown Revolution, 1917–1921*, Binghamton, NY: PM Press.

Woodcock, G. (2017[1991]) 'Introduction to the 1991 Edition', in P. Kropotkin, *In Russian and French Prisons*. Chico, CA: AK Press, pp ix–xx.

10

Anarchism and the Abolition of the Criminal Justice System: The Struggle for the Discourse on Evolution and Social Order in Spain

Alejandro Forero Cuellar

Introduction

When we speak of anarchism, just as when we speak of abolitionism, we must do so in the plural. There has never been a single anarchist discourse, just as there has never been a single abolitionist discourse. Therefore, the *voices* we study are plural and we should contextualize them in each historical moment and every geographical place (Scott, 2025). Regarding the *anarchist abolitionist voices* I study in this chapter, it is essential to reflect upon the profound influence that scientific debates on evolutionism and progress had on them in the historical period under discussion (the late 19th and early 20th centuries).

Why is this moment so important for understanding the anarchist abolitionist tradition? The scientific (and political) revolution brought about by the arrival of positivism shared its moment with the rise and organization of the anarchist movement in the sociopolitical order, especially in Spain. The relationship between these two elements gave rise to a framework for the production of political and legal debates that explain much of the current configuration of criminology and criminal law. Within criminal policy, on the one hand, the causes of social conflict were individualized and pathologized to a large extent, and criminology developed tools to diagnose who should be treated, locked up or eliminated from society. Political violence was also treated differently from the previous ('classical') period, reconceptualizing the relationship between political crime-terrorism-resistance and criminal exceptionality. On the other hand, anarchism's profound critique of the very foundations of criminology and prisons, as well as their latent functions, exposed the criminal justice system as a model that continually needed self-justifying discourses. From this moment on, it became evident that the narrative of the criminal justice system, as a system of social hygiene, was countered by an abolitionist one, based on denouncing the system as a means of oppression designed to prevent real social change.

This period heralded the beginning of using science as a tool for the study and treatment of social problems. Science featured not only in academic criminology but also in the production of anarchist ideology and its abolitionist perspective, not just with regard to the criminal justice system but also, as will be seen, to the bourgeois social model. Positivism and evolutionism both used the same tools to serve opposing goals. Darwinism is a good example, split between the social Darwinism of Spencerian trend and an anarchist Darwinism developed by the anarchist thinker Kropotkin. While during the First World War, much of the discussion on criminal anthropology lost momentum, the war did bring to light the clash of discourses that went beyond the analytical framework of crime control and punishment to address civilization, war and state criminality.

This chapter therefore examines how positivist criminology was built on the foundations of evolutionism and helped to build a first criminal law of the enemy, using the anarchists as scapegoat. It then determines how anarchist thought both drew on evolutionism and was in part configured in opposition to positivist criminology, leading to the emergence of the Spanish anarchist abolitionist tradition and its continuing struggle for emancipation.

Darwin versus Darwin: positivist foundations in the service of emancipation

The anarchist thought of the late 19th and early 20th centuries is a political and social ideology that cannot be separated from the historical context and the cultural environment in which it developed. Although it is a discourse that is radically opposed to the established order and the pillars that constitute it, it draws on the new scientific theories that were revolutionizing the social thought of the 19th century. Part of the anarchist ideology of that time is to a large extent positivist and evolutionist. It should not be forgotten that positivism and evolutionism were progressive sciences, born out of criticism of the established traditional and religious values (although they were also quickly adopted by some conservative defenders of that order) and to the enlightened, labelled as metaphysical.[1]

Like those who defended the established order and justified social inequality, the Spanish anarchists under discussion in this chapter quote the most renowned scientists of the time, such as Haeckel, Spencer, Darwin and Galton, and also representatives of positivist criminology, such as Lombroso, Ferri, Colajanni, Turati, Tarde and Quételet. Unlike the defenders of the existing social order, the interpretation of those theories in a libertarian way revealed the unnatural, unjust and barbaric character of bourgeois society. Anarchists tried to prove that the most just society was the libertarian one, drawing on positivism and science to show the way to get there.

Positive science was thus a fundamental part of the emancipatory mission of the anarchist abolitionist tradition in Spain. Anselmo Lorenzo (1895: 5), one of the most influential anarchists of that time, pointed out that 'positive science' was a part 'of the synthesis that constitutes the revolutionary worker'.[2]

This debate between worldviews, which drew support from the same scientific theories, is represented by the different uses made of Darwin's evolutionary theory: by Kropotkin, Huxley, Haeckel and Spencer. This debate largely took place on the pages of journal *The Nineteenth Century*, in which Kropotkin published a series of articles refuting the interpretation that Huxley had held in the same journal in an article from 1888 entitled 'The struggle for existence: a programme'.[3] From Kropotkin's (1989: 281) point of view, Darwin's struggle for existence is not primarily a struggle for the basic means of existence, but rather a struggle against all natural conditions unfavourable to the species (such as food shortages or natural disasters). The species that collaborate with each other are those that have more options for survival. Solidarity becomes a characteristic of progressive evolution. As will be seen later on, conceiving cooperation as the engine of progress would allow evolution to be understood in terms of revolution.

Anarchist thought and positivist criminology

It is key to emphasize that the development of Spanish abolitionist anarchism cannot be understood separately from the development of criminological positivism itself. Many of the most emblematic anarchist thinkers read, and were familiar with, the theories of Italian or French positivist criminology. Many anarchists recognized revolutionary ideas in these theories, which applied a scientific and rational methodology to explain crime as something produced by nature (and no longer a political and legal definition given by the liberal bourgeoisie). The crime and the offender could now be explained through environmental, meteorological, geographical and other causes. But, above all, they recognized that crime could be due to social causes or relations, to the way in which society was organized and to the conditions in which some people lived.

However, they soon adopted a critical approach to these theories. Anarchists were aware of how the bourgeoisie were using these 'progressive' theories to justify their new position of domination, through the positivist criminological construction of the 'anarchist threat'. Spanish anarchists thus began to respond to criminological theories and rejected their solutions to criminality, although they did recognize the importance of the scientific study of the problem of criminality.

One author who was very critical of the criminology of the time was Martínez Ruiz.[4] Clearly influenced by Kropotkin's *Prisons*,[5] he points out in his book *Sociología Criminal* that:

> The mission of criminal justice must be, to say it once and for all, completely analogous to that carried out by doctors. We reject, therefore, the theories that the determinist saviours of criminality have invented. We reject more than any other, in its present form, the theory of the utilitarians, of the Italian school, of the type of Garofalo and Ferri. (Martínez Ruiz, 1899: 131)

Martínez Ruiz (1899: 69–72) takes up the theories of Tarde to criticize the theories of Lombroso, concluding that the criminal typologies of Lombroso, and also of the 'more balanced' Ferri, and of Garofalo, are false and artificial, and therefore inadmissible (Martínez Ruiz, 1899: 74). For this author, therefore, the doctrines of those who pretend to define crime once and for all are vain, as are the definitions of crime itself, of *natural crime*, as advanced by Garofalo. Together with Dorado's doctrine, he criticized those who pretend to differentiate between the insane and the sane, such as Liszt or Tarde, explaining that it is not possible to find distinctions between the insane, the sick and the savage, and the healthy, the normal and the civilized, because in the end, everything is a problem of who defines these categories. Even crime: there is no *crime*, but a *definition of crime* (Martínez Ruiz, 1899: 142).

But the acceptance or rejection of the theories of positivist criminology depended on how they could be interpreted to align more closely with the libertarian ideology. Beyond the reception of Lombroso or Ferri, authors with a perspective based on a more environmental and socialist perspective were most widely accepted, as was the case for Colajanni, Niceforo or Sighele.

Despite their differences, Lombroso was one of the most referenced authors by anarchists when speaking in general terms of the criminal question. Lombroso's theories on anarchism (*The Anarchists*, 1894 – see Mella, 1978[1896]) triggered direct criticism from different anarchist authors in Spain. The most emblematic response can be found in Ricardo Mella.[6] Although this author had already responded to Lombroso in 1895 (with a critique of positivist scientific thought and the criminalization of anarchism), it was in 1896 when he criticized the subjectivity and ignorance shown by Lombroso. Mella branded his anthropological theory a hoax against anarchism, since Lombroso, without scientific rigour, identified anarchists by their jargon or their tattoos, for example, and denounced their ideas as illogical, close to madness. Lombroso proposed that anarchists should be locked up in mental hospitals, not prisons. Mella (1978: 130) criticizes Lombroso's methodology, accusing him of basing his studies only on the incarcerated population, as well as abusing statistics, drawing conclusions from isolated facts, to conclude, in short, that 'Lombroso as always affirms, but proves nothing'. Mella blames him for being a defender of the bourgeoisie and of the repressive means used to quash anarchism: 'Society is divided into two belligerent armies. Against the propaganda and constant action of revolutionary socialism, nothing remains for the bourgeoisie but violent repression, lynching, deportation and the madhouse, as Lombroso wants' (Mella, 1978: 146).

Martínez Ruiz would go on to criticize Lombroso and the methodology followed by the *Scuola*. Of Lombroso he says that:

> he does not leave the meter of the hand; he does not give peace to the weighing scale. He weighs and measures everything ... he studies and inspects everything ... For Lombroso there is no society; everything is anatomy. There is no such thing as economic struggle; everything is Nature. (Martínez Ruiz, 1899: 69–70)

Clearly influenced by Kropotkin, Ruiz recognizes Lombroso as having opened up the way to the study of the causes of crime and its treatment, but 'the Italian professor has seen these causes *mainly* in the factory of the human body; others have come later and have seen them in the miserable condition in which we live. That is the difference' (Martínez Ruiz, 1899: 72; emphasis in original).

The social question: social organization as a cause of degeneration and criminality

The Spanish anarchists' rejection of the positivist construction of the criminal (and of anarchists) led them to develop an abolitionist theory not only of the criminal justice system, but also of the entire model of social order. In this sense, the criminal question was understood as being just one part of the larger social question. The criminal justice system (based on criminological positivism) served as a pillar for the support and reproduction of the bourgeois order. In this order lay the true causes of crime. In this regard, as will be seen, the abolition of the criminal justice system was merely one step on the path towards emancipation and the end of criminality: what should be abolished was the entire bourgeois social order.

Positivist criminology defended the concept of determinism, through which it was understood that phenomena, such as crime, were predetermined by certain circumstances, especially natural or hereditary. For this reason, the offender was not free, but had to be controlled because he was dangerous; he was determined to commit a crime. However, the anarchists who also defended determinism argued that its causes were, above all, social. The perpetration of crimes is seen as a product of social organization itself. It is true that the environmental component was also emphasized by Italian – and especially French – positivist criminology, but the hallmark of anarchist ideology in this respect lies in the conception of the social organization of the moment as unnatural. Society, under capitalist and bourgeois principles, and under state hierarchy, determines humans in an unnatural way – that is, it makes them selfish, unequal and slaves. The main cause of criminality was to be found in the social structure. This understanding is the starting point for anarchist abolitionism.

Just like determinism, the idea of degeneration (through which a species worsens its qualities due to hereditary or environmental processes) is accepted both in its biological and social aspects. In a discourse where the boundaries are not always clear between both types of degeneration and the degree of relationship or dependence between them, the physical individual traits were understood as a consequence of social organization itself. Both types of degeneration – biological and social – were also thought to explain a large part of criminal activity.

Likewise, degeneration is attributed to the existence of punitive institutions such as prisons or asylums: 'The penitentiary regime, as well as the asylum regime, will leave traces on any face, just as the exercise of certain professions leaves them on an individual, but the existence of a criminal type cannot be deduced from this' (Mella, 1978: 155).

Thus, organic degeneration was interpreted by anarchists as a degeneration of class and of living conditions. In this sense, the anarchist ideology also explains symptoms of social degeneration in certain types of life or work that were interpreted by the discourses of positivist criminologists as 'bad life' (Niceforo and Sighele, 1897). But these groups and classes were not conceived in anarchist ideology as a threat or a social danger, and were far from representing that 'army of fundamental enemies of the social order' mentioned by von Liszt. These classes and groups were seen as victims of a defective economic and social organization, and although this affirmation could also be shared by some criminologists or politicians of the time (such as Ferri), what defined the anarchist point of view in a radically different way was its view of how to solve and overcome such phenomena. As will be seen, there would be no place for social reforms, but only for the abolition of the system, as, for example, was stated in the anarchist publication *Bandera Social* (1885): 'the basis [of crime] is the bad economic order that exposes and drives individuals on some occasions to commit crimes. A perennial source that persists and will persist as long as the social revolution does not modify this unjust order, a seedbed of injustice and moral disorders'.

Another explanation for criminality lay in traditional, bourgeois morality. This traditional, bourgeois and religious morality would explain the commission of crimes that did not respond solely to an economic cause or material necessity. From another important anarchist newspaper, *Tierra y Libertad* (1907), 'brutalizing' religious mentality and the irrational and authoritarian education system were proclaimed as causes of crime. 'Vicious' education and repression appeared intimately related in the pages of *La Federación Igualadina*: the current social order 'abandons thousands of children to a vicious education, thus forming thieves and murderers in order to have the pleasure of hanging them' (Álvarez Junco, 1976: 268).

In short, criminality, for one reason or another, is nothing more than an expression of the current civilization – thus declared Mella (1975: 59–61), who, against those who spoke of 'regression to barbarism' in response to a brutal crime of dismemberment in Madrid, warned that 'it is the fruit, it is the foam of civilization'. For that reason, from a clear libertarian Darwinist perspective, Mella (1975: 134) also noted: 'We are not thieves and murderers as much by atavism as by progressivism.'

To speak of oppression, misery and social inequality as the political basis of criminality was not confined to anarchist discourse, but was also evident in that of socialism in a broad sense, and was accepted by liberals. The difference of the libertarian discourse lies in its radicalism with regard to the conception of the state. To solve the problem of criminality, as will be seen later on, the state should not be reformed or improved; it should be abolished.

Undertaking conflict globally: the state and capitalism as producers of crime

One of the things that differentiates the anarchist thought of the time from other critical political ideologies is its global vision of the form of political and social organization, its view of which cannot lead it to any other place than abolitionism. Its vision of the state is of particular relevance here. When speaking of criminality, anarchist positions not only held the social organization itself (state and capitalist) responsible for the existence of crimes committed by the working and poor classes; in addition, this view pointed the finger at the state and capital as producers of criminality themselves. This vision, then, opposed the liberal and social construction of the state as guarantor of rights and liberties and as protector of its citizens. Let us consider now some ways in which this understanding has underscored the Spanish anarchist approach to abolitionism.

Economic violence: misery, death and social harm

The anarchist press in the late 19th and early 20th centuries devoted significant efforts to publishing articles, news and statistics on hunger and misery, highlighting their origin in the symbiotic relationship between public and private powers. It is difficult to find an issue within the dozens of libertarian newspapers in the period studied in which there is no reference to this subject. The anarchist press thus contributed to making social inequality visible and denouncing it. Death by hunger, disease, poverty or war were regarded as 'consequences' of the social order and were defined as crimes committed by the state and private interests against the poor.

Along with the criticism of religion and the state, there was another institution that was regarded the seed of violence and crime: private property. Not only was its existence per se a source of inequality, but the predatory actions of companies and factories were also regarded as a cause of crime. 'Criminal companies' were directly referred to as the cause of poverty (YO, 1913). In the anarchist publication *La Anarquía* (1890), the authors spoke of the fortune of the Rothschild family, calculating how many times it could go around the world in gold coins; it was said that another calculation should be made: 'The pile of misery that this illegal accumulation of wealth has undoubtedly produced' and 'the tears it will have caused to be shed, and the crimes of which it will have been the direct or indirect cause'.

Publications such as *El Corsario* and *El Porvenir del Obrero* opened specific sections with the title 'Bourgeois dynamite' or under other headings that appeared already in the 1880s such as 'Workers' martyrology' (in *Bandera Social*), or 'Labour martyrology' (in *El Productor*). In these sections, there was news about deaths and injured workers as a result of bad working conditions or accidents, such as mine explosions, building collapses or fires.[7]

Denouncing state violence and the dirty war against the labour movement

The anarchists' view of the role of the criminal justice system is critical. The role of the law as creator/preserver of the conditions of inequality was highlighted, as was the role of agencies such as courts and prisons for their repression of the dispossessed. The law and the criminal justice system were thus seen to reproduce the system of oppression and were labelled in the publications as 'criminal', both in its illegal and its legal action. Torture and ill-treatment were regarded as expressions of state violence that were widely denounced through the workers' press and other writings. This violence, perpetuated by the police and the military, was reinforced by censorship and state terror policies. An example would be the so-called 'Montjuic trials',[8] which portrayed Spain internationally as one of the cruellest and most barbaric countries in the world. The repression was so great that there was widespread talk of a new 'Inquisition' (Nettlau, 1897; Tarrida de Mármol, 1897).

The high level of social conflict that marked the advent of the 20th century was reflected in great acts of rebellion and their respective repressions, which led Barcelona to become one of the most important rebellious epicentres in Europe. The first general strike of the century in 1902 resulted in 300 wounded and 106 dead, as well as the arrest of more than 500 people (Fernández González, 2011: 27). Then came the famous Semana Trágica (Tragic Week) when the events of Cullera led to at least 500 activists from the Confederación Nacional del Trabajo (the National Confederation of Labour, the most numerous anarchist union of workers in the country) alone being detained (Íñiguez, 2008: 408). After a decade of intense conflict, the strike at La Canadenca (Catalana de Gas, Ferrocarrils de Sarria and Societat General d'Aigües) led to the arrest of around 58,000 workers (Fernández González, 2011: 27).

However, it should be noted that the political violence exercised by the state and its supporters cannot be reduced to large-scale repressive campaigns. Persecution was constant and acts of state violence were daily occurrences. That is why some newspapers opened special sections to denounce such events, using headlines such as 'The Spanish bourgeoisie to the pillory: its victims' (in *La Tribuna Libre*) and 'Spanish bourgeoisie's list of ignominies' published (in *Justicia!*). Lists of the names of imprisoned comrades and of the prisons in which they were held were published as an example of this continued repression.

War, colonialism and the civilization debate

The anti-authoritarian principle of the Spanish anarchists led them to analyse war and colonialism as part of the external criminal action of the state. They argued that the expansion of the *civilized world* by means of force to subdue and pacify the *barbarian* questioned the dominant state narrative of 'civilization' and 'barbarism': 'By violence the indigenous races have been annihilated by the European conquerors' (*Tierra y Libertad*, 1913). The anarchist press leaves no room for doubt about its vision of the colonial enterprise as one of death and destruction.

Criticisms were made not only of past imperial expansion but also of European policy at the time.[9] *La Idea Libre* (1898), which published an article by Calderón criticizing the Tonkin campaign, as well as that of England in Egypt, called them campaigns to 'open markets', expressing the idea that instead of bringing civilization to the colonized countries, the colonial companies slaughtered and subjugated entire populations in order to control their resources and secure European markets. In the same way, the anarchist publication *Acracia* (1887) declared: 'The opening of a new market for the products of French industry has caused a number of victims that exceeds what could be imagined', while 'the French workers suffer all sorts of miseries and privations, next to warehouses full of all kinds of merchandise that are waiting to be consumed'.

The abolition of the state as a solution to criminality

The abolition of the state finds its foundation in the anti-authoritarian principle, a true pillar of libertarian thought expressed by the most relevant anarchists at the international level, such as Godwin, Proudhon and Bakunin, whose influence in Spain was key in shaping anarchist thought. This anti-authoritarian vision proclaims the illegitimacy of the state to punish (see also Tuke, Chapter 2 in this volume, and Zorin, Chapter 4 in this volume).

Criticism of the death penalty finds a solid foundation in the anti-authoritarian principle. If the state does not have the legitimacy to punish, nor does it have the legitimacy to take life. Discussions about the functions of the death penalty are therefore irrelevant, because the negation is of the penalty itself. Lorenzo (1886) (another of the most influential anarchists of the time and the one who knew best the neo-Malthusian theories) clearly stated that 'anarchist socialism opts, contrary to historical justice, for the immediate abolition of the death penalty'.

The existence of prisons was a major object of criticism for the anarchists. Kropotkin (1977: 57), who also had great influence on this subject within Spanish anarchist thought, had already stated that 'the first duty of the Revolution would be to demolish the prisons; those monuments of hypocrisy and human vileness'. Prison was not only the object of criticism in the abstract, as a sanction and punishment, but so were the conditions of imprisonment itself, as well as its effects, for example, on the prisoners' relatives[10] (see also Weide, Chapter 9 in this volume).

As we have already seen, prison is also the focus of criticism due to its effects on the physical and mental health of the detainees and its classist character; indeed, it was one of the most important means of repression of the workers' movement. For this reason, many workers' journals of the time served as a channel of information for prisoners' relatives and organized collections to support the incarcerated.

From an abolitionist perspective, the anarchists demolished the argument that prisons provide security:

> 'Open the prisons, abolish the gendarmes and men will kill each other': an old fable, a bogeyman for children. Abolish prisons and police and humanity will continue its evolution towards the good, towards the best. So, positivists, determinists, materialists, do not tremble with fear ... before the death of criminal law. Its death will not bring us

barbarism, nor the right of the strongest as they imagine. (Molinari, 1907: 12)

The neo-Malthusian vision: solutions to criminality and libertarian society

The criticism of the structures of the bourgeois and capitalist state and its morality, as well as the rejection of its transformation, established that real change could only be brought about through a change of humanity, through the implementation of measures that would generate the *new man*. A basic principle was the abolition of the structures that generate criminality: bourgeois laws and morals. Martínez Ruiz (1899: 82) stated that 'having no law there will be no transgressions of the law. Not having bloodthirsty instincts there will be no homicides. Not having the need to steal, there will be no robberies'.

The destruction of the law should give way to anarchic government: in anarchy there should be 'no shadow of authority, no codes, no trace of preventive laws ... no magistracy, no lawyers, no curiales, but free and spontaneous pacts between individuals and collectives reciprocally' (*El Corsario*, 1892). It was with the support of neo-Malthusianism[11] that the anarchists could harness the regenerative and revolutionary power of science and libertarian ideals. With the implementation of its tools, measures could be found to put an end to many of the evils that were being denounced, such as infanticide, abortion and suicide.[12]

It is here that the neo-Malthusian principle of 'conscious generation' appears, and its relation to the reduction or elimination of criminality. This rhetoric had an important impetus from the famous writing of Luis Bulffi (the most important Catalan author within neo-Malthusianism), entitled *Huelga de Vientres* (*Strike of the Wombs*, 1905) and its slogan 'poverty does not breed rebels'. Reducing the size of the proletarian class could have benefits: the number of workers without employment and their resulting exploitation; the list of men called to war as 'cannon fodder'; the enslavement of women to the home and to motherhood, and sexuality understood solely as a means for procreation. Reproduction was thus reinterpreted in the political and anti-clerical sense of women's liberation, sexual freedom and reduction of the proletarian 'mass', the product of capitalism. For all these reasons, Bulffi advocated a 'womb strike' as a revolutionary strategy. The woman's womb appears as the place for the physical and spiritual regeneration of the working class.

The advantages of neo-Malthusianism can be summarized as: (a) a reduction of the proletarian mass and therefore greater dedication on the part of parents for the education and maintenance of their offspring; (b) a reduction of the labour reserve and therefore increased wages; (c) physical and intellectual improvements of the proletarian class who would thus be better prepared for revolution; (d) a reduction in the number of young men used as cannon fodder for wars; (e) the liberation of women; (f) the separation of sexuality from procreation; (g) 'more space, light and air for families in their hovels' (Hardy, 1904); and (h) preventing the physical deterioration of women by multiple pregnancies.

The strong evolutionist influence in anarchist discourse, as we have seen, had in its greatest representatives Kropotkin and Darwinist theory, developed mainly in *Mutual Aid* (1902) and *The Conquest of Bread* (1892). Darwinist and Malthusian theories took the debate of the social question into the terrain of the struggle for life. In this, the metaphor of the *banquet of life* represented how some (property owners) and others (the dispossessed) had different places around a table where the fruits of life, the products of nature and wellbeing were offered. The majority were not seated at the same table. The *banquet of life* was an expression of high significance in anarchist ideology, used by many authors, such as Lorenzo, who borrowed it for his book written in 1905: *El Banquete de la vida: concordancia entre la naturaleza, el hombre y la sociedad* (*The Banquet of Life: Concurrence between Nature, Man and Society*).

Criminality in the libertarian society?

As seems obvious, the proposal for a new society led critics of anarchist positions to ask how such a society would respond to crimes or harmful actions. Ferri stated that even if it were true that the disappearance of institutions such as private property or marriage would put an end to crimes related to them, there would still be physical and personal factors that would lead to crime. For him, even in collective or communist societies, there would be born vagabonds who, due to their *organic* repugnance for work, would steal food stamps to provide for himself.[13]

The pages of *La Anarquía* (1892), which reproduce a text from the London anarchist newspaper *Freedom*, also reflect that continuous concern about the libertarian project: 'What are you going to do with the thieves and murderers?' Faced with that question, the solution of killing them, deporting them or locking them up is rejected by the anarchists, who regard prison as a school of criminality which causes harm not just to the wrongdoer but also to his family (see discussion in Weide, Chapter 9 in this volume). From that text of *Freedom* reproduced in *La Anarquía*, the solution was to 'resign ourselves to convert criminals into honest men'. They believed this could be achieved in a simple way: they argue that with what is spent on 'wars, police and prisons there would be more than enough to redeem the ignorance and poverty of those who today are driven to crime'. Furthermore, given that crime is not an exception in society, but the general rule, committed by rich and poor, the solution must lie in regenerating society as a whole.

From the anarchist perspective, denying punishment did not mean denying all types of jurisdiction or intervention. In 1886, Lorenzo argued:

> In the society of the future, we are certain, and no one will dare to contradict us, that, having destroyed the causes that promote crime by true enlightenment, by attractive work and by sublime solidarity, crime will disappear, and if in a rare case some *criminal, mad or wicked*, should recall these times of barbarism in which we live, the whole social mass will be moved, wounded in the fibre of feeling, wounded in the immense love that will unite in a fraternal bond all humanity, and would opportunely apply *the pathological or moral treatment to obtain the cure or rehabilitation of the unfortunate.* (Lorenzo, 1886, emphasis added to show how anarchist thought of the time was also influenced by positivist thought)

The anti-authoritarian principle led to the denial of coercion, but it opened up the way to accepting methods that arose spontaneously and that had, above all, a curative or therapeutic purpose. According to *Acción Libertaria* (1911), jails and prisons were to be replaced by work farms and health homes, with all the improvements that progressive science advised. The stick and the shackle were to be replaced by the book and the pen. Only then could the moralization, the dignification and the relative improvement of the so-called delinquent begin to bear its beneficial fruits for society.

Other anarchists such as Albert (1909) expressed themselves in the same way:

> Bourgeois society contributes greatly to making the criminal before punishing him. And that is why the punishment revolts us more than the crime itself. To stop this rising criminality there is no other remedy than the society of justice, equality and free labour that we want to found. We do not say that this remedy will be sovereign, that it will straighten out all deviations as if by magic. *Perhaps there will always be abnormal and maladjusted people.* There will be sick people who we will have to take care of with patience, to cure with gentleness, with interest. And we will not throw them like beasts to the chopping block of the guillotine. (Emphasis added)

As can be seen, the critique of bourgeois terminology and a reappropriation of certain labels did not really lead to an abolition of certain kinds of concepts. 'Criminal', 'crime', 'sick' and 'abnormal' continued to be part of the anarchist language in their proposals for the future society.

Repeating arguments expressed in other areas, the anarchist justification and defence of certain postulates relies on science. When speaking of the confinement or separation of a member of the community, it is defended on the grounds that he will be treated 'scientifically, in healing establishments, not in infamous prisons, not with life or temporary sentences'.[14] It is also understood that with the 'establishment of a rational educational system, these cases would decrease' (Giner de los Ríos, 1902).

Here we can also observe a convergence with so many other criminological postulates that defended scientific and educational treatments. The difference, once again, lies in the content and perspective of *libertarian* education and science.

What can we learn from these positions for abolitionism today?

After this historical review that demonstrates the relationship between anarchism, positivism and abolitionism, we can ask ourselves what relevance it may have today for those engaged in the political struggles of the present.

It is evident that not everything pointed out in this epoch is reproducible in the present. In the first place, it must be made clear that the adoption of much of the anarchist discourse of positivism led to insurmountable contradictions, notably the idea that those people who could not adapt to a new order should be 'treated', through science and care. But in the end, defending scientific theories that were reinterpreted in an anarchist mode did not cease to reinforce tools that were being used precisely by the bourgeois order to repress the poor and the workers' movements. Although the anarchist discourse of evolutionism was clearly based on the principles of Kropotkin – that is, solidarity as a revolutionary mechanism – these postulates, in large part, are incompatible with libertarian and emancipatory thinking today. It is not possible to generalize an alternative discourse by taking the same (liberal) principles and the same tools (from positive science) as the ruling class.

Beyond this warning, the convergence between anarchist ideology and penal abolitionism continues to be relevant. Both discourses, taken broadly: (i) conceive of the penal system as a social problem in itself; (ii) make harsh criticisms of the role of the law and its regulatory function in social relations; (iii) deny the legitimacy of the state to punish; and (iv) agree that abolitionism, more than a concrete programme, is a political attitude. In relation to this, a change in the model of justice must involve a change in the way we conceive of punishment in both social and cultural terms.

These obvious theoretical links between libertarian ideology and penal abolitionism might lead us to ask why the latter has not relied more on the rich theoretical and epistemological material provided by anarchism. One reason may lie in the fact that both are widely discredited, inside and outside academia, as utopian, impractical and unrealistic, which has clearly marginalized them. To this is also added the self-marginalization that anti-institutional criticism entails.

But the key, then and now, lies in the fundamental denial of the State's power to punish (see also Zorin, Chapter 4 in this volume). The constant denunciation of that power to punish, in whatever form it materializes (softer or harsher, penal or administrative, legal or illegal), was and must remain the task of an abolitionist critique of the criminal justice system and of state-sponsored criminology. Although it is only one of the manifestations of that power, prisons must continue to be denounced, especially when we see that after decades of criticism and unveiling the ineffectiveness of its (changing) official functions, prison continues to have a central power in the culture of punishment. Prison has never been, and can never be, more than an exercise in violence. Scott has said that a common language is needed in order to bring together all the fragmented anti-hegemonic and anti-prison thinking. This language entails understanding prisons within the concept of state violence: 'This is not to say that violence is the only way that prisons can be analysed and conceptualised, but it may be a politically significant way of expressing the inherent harms of penal confinement and mobilising resistance' (Scott, 2016: 4).

Finally, we cannot ignore the fact that part of the discourse of institutional power highlighted in this chapter continues to be present. In Catalonia and Spain we have experienced this in recent years with the police operations ('Ice', 'Pandora', 'Piñata', 'Araña' and so on)[15] against the anarchist movement. The discourse continues to repeat a standard that identifies 'anarchism' with radicalism, with explosive devices, with the reading and propagation of dangerous ideas, and that has served as a justification for the repression of social movements. More broadly, this is repeated in the dichotomy that is often drawn between civilization (the West) and barbarism (everything else). That is why the anarchist thinking of the 19th and early 20th centuries which denounced the criminal power of the capitalist state form and its production of massive social harm continue to be valid today in an abolitionist critique of the criminal system.

Notes

[1] Following the progressive line of thought developed by Auguste Comte (of the three stages of knowledge), the Enlightenment – and therefore criminal law – belonged to the metaphysical stage of knowledge (the second, after the theological, both not scientific). The next, higher, stage of knowledge was the positivist one.

[2] In Spanish in the original. All translations from Spanish are mine.

[3] Kropotkin's articles, published between 1890 and 1896, would serve as a basis for the publication of his most important book in this sense, *Mutual Aid: A Factor of Evolution* (1989[1902]). This theory had a great influence on Spanish anarchist thought, since the articles from *The Nineteenth Century* had been translated in large part throughout 1892 by the anarchist publication *El Productor*. The book was translated by Josep Prat and published in 1906.

4 He was one of the most important Spanish writers of the so-called Generation of 98. Despite this time of great anarchist influence, his thought became increasingly conservative until he became 'Azorin', which is how the great Spanish writer is known by conservatives.
5 *In Russian and French Prisons*, London: Ward and Downey, 1887.
6 Mella was one of the most important anarchist theorists in Spain at that time. He was one of those who knew the most about the theories of positivist criminologists (he came to answer directly to Lombroso for his book on anarchism), of the debate on Darwinian evolutionism, and of the most active authors in the task of anarchist propaganda through the publication of texts, books and through talks and participation in meetings and congresses.
7 See *El Corsario*, for example, nos. 219 and 234 of February and June 1896; *El Porvenir del Obrero*, nos. 153 (24 March 1903), 195 (14 April 1905) and 196 (21 April 1905); 'Martirologio obrero', in *Bandera Social*, no. 92, 23 December 1886; *El Productor*, different issues of 1887.
8 The Montjuic trials entailed the arrest of around 400 people, many of whom were tortured, and ended with the murder of five workers, after trials conducted with a clear lack of evidence and respect for due process. Among those repressed and tortured, or who had to run away because of the persecution were important figures in the libertarian movement such as Montseny, Lorenzo, Tarrida de Mármol, Sunye, Clarmunt, Prat and Gustavo. See, among others, Mella and Prat (1897) *La barbarie gubernamental en España*, Brooklyn.
9 In relation to massacres in America, several articles of *El Libertario* referred, for example, to the massacre and exploitation of rubber tappers in Putumayo ('Relato del Libro Azul', no. 2, 17 August 1912; 'La obra de la civilización burguesa. Los crímenes del Putumayo', No. 25, 1 February 1913; 'Frescura gubernamental. Los crímenes del Putumayo', No. 33, 29 March 1913).
10 See, for example, the description of the Ceuta prison given in 1903 by Francisco Prieto, one of the prisoners released from the Jerez event, where he describes beatings, filthy dungeons, rotten food, punishments of deprivation of drink and food, physical restraints and so on. As a result of these conditions, many did not survive. Letter published by *El Productor*, No. 18, 28 March 1903.
11 Malthusianism, a school of thought based on the ideas of Thomas Malthus, maintains that human population growth will exceed available resources, leading to scarcity and environmental deterioration. This led to eugenicist proposals to control the population, such as birth control, sterilization, the prohibition of mixed marriages or even death. From an anarchist point of view, neo-Malthusianism emphasizes that scarcity is not due to the number of inhabitants, but to the hoarding of resources by the rich and proposes a series of measures to improve the living conditions of the working class through birth control.
12 This is reported in *Acción Libertaria*, which reproduces an editorial of *Salud y Fuerza* signed by Rafael Zuriaga in which he defends neo-Malthusianism as a solution to these behaviours (see 'Opiniones y juicios', No. 18, 14 April 1911).
13 Ferri puts it this way in 'Educación, ambiente y criminalidad', published in *Nuevos estudios de Antropología criminal* (see Peset and Peset, 1975: 338–340).
14 'El presidiario', *Bandera Social*, no. 38, November 1885; see Álvarez Junco, 1976: 270.
15 Police operations in Spain between 2014 and 2015 targeted the anarchist movement and uncovered 'indications' of guilt such as having anarchist books or posters of anarchist events. In other words, those targeted were criminalized not for criminal acts, but for professing anarchist beliefs that were seen as radical.

References

Acción Libertaria, (1911) no. 10, 20 January.
Acracia (1887) 'Miscelánea', no. 18, June.

Albert, C. (1909) 'El crimen y el castigo', in *Acracia. Suplemento de Tierra y Libertad*, no. 5.
Álvarez Junco, J. (1976) *La ideología política del anarquismo español (1868–1910)*, Madrid: Siglo XXI.
Bandera Social (1885) 'El Presidiario', 1 November.
Bulffi, L. (1918[1905]) *Huelga de vientres*, Barcelona: Biblioteca Salud y Fuerza.
Calderón, A. (1898) 'Abriendo mercados', *La Idea Libre*, no. 152, 17 December.
El Corsario (1892) 'Gobierno anárquico', no. 89, 7 February.
Fernández González, M. (2011) *Del odio al bien. Misericordia, higienismo, urbanismo y civismo como culturas de control en el Raval de Barcelona*, Memòria de Màster en 'Criminología y Sociología Jurídico-Penal', Universitat de Barcelona.
Giner de los Ríos, F. (1902) 'La escuela que cerrará los presidios' in *Almanaque de la Revista Blanca*, Madrid.
Hardy, G. (1904) 'La lucha por la existencia y el neomaltusianismo', in *Salud y Fuerza*, no. 1, Barcelona.
Íñiguez, M. (2008) *Enciclopedia histórica del anarquismo español*, Asociación Isaac Puente, Vitoria.
Kropotkin, P. (1977[1887]) *Las Prisiones* (intro. by M. Morey; trans: E Heras), José J. de Olañeta, Barcelona.
Kropotkin, P. (1989[1902]) *El apoyo mutuo* (intro. A. J. Cappelletti), 3rd edn, Madre Tierra, Cali.
Kropotkin, P. (1907[1892]) *The Conquest of Bread*, Putnam.
La Anarquía (1892) 'The abolition of crime', 3 March.
La Anarquía (1913) 'Misceláneas', 28 September.
La Anarquía (1890) 'Misceláneas', no. 7, 28 September.
Lorenzo, A. (1886) 'La pena de muerte', in *Acracia. Revista sociológica*, no. 6, June, Barcelona.
Lorenzo, A. (1895) 'El obrero revolucionario', in *La Idea Libre* no. 36, 5.
Martínez Ruiz, J. (1899) *La Sociología Criminal* (Foreword by. F. Pi y Margall), Librería de Fernando de Fé, Madrid.
Mella, R. (1975[1925]) *Ideario*. (Intro: F. Montseny; Foreword. Ed 1925: J. Prat; Foreword. Ed 1953: F. Alaiz), CNT, Toulouse.
Mella, R. (1978[1896]) *Lombroso y los anarquistas* (Joint edition with Mella, R 1896, *Lombroso y los anarquistas. Refutation* and Lombroso, C., 1894, *Los anarquistas*), Biblioteca Júcar, Madrid.
Molinari (1907) *Páginas Libres (Revista mensual de filosofía, ciencia, sociología, literatura, arte y critica)*, Barcelona), no. 8, 15 September.
Nettlau, M. (1897) *Revival of the Inquisition: Details of the Tortures Inflicted on Spanish Political Prisoners*, London: J. Perry.
Niceforo, A. and Sighele, S. (1897) *La mala vita a Roma*, Turin: Roux & Frassati.

Peset, J. and Peset, M. (1975) *Lombroso y la escuela positivista italiana*, Madrid: CSIC.

Scott, D. (2016) 'Speaking the language of state violence: an abolitionist perspective', *European Group for the Study of Violence and Social Control Newsletter*, February, pp 4–20.

Scott, D. (ed.) (2025) *Abolitionist Voices*, Bristol: Bristol University Press.

Tarrida del Mármol, F. (1897) *Les inquisiteurs d'Espagne, Montjuich, Cuba, Philippines* (París).

Tierra y Libertad (1907) 'Crímenes y criminales', 7 November.

Tierra y Libertad (1913) 'La violencia y el miedo', Editorial, 23 April.

YO (1913) 'Why misery exists', in *Acción Libertaria*, 30 May.

11

Fear or Freedom? Errico Malatesta on Crime and Punishment

Davide Turcato

Introduction

The Italian anarchist Errico Malatesta (1853–1932) was a major figure in the history of the international anarchist movement and the author of hugely popular pamphlets, such as *Between Peasants* (1884), *Anarchy* (1891) and *At the Café* (1897). His militancy spanned the first six decades of that movement, from its foundation at the St Imier Congress in 1872 to the rise of the Second Spanish Republic, which marked one of the highest points in that movement's history. This chapter discusses Malatesta's views on crime and punishment that underlay his penal abolitionism. After a preliminary overview of his anarchism, the main body of the chapter will contrastively describe those views by outlining what may be termed a 'competing contradiction' – to use Thomas Mathiesen's phrase (Mathiesen, 1974: 14) – between the statist approach to punishment and Malatesta's anarchist approach, in pursuit of the equally asserted aim of spreading moral behaviour among social actors. The two final sections will spell out the implications of Malatesta's ideas, respectively, for his short-term practices and for penal abolitionists today.

Malatesta's anarchism

A good starting point for outlining Malatesta's anarchism is his definition of anarchy, which is as concise and seemingly obvious as it is enlightening: 'Anarchy, in common with socialism, has as its basis, its point of departure, its essential environment, *equality of conditions*; its beacon is *solidarity* and *freedom* is its method' (Malatesta, 1974: 47). Equality of conditions means primarily equal access to the means of production – that is, socialism. Solidarity is a beacon, an intentionally pursued value that drives social action. And freedom is a method. The concept of method is central for Malatesta: 'A programme which is concerned with the bases of the social structure cannot do other than suggest a method.' Method is what primarily makes the difference between parties. Therefore, 'one must consider anarchy above all as a method' (Malatesta, 1974: 45). The anarchist method is the method of freedom – that is, free initiative and free agreements. According to this method, the best solutions to social problems can be experimentally and pluralistically found. Anarchy is thus defined not as a static blueprint, but as a process. Thus, immediately after defining anarchy, Malatesta explains that 'it is not perfection, it is not the absolute ideal which like the horizon recedes as fast as we approach it; but it is the way open to all progress and all improvements for the benefit of everybody' (Malatesta, 1974: 47).

The definition of this process in terms of the individual disposition of solidarity and the method of freedom highlights a fundamental presupposition in Malatesta – that is, the construal of society in methodologically individualistic terms: society is the resultant, the composition effect, of the intentional actions of all its members. This presupposition underpins Malatesta's distinctive *voluntarism* – that is, the idea that society has no inexorable direction, but takes the direction that the combined wills of its members give to it. This presupposition also sheds light on Malatesta's principle of *coherence between ends and means*. This was his antidote to a danger that has become well known in sociology – the *displacement of goals*, the phenomenon of means becoming ends in themselves. Anarchism as a method, methodological individualism and coherence between ends and means are the theoretical pillars of another distinctive trait of Malatesta's anarchism, his *gradualism*. On the one hand, the anarchists' present means are ends in the making; on the other hand, anarchy is quite simply a society of anarchists, of individuals practising the method of freedom. Since, in methodological individualistic terms, the anarchists' influence on society is progressively felt as they grow in number and strength, anarchy is gradually approached as anarchists spread their influence on society. In this spirit, for Malatesta, no struggle was too partial to be worth fighting: 'Every blow given to the institutions of private property and to the government is a step towards Anarchy' (Malatesta, 2014c: 300). What mattered was not so much the scope of a struggle, but the method by which it was fought – direct action rather than parliamentary means.

Many of those partial struggles concerned the penal system. What was Malatesta's appraisal of that system? What was his ground for advocating its abolition? Malatesta's focus on method lends itself to answer these questions by comparing his method with the antithetical statist method of deterrence as the primary way of ensuring security and peaceful coexistence. This comparison is carried out in the next four sections: after outlining the statist view and its critique by Malatesta, his alternative to a coercive order and his approach to crime and punishment are discussed.

The statist view

The traditional justification of the state is that its rise marks the transition from a condition of insecurity and universal war to one of security and peace. In the classical account set out in 1651 by Thomas Hobbes in his *Leviathan*, the natural condition of humanity 'during the time men live without a common Power to keep them all in awe' is a state of war of every man against every man, where everyone lives in continual fear of violent death (Hobbes, 1965[1651]: 62). The state is established to tie men by fear of punishment to the observation of the laws of nature summarized by the maxim of 'doing to others, as wee [sic] would be done to' (Hobbes, 1965[1651]: 85).

Thus, the concepts of state and punishment are coextensive. It is only when a power arises that ties all men by fear of punishment that peace can be secured. Conversely, punishment is not just any harm inflicted upon any wrongdoer; it must be inflicted by a public authority to transgressors of the law and it cannot exceed what the law prescribes, on pain of turning from a punishment to a mere act of hostility (Hobbes, 1965[1651]: 161–162). The Italian penologist Cesare Beccaria frames punishment as a safeguard of liberty. In society, he argues, men surrender a share of their natural liberty to the sovereign so that they might enjoy the rest of it in peace and safety. However, every individual 'always tries not only to withdraw his own share, but also to usurp for himself that of others'. Punishments are the 'tangible motives' required to 'prevent the despotic spirit, which is in every man, from plunging the laws of society into its original chaos' (Beccaria, 1963: 11–12).[1] The link between state and punishment is most explicitly asserted by the exponent of legal positivism Hans Kelsen, who equates state and law, and defines the state as a 'relatively centralized coercive order' (Kelsen, 1970: 318) – that is, an order that reacts against events regarded as detrimental to society with a coercive act, which inflicts evil on the culprit (Kelsen, 1970: 33).

The fundamental aim of punishment is not so much retribution or individual prevention as general prevention in the form of deterrence. 'Hurt inflicted', Hobbes writes, 'if lesse than the benefit of transgressing, is not Punishment', because the end of punishment is 'the disposing of men to obey the Law' (Hobbes, 1965[1651]: 162). In a similar vein, the utilitarian Beccaria argues that punishments should be chosen so as to 'make the strongest and most lasting impression on the minds of men, and inflict the least torment on the body of the criminal'. In order for a punishment to attain its end, 'the evil which it inflicts has only to exceed the advantage derivable from the crime ... All beyond this is superfluous and for that reason tyrannical' (Beccaria, 1963: 42–43).

In sum, the state acts as a moralizer of its subjects through the incentive of threatened punishment. The statist perspective is thus entirely inscribed in the horizon of fear. The progress from the natural state of war and insecurity to the civil state of peace and security is a transition from fear of everyone to fear of the sovereign alone. Thus, Beccaria recommends: 'See to it that men fear the laws and fear nothing else. For fear of the laws is salutary, but fatal and fertile for crimes is one man's fear of another' (Beccaria, 1963: 94). As much in the state of nature as in the civil state, fear is the fabric of human relations. This presupposition, both descriptive and normative, is utterly rejected by Malatesta.

A critique of the state

Malatesta, like Hobbes, aspires to a society where individuals peacefully cooperate, and wishes, with Beccaria, that all human beings equally enjoy as much liberty as possible. For him, however, the state is part of the problem, not of the solution.

To begin with, Malatesta sees continuity rather than contrast between the state of nature and the commonwealth, as described by Hobbes: 'If human existence is a struggle between men, there must obviously be winners and losers, and government ... will certainly never fall into the hands of those who lose' (Malatesta, 1974: 23). Indeed, Hobbes himself had maintained that a commonwealth can be established not only by mutual agreement of the subjects but also by conquest. The difference consists only in the source of the subjects' fear: they can submit to a sovereign for fear of one another or for fear of the conqueror himself (Hobbes, 1651: 102). And while the social contract is a fictional device, there is no lack of examples of states established by force.

At the heart of Malatesta's critique is the argument that the logic underlying the rise of the state is self-defeating. In attributing the monopoly of force to a minority to the end of curbing everyone's evil passions, the subjects give free rein to that minority's very same passions. Beccaria claims: 'No man ever freely sacrificed a portion of his personal liberty merely in behalf of the common good.' This, he continues, is a chimera that exists only in romances. If it were possible, 'every one of us would prefer that the compacts binding others did not bind us' (Beccaria, 1963: 11). This is the well-known 'free-rider' problem, which political theorists regard as the chief reason why a government is required to ensure everyone's cooperation in the provision of collective goods. However, government is the ideal place for free-riders, as they can seek to maximize their own benefit – as anyone would do in the absence of constraints – while being able to force everyone else to cooperate. Malatesta thus summarizes the point: 'The realisation of the usefulness of cooperation, which should have led to the triumph of solidarity in all human relations, instead gave rise to private property and government.' It was still association and cooperation, 'but it was a way of cooperation, imposed and controlled by a few for their own personal interest' (Malatesta, 1974: 28). Beccaria himself, a century earlier, had to acknowledge that most laws are 'a tribute paid by all to the convenience of some few' (Beccaria, 1963: 94). In brief, punishment is the means by which rulers, rather than moralizers, become monopolizers and even enforcers of immoral behaviour.

A moral social order

In step with his critique of the state, Malatesta's way to the spread of morality, in a full reversal of the statist logic, involves no use of punishment. From the statist perspective, giving up a coercive order amounts to plunging society into chaos. However, in rejecting a coercive order, Malatesta does not reject order; he rejects coercion. As Kelsen explains, there are social orders that do not prescribe sanctions, such as moral orders (Kelsen, 1970: 27). Malatesta objects to coercive laws, not to norms. He agrees that everyone should submit to universal norms – that is, norms that are valid for everyone. Moral norms are social norms, as they regulate the behaviour of men to each other. However, different individuals can uphold different, and equally universal, moral norms. Thus, Malatesta does not object to norms, but to their monopoly. In its place he advocates a distributed model, where social order arises in the form of customs and habits, in a continuous and spontaneous process of uncoerced interaction and mutual adjustment among equals.

Anarchist reliance on spontaneous processes tends to be uncharitably interpreted as a fideistic belief in a pre-established harmony. However, spontaneous processes are ubiquitous and unproblematically accepted when advocated by non-anarchists. It suffices to mention Friedrick Hayek's 'extended order of human cooperation' – better known as 'capitalism' – which 'resulted not from human design or intention but spontaneously ... from unintentionally conforming to certain traditional and largely *moral* practices' (Hayek, 1989: 6). An even more fitting example in the present context is the account of language provided by the American philosopher Donald Davidson, who emphatically argues that 'there is no such thing as a language' if, as many philosophers and linguists maintain, we mean by 'language' a precise and specifiable set of syntactic and semantic rules and conventions – as usually encoded in grammars and dictionaries – to which speakers of the language must conform. Rather, Davidson argues, language does not need a centralized set of norms to work, but is distributed over (and constantly remoulded by) a myriad of independent, cooperative interactions (Davidson, 2005a, 2005b). Likewise, Malatesta's social order – as per his definition of anarchy in terms of equality, freedom and solidarity – retains the equality and freedom of Hobbes' state of nature, while realizing his moral law of 'doing to others, as we would be done to' through voluntary cooperation rather than coercion.

Malatesta's views on crime and punishment

Malatesta's advocacy of a moral social order shares two premises with the statist view: the first is that the spread of moral behaviour is the mainstay of a peaceful and cooperative society; the second is that state and punishment are coextensive. However, his horizon is antithetical and mutually exclusive with the statist one: freedom, not fear defines that horizon. Accordingly, his views are based on a blanket rejection of both state and punishment and on a redefinition of the question of crime. It is this combination of shared premises and radically alternative approaches that makes this contrast reminiscent of Mathiesen's 'competing competition'. This section illustrates Malatesta's views by discussing first his replacement of the notion of 'crime' with that of 'anti-social behaviour' and then his noncoercive approach to anti-social behaviour in the anarchist society. Malatesta's point of view is further enlightened by discussing some criticisms to which it has been submitted and by clarifying its methodological humanistic foundations.

Anti-social behaviour

Malatesta's point of departure is that individual freedom finds its limit in everyone else's equal freedom. This condition sets apart his self-sustainable version of freedom — which is simultaneously enjoyed by everyone, in line with the reciprocity of Hobbes' moral law — from the unrestrained freedom of Hobbes' state of nature. Violation of freedom thus conceived is what defines anti-social behaviour. To the extent that Malatesta talks about 'crime', it is in this sense rather than in the sense of acts punished by the criminal code 'because they offend the privileges of the ruling classes' (Malatesta, 2021a: 347).

For Malatesta, the main path to removing anti-social behaviour is to remove its causes. Crimes, he argues, 'derive either from natural causes (congenital or acquired defects of constitution) or from social causes (poverty, ignorance, vices, etc.)'. The former must be entrusted to the care of physicians and alienists, while the latter, which are by far predominant, will disappear with better social organization (Malatesta, 2021a: 347). However, in addition to determining immediate criminal acts, social conditions 'produce habits, dispositions and incapacities that cannot suddenly and completely disappear as soon as the conditions that produced them have changed' (Malatesta, 2021b: 351). And as long as anti-social behaviour exists, people must defend themselves.

Everyone has a right to resist anti-social behaviour — that is, encroachment upon one's own freedom. In fact, resisting evil is not just a right; it is also a duty, in step with the moral law of 'doing to others, as we would be done to'. Just as we would wish to be helped if we were under threat, so we should help those under threat. Thus, in critiquing Tolstoyism, Malatesta acknowledges its morality, but at the same time argues that one would be 'terrifically selfish if he were to let others suffer oppression without trying to come to their defence' (Malatesta, 2014b: 204; see also Zorin, Chapter 4, in this volume). Viewing resistance to anti-social behaviour as a duty turns it from individual resistance to social resistance. However, viewing such resistance as a social task does not mean that it befalls 'society' as an undivided whole. Society is made up of individuals, and accordingly social defence is mutual defence among individuals.

Malatesta's approach to contrasting anti-social behaviour can be qualified as minimalistic because its scope is limited to resistance. This is the only legitimate purpose for the use of force. The 'constructive' use of force for positive goals – 'doing good by force', as Malatesta calls it – is firmly rejected: 'For us, violence only serves and can only serve to repel violence, and when it is used to achieve positive ends, it either fails completely, or succeeds in establishing the oppression and exploitation of one over the other' (Malatesta, 2021i: 632). This attitude towards violence extends to Malatesta's outlook on revolutions as well. Violence, he argues, is necessary to resist the opponent's violence, but it contains the danger of 'transforming the revolution into a brutal melee without the light of an ideal'. Hence, anarchists 'must insist on the moral aims of the movement and on the necessity, on the duty to contain violence within the limits of strict necessity' (Malatesta, 2021j: 649).

Any punitive intent is alien to Malatesta's views. In the 'terrible age-old duel between so-called crime and so-called justice', he argues, 'one can see how the most barbarous tortures do not serve to eliminate or diminish crimes'. Even the reforms of the punitive system 'always leave unchanged the principle of vengeance, the system of inflicting new suffering on those most in need of loving help' (Malatesta, 2021f: 422). Therefore, anarchists, 'inspired only by the need to defend and the desire to correct and benefit … must seek the means to achieve the goal without stumbling into the dangers of authoritarianism' (Malatesta, 2021b: 352). Malatesta's reference to the principle of vengeance shows that he is opposed to punishment not only as a means of deterrence, but also of retribution. In fact, justice itself, which underlies retribution and is central to many abolitionists, does not rank highest in Malatesta's value system. In a letter of 1931 to his friend Luigi Fabbri, he maintains that the anarchist programme, being based on solidarity, goes beyond justice itself. Justice, he argues, means giving others the equivalent of what they give you. It means 'reciprocity, exchange, proportion, and consequently implies calculation, measurement. Its symbol is the scale'. In contrast, love means giving all one can give, without any calculation. In economics, justice corresponds to the collectivist formula 'to each according to his contribution' and love to the communist formula 'to each according to his needs'. In the human soul, Malatesta concludes, there are two opposing feelings: the feeling of love for one's fellow human beings, which always works for the best, and the feeling of justice, 'which is a constant cause of struggle, because each person finds just what suits him best' (Malatesta, 1984: 316–317).

Within the boundaries outlined earlier – the definition of anti-social behaviour as encroachment upon the equal freedom of others, the universal right to resist anti-social behaviour and the minimal use of force in resisting it – any means of defence are legitimate for Malatesta. Moreover, the right – or rather the moral duty – to resist anti-social behaviour equally holds in the present and in the future society. In both cases, whoever hinders a moral social order based on respect for each other's freedom and equal access to the means of livelihood is to be resisted. The difference between the two scenarios is only of scale – though it is clearly a significant one. The solutions concerning the anarchist society, Malatesta writes in 1922, presuppose that 'delinquency is reduced to sporadic, individual, truly pathological cases. For if delinquents were too numerous and powerful, if they were, for example, what the bourgeoisie and fascism are today, then it is not yet a question of discussing what to do in anarchy: it is a question of fighting and winning' (Malatesta, 2021h: 628). In such a scenario, fighting and winning delinquents takes nothing less than armed insurrection. However, the scenario that most concerns the pragmatist Malatesta is the aftermath of a revolution.

Anarchy and 'crime'

In fact, most of Malatesta's writings on the subject of crime date from the early 1920s, shortly after a socialist revolution had seemed a practicable prospect, in the wake of the Russian Revolution, and therefore the problems of a postrevolutionary society had been posed with a novel sense of urgency. Malatesta's concern is not so much with a full-fledged socialist society, but with the aftermath of a successful insurrection, when anti-social habits are still lingering (Malatesta, 2021c). However, the ideas put forward by him are not contingent proposals confined to a specific – and presently unlikely – scenario, but rather are illustrations of the broadly applicable workings of the method of freedom.

Just as Malatesta advocates a distributed model for social norms, so he does for social defence: 'We see no other but to leave it to those concerned, leave it to the people, that is, to the mass of citizens, who will act differently according to circumstances and according to their varying degrees of civilisation' (Malatesta, 2021b: 353). Leaving social defence to the people means persuading people that everyone must intervene in defence of the weak and possibly 'become judges and, in extreme cases … entrust those found guilty to the custody and care of an asylum, always open to public scrutiny' (Malatesta, 2023c: 210). As an example of an extreme case of irreducible offender who 'must be put in a position to do no harm', he mentions 'a *satyr* who rapes and tears the little bodies of poor girls' – what would be called today a 'serial killer' (Malatesta, 2023b: 199). These views led a commentator to present Malatesta as an advocate of a 'gendarme society' (Marconi, 1979: 116). The phrase may be catchy, but it is more confusing than explanatory. A *gendarme* is by definition an agent of the monopoly of force, whereas Malatesta is precisely advocating the abolition of that monopoly, and equating society to an individual hints at a view of society as an undivided whole, which is the exact opposite of Malatesta's view of society as an aggregate of interacting individuals.

The latter is the view that underlies Malatesta's outlook on social defence as a spontaneous, pluralistic and experimentally evolving process. He acknowledges the complexity of the problem and maintains, accordingly, that 'everything that can be said and done to combat crime can only be of relative value – relative to time, place and above all to the degree of moral development of the environment in which the events take place' (Malatesta, 2021d: 372). As in Davidson's account of language, speakers come to the communication process with different 'theories' of their language, but tend to converge on a shared understanding, so do social actors in Malatesta's account of social defence (see also Testa, Chapter 8, in this volume). So, even for those who share the anarchist definition of anti-social behaviour, opinions vary as to what is criminal or not. Nevertheless, the needs of collective life give rise in every society to 'a certain morality, which recognizes for each person certain rights, the violation of which, by fraud or violence, is considered a crime, and as such is condemned and persecuted by public opinion' (Malatesta, 2023a: 76). The concept of social duty, and accordingly of anti-social behaviour, is constantly evolving, so that many actions that were considered as pertaining to individual rights – such as the education of children or the basic rules of hygiene – will acquire 'the character of things that concern everyone and must be regulated in accordance with the general interest'. However, social duties must 'develop freely, without any external sanction other than the esteem or dislike of fellow citizens' (Malatesta, 2021b: 352).

Malatesta was aware of the pitfalls of entrusting social defence to the people, as he cast a realistic eye on the fickleness of popular masses: 'But what to do about it? We have to work with the material at hand and try to get the best out of it' (Malatesta, 2021d: 373). In fact, his main preoccupation was to avoid the creation of a specialized body devoted to social defence. Hence, he rejected the proposal of his friend and former anarchist Francesco Saverio Merlino to organize social defence like any other public service. He approved in general specialization and division of labour, for example, in railways or hospitals, but he argued that 'it is dangerous and corrupting, though technically it might be advantageous, to allow someone to be a policeman and a judge' (Malatesta, 2021d: 373). Long-term consequences trumped immediate practical advantages. It would always be better, he declared, to have 'the injustice, the transient violence of the people than the leaden cloak, the legalized violence of the judicial and police state' (Malatesta, 2021b: 353).

Malatesta's key concern is what Karl Popper calls the 'paradox of freedom'. It was first formulated by Plato, to whom Popper attributes the following question: 'What if it is the will of the people that they should not rule, but a tyrant instead?' (Popper, 1945a: 109). Freedom, Popper argues, defeats itself if it is unlimited: 'Unlimited freedom means that a strong man is free to bully one who is weak and to rob him of his freedom' (Popper, 1945b: 116). According to him, the paradox 'was solved by Kant, who demanded that the freedom of each man should be restricted, but not beyond what is necessary to safeguard an equal degree of freedom for all' (Popper, 1945b: 42). Likewise, Malatesta's concern is to ensure that the method of freedom do not defeat itself by either allowing a de facto monopoly of force or the encroachment by some on the equal freedom of others. His focus is on the process: he knows that the process is fallible and can lead to excesses, but it can correct itself as long as it aims to steer clear from either pole of the Hobbesian horizon – the monopoly of force or 'anarchy' in its pejorative sense. Thus, social defence can neither be delegated nor neglected.

There is a reason why Malatesta describes the anarchist approach to social defence without providing much detail about specific proposals. He acknowledges the vagueness and diversity of anarchist views. However, he adds, this is not a bad thing, but rather 'the characteristic and the merit of anarchism', which does not intend to predetermine the ways of the future, but simply 'to ensure that social evolution will have the conditions of freedom necessary for it to achieve the maximum well-being, the maximum material, moral and intellectual development for all' (Malatesta, 2021d: 372). The framework that Malatesta describes constitutes all that is both necessary and sufficient to outline the anarchist approach to social defence. Thus, responding to Merlino's charge that anarchists refuse to detail the forms and norms of their organizations for social defence, Malatesta agrees that it is necessary to specify such forms and norms, but at the same time he makes it clear that 'this must be done as a proposal and an experiment, without anyone having the power to impose their own solutions' (Malatesta, 2021e: 389). All such proposals would be anarchist proposals, as long as they conform to the method of freedom, but none of them could be inscribed in the anarchist programme.

Criticisms of Malatesta's views

In recent times, Malatesta has been subjected to two criticisms, both levelled from self-proclaimed anarchist positions, but heading in opposite directions: one charged Malatesta's account of social defence with stopping too short, and the other with going too far. Marco Cossutta contrasts Malatesta's ideas with those of Merlino: Malatesta entrusted social defence to the people – while admitting people's shortcomings – whereas Merlino rejected the dilemma between government and mob's rule, and proposed intermediate forms, such as people's courts and public security services. Cossutta considers Malatesta's viewpoint contradictory and his refusal to be more specific dogmatic. After remarking that he preferred the transient violence of the people to the legalized violence of the state, Malatesta had added that anarchists, at any rate, 'are but one of the forces acting in society, and history will walk, as always, according to the resultant of forces' and had concluded: 'In practice, what can happen will happen' (Malatesta, 2021b: 353). Latching on to this last remark, Cossutta brands Malatesta's position as facile, irresponsible and 'worthy of Pontius Pilate', as anarchists wash their hands of social defence by leaving it to the people (Cossutta, 2015: 178).

The key to understanding Malatesta's position is the *indeterminacy in social interaction*. In a book on the subject, Russell Hardin remarks that in contexts of strategic interaction – that is, in virtually all social contexts – 'I cannot simply act in a way that determines my own outcome. I can choose only a strategy, not an outcome. All that I determine with my strategy choice is some constraints on the possible array of outcomes I might get' (Hardin, 2003: 1). The difference between Malatesta and Merlino is the former's greater awareness of this theme. With his 'pragmatic' proposal, Merlino is aiming to strike a middle ground between the method of fear and the method of freedom. He is choosing an outcome. However, in terms of strategies, the two methods are incompatible. One must choose one or the other strategy. This is what Malatesta is doing. He is aware that the outcome is indeterminate and that it will likely be some middle ground between the two methods. It is this kind of awareness that he expresses with his remarks that anarchists 'are but one of the forces acting in society' and that 'what can happen will happen'. Yet he chooses the method of freedom as his strategy to constrain the possible outcomes – the middle ground – as best he can in his preferred direction.

Peppe Aiello detects an authoritarian deviation in Malatesta's contemplating the confinement of serial killers in an 'asylum'. He argues that if there is even a single person that the community decides should be locked up, there will have to be jailers; that if the mechanism of control 'is applied at one point it is bound to expand metastatically to all human relations', and that in assessing the dangerousness of individuals, 'we move from questioning one's actions to questioning one's motives' (Aiello, 2007). With some overemphasis, Aiello makes arguments that were known to Malatesta. His point about asylums was raised by Malatesta as early as 1897, in debate with Merlino. He admitted that there might be a technical advantage in having 'a corps of specialists charged with diagnosing dangerous neuroses and hauling the lunatics away to the asylum'. Unsurprisingly, though, anarchists were 'afraid of such learned doctors and orderlies pronouncing mad everyone who does not think as they do'. And he concluded mentioning the example of Lombroso, 'who would lock every one of us up, Merlino included!' (Malatesta, 2016: 96). However, Aiello seems to overlook a concern that is instead foremost in Malatesta, the paradox of freedom: practising the method of freedom means not only preventing any delegation of social control to a specialized body, but also preventing any practice of 'freedom' that amounts to trampling over the equal freedom of others. Neglecting either task ends up in the same result: the resurgence of the method of fear. This is how Malatesta puts the matter. The policeman, he argues, is more dangerous and harmful to society than the delinquent, in the sense of the ordinary petty criminal. However, 'it is certain that if people do not find themselves sufficiently protected by the public, they immediately call for the policeman's help'. Hence, the only way to prevent the existence of the policeman is 'to make him useless by replacing him in those functions in which he really does exercise a protective action for the public' (Malatesta, 2021d: 373). Aiello concludes his article by claiming that genuine freedom 'has a price and it is to be seen whether one is willing to pay it' (Aiello, 2007: 94). Yet, however high that price may be, it cannot possibly be self-defeat.

A humanistic perspective

What guarantee does Malatesta have that things will go his way, that people will behave morally in the absence of a 'power to keep them all in awe'? None.

There is a common misconception that anarchists believe in a benign human nature, such that harmony would naturally result after the abolition of the state. In fact, the opposite is the case. It is the statist view that is based on a Hobbesian negative anthropology, such that the state of nature is a state of universal war. In contrast, Malatesta holds a humanistic view. In his *Oration on the Dignity of Man,* which is considered a sort of manifesto of European humanism, Giovanni Pico della Mirandola depicts an anthropogony where man, God's last creature, is placed at the centre of the world and instead of being assigned a specific nature, like every other creature, is made free to acquire any nature by his own will, thus being able to degenerate into a beast as much as regenerate into an angel (Pico della Mirandola, 1956: 5–8). A contemporary version of the humanistic view can be found in the approach to social sciences known as *methodological individualism*. The central assumption of this approach, in the words of one of its foremost exponents, is that 'no social tendency exists which could not be altered if the individuals concerned both wanted to alter it and possessed the appropriate information' (Watkins, 1994: 443). From this perspective, the direction society takes is the resultant, the composition effect, of the intentional actions of all its members. This is also Malatesta's perspective.

Different views of human nature reverberate upon the respective consistency of statism and anarchism. Statists claim that the state is necessary because men cannot be spontaneously virtuous. This is the chimera that for Beccaria exists only in romances (Beccaria, 1963: 11). Yet they expect rulers to be spontaneously virtuous at the very time they are placed in the best position to unleash their passions. In contrast, anarchists self-fulfillingly but consistently falsify Beccaria's claim by their very existence. If being spontaneously virtuous is possible for some, it is possible for everyone. And, as Thomas Hobbes claimed, if a multitude of people could live morally, 'we might as well suppose all Man-kind to do the same; and then there neither would be, nor need to be any Civil Government' (Hobbes, 1965[1651]: 86). Indeed, as methodological individualists assume, 'no social tendency exists which could not be altered'.

Malatesta's anarchist practices

Anarchists not only prove the possibility of anarchy by their existence, but they also impact present society by their action, in proportion to their strength. The method of freedom not only characterized the anarchists' moral order, but also informed Malatesa's life, struggles and outlook on social issues, including crime. When, in 1899, he was shot in a leg by an opponent, he did not pursue his assailant, legally or otherwise. And when he and other London anarchists caught spies red-handed – for example, the French police spy Eugène Cotin in 1895 and the Italian Gennaro Rubini in 1902 – they sought no revenge, but simply put the spies 'in a position to do no harm' by publicly exposing them and letting them leave the country.

The method of freedom also characterized anarchist collective action. Malatesta was supportive of any struggle against the penal system, as long as its aim was to reduce human suffering and not to make prisons more acceptable. 'Certainly', he wrote 'we have an interest, as long as there is a government, that this be the least oppressive, that is, the least government possible' (Malatesta, 2023c: 211). Direct action, whether by legal or illegal means, was the anarchists' tactics. For instance, in 1897 Malatesta and the Italian anarchists were in the frontline in a campaign against a bill that made *domicilio coatto* (forced residence) part of the permanent legislation, de facto introducing deportation for political reasons as an ordinary procedure.

Likewise, the method of freedom gave a distinctive character to Malatesta's views on current issues pertaining to the penal system. For example, in 1922 he wrote an article advocating drug liberalization. The article, which was ahead of its time by at least half a century, bore the eloquent subtitle 'a proposal ... that will not be accepted' (Malatesta, 2021g). To illustrate the distinctiveness of Malatesta's outlook on penal issues, it is also instructive to compare his views on the death penalty with those of the capital punishment abolitionist Cesare Beccaria. The latter's argument against death penalty was that the death of a criminal is a terrible but momentary spectacle, and therefore a less effective method of deterring others than the continued example of a man deprived of his liberty (Beccaria, 1963: 47). Unsurprisingly, Malatesta also opposed the death penalty, but on a different ground. He acknowledged that there are rare 'moral monsters' whose death could not be mourned. When these were a constant danger to everyone and there were no other means of defence but to kill them, 'one might even admit the death penalty'. The trouble, though, is that the death penalty requires an executioner. 'Now', Malatesta concluded, 'the executioner – the one who orders and the one who executes – is or becomes a monster; and, monster for monster, it is better to let those who exist live than to create others' (Malatesta, 2023d: 232; see also Zorin, Chapter 4, in this volume). Beccaria is arguing from the perspective of the method of fear, Malatesta from that of the method of freedom.

The two methods are polar opposites. Ultimately, the hallmark of the method of freedom is the absence of fear. There is no telling what the anarchists' moral order will be like: what ideas of common good will be held, what social experiments will be attempted, what norms will apply, what institutions will be established. No idea of common good, social experiment, norm or institution is inherently anarchist; any of them can be, as long as no one accepts it out of fear. This is what freedom is about. However, and perhaps more importantly, absence of fear is also the hallmark of anarchist practices. In his daily life and struggles, Malatesta acted on moral norms and pursued the common good to the best of his ability, even when this was considered a crime.

Malatesta and abolitionism today

Just as the principle of coherence between ends and means dictates that anarchist practices be informed by their ultimate goal, so Malatesta's abolitionist strategy, and therefore his message to abolitionists today, is best summarized by his succinct definition of anarchy in terms of equality of conditions, the method of freedom and the beacon of solidarity. Equality of conditions, which entails abolishing the monopoly of the means of production, is the high road to the removal of crime through the removal of its main cause: social inequality. The spread of solidarity, more than the pursuit of justice – and all its corollary concepts of redress, reparation and restoration – is the best antidote to competitive and therefore possibly anti-social attitudes. Above all, the method of freedom is the antithesis of the method of fear, the backbone of all penal systems and coercive orders.

Malatesta's key point is that punishment cannot be removed without removing the state, because he believed the two concepts are interdependent. The inherently coercive nature of the state, asserted by such political theorists as Thomas Hobbes, Max Weber and Hans Kelsen, has been reaffirmed more recently by Enrique Dussel, the 'philosophy of liberation' theorist that has been highly influential among abolitionists (Scott, 2020). Dussel claims that 'any prevailing institution … must be supported by a legitimate kind of coercion, which allows for guiding those not willing to comply with the validly accepted agreements' (Dussel, 2013: 400). He maintains that 'the prevailing order has the right (legality) to the monopolistic exercise of coercion' and, in contrast with such legitimate use of force, he tellingly 'reserve[s] the word *violence* … exclusively for the illegal and illegitimate rebellion of the anarchist, or legal coercion turned illegitimate' (Dussel, 2013: 407, 409). The explicit contrast between legitimate coercion and anarchism makes one wonder whether abolitionism is not really on the anarchist side, rather than on Dussel's.

Equating state and punishment exposes the oxymoronic nature of the concept of 'noncoercive state', which abolitionists sometimes advocate. For example, as part of his abolitionist strategy, David Scott questions 'the legitimacy of the coercive state', argues that 'socialist conceptions of the state … are also often conceived as non-coercive' and takes inspiration from G.D.H. Cole's guild socialism as an aspirational model of a 'non-coercive state grounded in genuinely democratic principles' (Scott, 2020: 227). In fact, Cole's blueprint of a socialist society does not remove coercion, but decentralizes it: 'So far as coercive machinery, such as a police force, remained, it should be controlled, not by any single functional body, but by all jointly – that is by the Commune' (Cole, 1920: 128). Of course, there are degrees in coercion, and Cole's model stands on the more 'libertarian' side of the spectrum. However, this is where Malatesta's focus on method becomes crucial.

One can aim for any middle ground between coercion and freedom. However, as Malatesta claimed, 'in sociology as in topography, one does not go wherever one *wishes*, but wherever the path one is on may lead' (Malatesta, 2014a: 99), which is another way of expressing the principle of strategic interaction – that one can choose only a strategy, not an outcome. This was the point at the heart of Malatesta's debate with Merlino, who advocated a 'realistic' version of libertarian socialism. One can only choose a method, and the methods of fear and freedom are incompatible, though the outcome will be the resultant of both. In brief, in the abolitionist struggle, the method by which it is conducted is all that can be chosen and that matters.

Malatesta's way of framing the abolitionist struggle, which, in his view, is at one with the anarchist struggle, finds a powerful echo in some of

Thomas Mathiesen's themes. Mathiesen claims that the alternative lies in the 'unfinished'. To be a competing contradiction, its message must be *foreign* (as opposed to *integrated*) and *suggested* (as opposed to *fully formed*). He argues that working for short-range improvements on the premises of the old system is prone to absorption and departure from the long-range goal. Short-term goals can be set, but 'the point is that you should not make these short-term goals your final ones, but let them remain steps on a road which still is foreign and suggested only – unfinished'. The inception of the unfinished takes place through 'abolishing the established order' and 'entering unbuilt ground': 'freedom is the anxiety and pleasure involved in entering a field which is unsettled or empty'. In the dialectical relationship between reform and revolution, Mathiesen concludes, 'it is decisive that the work for the abolition, and thereby for the unfinished – the alternative – is not only seen as long-range, but that it *takes place always, as directly and concretely as possible*' (Mathiesen, 1974: 13–28).

By defining anarchy as a method rather than a blueprint and by regarding it as an open process that indefinitely approaches perfection without ever attaining it, Malatesta strikingly foreshadows Mathiesen's 'unfinished'. His principle of coherence between and means exhibits the same awareness of the displacement of goals that we find in Mathiesen's concern over absorption. In his reluctance to specify in advance the forms of the postrevolutionary society and his insistence on committing them to free experimentation, Malatesta shares Mathiesen's expectancy in 'entering unbuilt ground'. Finally, his focus on direct action and on always struggling 'as anarchists' even for short-term goals is akin to Mathiesen's recommendation to always keep the long-range goal, the unfinished, in sight and struggle for its direct and concrete realization. It was Max Weber who claimed that, in history, 'man would not have attained the possible unless time and again he had reached out for the impossible' (Weber, 1965: 55). Indeed, Malatesta reached out for the impossible to attain what was possible, but all that was possible.

Note
[1] Cesare Beccaria's book *On Crimes and Punishments* was published anonymously in Italian in 1764 and two years later in French, with numerous changes. Accordingly, English editions also vary, depending on their source.

References
Aiello, P. (2007) 'Malatesta e il satiro: Delinquenti e pazzi nella società liberata', in *Errico Malatesta: A centocinquant'anni dalla nascita*, Ragusa: La Fiaccola, pp 91–93.
Beccaria, C. (1963) *On Crimes and Punishments*, Indianapolis: Bobbs–Merrill.
Cole, G.D.H. (1920) *Guild Socialism Re-stated*, London: Leonard Parsons.
Cossutta, M. (2015) *Errico Malatesta. Note per un diritto anarchico*, Trieste: Edizioni Università di Trieste.

Davidson, D. (2005a) 'A nice derangement of epitaphs', in *Truth, Language, and History*, Oxford: Oxford University Press, pp 89–107.

Davidson, D. (2005b) 'The social aspect of language', in *Truth, Language, and History*, Oxford: Oxford University Press, pp 109–125.

Dussel, E. (2013) *Ethics of Liberation in the Age of Globalization and Exclusion*, Durham, NC: Duke University Press.

Hardin, R. (2003) *Indeterminacy and Society*, Princeton: Princeton University Press.

Hayek, F.A. (1989) *The Fatal Conceit: The Errors of Socialism*, Chicago: University of Chicago Press.

Hobbes, T. (1965[1651]) *Leviathan*, Oxford: Oxford University Press.

Kelsen, H. (1970) *The Pure Theory of Law*, Berkeley: University of California Press.

Malatesta, E. (1974) *Anarchy*, London: Freedom Press.

Malatesta, E. (1984) *Epistolario: Lettere edite e inedite 1873–1932*, Carrara: Centro Studi Sociali Avenza.

Malatesta, E. (2014a) 'Our plans: union between communists and collectivists', in *The Method of Freedom: An Errico Malatesta Reader*, Oakland: AK Press, pp 95–99.

Malatesta, E. (2014b) 'Errors and remedies', in *The Method of Freedom: An Errico Malatesta Reader*, Oakland: AK Press, pp 199–204.

Malatesta, E. (2014c) 'Toward anarchy', in *The Method of Freedom: An Errico Malatesta Reader*, Oakland: AK Press, pp 299–302.

Malatesta, E. (2016) 'Polemic', in *The Complete Works of Errico Malatesta*, vol. 3, Chico: AK Press, pp 94–97.

Malatesta, E. (2021a) 'Ancora del diritto penale nella rivoluzione,' in *Opere Complete*, vol. '"Fronte unico proletario": Il bienno rosso, *Umanità Nova* e il fascismo, 1919–1923', Milan: Zero in Condotta and Ragusa: La Fiaccola, pp 346–348.

Malatesta, E. (2021b) 'La difesa sociale contro il delitto', in *Opere Complete*, vol. '"Fronte unico proletario": Il bienno rosso, *Umanità Nova* e il fascismo, 1919–1923', Milan: Zero in Condotta and Ragusa: La Fiaccola, pp 351–353.

Malatesta, E. (2021c) 'Sulla questione del delitto', in *Opere Complete*, vol. '"Fronte unico proletario": Il bienno rosso, *Umanità Nova* e il fascismo, 1919–1923', Milan: Zero in Condotta and Ragusa: La Fiaccola, p 363.

Malatesta, E. (2021d) 'Ancora sulla questione della criminalità', in *Opere Complete*, vol. '"Fronte unico proletario": Il bienno rosso, *Umanità Nova* e il fascismo, 1919–1923', Milan: Zero in Condotta and Ragusa: La Fiaccola, pp 370–373.

Malatesta, E. (2021e) 'Sulla questione della criminalità', in *Opere Complete*, vol. '"Fronte unico proletario": Il bienno rosso, *Umanità Nova* e il fascismo, 1919–1923', Milan: Zero in Condotta and Ragusa: La Fiaccola, pp 386–389.

Malatesta, E. (2021f) '"Abolite le carceri" di Giovanni Forbicini', in *Opere Complete*, vol. '"Fronte unico proletario": Il bienno rosso, *Umanità Nova* e il fascismo, 1919–1923', Milan: Zero in Condotta and Ragusa: La Fiaccola, pp 421–422.

Malatesta, E. (2021g) 'Il pericolo della cocaina', in *Opere Complete*, vol. '"Fronte unico proletario": Il bienno rosso, *Umanità Nova* e il fascismo, 1919–1923', Milan: Zero in Condotta and Ragusa: La Fiaccola, p 598.

Malatesta, E. (2021h) 'Libertà e delinquenza', in *Opere Complete*, vol. '"Fronte unico proletario": Il bienno rosso, *Umanità Nova* e il fascismo, 1919–1923', Milan: Zero in Condotta and Ragusa: La Fiaccola, pp 626–628.

Malatesta, E. (2021i) 'La rivoluzione in pratica', in *Opere Complete*, vol. '"Fronte unico proletario": Il bienno rosso, *Umanità Nova* e il fascismo, 1919–1923', Milan: Zero in Condotta and Ragusa: La Fiaccola, pp 631–634.

Malatesta, E. (2021j) 'Morale e violenza', in *Opere Complete*, vol. '"Fronte unico proletario": Il bienno rosso, *Umanità Nova* e il fascismo, 1919–1923', Milan: Zero in Condotta and Ragusa: La Fiaccola, pp 647–650.

Malatesta, E. (2023a) 'Opinione popolare e delinquenza: Un effetto moralizzatore del Fascismo', in *Opere Complete*, vol. '"Anarchismo realizzabile e realizzatore": *Pensiero e Volontà* e ultimi scritti, 1924–1932', Milan: Zero in Condotta and Ragusa: La Fiaccola, pp 76–78.

Malatesta, E. (2023b) 'Demoliamo. E poi?' in *Opere Complete*, vol. '"Anarchismo realizzabile e realizzatore": *Pensiero e Volontà* e ultimi scritti, 1924–1932', Milan: Zero in Condotta and Ragusa: La Fiaccola, pp 197–200.

Malatesta, E. (2023c) 'Chiarimenti', in *Opere Complete*, vol. '"Anarchismo realizzabile e realizzatore": *Pensiero e Volontà* e ultimi scritti, 1924–1932', Milan: Zero in Condotta and Ragusa: La Fiaccola, pp 209–212.

Malatesta, E. (2023d) 'Il ristabilimento della pena di morte', in *Opere Complete*, vol. '"Anarchismo realizzabile e realizzatore": *Pensiero e Volontà* e ultimi scritti, 1924–1932', Milan: Zero in Condotta and Ragusa: La Fiaccola, pp 231–232.

Marconi, P. (1979) *La libertà selvaggia: Stato e punizione nel pensiero anarchico*, Venice: Marsilio.

Mathiesen, T. (1974) *The Politics of Abolition*, New York: John Wiley & Sons.

Pico della Mirandola, G. (1956) *Oration on the Dignity of Man*, Chicago: Henry Regnery.

Popper, K.R. (1945a) *The Open Society and Its Enemies. Volume I: The Spell of Plato*, London: Routledge.

Popper, K.R. (1945b) *The Open Society and Its Enemies. Volume II: The High Tide of Prophecy: Hegel, Marx, and the Aftermath*, London: Routledge.

Scott, D. (2020) *For Abolition: Essays on Prisons and Socialist Ethics*, Sherfield on Loddon: Waterside Press.

Watkins, J.W.N. (1994) 'Historical explanation in the social sciences', in M. Martin and L.C. McIntyre (eds) *Readings in the Philosophy of Social Science*, Cambridge, MA: MIT Press, pp 441–450.

Weber, M. (1965) *Politics as a Vocation*, Philadelphia: Fortress Press.

12

Envisioning a New Society: Pietro Gori and the Problem of Criminal Justice

Marco Manfredi

Introduction

Pietro Gori (1865–1911) may have been the best-loved, if not the most politically important, of all Italian anarchist leaders of his time (Antonioli, 1996; Antonioli and Bertolucci, 2001; Manfredi, 2017). He was a hugely popular figure, though mostly forgotten today, and this popularity extended beyond the circles of libertarian socialist militants. A man of many talents, he was known above all as a revolutionary propagandist who could speak to the people through his ability to mix politics with other languages: poetry, song and theatre. However, as mentioned in the first section of this chapter, Gori was also a brilliant criminal lawyer. His work and thinking in this field is one of the lesser-known aspects of his story, and was influenced not only by his studies and profession, but also by his firsthand experience of prison and exile.

This chapter aims to reintroduce Gori to a global abolitionist audience. Engagement with Gori will be of assistance to abolitionist scholars and activists today because he wrote about penal change in pamphlets and newspaper articles, in dialogue with the most advanced penal criticism of his time. Reflecting on issues that are still debated in abolitionist circles today (Ruggiero, 2010; Scott, 2013), he went so far as to criticize institutions such as prison and the death penalty in the name of a broader condemnation of the punitive logic at the heart of modern legal systems. Influenced by legal positivism, which in Italy included such well-known theorists at the time as Cesare Lombroso and which asserted the non-individual nature of crime, he argued that the causes of crime lay in the pathologies of a capitalist society that was a source of inequality and misery. In line with the anarchist thought he had been following since his university days, he attributed another cause of delinquency to the authoritarian nature of a society based on an institution like the state with its coercive apparatuses, starting with the military. The end of the capitalist economy and state authority would lead as an immediate consequence to a drastic reduction in criminal offences, while those that did not disappear would be 'cured' and not 'punished'. It was a treatment-orientated approach to wrongdoing that was part of a school of thought at the forefront of which was Pyotr Kropotkin (see Weide, Chapter 9 in this volume). Gori developed this approach further during the years of his second exile in Argentina, as will be discussed in the second section of this chapter.

Although Gori is not an obvious abolitionist, the final section of this chapter will show that abolitionist ideas were always present in the background of his own legal defences, and in more utopian and political forms, such as in the varied literary production (poems, ballads and theatrical sketches) that made him a revolutionary celebrity at the turn of the century.

La miseria e i delitti *(Poverty and Crimes)*

Gori was born in 1865 in Messina, Sicily, to parents of Tuscan origin. His father served as an army officer, while his mother belonged to a noble Tuscan family. His family's political traditions had links with the democratic movement of the Italian Risorgimento. After finishing school in Livorno, his family's financial resources enabled him to enrol at the University of Pisa. There he became involved in politics and was prosecuted for distributing a pamphlet promoting social revolution and defending the principles of anarchist internationalism.[1]

He quickly became a prominent leader of the new generation of anarchists emerging on the scene alongside important First International figures, including Francesco Saverio Merlino and Errico Malatesta (see Turcato, Chapter 11 in this volume). A rapid shift to active political commitment led him to take part in the Congress of Capolago, where the Anarchist Revolutionary Socialist Party was established in 1891. The following year, he attended the Congress of Genoa as a delegate for the anarchists, where the Socialist Workers' Party was formed, and a definitive divide occurred between the legalitarian socialists, headed by Filippo Turati, and the libertarian factions of the Italian workers' movement. In the meantime, Gori graduated in law in 1889 and his sympathies for socialism, by now already clear, also emerged in his dissertation. The title of this courageous, if rather bitter, writing was *La miseria e i delitti* ('Poverty and crimes').[2] Influenced by the positivist legal culture of the time, which limited the concept of personal responsibility for criminal behaviour, this essay argued that the crime was merely the consequence of an unjust society. According to Gori, 'poverty, without being the sole cause of the sad social phenomenon of delinquency, has an infinite number of direct and indirect links with crime' (Gori, 2001: 72). In contrast to the Classical School of Criminal Law (represented by his initial mentor Francesco Carrara), crimes were therefore to a certain extent a false problem, as society's significant social inequalities needed to be addressed first.

The following year, Gori was himself arrested in Livorno and imprisoned for several months after attempting to organize a strike on May Day with some workers. This incarceration was the beginning of several prison sentences that would shape his entire lifetime. Once free, he moved to Milan and began to work as a lawyer in the office of the socialist Turati. He established himself as a skilled criminal lawyer. In this role, he distinguished himself by defending important trials of anarchist militants and political prisoners, increasingly oppressed by the kingdom's repressive laws against the revolutionary left and political dissent more generally (Diemoz, 2011; Colao, 2007). Throughout the 1890s, apart from the interlude of his first exile, which he spent between 1894 and 1896 travelling between Europe and North America, he took part in some important political trials that helped to increase his popularity.

In Italy at that time, the criminal courts were a great stage and an excellent forum for propaganda. The growing influence of public opinion and the introduction of the institution of popular juries, as Gori himself noted (Gori,1905a), made courtrooms much more prone to emotional involvement and much more sensitive to the language of sentiment. As a result, the great criminal trials of the turn of the century became some of the greatest spectacles of the age and a formidable arena for legal oratory (Colao, Lacchè and Storti, 2008; Minuto, 2011; Seymour, 2012; Minuto, 2017; Papadia, 2018). Gori's long and theatrical defence arguments were therefore taken up by revolutionary newspapers and printed as effective popular propaganda pamphlets.

It was precisely in Gori's work as a militant lawyer defending comrades and workers repressed for their ideas and struggles that the critical approach to the question of punishment advocated in his university thesis became even more explicit and clearly defined. In his courtroom speeches, he used imaginative language, extensive historical references and numerous examples from everyday life to argue that it was impossible to prosecute a 'utopia' and its ideas. At the same time, he argued that the only real and effective remedy for the problem of crime was to cure society (Gori, 1905b, 1907). In 1894, after the anarchist Sante Caserio had attempted to assassinate the French President Sadi Carnot, he recalled his acquaintance with the unfortunate young man to whom he had offered his legal aid some time before and gave a detailed account of the difficult life of the poor Milanese worker:[3] the bleak poverty in which he had lived since childhood; the madness of his father, who was interned in an asylum; the hard and heavy work; and the constant and arbitrary harassment by the police. This 'bitter and difficult struggle for life' had thus armed his hand (Gori, 1945: 32). Caserio's criminality was therefore the same as that of so many members of the subaltern classes who were victims of an unbalanced and unequal social order. The context should therefore always be placed at the centre of the criminal theory, even more and even before the offender. The perspective that the social factor was more 'scandalous' than the crime enabled Gori to strongly criticize bourgeois society and its economic order, of which the state and its laws were the guardians.

In the aforementioned 'political trials' at the turn of the century, it was particularly easy to fall back on this pattern of reasoning, because the state was presenting itself in a public hearing with the naked face of repression. In one of his most famous legal defences, on behalf of the editors of *L'Agitazione*, who were accused of inciting the anti-caravan riots in Ancona in January 1898, he escaped the juxtaposition of anarchism, violence and the legitimacy of repression by suggesting a play on the antithesis of anarchist and bourgeois morality;[4] a juxtaposition of moral codes that gave rise to two very different political and socioeconomic systems, destined to alternate in a natural evolutionary cycle of historical movement towards the progressive triumph of humanity. Assimilated to the 'barbaric' morality of the indigenous peoples, the bourgeois morality remained, in Gori's words, a morality eminently marked by violence, nourished by the theft of the wealth produced by others and by the militarism of the state. The deep roots of the violence therefore lay in a distorted and flawed social and productive organization. Immediately after Gori, the main defendant, Errico Malatesta, editor of the anarchist journal, spoke, completing and explaining the argument of his friend and comrade lawyer. Having affirmed in his self-defence the 'political nature of a trial conducted by men whose functions I do not recognise, because I do not recognise the law', he foreshadowed an ideal future world in which 'your function as judges would be abolished'. 'In an organised society', he concluded, addressing the court directly, 'the function you now perform will become useless, because there will no longer be crimes that depend on the economic imbalance of populations, and those that do exist will be entrusted to the care of psychiatric science.'[5]

In this way, Malatesta expressed in decidedly futuristic terms what the most advanced criminologists in the socialist sphere were advocating in those years (see chapters by Forero Cuellar, Chapter 10 in this volume, and Turcato, Chapter 11 in this volume). For them, which at that time had already gone beyond the positions of Enrico Ferri[6] the founder of criminal sociology and leader of the newly formed Italian Socialist Party, the issue of crime would be first and foremost a matter of social transformation (Sbriccoli, 1974/1975). It was so closely linked to the socioeconomic dimension that only a paradigm shift could resolve it – that is, by means of a historical and political upheaval of bourgeois society and the consequent construction of a future characterized by a tendency towards the disappearance of the need for a penal system as such. In this sense, it was necessary to 'give the most terrible shock to this old carcass that is the criminal society that oppresses us' (Gori, 1911a: 79) in order to achieve, as anarchists, as Gori himself said in another famous defence of a group of well-known comrades at the Genoa court in 1894,[7] 'a society in which theft and murder are impossible'. The allusion was clearly to a reality inspired by the principle of radical freedom of the anarchist idea. It was no longer a question, as in the legal positivism of the university years, of registering that an unequal material reality was the origin and explanation of the criminal tendencies of the so-called 'dangerous classes', but of affirming that the penal system was no guarantee, even in the abstract, because it conveyed, and in some respects reproduced, precisely these inequalities. The problem was therefore not only to be found in society, but also in the law itself. It was enough to note the disparity between the severity with which the crimes of the poor were punished and the mildness reserved for the crimes of the powerful – the 'thieves in gloves' – as Gori called them (Gori, 1905b: 9). More than any other branch of law, criminal law was socially influenced, the result of power relations that decided what was good and what was bad, which revealed its class-based and not universal nature and therefore its profile as 'unjust law'.

Criminal sociologist

In the summer of 1898, Gori, along with other anarchists and socialists, was again convicted, on purely circumstantial evidence, of being one of the main instigators of the important and bloody popular uprisings in Milan, which were harshly repressed by the army. To avoid having to spend several years in prison, he once again decided to leave Italy and sailed from Marseille to Argentina. If the forensic practice of the previous years had been an important step in the strengthening of his criticism of the criminal justice system that had matured during his university years, the experience of the second exile would be another fundamental moment in this direction. The four years spent in South America, in addition to the political activity useful for the spread of anarchism in this part of the American continent, would in fact see him particularly engaged in the discussion and deepening of the theoretical profile of penal matters.

Gori settled in Buenos Aires, opened a law firm with a partner and for a few months, before he was explicitly banned, even managed to get the opportunity to teach a free course in the 'sociology of crime' at the university in the Argentine capital. In connection with this activity, he was the founder and director of a monthly review, *Criminalogia Moderna* (*Modern Criminology*). It was the first periodical on criminology to be published in South America and ran continuously from the end of 1898 to the beginning of 1901 (Rotondo, 2014; Quinto, 2020). An immigrant sentenced to imprisonment in his homeland thus placed himself at the centre of the penal debate in a large new country that was reforming and modernizing its legal systems, in dialogue with locals who were interested in the new developments, in order to disseminate and introduce the most important and recent trends in European legal positivism. It was not by chance that the new journal was conceived as a forum in which to translate into Spanish the contributions of leading European exponents of positive science and in which to publish previously unpublished articles penned by young local jurists interested in new developments in criminology.

Different topics and different approaches found their place in the criminological reflection of the journal. In several issues it published translations and contributions by Cesare Lombroso, the founder of criminal anthropology, or other representatives of his school. Gori particularly appreciated the author of *L'uomo delinquente*'s criticism of the doctrinaire abstractionism of the classical school (Lombroso, 1876), which viewed crime from an exclusively moral perspective as a pure manifestation of the free will of the criminal. But compared to the Lombrosians, the editor of the journal seemed far less constrained by the biological data and the obsessive desire to define criminal types (Darmon, 1989; Gibson, 2002), and far more interested in stressing the weight of the social environment on the causes of crime. The focus on the criminal in order to classify him and reveal his natural tendency to commit crime according to the Lombrosian theory of atavism, which linked character to physical features, was explicitly criticized by Gori (Gori, 1911c: 16–17).[8] Knowledge of the motives of crime was not exclusively linked to the anthropological study of the offender and his inner drives,[9] but the horizon had always to be broadened to include the social environment and the problems he had to face there on a daily basis. This was the path that led him, through the mediation of Enrico Ferri, towards criminal sociology rather than criminal anthropology.

Among the topics covered in *Criminalogia Moderna*, the one that received the most attention was that of prisons. The prison problem was particularly acute in the legal culture in which Gori had received his training in Italy (Sbriccoli, 1974/1975: 636–637). As he had done in other European countries and in the US, Gori visited the penitentiary system in Argentina, in particular making a long journey to Tierra del Fuego, to which he devoted an extensive series of articles in the magazine in order to get to know the large prison complex of Sierra Chica.[10] Although he presented his visit in the magazine as motivated by purely analytical intentions, with the aim of gathering data on the reality of Argentine prisons, behind the pretence of objectivity there were moments of sincere empathy for the people who experienced the suffering and deprivation of imprisonment in an institution that he described on entering with a literary reference to Dante's descent into hell. He reserved a long excursus for a meticulous analysis of the poor social conditions shared by almost all convicts – conditions whose cure would have required good food for the stomach and, above all, intellectual and emotional education. The remote region of Argentina, with its wide-open spaces and lush nature, nevertheless allowed the prisoners a degree of freedom that made it more akin to an agricultural colony, an experience that in Italy had only one comparison: the penal colony on the small island of Pianosa, where prisoners worked in the open air and lived in relative freedom. The agricultural penal colonies were certainly to be preferred to the repressive experience of the cellular jail, a model of solitary confinement that prevailed on the European continent: 'Confining convicts ... in solitary cells (as unfortunately happens in many European prison systems) is a real crime, even if it is committed by society and in the name of the law.'[11]

Unlike the more militant socialist penologists, for Gori it was not only the misery produced by capitalism that was the source and explanation of crime. In fact, as an anarcho-communist, he believed that the enormous economic imbalances were only one of the two great distortions on which social organization was based. Indeed, it was necessary not to forget the 'authoritarian bias' of a society entirely dependent on the coercive apparatus of the state (Gori, 1906b). In line with the anti-authoritarianism of the anarchists, much of the violence perpetrated in society was due to the existence of a state power contrary to the human tendencies inherent in human nature.[12] The end of state institutions and their legal systems and political apparatuses would have been another powerful driver of crime reduction. The ways of dealing with the residual delinquency that would remain in a definitively transformed society would also be radically changed, with punishment finally being replaced by other means, and the blind pain of chains being replaced by loving care. In particular, with regard to the problem of punishment and its execution, Gori called for a move away from the logic of punishment in favour of a medical model of crime, setting as an ultimate goal the duty, with the progress and evidence brought by science, to abandon the practice of burying the criminal alive in a cell[13] (see further discussion on the influence on anarchism of criminological positivism in Forero Cuellar, Chapter 10 in this volume).

From Gori's point of view, the prison did not reduce crime, nor did it improve the offender; in fact, it had the opposite effect. The exasperating segregation of the cell led to 'a destruction of the last instincts of benevolence and sociability, together with the ever-increasing development of antisocial impulses'. Not only was the prison based on a purely punitive logic, but it also did not allow prisoners to be reintegrated into society. In the future, it would be desirable for the codes of the various countries to provide for a specific 'rational therapy' for offenders, offering judges alternatives to penal institutions. The critique of the prison was certainly not new in the anarchist movement, so much so that in some of the arguments used by Gori, it was evident that they were in keeping with ideas and theses such as those put forward by Kropotkin, who had been engaged in an abolitionist reflection on penal institutions since the mid-1880s (Noccella, Seis and Shantz 2020; see also Weide, Chapter 9 in this volume). The same insistence on the alternative role of the practice of medical therapy in penal institutions reflected a well-established approach of libertarian penal reflection, which, beginning with the Russian prince of anarchism, is also found, for example, in Malatesta (Marconi, 1979; Ruggiero, 2012; see also Turcato, Chapter 11 in this volume). The treatment of the criminal, and therefore the preservation and defence of society, was to be entrusted not to 'judicial vengeance', but to 'science' (see Forero Cuellar, Chapter 10 in this volume).

It is not by chance that, despite the different orientations on the subject within the ranks of penal positivism (Rotondo, 2014: 162–65) and the journal's claim to a kind of objective neutrality in the name of science, one issue on which it adopted a very 'political' stance was precisely that of the decisive rejection of the use of corporal punishment, starting with torture, which was considered typical of the inquisitorial process. This was a criticism that extended in this context to state justice institutions such as preventive detention, considered as an unjustified restriction of personal freedom for the mere organizational needs of justice and defined by Gori as a veritable moral torture that, moreover, tended to overcrowd prisons by fomenting delinquency in the prisons themselves.[14] The magazine and its editor in particular took a clear position against the death penalty, which was regarded as the most manifest expression of the punitive tradition underlying legal systems. In fact, the perpetuation of the 'sad use of the gallows', against which the journal waged a full-blown abolitionist campaign, deserved special and articulate disapproval.[15] The practice, which was still in force in many countries considered civilized, starting with France 'to which so much affection of revolutionaries connect us', was to be seen as an act of 'pure revenge'.[16] As murder, rightly denied to the individual, it had nothing to do with legal civilization and respect for the law. Moreover, from a sociological point of view, no practical basis for the death penalty could be found, since observations and data from the positive sciences showed that it had no real deterrent effect, resulting in a gratuitous display of pure wickedness that accentuated the cruelty and violence in society itself. In conclusion, from an ethical and legal point of view, as well as from the point of view of social effectiveness, one could affirm the 'immorality, illegitimacy and uselessness' of the maximum criminal sanction.[17]

Between science and propaganda

In Argentina, more than anywhere else, Gori's history moved along the difficult line between the dimension of political activism, working with anarchist periodicals or promoting political circles and groups (Zaragoza Rovira, 1996), and the more specialized dimension of criminological studies. The libertarian ideal preached a radical rupture, a revolutionary paradigm shift that would eliminate inequalities between men, while the criminological reflections focused on crime and society, proposing concrete transformations in the wake of thoughtful evaluations. While the first horizon, full of expectations of change, aimed at the eradication of relations of authority and control, the scientific discourse, mediated by Gori's own journal, discussed the forms and experiences of social control.

In particular, the space given to the assumptions and theories of Lombroso, who was no friend of the anarchists[18] and whose positions were certainly not detached from the dominant system of power, ultimately left even some anarchist circles with a feeling of disorientation, if not ambivalence, towards the journal and its director (Geli, 1992: 14; Albornoz, 2014). *Modern Criminology* was a kaleidoscope open to the contribution of different tendencies within the positive current, discussing and reflecting upon the positions of a new discipline. However, if it accommodated both anthropological and sociological positions, it did not, like its founder, hide its sympathy for the latter to the detriment of the former and its claims to explain moral behaviour in physical-biological terms.

Neither in tone nor in form did its pages proclaim a true *Tramonto del diritto penale* ('Sunset of the criminal law'), according to the eloquent title of a pamphlet written at the time by an anarchist propagandist and former university classmate of Gori's in Pisa. In 1904, the Lombard anarchist and lawyer Luigi Molinari, although always starting from Kropotkin's foundations, had in fact strongly supported a proposal for total abolitionism (Molinari, 1904; Marconi, 1979), the echo of which could be heard in many Italian anarchist publications of the time, such as the pamphlets and the articles of the two main libertarian *pasionarie* of the time, Leda Rafanelli and Nella Giacomelli (Rafanelli, 1907, Masini, 1973; Masini, 2005; Ongaro, 2019).

In contrast to the frontal attack in Molinari's essay, the abolitionist positions in Gori's review are more nuanced and, as we have seen, preferable in relation to individual issues, from prisons to the death penalty. However, the strictly positivist background and often reformist rather than revolutionary framework that Gori seemed to have accepted as the game plan for his journal did not prevent the emergence of criticism and perplexity towards the anthropological mainstream or the widespread use of its principles. And although he dealt with specific questions, such as the relationship between crime and a set of physical characteristics or psychological causes, the influence of the external social environment or the inventory of penalties, with a degree of technicality, behind the role of sociology of crime in denouncing economic inequality and legal injustice, Gori never failed to explicitly refer to a broader horizon in some criminological texts.

In fact, Gori's sociology of crime could only take on real meaning when it broadened its vision to a new project of society, to give rise to an anarchic sociology, rather than mere 'social therapy' (Gori, 1905d: 99) aimed at studying and measuring the causes of crime with supposed objectivity. For him, the real work of curing this social plague would only be achieved with the complete renewal of collective life on the basis of altruism and solidarity, in accordance with the deepest essence of man and the humanitarian philosophy par excellence that anarchism represented for him. This was a result that could only be achieved by 'convincing the majority', still 'deceived by the sophistry of misunderstood individual self-interest', to establish a new 'collective psychology', 'which must surround the new social world like a pure atmosphere' (Gori, 1906a):

> The two fundamental characters of the moral sense – honesty and piety – in their highest and most human sense, will find in the new purer environment new forces and favourable elements to expand and take root more and more in the human psyche.
>
> Honesty and mercy, from their negative meaning of the dying morality: *do not do to others what you do not want to be done to you*, will dictate to the hearts of men a more perfect maxim that will guide their good charity: *do to others what you would like to be done to you*, as the logical and ethical crowning of *all the brothers of each one*. (Gori, 1906a: 52)[19]

The imagined society would be based on a principle of living together in solidarity, which for Gori was already inherent human nature. A harmonious coexistence, Gori intuited, that would be the real form of law, without the need for an authority to which the exercise of power could be delegated. He was still writing these sentences in the guise of a 'sociologist' who, unlike the 'agitator, the poet, the militant', had, in his words, 'to try to place himself far outside the deafening clamour of the political and social struggle' (Gori, 1906a: 51). It is no coincidence that the text containing them was collected in the 12 small volumes of *Opere* published after his death in the book *Sociologia anarchica* (Gori, 1912). With their biblical lexicon, their messianic intonation and their millenarian sense of expectation, these reflections nevertheless seemed more reminiscent of the 'poet of anarchy', one of the agitator Gori's best-known nicknames, than of the scientific analyst. In other words, they came close to that vast poetic-literary production of which he was at the same time an inexhaustible proponent, and to which, in the subversive imagination of the time, he owed all his fame as a revolutionary political celebrity, as well as his legendary pseudonyms ('Wandering Knight of Anarchy', 'Apostle of the Ideal' or, more precisely, 'Poet of Anarchy') (Antonioli, 1996; Manfredi, 2018). The relationship between scientific intentions and libertarian militancy thus concealed an unresolved tension, a difficult balance between the magazine's underlying idea of history's natural tendency towards an anarchist society and the demands of ideological propaganda and popular consumption. The revolutionary of the Ideal, holding the flag and his dreams of change, tended to take the place of the social analyst, and the latter faded into the Gori who was best known and loved by militants. This was the multifaceted and 'multimedia' politician whose compositions were expressed in more popular forms and were not intended for an academic and expert audience. In the latter capacity, he was in fact able to speak a language strongly based on emotions, using literary genres such as poetry, theatre and song.

In the Argentinean review's experience, the libertarian identity of its director, although not absent, could thus appear more attenuated behind the technicalities imposed by the scientific and positivist discourse and filtered through the criticism of specific issues and the frequent emphasis on the importance of the social factor in crime. In the role of the lawyer, through that veritable political-literary genre that became his defence speeches, Gori's approach to criminal matters was coloured by his desire to strike at the emotionality of popular juries and the growing importance of public opinion (Gori, 1905a). With bold historical comparisons and numerous literary quotations, his tone of criticism became more acute and, as we have seen, frontally attacked not the 'criminal' nature of the accused, but that of existing society and its penal system.

However, it was in the various popular texts, designed to propagandize the masses and dripping with revolutionary passion, that the criticism of an unjust order was most explicit and radical alternative visions were advanced. Poems, social sketches for the theatre, and songs with vivid images of the future advanced a new idea of justice that echoed his abolitionist ideal of a society finally free of crime and punishment. Thus, for example, in the well-known folk song, written to the tune of a traditional Tuscan folk ballad, 'Ballata di Sante Caserio' (1900), the dark and bitter atmosphere of the opening verses, which recall the sad end of the young anarchist who ended up on the guillotine, dissolves in the last two octaves into the bright and imminent arrival of a world in which there would be no more Sante Caserio – a world 'purified' from injustice where human lives would be 'sacred' and the basis of law would be informed only by 'science and bread'. This visionary and literary abolitionism, consisting of promised lands finally emancipated from the coercive yoke of authority, is also often found in the background of the social sketches, simple working-class or peasant dramas performed in those years in the countless proletarian theatres of the peninsula and in those of immigrant communities abroad. Here, too, a present of misery, exploitation and persecution was counterbalanced by a mythical, utopian future, characterized by the establishment of a new humanity, inspired in its concept of justice only by egalitarianism and fraternity (Gori, 1911d).

Conclusion: Gori and penal abolitionism today

The human and intellectual history of a figure such as Pietro Gori is thus a further confirmation of the very long genealogy that lies behind the tradition of abolitionist thought. His forensic work in the courts is not divorced from his ideas as a libertarian socialist, which led him to question legal and social practices from an anthropological, historical and philosophical perspective. His reflections addressed profound issues, such as the inner meaning of the criminal act, the function of punishment, and the close link between delinquency and a specific model of society. This critical approach to the question of punishment increasingly led him over time to denounce a criminal process that did not cure bad behaviour, but in fact encouraged it. His criticisms were clearly laid out in his theoretical pamphlets and editorial initiatives, originally inspired by a comparison with the theses of the new criminal sociology of the time.

Throughout his life, Gori found himself on both sides of the fence. He entered courts and prisons not only as a defence lawyer, but also as a defendant and a convict. Prosecuted by the Kingdom of Italy and other governments for his ideas, which in the world of the turn of the 20th century were mainly associated with terrorism, his reflections on these themes were therefore also influenced by an inside knowledge of the prison environment, an experience that he often recalled in his autobiographical writings as well as in collections of lyric poetry (Gori, 1891; Gori, 1911e). The trials brought against his anarchist beliefs, his bewilderment at the authorities' moral code, which preached destruction rather than love and humanity, or constant and gratuitous police harassment, informed his personal beliefs. Indeed, his life experience must have been no less influential than his reading and study in maturing his attitudes towards justice and the penal system.

It is no coincidence that the theme of imprisonment, experienced firsthand, is one of the most recurrent in Gori's criminological interventions, being drawn on to refute the usefulness of the prison institution for society and for the offender himself. For him, prisons and their overcrowding were the mirror of a distorted and sick society that, while pursuing crime, ended up feeding it. A first element of criticism, which came from his fascination with the anarchist ideal breathed in student circles, was his denunciation of the authoritarian nature of an institution like the state, which was supported by coercive powers (prisons, the army, the police and bureaucracy). However, more often, he emphasized the weight of the pernicious link between social and economic inequalities on the one hand, and high crime rates and prison populations on the other hand, in the light of the socialist-inspired penal doctrine he had begun to embrace since his university dissertation. These were critical insights that continue to resonate in the debate on penal abolitionism today (Scott, 2013). And in terms not very different from those of contemporary libertarian and socialist criminology (Scott, 2020), Gori's vision of a change of social paradigm would also have favoured an important ethical reversal in the hierarchy of prevailing values. While capitalist society promotes individualism by strengthening man's selfish tendencies and weakening social bonds and the sense of solidarity, the society imagined by Gori is presented as a community capable of promoting the best of the sense of humanity inherent in man: brotherhood, friendship, mutual aid, love and trust in one's neighbour. In line with this, the narrative of his propaganda writings often followed a rigid and established binary pattern. Disturbing and bleak images in the first part gave substance to the sad condition of the imprisoned or exploited, only to give way to metaphors and symbols of regeneration which, in an unspecified future, heralded the coming of a fruitful and hopeful system of true justice.

Notes

[1] This radical pamphlet was entitled *Pensieri Ribelli*, Pisa: Il Folchetto, 1889.

[2] Gori, 2001. For an exhaustive picture of Gori's life story, see especially Antonioli and Bertolucci (2001).

[3] For his relations with Caserio and for this lenient attitude, Gori was unjustly accused by a fierce press campaign of being a sort of instigator of the young Italian baker's act of terrorism, so much so that he decided to go into his first exile abroad (Antonioli and Bertolucci, 2001: 56–58).

[4] This claimed moral alternative was also developed in binary terms from the title in a political lecture later published in Gori (1905c).

[5] *Il processo Malatesta e Compagni innanzi al tribunale penale di Ancona e i vecchi processi di Ancona, Castelferretti e Milano per le bombe ammaestrate*, Pescara: Di Sciullo, 1908: 151.

[6] On Ferri, also a brilliant lawyer, a former defence lawyer in Gori himself and a professor of criminal law at several Italian universities, see Bisi (2004).

[7] Among them was Luigi Galleani, who would become the most feared anarchist in America. He was also involved in the Sacco and Vanzetti case and a number of attacks on US soil.

[8] The paper 'Evolution of criminal sociology' is the text of the opening lectures of his course at the University of Buenos Aires and was first published in the journal *Il Pensiero* (Gori, 1905d). It was later collected with other writings in Gori (1911c).

[9] On his distance on this topic, see Bruno [P. Gori] (1899) 'Guia del Estudiante, los datos de la Antopologia criminal', *Criminalogia Moderna*, II(5): 144–147.

[10] Gori, P. (1898) 'Estudios carcelarios. Visita à la Penitenciaria de la Sierra Chica', *Criminalogia Moderna*, II (6): 176–182; Gori, P. (1899) 'II. Trabajos', II (7): 205–212; Gori, P. (1899) 'III. Los penados', II (8): 228–233. On his visit to Sierra Chica Rotondo, 2014: 36–39.

[11] 'Encerrar a los condenados ... al aislamiento ocioso de las celdas (como sucede, por desgracia, en muchos sistemas penitenciarios de Europa), es un verdadero delito, dunque

cometido por la sociedad y en nombre de la ley.' Gori, P. (1899) 'II. Trabajos' II (7): 206 (author's translation)
12   See, for example, Gori, 1911b.
13   'Clinica o castigo?' ('Clinic or punishment?') in Gori (1911c: 145–152), to which reference will also be made for subsequent quotations.
14   Gori, P. (1900) 'Recuerdos forenses. Cárcel preventiva', *Criminalogia Moderna*, 17 y 18 (III): 518–524.
15   In a letter to his friend Edoardo Milano a few years earlier, Gori referred to his participation in meetings in favour of prisoners condemned to death in the US (Bertolucci, 2012: 310).
16   See, for example, Gori, P. (1900) 'Pro y contra el verdugo', *Criminalogia Moderna*, III (19): 565–69; Gori, P. (1900) 'En defensa de la vida', *Criminalogia Moderna*, III (20): 597–99; 'Contro la pena di morte' (Against the death penalty) in Gori, 1911c: 153–56, referred to for quotations.
17   La dirección (1900) 'La pena de muerte', *Criminalogia Moderna*, 17 y 18 (III): 559–560.
18   In his essay *Gli anarchici* (Lombroso, 1894), written at the time of the bombings, he used a series of physiognomic observations to place anarchists in the ranks of the mattoid or delinquent races, making them the first sign of the abnormality of political dissent.
19   I due caratteri essenziali del senso morale – onestà e pietà – nel loro significato più alto e più umano, troveranno nel nuovo ambiente più puro nuove forze e condizioni favorevoli per espandersi e radicarsi sempre più nella psiche umana.
   L'onestà e la pietà, da com'è nel suo significato negativo della morale moribonda: *non fare agli altri ciò che non vorresti fatto a te*, detteranno al cuore degli uomini una massima più perfetta che ne guiderà l'opera buona: *fa agli altri ciò che vorresti fatto a te*, come coronamento logico ed etico del *tutti fratelli di ciascuno*. (author's translation; italics in original text).

References

Albornoz, M. (2014) 'Pietro Gori en la Argentina (1898–1902): anarquismo y cultura', in P. Bruno (ed.) *Visitas culturales en la Argentina, 1898–1935*, Buenos Aires: Biblos, pp 23–48.
Antonioli, M. (1996) *Pietro Gori*, Pisa: BFS.
Antonioli, M. and Bertolucci, F. (2001) 'Pietro Gori: Una vita per l'ideale', in P. Gori, *La miseria e i delitti*, Pisa: BFS, pp 5–117.
Bertolucci, F. (2012) 'Pietro Gori: Epistolario edito e inedito 1889–1902', in M. Antonioli, F. Bertolucci and R. Giulianelli (eds) *Nostra patria è il mondo intero: Pietro Gori nel movimento operaio e libertario italiano e internazionale*, Pisa: BFS, pp 281–359.
Bisi, R. (2004) *Enrico Ferri e gli studi sulla criminalità*, Milan: Franco Angeli.
Colao, F. (2007) 'Il principio di legalità nell'Italia di fine Ottocento tra "giustizia penale eccezionale" e "repressione necessaria e legale … nel senso più retto e saviamente giuridico, il che vuol dire anche nel senso più liberale"', *Quaderni fiorentini per la storia del pensiero giuridico moderno*, 36: 697–742.
Colao, F., Lacchè, L. and Storti, C. (eds) (2008) *Processo penale e opinione pubblica in Italia tra Otto e Novecento*, Bologna: Il Mulino.
Darmon, P. (1989) *Médecins et assassins à la Belle Epoque. La médicalization du crime*, Paris: Le Seuil.
Diemoz, E. (2011) *Morte al tiranno. Anarchia e violenza da Crispi a Mussolini*, Turin: Einaudi.

Geli, P. (1992) 'Los anarquistas en el gabinete antropométrico. Anarquismo y criminología en la sociedad argentina del 900', *Entrepasados. Revista de Historia*, 2(2): 7–24.
Gibson, M. (2002) *Born to Crime: Cesare Lombroso and the Origins of Biological Criminology*, London: Praeger.
Gori, P. (1891) *Prigioni e battaglie*, Milan: F. Fantuzzi.
Gori, P. (1905a) 'Giustizia popolare e giustizia togata', *Il Pensiero*, 3(13): 194–196.
Gori, P. (1905b) *Gli anarchici sono malfattori? Difesa pronunciata il 27 aprile 1898 innanzi al tribunale penale di Ancona nel processo Malatesta e Compagni*, Florence: F. Serantoni.
Gori, P. (1905c) *Il nostro ordine e il vostro disordine. Conferenza tenuta il 15 marzo 1896 nella 'Bersaglieri Hall' di S. Francisco Cal. (Stati Uniti d'America)*, Florence: F. Serantoni.
Gori, P. (1905d) 'L'evoluzione della sociologia criminale', *Il Pensiero*, 3(7): 99–101.
Gori, P. (1906a) 'Come sarà la società futura?', *Il Pensiero*, 4(4): 51–52.
Gori, P. (1906b) 'La delinquenza all'indomani della rivoluzione', *Il Pensiero*, 4(6): 83–85.
Gori, P. (1907) *Gli anarchici e l'articolo 248. Difesa dell'Avv. Pietro Gori innanzi al tribunale penale di Genova*, Rimini: L'iniziativa editrice.
Gori, P. (1911a) 'Il martirio di Chicago', in *Opere, II. Ceneri e faville*, II, La Spezia: Tipografia La Sociale, pp 78–80.
Gori, P. (1911b) 'I delinquenti dell'ordine', in *Opere, II. Ceneri e faville*, II, La Spezia: Tipografia La Sociale, pp 14–15.
Gori, P. (1911c) *Opere*, VI. *Sociologia criminale*, La Spezia: Tipografia La Sociale.
Gori, P. (1911d) *Opere*, VII. *Bozzetti sociali*, La Spezia: Tipografia La Sociale.
Gori, P. (1911e) *Opere*, I. *Prigioni*, La Spezia: Tipografia La Sociale.
Gori, P. (1912) *Opere*, VIII. *Sociologia anarchica*, La Spezia: Tipografia La Sociale.
Gori, P. (1945) *In difesa di Sante Caserio*, Rome: La Rivolta.
Gori, P. (2001) *La miseria e i delitti*, Pisa: BFS
Lombroso, C. (1876) *L'uomo delinquente*, Milan: Hoepli
Lombroso, C. (1894) *Gli anarchici*, Turin: Bocca.
Manfredi, M. (2017) *Emozioni, cultura popolare e transnazionalismo. Le origini della cultura anarchica in Italia (1890–1914)*, Florence/Milan: Le Monnier/ Mondadori Education.
Manfredi, M. (2018) '"An anarchiste comédien". Pietro Gori, un canone per il movimento anarchico italiano', in M. Manfredi and E. Minuto (eds) *La politica dei sentimenti. Linguaggi, spazi e canali della politicizzazione nell'Italia del lungo Ottocento*, Rome: Viella, pp 191–220.
Marconi, P. (1979) *La libertà selvaggia. Stato e punizione nel pensiero anarchico*, Venice: Marsilio.

Masini, P.C. (1973) 'Le due Pasionarie dell'Anarchia in Italia', *Storia Illustrata*, 191: 119–128.

Masini, P.C. (2005) 'Irèos e Djali. Nella Giacomelli e Leda Rafanelli da "Il Grido della folla" a "Sciarpa nera": due donne nel movimento libertario, 1901–1914', in R. Giulianelli (ed.) *Luigi Fabbri. Studi e documenti sull'anarchismo tra Otto e Novecento*, Pisa: BFS, pp 105–120.

Minuto, E. (2011) 'Gli anarchici nella crisi di fine '800. L'attività di Pietro Gori in difesa della libertà', *Storia e Futuro. Rivista di storia e storiografia*, 26. Available from: http://storiaefuturo.eu/gli-anarchici-crisi-800-lattivita-pietro-gori-in-difesa-liberta [Accessed 23 February 2024].

Minuto, E. (2017) 'Pietro Gori's anarchism: politics and spectacle (1895–1900)', *International Review of Social History*, 62(3): 425–450.

Molinari, L. (1904) *Il tramonto del diritto penale*, Milan: Tipografia dell'Universita popolare.

Noccella, A J., Seis, M. and Shantz, J. (2020) *Classic Writings in Anarchist Criminology: A Historical Dismantling of Punishment and Domination*, Berna: AK Press.

Ongaro, E. (2019) *Nella Giacomelli. Un'anarchica controcorrente*, Milan: Zero in condotta.

Papadia, E. (2018) 'I processi come "scuole di anarchia". La propaganda sovversiva nelle aule dei tribunali (1876–1894)', *Memoria e Ricerca*, 26(2): 277–294.

Quinto, H. (2020) 'Os estudos do crime sob a ótica de um anarquista: Pietro Gori e a revista Criminalogía Moderna', *Crítica Historica*, 11(21): 232–264.

Rafanelli, L. (1907) *Valide braccia. Opuscolo di propaganda contro la costruzione di nuove carceri*, Florence: Libreria Rafanelli-Polli.

Rotondo, F. (2014) *Itinerari alla periferia di Lombroso. Pietro Gori e la 'Criminalogia moderna' in Argentina*, Napoli: Editoriale Scientifica.

Ruggiero, V. (2010) *Penal Abolitionism*, Oxford: Oxford University Press.

Ruggiero, V. (2012) 'Anarchismo e criminalità', in M. Antonioli, F. Bertolucci and R. Giulianelli (eds) *Nostra patria è il mondo intero: Pietro Gori nel movimento operaio e libertario italiano e internazionale*, Pisa: BFS, pp 151–161.

Sbriccoli, M. (1974/75) 'Il diritto penale sociale (1885–1912)', *Quaderni fiorentini per la storia del pensiero giuridico moderno*, I(3–4): 558–642.

Scott, D. (2013) 'Unequalled in pain', in D. Scott (ed.) *Why Prison?*, New York: Cambridge University Press, pp 301–324.

Scott, D. (2020) *For Abolition. Essays on Prisons and Socialist Ethics*, Hook: Waterside Press.

Seymour, M. (2012) 'Emotional arenas: from provincial circus to national courtroom in late nineteenth-century Italy', *Rethinking History*, 16(2): 177–97.

Zaragoza Rovira, G. (1996) *Anarquismo argentino (1876–1902)*, Madrid: De La Torre.

13

'Cemeteries of the Living Dead'[1]: Eugene V. Debs, Prison Abolitionist

Lisa Phillips

Introduction

Eugene V. Debs, five-times candidate for US president on the Socialist Party's ticket, internationally renowned labour leader, president of the American Railway Union (ARU) and a founding member of the Industrial Workers of the World (IWW), developed an understanding of criminal behaviour that countered just about everything the emerging professionals believed to be true. Over the course of Debs' lifetime (1855–1926), 'criminals' were increasingly understood as simply defective, either genetically or through a problematic upbringing, or a combination of both (see Forero Cuellar, Chapter 10 in this volume). The emphasis was almost exclusively on an individual's defects and failings. Few invoked the possible structural or systemic reasons why someone might be forced, as Debs understood criminality, into problematic or illegal behaviour.

Debs spent a total of three years in prison over two separate convictions. The first, in 1894, was a result of his having led a national strike and ignoring a court-ordered injunction; the second, a longer stay in the Atlanta Penitentiary, for having encouraged people to avoid the draft during the First World War. Both times Debs said he felt a deep kinship with his fellow prisoners. He believed they had all been incarcerated for society's failings rather than their own. As he left the Atlanta Penitentiary in 1921, with tears in his eyes, his fellow prisoners applauded him for over five minutes. Most prisoners would have cried with relief on their release, but Debs' tears were for the prisoners he left behind. He treated his fellow prisoners as human beings, not defective at all, but imprisoned through the fault of a legislative system designed to criminalize people for crimes more appropriately attributed to 'the capitalist class'.[2]

The capitalist understanding of the criminal

The 'defective-individual' understanding of crime developed concurrently with capitalism and was relatively new to Debs and his contemporaries. For at least 200 years in North America, until industrial capitalism took hold, crime was simply not understood as being committed by deeply flawed individuals (with the notable exception of women 'witches' who were believed to be possessed by the devil). Rather, most crime was understood as the result of someone temporarily having lost their way. Deterrents were the answer. Fines, hard labour, corporal punishment and executions were brutal forms of punishment designed to remind people to avoid sinful (criminal) behaviour. Invoking someone's upbringing, their racial and/or ethnic backgrounds, or their class status as explanations of crime would not become the dominant paradigm until the late 19th century. Eugene Debs vehemently opposed these hyperindividualized explanations of errant behaviour in favour of a systemic understanding rooted in the failings of capitalism.[3]

How did the focus on an individual's inherent characteristics develop? After the Revolution, Americans were overwhelmingly concerned with creating a moral, upstanding 'American' citizenry. The country's first appointed judges created a penal code designed not to administer swift and harsh punishment as a deterrent to crime but, rather, to provide the criminal with time to spend in quiet contemplation (Smith, 2020). Americans believed theirs to be more humane than the British system that preceded it. This early 19th-century understanding began a process that cemented criminal behaviour to the 'individual's failings' (Rothman, 1995, 2002). The next few decades witnessed an extension of this thinking in the creation of the Pennsylvania and Auburn systems (Rubin, 2021). Both emphasized versions of solitary confinement – the method by which criminals would rehabilitate themselves through long periods of contemplative silence – which represented a few more steps towards the hyperfocus on the individual that Debs so detested. In reality, brutal corporal punishment was what was actually practised, and solitary confinement proved no better than harsh deterrents in producing upstanding 'moral citizens' (Rubin, 2021: 43).

The years leading up to the American Civil War saw a continued emphasis on the individual, now further justified by the fact that the US saw its first influx of immigrants, the development of the urban population and its first police force. Newly arriving immigrants, particularly the Irish, drew the ire of the white, native-born, Anglo population. New York City's infamous Irish gangs generated what we might recognize as the first urban criminal element, their behaviour allegedly being bad enough to result in the creation of the first formalized professional police force (Jenkins, 2003; Barrett and Roediger, 2005; Barnett, 2012). Americans understood criminals, just like foreigners, as needing a good dose of religion, a chance to recalibrate toward their moral centre, and to refocus their efforts on productive work, forcibly if necessary. Criminals were best isolated for their own good, as well as that of wider society, until they proved themselves capable of being God-fearing and hardworking citizens. Prison reformers led by Dorothea Dix brought the reality of the prison situation to light, as Debs would do 50 years later, but her efforts were not enough to prompt an ideological shift away from the individual and towards a systemic analysis (Sullivan, 1990; Dix and Lightner, 1999). The system we now have in place was coming into being. As the historian David Rothman writes: 'Prisons in the post-Civil War era became modern, that is, characterized by overcrowding, brutality, and disorder' (1995: 112).

The immigrant criminal element put yet another layer of emphasis on the individual and also served to reinforce ideas surrounding white native-born superiority. If criminals were predisposed to crime, society as a whole was not really responsible for it and did not have to confront the economic realities facing immigrants or Black Americans. The hyperfocus on the individual fit the country's collective determination to support what was in the making: a capitalist economic system based on class, racial and gender inequality. Penologists, reformers and scholars wholeheartedly believed that the changes they instituted were for the betterment of the prisoner. They were incapable of seeing the hierarchical lens they were using to define criminality, based on innate characteristics, as at all problematic. Writing in 1927 about the previous decades' progress, Harry Barnes, a historian commissioned by the Prison Investigating Commission, wrote:

> It has long been recognized that certain members of this legal class of criminals are amendable, though in different degrees, to reformatory influences, and that it is, therefore, the duty of society to supply these influences for its own welfare, as well as for that of the individual offender. On the other hand, it is admitted with equal frankness that others of the class of so-called criminals are, by reason of unfavorable biological heredity or unfortunate individual experience, so hopelessly defective or abnormal as to defy any hope of ultimate reformation, and, as a consequence, demand permanent segregations and the prevention of propagation. (Barnes, 1927: 7)[4]

While Barnes clearly believed some criminals to be beyond reform, Debs, in essays published the same year, believed the exact opposite: that prison itself and the ideas surrounding crime were what created the criminal. The answer was to end the system itself by adopting socialism. 'Capitalism', he wrote, 'needs and must have the prison to protect itself from the criminals it has created' (Debs, 1927: 174) and 'the prison ... is not only anti-social, but anti-human, and at best is bad enough to reflect the ignorance, stupidity and inhumanity of the society it serves' (Debs, 1927: 187). Socialism would not depend upon an imprisoned class, he argued, but rather would eliminate the very need for crime by more equally distributing wealth and eliminating poverty: 'Socialism will abolish the prison by removing its cause and putting an end to the vicious conditions which make such a hideous thing as the prison a necessity in the community life' (Debs, 1927: 233).

From petit-bourgeois to socialist

Debs came to socialism and prison abolition in mid-life. The turning point for him was the 1894 Pullman Strike. The members of the American Railway Union (ARU) called what was initially a wildcat strike to protest against the conditions under which they worked, but also against the overall power railroad companies and owners had over people's lives, their futures and their children's futures. The strike, described one historian in 1948, was not only 'an attack upon the incident evils of capitalism but on the very system itself' (Varg, 1948).[5] Debs was of a generation that could remember small producer-ownership now completely taken over by the corporation. The transition to corporate capitalism was led in the US by the railroad industry, organized nationally, horizontally and vertically by men who privately owned large portions of it. The railroad magnates controlled the Congressional purse strings informally behind the scenes. So entrenched was their power that nothing less than a labour revolution was necessary, as Debs and others would go on to argue. During the commission hearings called by President Grover Cleveland to investigate the conditions that led up to the strike, Debs declared that 'government ownership of the railroads is decidedly better than railroad ownership of the government' (Lindsey, 1942: 352). Debs' labour activism predisposed him to the systemic critique that would result in his prison abolitionism, something he first contemplated while serving time in jail in Woodstock, Illinois, in 1894 because of the strike (see also Bell and Scott, Introduction, this volume).

Debs grew up along with the development of industrial or corporate capitalism. After the industrial north defeated the agriculturally driven plantation south, the whole of the country was open for business, literally. Southern planters, disenfranchised at least temporarily, could no longer block the building of railroad tracks and the subsequent transportation of goods across the country, transforming small local markets to regional, national and international ones and, in the process, transforming the majority of the country's small producers into wage earners now working for members of the growing capitalist class.[6] As the golden spike was driven into the ground at Promontory Point connecting the first cross continental railroad track in 1869, Debs took his first job painting signs and railroad cars for a local, Terre Haute, Indiana, railroad owner. This unusual job proved fortuitous. Debs came into contact with the men who now worked, at least part of the year, for wages on the railroad. Many were local farmers, small businessmen and owners of small front-room stores selling dry goods, who took the railroad jobs to earn a small amount of cash. Others were recently arrived immigrants. None, at least in 1870, expected to lose their independence to the big corporate railroad bosses who paid them. It was this transition, from small producer to wage earner, through which Debs came of age and the very one that informed both his labour activism and, eventually, his advocacy of the abolition of prisons.[7]

Debs' parents, immigrants from Colmar, Alsace, owned a small but successful grocery store in Terre Haute, Indiana, one of hundreds scattered throughout the bustling and fast-growing midwestern town. With a population of over 16,000 people in 1870, Terre Haute had doubled in size in just ten years. The fourth-largest town in Indiana, it boasted an emerging business elite and enough of a religious presence to make it an appealing place to live. It was not, as one historian explained, a 'Midwestern backwater', but the 'bustling activity on its streets and the resounding affirmation heard in its pulpits and papers' indicated that it was indeed a good place to raise a family. Terre Haute was situated at the 'crossroads of America': as a distribution point for all railroad tracks emanating north, south, east and west, it was already a railroad hub and it sat on the banks of the Wabash River with connections to the Erie Canal and the Ohio River (Salvatore, 1982: 8–9).[8]

Early on, Debs, his parents' oldest son, seemed destined to inherit the family business, not found the Socialist Party of America (SPA). The budding grocer was a good student who was well liked and personable. When he quit high school to take a job with the Vandalia Railroad as a locomotive paint-scraper, historian Nick Salvatore tells us that the decision caused a great deal of dissension within the family, as neither of his parents supported the choice. Yet, 'if Debs' parents envisioned a petit-bourgeois position for their son in the family business, Eugene's choice of occupation was not without its own prestige or avenues of mobility' (Salvatore, 1982: 17). After losing the job to the 1873 depression, Debs hunted for stable employment as far away as St Louis. His father intervened on behalf of 'the tramp' and got him a job as an accountant for the wealthy Hulman family back in Terre Haute. Debs, still drawn to the railroad, joined fellow Terre Hautians in organizing Local 16 of the Brotherhood of Locomotive Firemen (BLF). At the age of 19, he became its recording secretary. The BLF was not at all 'anti-capitalist', but rather functioned as a 'benevolent association' providing insurance and burial expenses for its members. Accidents were so common among locomotive firemen that these became the association's sole reason for being and its justification for collecting dues. BLF members agreed that saddling widows with burial costs was an undue burden. Rather than take up a collection at the railroad locomotive firemen's funeral, the union built up a coffer through dues paid to provide a more stable funding mechanism for the burials they knew were coming. Debs, the accountant, took it upon his 20-year-old self to 'manage the books' (Salvatore, 1982: 20).

In his early twenties, Debs ran as a Democrat for the position of city clerk. He won the 1879 election easily and served two terms. In his youthful idealism, again not at all yet anti-capitalist, he envisioned a world in which 'harmony' between the labouring and business classes might be achieved. He was a young, charismatic, idealistic, well-liked son of a small grocer who had worked for one of the small town's leading businessmen, not at all yet a socialist or prison abolitionist. After having served as city clerk and continuing now as general secretary of the BLF and editor of its magazine, he ran and won election as state representative in 1884 as a Democrat.[9] While in the Indiana State Assembly, he introduced minor bills that would have required the railroad companies to pay for railroad workers' funerals and burial expenses rather than through the BLF's union-collected dues – that is, rather than workers' families paying for job-related injuries and deaths themselves. Debs and the American public were beginning to think about corporate responsibility. Upton Sinclair's *The Jungle* (1905), the muckraking exposé that revealed the types of body parts Americans were consuming in the processed meat they now bought at regional grocery stores, like the one Debs' parents owned, was still 20 years way, while legislation requiring businesses to pay for burial or injury costs was over 40 years away.

Debs was disillusioned to say the least. Men he respected refused, in his mind, to take responsibility for business 'excesses' that ruined an untold number of lives. It was at this point, in the 1880s, that he devoted himself full time to building a labour movement designed to counter the growing power of capital. It was a tall order, but he was not alone. By 1890, the US boasted thousands of union members in all walks of life who were all similarly disaffected by the shift over the 19th century from a producer to a corporate capitalist economy. Still living in the railroad hub of Terre Haute, Indiana, Debs continued to focus his attention on railroad workers. It was *the* industry, at the time, to organize, as it constituted the foundation of the growth of both 'horizontally' and 'vertically' organized business models that provided the foundation for men like Cornelius Vanderbilt to ascend to the top of the heap and create 'monopoly' capitalism by using the wealth he generated for himself to buy up subsidiary businesses (lumber for railroad tracks, for example). Vanderbilt then used the wealth to further monopolize so that wealth was increasingly concentrated in fewer and fewer hands.[10]

To counter this organizational 'scheme', Debs envisioned a counter in a nationally organized – top to bottom – labour movement. Nothing less, he argued, would be powerful enough to push back. Working with railroad workers, he organized the ARU, the first national industrial union in the US. Headquartered in Chicago, Debs and his fellow organizers managed hundreds of local branches nationwide, eventually including everyone from the top-paid engineers to the lowest-paid painters and sweepers. This was what made it an industrial rather than a skills-based union. Debs tried but was unable to break through the colour line, a racial divide that he knew, at the time, would weaken the union overall. The vote to do so was only two shy of carrying. Debs said later that that vote was 'was one of the factors in our defeat' (Salvatore, 1982: 227). It is important to put his perspective on race into context. Indeed, the 1890s saw thousands of strikes organized by white workers who refused to work alongside or organize unions with Black workers. Debs' stance, as president of a powerful union, was significant, even if it failed (see Wilson, Marable and Ness, 2006: 29).

The ARU was put to the test in 1894 when workers just outside of Chicago went out on what was, initially, a wildcat strike. At issue were low wages and long hours, and George Pullman's complete control over food prices, housing costs and religious services, as his striking workers lived in Pullman, the company town (which is still in existence today). Reluctantly, Debs supported the strike. Despite his misgivings, this was just the sort of pushback power he had envisioned when he helped organize the ARU, but the timing was off and this, he thought, was not the right context in which to 'lead a revolution'. When, on 4 July, President Cleveland sent in 'regulars', US troops to break up what was at this point still a Pullman-localized strike, Debs attempted to call the strike off for fear of an all-out class war on the condition that Pullman reinstate the strikers. Pullman refused. It was then that Debs went to the ARU membership to ask for a vote for a general strike; the vote was a resounding 'yes' and a general-national strike was called. Just one of a few such strikes in US history, it proved weak and ineffectual largely because the other national labour union in existence at the time, Samuel Gompers' American Federation of Labor (AFL), took the opportunity to predicate its support on commandeering control over the strike from the ARU and Debs, with which (and whom) they had been at odds over the very nature of union organizing. The ARU was organized as more of an anti-railroad, anti-industrial capital organization while the AFL, representing workers based on their skill, such as the 'Locomotive Engineers' Union', explicitly accepted much of the capitalist framework and worked for mere bread-and-butter issues.[11]

President Cleveland was incensed that the leader of a labour union had the power to bring the economy to a grinding halt. He ordered Debs to get the ARU members and, by extension, everyone else who went out in support back to work. The Illinois State Supreme Court issued an injunction. Debs refused again because Pullman would not reinstate the striking workers. He was arrested twice, first 'on charges of conspiracy to obstruct interstate commerce' and then, again, for violating a court order (Salvatore, 1982: 135). For the second charge, he was sentenced to six months in prison. Eventually, the case went all the way to the US Supreme Court. In *Re Debs*,[12] Supreme Court Justice David Brewer argued that the US government had the authority to regulate the distribution of commerce and the mail, both of which were obstructed by Debs and the ARU. By calling a nationwide strike and violating the subsequent injunction, Debs had violated the Commerce Clause. Brewer argued further that no one man presiding over a nationally organized labour union should have such power. None other than Clarence Darrow (see Kersten, Chapter 14 in this volume), who represented Debs and the other ARU leaders, countered that the Commerce Clause and the Sherman Anti-Trust Act were *not* intended to infringe upon workers' rights, but were passed to limit corporate power and prevent monopoly formation. As it had throughout the 1890s, the Supreme Court came down on the side of the railroads; nationwide strikes were now effectively banned by giving the courts liberal use of the injunction to stop coordinated labour action (Papke, 1999).

Debs turns prison abolitionist

Debs went to prison. Like so many other later famous prisoners, he came to an epiphany while serving his six-month sentence in Woodstock penitentiary: perhaps this was something akin to prisoner self-reflection in the early 19th-century way of thinking, but it backfired in the sense that Debs did not 'mend his ways', 'see the light' or otherwise succumb to the authority structure in place; instead, he began to thoroughly reject it. He read Edward Bellamy, Victor Berger and Karl Kautsky's popularization of Marx. 'The Woodstock experience', Salvatore tells us, 'is critical in any evaluation of Debs' life and career. It remains the portal through which one understands the meaning of Socialism for Debs and other Americans in the decades to come' (Salvatore, 1982: 50). Debs spent a great deal of time thinking about the US legal and economic systems, about the ways in which they were intertwined, and about how the political system, in his opinion, existed to prop up the power of the growing corporate elite, all at the expense of the working class.[13]

In *Walls and Bars* (1927), the only book Debs wrote, he discusses these connections in stark terms. It was while he was in prison in Woodstock that he connected the dots, so to speak, between the economy, evolving as it was into one that supported and revolved around corporate capitalism; local, state and federal political systems, in reality all branches of the government that also supported the rise of the corporation; and, even more insidiously, the growing ideology around 'the criminal element' that resulted in his being criminalized for leading a strike to advocate for workers' rights. Together, the corporate capitalist paradigm held a tight grip on the American psyche. It was at this moment that Debs became a prison abolitionist. 'I sense the solemn duty', he wrote, 'to join and persist in the demand for the release of all other comrades still immured in dungeon cells until the last prisoner of the class war has secured his liberation' (Debs, 1927: 17; Tussey, 1970).

It was also in the Woodstock jail that Debs rejected capitalism and adopted socialism. He made a pact with himself, his brother Theodore and his politically likeminded friends to launch the SPA . Labour union action, as coordinated as it had to be to have any kind of effect, was easily thwarted by a judicial system that simply rendered strikes illegal. The only solution, given the clarity Pullman provided, was to try and change the political structure. A new class-conscious party was the answer, Debs thought. He was joined by intellectual activists Upton Sinclair, Emma Goldman, Victor Berger, Walt Whitman and others who rejected capitalism in this era (Ross, 2015; see also Weiss, Chapter 15 in this volume). Black intellectuals like W.E.B. Du Bois, Ida B. Wells-Barnett and Booker T. Washington were not anti-capitalist in the same way, but rather sought some version of inclusion in the economic structure their ancestors helped to build. They were, in a word, conflicted.[14] Debs was not ambivalent. He rejected capitalism outright because members of the 'working-class', regardless of their racial or ethnic backgrounds, paid for 'crimes' not of their own doing, but created by the economic system that impoverished them, writing:

> The prison in our modern life is essentially a capitalistic institution, an inherent and inseparable part of the social and economic system under which the mass of mankind are ruthlessly exploited and kept in an impoverished state, as a result of which the struggle for existence, cruel and relentless at best, drives thousands of its victims into the commission of offenses which they are forced to expiate in the dungeons provided for them by their masters. (Debs, 1927: 23)

The year 1900, then, would see the first of Debs' campaigns for President on the SPA's ticket. He ran after a bitter dispute with a rival party faction was resolved when they all agreed to tentative unity for the purpose of the campaign. Socialism was not at all popular in the US. Debs described the challenges the party faced, writing, 'it would be difficult to imagine a more ignorant, bitter and unreasoning prejudice than that of the American people against Socialism during the years of its introduction by European immigrants' (Debs, 1908: 86). The 1900 campaign was an abysmal failure. Debs and leading members of the party responded by working hard to make American socialism more 'American'. Over the next two decades, in speeches and in its circular, he and the SPA emphasized the US' small producer, yeoman farmer roots. Turned into industrial workers, the capitalist class was responsible for the demise of American democracy. While the founding fathers had not, Debs explained, lived in the (Debs') current context, the US Constitution nevertheless contained within it the ability to recognize the all-encompassing power of a class grown too big. Socialism was the logical outgrowth of what were 'real' American values and the rejection of a corporate oligarchy which had replaced the monarchy as an overpowerful entity. The 'individual' needed to be able to reach his full potential unfettered by capitalism and the poverty and crime the system created. Debs was a product of the era's emphasis on the individual, but, unlike the penologists and other advocates for the prison system, he recognized the ways in which the capitalist system was responsible for limiting people's ability to realize their full potential. Socialism would right the American ship.[15]

The links to American democracy now better elucidated, the 1908 and 1912 presidential campaigns saw greater success for Debs and the SPA Both times Debs campaigned for an eight-hour day, a minimum wage, a rejection of capitalist private ownership and government control of industry. Nationalized railroads, for example, would enable the US government to take the money generated from ticket sales to pay railroad workers a living wage, mandate safety protocols, enact an eight-hour day and reduce the concentration of wealth in the hands of corrupt capitalists, the hated Vanderbilts and Rockefellers of the era. Debs framed the party's platform in the Marxist understanding that socialism was the next stage in economic evolution – that is, that capitalism would collapse and socialism would replace it. The power in his speeches was there, in the envisioning of a different world, in which class conflict was eliminated. His was a kind of unique, American, social democratic, utopian and almost religiously infused vision. People turned out in their thousands to hear him speak, and more and more of them voted for the SPA, both federally and locally. Debs concluded his speeches by invoking Abraham Lincoln and reaffirming the necessity of industrial unions like the ARU and the IWW to enable workers to 'control their own jobs ... their own labor and be free men instead of industrial slaves' (Salvatore, 1982: 293).[16] 'When poverty goes out of the world the prison will remain only as a monument to the ages before light dawned upon darkness and civilization came to mankind', he wrote (Debs, 1927: 190).

While not a part of his stump speeches, Debs argued in the *Appeal to Reason* newspaper and *Walls and Bars* that the economic stability workers would gain from the new socialist system would reduce crime, if not eliminate it completely. In his view, crime was a byproduct of the priorities, namely profit, put in place by the capitalist class:

> The capitalist of our day, who is the social, economic, and political successor of the feudal landlord of the Middle Ages, and the patrician master of the ancient world, holds the great mass of people in bondage,

not by owning them under law, more by having sole proprietorship of industry, the tools and machinery with which work is done and wealth produced. In a word, the capitalist owns the tools and the jobs of workers and therefore they are his economic dependents. In that relation the capitalist has the power to appropriate to himself the products of the workers and to become rich in idleness while the workers, who produce all the wealth that he enjoys, remain in poverty. Capitalism needs and must have the prison to protect itself from *the criminals it has created* [emphasis added]. It not only impoverishes the masses when they are at work, but it still further reduces them by not allowing millions to work at all. (Tussey, 1970: 306–307)

In the 25 years after Pullman and Woodstock, Debs pulled no punches. He critiqued the system from top to bottom, highlighting the ways in which it hurt the working class generally and women and people of colour specifically. At the same time, penologists were hard at work creating an understanding of the criminal that was hyperfocused on the individual. Social Darwinism and the new field of eugenics ran completely counter to Debs' critique, in that both emphasized race and ethnicity (and, to a lesser extent, gender) in their explanations of what caused crime. The moral upstanding citizen was still the focus in the late 19th and early 20th centuries, the ideal now complicated by the need to define just who the ideal citizen was in the context of an influx of millions of foreign-born immigrants and the first generation of free Black Americans trickling up to northern cities. The more nuanced understanding of the 'criminal' and criminal behaviour contained none of Debs' systemic analysis.

What is so interesting about Debs' understanding is how against the grain it was. How could it be that most of the people who studied crime and criminals at this time were blind to the economic arguments regarding the causes of crime? What was it about the US at the turn of the 20th century that created some kind of wilful ignorance or even an actual inability to see the straight line Debs drew between capitalism and crime? All generations are similarly blind, with outliers, like Debs in this case, labelled radical or crazy for their interpretations of reality, only later to be seen. Over 100 years later, Debs' critique is just as valuable, yet just as ignored by the authorities, including congressional representatives, the Supreme Court, the wider judicial system, local police and most members of the public.

In order to understand the marginalization of Debs' and subsequent prison abolitionists' critiques, we need to understand what was so threatening about what he was arguing. The growing middle class of professionals, political activist-reformers, factory foremen, police/hospital/asylum wardens, medical doctors and lawyers, and the managerial class now in charge of running regional and national companies increasingly benefited in some way from the existence of a poor and criminal element. The criminals became proof of the virtuosity of the middle class, of their living well and successfully. The poor became the basis of many a career as members of the emerging middle class devoted their lives to the less fortunate. For these elites, criminals did not steal to eat; rather, they stole because of some deeply rooted issues that were studied, discussed, legislated and observed. The middle class debated how to solve the 'the negro problem', 'the labour problem' and the 'Indian problem'. Never did the emerging middle class of reformers and professionals talk about the 'wealth problem' or the 'class problem', and never was the root of any of the era's 'problems' considered to be economic, at least from a systemic point of view. Laziness was cited as the principal reason for a man's inability to, for example, support his family rather than his boss' unwillingness to pay him enough (Monkkonen, 1981).[17]

In Debs' eyes, all of these expensive efforts propped up the system while never addressing the root causes of criminality: the unequal distribution of wealth. It must have been so incredibly frustrating for him to speak to business leaders in Terre Haute, to politicians, to the authorities who determined criminal behaviour, all constantly greeting him with arguments about how people were innately bad or of 'criminal stock' when there was obvious evidence all around them of the simple maths that showed that most people were poor and that (legally defined) criminal behaviour originated from the simple lack of money. Debs' supporters, not surprisingly, were members of the working class for whom his message not only rang true, but also relieved them of the internalized stigma associated with the day's thinking. For that, Debs was loved and revered by his fellow prisoners both times he was imprisoned, and by members of the working class more generally, who viewed themselves as more likely to be criminalized by the legal and judicial systems than their wealthy bosses. There is no such thing, he argued, as a 'criminal countenance'. Prison was simply 'the outgrowth of the capitalist system for the poor'. 'If', he asked his audiences, 'society deprives a family of its provider, should it provide?' (Debs, 1927: 23, 33 and 35).

Just as Debs was leading the charge to confront the system as a whole, progressive-era reformers were engaged in massive efforts to prevent degeneracy and crime among immigrants by continuing to de-emphasize the systemic in favour of a social Darwinist and eugenics-oriented understanding of an individual's propensity to crime. Historian Khahlil Muhammad (2010) has done more to explain this late 19th and early 20th-century phenomenon than any other scholar. He argues that reformers and newly professionalized police forces were, together, quite influential in shaping an ideology around degeneracy and crime. They rendered the immigrant childlike and inferior, prone to impatience, anger and violence, to undue outside influence and in need of supervision and education. The public school system and professional police forces, complete with vice squads, all funded out of the cities' coffers, were products not of altruism, but of the condescension implicit in the anti-immigrant understanding that drove the mostly native-born reformer class (Muhammad, 2010).[18] The criminal profile was rooted in the same late 19th and early 20th-century assumptions about 'natural' racial and ethnic predispositions to criminal behaviour. Profiling was considered cutting-edge at the time, albeit pseudo-science steeped in racism as we now understand it (see also Forero Cuellar, Chapter 10 in this volume).[19] Debs' call to abolish prisons depended on his rejection of the very ideological paradigm through which most of his generation explained crime.

Conclusion: Debs' systemic critique still applies

The understanding of the 'criminal' we carry with us today, in the early 21st century, has its roots in this thinking, in the philosophy that grew up with corporate capitalism. This pitted the hero, the successful businessmen, against his alter ego, the degenerate, less-than-intelligent, slacker-immigrant who, because of a bad mix of genetics, was predisposed to criminal behaviour. Reformers believed themselves to be doing their very best to help immigrants and the lower classes more generally move into the role of productive citizen. The entire public school system was rooted in the need to Americanize and educate immigrants. Corporate capitalism's emphasis on private ownership worked in tandem by reinforcing the significance of the individual. Had corporate capitalism been attenuated or even rejected, as Debs and the socialists advocated; had reformers studied the system's weaknesses and made the capitalist-driven need for profit their focus, *systemic* changes would have become the obvious solution to crime rather than fixing the *individual*. As things stood, crime as it was continually being defined and redefined in the court system supported capitalism's further entrenchment and enabled people who were increasingly invested in the system to gain access to professional careers, driven by the need to understand the individual criminal. Debs became a 'criminal' for criticizing the very system that made criminals out of the individuals it forced into poverty and consequent 'crime'. No one was allowed to take capitalism's failings on and advocate an alternative without risk of imprisonment.

Debs' critique still applies. His systemic analysis, leading as it did to his wholehearted adoption of American socialism and prison abolitionism, has remained too anti-capitalist to be taken seriously by any US leading politician. Radicals continue to try. Angela Davis (2005), writing a century after Debs, encapsulates the connection between largely unfettered capitalism and imprisonment: 'Because of the extent to which prison building and operation began to attract vast amounts of capital – from the construction industry to food and health care providers – in a way that recalled the emergence of the military-industrial complex, we began to refer to a "prison industrial complex'" (Davis, 2003: 4). The prison industrial complex is now so inextricably intertwined in our American political and economic systems that it is virtually impossible to imagine anyone campaigning successfully to abolish it. The 'Defund the Police' movement has perhaps come the closest in recent years through its focus on systemic change. Yet, too many Americans are unable to see capitalism as responsible for crime. Nor do they understand the connections between race, purposeful impoverishment, and 'criminality' as they developed together in Debs' time period. In hindsight, Debs came perhaps the closest to imagining a country in which profit and crime might be *un*linked and may thus provide inspiration to contemporary campaigners.[20]

Notes

1. Debs, 1927: 236.
2. Several biographies detail Debs' involvement in prison reform. More recent treatments include Jones (2008) and Cole, (2021). Ernie Freeberg looked specifically at Debs' influence in ushering in the American Civil Liberties Union; see Freeberg (2008). Classic works include Ginger (1949) and Salvatore (1982).
3. David Rothman (1995) continues to be the guru of all US prison-related history.
4. Barnes was less a social Darwinist in his thinking than Herbert Spencer, the theorist most widely associated with its origins, but his assessment of the prisoner, criminality and rehabilitation programmes were nevertheless similarly steeped in the individual and his failings; see, for instance, Barnes (1921).
5. For a recent treatment of the ARU with an emphasis on the railroad owners' perspective, see Miller (2023); the definitive treatment remains Schnierov, Stromquist and Salvatore (1990).
6. While the development of the railroad is what, traditionally, historians have argued transformed the plantation south into something 'new' and more 'industrial', there has been a significant shift in our understanding of the relationship between slavery and industrial capitalism in the last ten years. See Baptist (2014) and Beckert and Rothman (2016), who argue that the roots of industrial capitalism can be found in the plantation agriculture, particularly in the way it was reorganized in a kind of routinized early version of the assembly line after the cotton gin pressured production.
7. Glickman (1997) provides the best explanation of the transition from artisan to wage worker.
8. See also McCormick (2005) and Madison (2006).
9. See Salvatore (1982) and the other biographies and the timeline maintained by the Eugene V. Debs Foundation. Available from: https://debsfoundation.org/index.php/landing/debs-biography [Accessed 25 September 2024].
10. The as-yet unchallenged trajectory of corporate capitalism's 'take over' in the US can be found in Sklar (1988). If anything, the same trajectory Sklar laid out is now being written about globally as historians are arguing about similar developments in other countries; see Johnson (2010). For the untoward influence of the railroads in the development of the industrial US and corporate capitalism, see White (2011).
11. Labour historians debate the degrees of anti-capitalism embedded in union philosophy constantly – see Salvatore (1982: 134–137) – but treatments of all AFL-affiliated unions grapple with Gompers' conservative positioning of the AFL in this era.
12. *Re Debs* 158 US 564 (1885).
13. Salvatore has the best discussion of Debs' 'conversion' process, see Salvatore (1982: 150–151).

14. Mark VanWienen has written a great book on interest book on the ways in which socialism attracted a diverse set of thinkers in this period, some, like DuBois, influenced by it but not able to fully embrace it; see VanWienen (2012).
15. For more on Debs' grafting socialist ideals to American tradition, see Salvatore (1982: 192–94).
16. An important feature in Debs' history is his helping to found the Industrial Workers of the World (IWW), which I do not mention much here, but which was an outgrowth of his growing insistence on the need to overthrow capitalist systems with the IWW globally. Founded in 1905, the IWW became a radical expression of working-class radicalism and one that was partially responsible for Debs having been arrested for inciting opposition to the draft in 1918; for more on the history of the IWW, see Struthers, Zimmerman and Cole (2017).
17. There are so many good books now on the history of progressive-era reform. On the reformers' take on the labour question, see Currarino (2010); for the 'Negro Question', see Southern (2005); for women, race and class, see the classic Frankel and Dye (1991); and, on the 'Indian Question', see Maddox (2005).
18. Frank Dikotte wrote a review article in which he linked the eugenics movement to the broader 'race culture' of the late 19th and early 20th centuries; see Dikotte (1998) and Mottier (2010).
19. Good histories of the development of forensic science are hard to come by as most treatments spill over into sensationalist accounts of trial cases and into 'true crime' (there are better histories for the UK and India); see Bell (2008).
20. See Davis (2003), Harvel and Wright (2011), and Alexander (2020).

References

Alexander, M. (2020) *The New Jim Crow: Mass Incarceration in the Age of Color Blindness*, New York: New Press.

Baptist, E. (2014) *The Half Has Never Been Told: Slavery and the Making of American Capitalism*, New York: Basic Books.

Barnes, H. (1921) 'The Historical Origin of the Prison System in America', *Journal of the American Institute of Criminal Law and Criminology*, 12(1): 35–60.

Barnes, H. (1927) *The Evolution of Penology in Pennsylvania*, Indianapolis: Bobbs-Merrell.

Barrett, J. (2012) *The Irish Way: Becoming American in the Multiethnic City*, New York: Penguin.

Barrett, J. and Roediger, D. (2005) 'The Irish and the Americanization of the new immigrants in the streets and in the church of the urban United States, 1900–1930', *Journal of American Ethnic History*, 24(4): 3–33.

Beckert, S. and Rothman, S. (eds) (2016) *Slavery's Capitalism: A New History of American Economic Development*, Philadelphia: University of Pennsylvania Press.

Bell, S. (2008) *Crime and Circumstance: Investigating the History of Forensic Science*, Westport, CT: Praeger.

Cole, P. (2021) 'Prisoner No. 9653: Eugene Debs on capitalism, incarceration, and solidarity', *North Meridian Review*, 2(1): 64–81.

Currarino, R. (2010) *The Labor Question in America: Economic Development in American during the Gilded Age*, Urbana: University of Illinois Press.

Davis, A. (2003) *Are Prisons Obsolete?*, New York: Seven Stories Press.

Davis, A. (2005) *Abolition and Democracy: Beyond Empire, Prisons, and Torture*, New York: Seven Stories Press.
Debs, E.V. (1908) *Debs: His Life, Writings, and Speeches*, Chicago: Kerr.
Debs, E.V. (1927) *Walls and Bars*, Chicago: Socialist Party.
Dikotte, F. (1998) 'Race culture: recent perspectives on the history of eugenics', *American Historical Review*, 103(2): 467–478.
Dix, D. and Lightner, D. (1999) *Asylum, Prison, and Poorhouse: The Writings and Reform Work of Dorothea Dix in Illinois*, Carbondale: University of Southern Illinois Press.
Frankel, N. and Dye, N. (eds) (1991) *Gender, Race, Class, and Reform in the Progressive Era*, Lexington: University of Kentucky Press.
Freeberg, E. (2008) *Democracy's Prisoner: Eugene V. Debs, The Great War, and the Right to Dissent*, Cambridge, MA: Harvard University Press.
Ginger, R. (1949) *The Bending Cross*, New Brunswick, NJ: Rutgers University Press.
Glickman, L. (1997) *A Living Wage: American Workers and the Making of Consumer Society*, Ithaca, NY: Cornell University Press.
Harvel, T. and Wright, P. (2011) *Who Makes Money from Mass Incarceration*, New York: New Press.
Jenkins, W. (2003) 'Patrolmen and Peelers, immigration, urban culture and the Irish police in Canada and the United States', *Canadian Journal of Irish Studies*, 28–29: 10–29.
Johnson, P. (2010) *Making the Market: Victorian Origins of Corporate Capitalism*, Cambridge: Cambridge University Press.
Jones, W. (2008) '"Nothing special to offer the negro": revisiting the Debsian view of the Negro Question', *International Labor and Working Class History*, 74(1): 212–224.
Lindsey, A. (1942) *The Pullman Strike: The Story of a Unique Experiment and of a Great Labor Upheaval*, Chicago: University of Chicago Press.
Maddox, L. (2005) *Citizen Indian: Native American Intellectuals, Race and Reform*, Ithaca, NY: Cornell University Press.
Madison, J. (2006) *The Indiana Way: A State History*, Bloomington: Indiana University Press.
McCormick, M. (2005) *Terre Haute: Queen City of the Wabash*, Charleston, SC: Arcadi.
Miller, B. (2023) 'The failed fight for workers' rights: Eugene V. Debs and the American Railway Union in the Pullman strike of 1894', *The Alexandrian*, XII(1).
Monkkonen, E. (1981) 'A disorderly people? Urban order in the 19th and 20th century', *Journal of American History*, 68(3): 539–559.
Mottier, V. (2010) 'Eugenics and the state: policy making in comparative perspective', in A. Bashford and P. Levine (eds) *Oxford Handbook of the History of Eugenics*, Oxford: Oxford University Press, pp 134–153.

Muhammad, K. (2010) *The Condemnation of Blackness: Race, Crime, and the Making of Modern Urban America*, Cambridge, MA: Harvard University Press.

Papke, D. (1999) *The Pullman Case: The Clash of Labor and Capital in Industrial America*, Lawrence: University of Kansas Press.

Ross, J. (2015) *The Socialist Party of America: A Complete History*, Lincoln, NE: University of Nebraska Press.

Rothman, D. (1995) 'Perfecting the prison, United States, 1789–1865', in N. Thomas and D. Rothman (eds) *The Oxford History of the Prison: The Practice of Punishment in Western Society*, New York: Oxford University Press, pp 100–116.

Rothman, D. (2002) *The Discovery of the Asylum: Social Order and Disorder in the New Republic*, London: Routledge.

Rubin, A. (2021) *The Deviant Prison: Philadelphia's Eastern State Penitentiary and the Origins of America's Modern Penal System, 1829–1913*, Cambridge: Cambridge University Press

Salvatore, N. (1982) *Eugene V. Debs, Citizen and Socialist*, Urbana: University of Illinois Press.

Schnierov, R., Stromquist, S. and Salvatore, N. (eds) (1990) *The Pullman Strike and the Crisis of the 1890s: Essays on Labor and Politics*, Urbana: University of Illinois Press.

Sklar, M. (1988) *The Corporate Reconstruction of American Capitalism, 1890–1916*, Cambridge: Cambridge University Press.

Smith, P. (2020) 'Solitary confinement: effects and practices from the nineteenth century until today', in J. Lobel and P. Smith (eds) *Solitary Confinement: Effects, Practices, and Pathways toward Reform*, New York: Oxford University Press, pp 21–42.

Southern, D. (2005) *The Progressive Era and Race: Reaction and Reform, 1900–1917*, New York: Wiley.

Struthers, D., Zimmerman, K. and Cole, P. (eds) (2017) *Wobblies of the World: A Global History of the Industrial Workers of the World*, London: Pluto Press.

Sullivan, L. (1990) *The Prison Reform Movement: Forlorn Hope*, New York: Twayne.

Tussey, J. (ed.) (1970) *Eugene V. Debs Speaks*, New York: Pathfinder.

VanWienen, M. (2012) *American Socialist Triptych: The Literary-Political Work of Charlotte Perkins Gilman, Upton Sinclair, and W.E.B. DuBois*, Ann Arbor: University of Michigan Press.

Varg, P. (1948) 'The political ideas of the American Railway Union', *The Historian*, 10(2): 85–100.

White, R. (2011) *Railroaded: The Transcontinentals and the Making of Modern America*, New York: W.W. Norton.

Wilson, J., Marable, M. and Ness, I. (eds) (2006) *Race and Labor Matters in the New US Economy*, Lanham, MD: Rowman & Littlefield.

14

Altgeld's Protégé: Clarence Darrow and the Abolition of Prisons and Capital Punishment in the United States

Andrew E. Kersten

Introduction

Clarence Seward Darrow (1857–1938) was born in the small farming town of Kinsman, Ohio, on 18 April 1857, at a moment when the US stood at the precipice of a violent, cataclysmic and transformative epoch. Darrow's family not only bore witness to this change but was also a part of it. His parents were integrated into the antebellum abolitionist and freethinking movements, and the young Darrow reaped the rewards of having luminaries such as Frederick Douglass (c. 1817–1895) and Robert Ingersoll (1833–1899) stay at his family's home on their itinerate journeys to spread the word of revolutionary reform. These experiences constitute an important part of Darrow's intellectual inheritance. The other part of his family's inheritance – the business of carpentry and casket making – he rejected. Instead, after the Civil War, he forged his own path, studying law at the University of Michigan, and then without the degree, passing the bar in Ohio in 1872. As a lawyer working in nearby Ashtabula, Ohio, he quickly outgrew the confines of rural life, and in 1887, he headed west to Chicago, which was his home base of operations for his 50-year fight on behalf of the poor and downtrodden who were ensnared in a criminal justice system that was stacked against them. Living in America's Windy City also provided him with the opportunity to engage in the world of ideas, politics and reform. Among other things, he became a leading voice in the US for the abolition of jails and prisons and for the abolition of capital punishment. This chapter focuses on Darrow's penal and death penalty abolitionism. It starts with a discussion of one of the main influences on his life and work, and then proceeds to explore his ideas, cases and writings in more detail. It concludes by reflecting on ways in which his abolitionism can be of inspiration today.

As a lawyer, Darrow's embrace of abolitionist ideas regarding the penal system and death penalty had little connection to his legal career in Ashtabula. Mostly, his work there was about collections, contracts and the grievances that one farmer sometimes holds against another. However, it was in that town that he received a book as a gift from a local judge. Reading John P. Altgeld's *Our Penal Machinery and Its Victims* (1886) changed Darrow's life forever. He became his protégé. Let us then reflect in some detail on the work of Altgeld as this provides an important stepping stone in our journey to understand the emergence of penal and death penalty abolitionism in Darrow's thoughts and career.

John Peter Altgeld and victimization in the penal machine

Born in the independent Germanic state of the Duchy of Nassau, John Peter Altgeld (1847–1902) emigrated to the US as an infant, settling in Lexington, Ohio. When he was 16, he joined the Union Army as a member of the Ohio Infantry. Following the Civil War, he became a lawyer and made a fortune in real estate and economic development in Illinois. He also became quite politically active as a member of the reinvented Democrat Party. Inspired by a farmers' movement, known as the Granger Movement, he began running for public office in the 1870s. In 1884, he tried unsuccessfully to be a US Congressmen from Illinois. His platform centred on several reform ideas to make life better for the average worker and the poor. Although he did not win, his progressive thoughts on crime and punishment had a profound effect through the publication of his book, *Our Penal Machinery and Its Victims* (Barnard, 1938).

As Altgeld engaged in his ill-fated 1884 congressional campaign, he talked to Illinois families and encountered a vast and complex social crisis, one that few Americans were discussing, but many were experiencing daily. Thousands were trapped and victimized by the state and local penal systems. As he began to investigate, he discovered that this was not a localized problem, but one that affected the entire US. He estimated that there were nationally 2,500,000 arrests each year, which represented about 5 per cent of the US population (Altgeld, 1886: 8). He assumed further that about 40 per cent of these people had prior arrests, leaving about 1,500,000 new arrests annually. In other words, every year, more than a million men, women and children were 'broken into what may be called a criminal experience' (Altgeld, 1886: 8). It had nothing to do with justice. He estimated that for each individual arrested, jailed and convicted, another five people close to the incarcerated were directly and adversely affected. 'The disgrace, the odium, the pain, reaches out remorselessly to [the fathers, mothers, brothers, sisters, sons and daughters], and to a greater or less extent they suffer on account' of those in the penal machinery (Altgeld, 1886: 11). This meant that millions upon millions were connected to the trauma of the legal system. Altgeld resolved to change the situation through political activism and by publicizing the problem and possible solutions. As he wrote, in 1886, the sole purpose in publishing *Our Penal Machinery and Its Victims* was 'to call attention briefly to the character of our penal machinery and if possible lead others to examine it; feeling confident that, when once generally understood, improvements will be made therein which will benefit society and will greatly lessen the sum of human misery' (Altgeld, 1886: iii).

Altgeld was one of many Americans seeking to transform the nation's penal systems. Among the leaders was Enoch Cobb Wines (1806–1879), who rose to national prominence as the convening secretary of the National Prison Association (NPA) which he helped to found in Cleveland, Ohio, in 1870. The NPA was dedicated to making the justice and incarceration systems more humane, with the gaols improving lives and building pathways toward remunerative work (Titus, 1906: 6). Wines and the Association held annual conventions. In 1885, Altgeld spoke at the Detroit convention, laying out the basic arguments in *Our Penal Machinery and Its Victims*, which became one of the bestselling and most influential books on justice and prison reform in US history (Altgeld, 1886: 136–151; Titus, 1906: 147).

In much the same way as English prison reformer John Howard (1726–1790) or American reformer Dorothea Dix (1802–1887) went about their work, Altgeld took a clinical approach to the investigation of crime and punishment, asking what their effects were and, pointedly, who the machinery served (Brown, 1998; Howard, 1777). He discovered that America's prisons, jails and houses of correction were what they had always been. He would have agreed with Enoch Wines, who wrote in his 1880 magnum opus *State of Prisons* (1880) that in the main prisons were an earthly manifestation of Dante's hell: the phrase 'Let all who enter here leave hope behind', Wines opined, 'stood, through the centuries and cycles, over all the prison gates of the world, crushing every aspiration and paralyzing all efforts, except the effort to escape from the hated hell' (Wines, 1880: 1). Mincing no words, it was institutionalized 'evil' that profited the jailers, not the jailed (Wines, 1880: 13–14). Altgeld's analysis supported Wines' lyrical conclusions. Tens of thousands were employed as policemen, constables, magistrates, sheriffs, judges, jailers, lawyers and tradesmen who built, maintained and serviced the jails, prisons, reformatories and workhouses. Altgeld estimated that the total cost of America's penal infrastructure was at least US$400,000,000 annually (more than US$12 billion in today's money). This annual investment was 'dead capital' as it did not improve society or the economy (Altgeld,

1886: 13). The vast network of enforcers and penal institutions did nothing to 'deter the young offender' or 'reform nor restrain the old offender'. In other words, Altgeld argued that the system made 'criminals out of many who are not naturally so'; rendered 'it difficult for those once convicted… to be anything else than criminals'; and failed 'to repress those who do not want to be anything but criminals' (Altgeld, 1886: 15). Given this, Altgeld asked the logical next questions: 'whether there is not something wrong with the system; whether it is not based on a mistaken principle; whether it is not a great mill which, somehow or other, supplies its own grist, a maelstrom which draws from the outside and then keeps its victims moving in a circle until swallowed in the vortex' (Altgeld, 1886: 14–15).

Altgeld knew precisely those trapped in the vortex. Of the 7,566 people incarcerated in the Bridewell House of Correction in Chicago in 1882, all but 190 had been imprisoned because they could not pay their court fines. Nearly one in four were women, and a similar ratio was under the age of 25 (Altgeld, 1886: 16–17). In that year there was one prisoner who was eight years old, five who were nine years old, and fourteen who were ten years old (Altgeld, 1886: 17). Most of the prisoners had either no living parent or only one close to them, had little formal schooling and were addicted to alcohol (even the children) (Altgeld, 1886: 19). Furthermore, more than half of all prisoners had been in Bridewell before. This 'repeater' rate was higher than the national average (Altgeld, 1886: 23–24).

Altgeld believed that the scourge of incarcerating Chicagoans for outstanding fines provided one main explanation. That said, penal systems in the US were capricious, which directly led to high recidivism rates. In one of his rare examples that dealt with race, he noted that in Southern states, Black Americans had higher repeater rates as they were 'frequently re-committed for rather trivial offenses' (Altgeld, 1886: 24). Simply put, 'our penal machinery seems to recruit its victims from among those who are fighting an unequal fight in the struggle for existence' (Altgeld, 1886: 21). The machinery warehoused them in inhumane conditions. Altgeld referenced an 1876 report from Unitarian minister, abolitionist and reformer William Greenleaf Eliot (1811–1887), whose description of St Louis' crowded primary prison was blunt and accurate: 'What school-houses of crime are these! The city's public schools of vice and profligacy, open for men, women, and children, every day in the year, with a double accumulated crowd for the Lord's day!' (Altgeld, 1886: 26).

The Gilded Age's cynics, of which there were many, concluded that these schools for teaching vice and crime existed only to provide more sources of revenue for those employed by the machine. Growth in the industry depended on creating more crimes and more poor people. Reformation and redemption had no relation to the system. Those who saw opportunities to help the imprisoned were few and far between. Prison libraries and schools (including Sunday Schools) were rare. Occasionally a minister visited prisoners.

As American prison lore has it, 'the first sermon preached in an American prison was under the protection of a loaded cannon, with a fuse in readiness to be touched off at any moment' (Wines, 1880: 24). The light of God, let alone the light of knowledge, was unwelcomed in the closed shuttered jails or houses of correction.

To ameliorate the situation, Altgeld proposed a series of reforms. In concert with the larger tradition of American prisons, some of which like the Auburn and Pennsylvania systems held out hope of redemption, he did not propose abolition, but rather changing it to make it more humane and more productive. He asked his readers to consider crime to be a symptom of a social illness. With that in mind, his reforms would allow for all 'patients' to have a full recovery. In short, better social medicine would mean less social disease. Six measures were key. First, he called for the standardization of sentencing so that a bank teller who stole $500 would not get a nominal sentence while an impoverished teenager would get three years for stealing needed clothing. Second, he proposed that workers in the penal machinery labour for a competitive wage paid by the state to eliminate the fee system whereby those accused and convicted of crimes paid fees to support their upkeep. Third, he recommended eliminating pre-trial incarceration, except for those deemed dangerous to others. His fourth measure, which was based on the first three, entailed the reduction in the number of police, jailers and judges. Magistrates and juries should speedily handle all 'lighter offensives' with treatment, not incarceration. Fifth, he asserted that should a person be found responsible for a crime, they should be sent to a house of correction or a reformatory until such time 'when again set free he will not be in a condition in which he can scarcely do anything except beg, starve, or steal' (Altgeld, 1886: 60–93). Finally, his sixth recommendation was that the prison system should be a means of restoring lost capital for prisoners. He wanted to replace the oppressive prison labour systems, particularly those in the South, that exploited the incarcerated, especially Black prisoners, to the advantage of the jailers, with systems that help prisoners to build personal material wealth.

Becoming Altgeld's protégé

Altgeld's book sparked a resurgence in American prison reform and influenced a new generation of thinkers and activists. Clarence Darrow was among them, saying late in life that Altgeld and his book 'came to have a marked influence upon me and my future' (Darrow, 1932: 41). After reading it for the first time, Darrow put the book on the desk of his quaint, country law office in Ashtabula, Ohio, and resolved to move to Chicago. Not only was it Altgeld's hometown, but Darrow also imagined it would be a better environment for a lawyer on the make and a budding intellectual and activist who wanted to do more in life politically than attend county fairs. In

1887, Darrow packed up his life and family and moved to the Windy City, America's second-largest metropolis whose population had been doubling every ten years. The city was, however, not a welcoming or nurturing place. It could be quite repulsive. German sociologist Max Weber (1864–1920) once compared it to 'a human being with his skin removed' (Weber, quoted in Altgeld, 1886: 74). Poet and historian Carl Sandburg (1878–1967) was more blunt: 'Here's the difference between us and Dante: He wrote a lot about Hell and never saw the place. We're writing about Chicago after looking the town over' (Sandburg quoted in Lindberg, 1996: 81).

In the hustle and bustle of an ugly city that had lots of lawyers already, Darrow initially found it difficult to make connections, or to find paying clients. Moreover, Chicago was a foreign and lonely place to be a stranger. Towards the end of his career, Darrow recalled standing on the street corner outside his downtown law office futilely 'watching the passers-by for some familiar face' (Darrow, 1932: 42). No friend from Kinsman or Ashtabula ever appeared. Moreover, he learned that everything he had read about the Chicago penal system was depressingly true. That said, in his book, Altgeld made one glaring omission. The elite and their enforcers used Chicago prisons to punish political opponents. A case in point was the Haymarket affair.

In early 1886, two labour federations, the Knights of Labor and the Federation of Organized Trades and Labor Unions, organized in Chicago a protest and strike for an eight-hour workday. The demonstration began on May Day. The first two days passed quietly. But on 3 May, police attacked strikers at the McCormick farm implement factory, killing four workers. Unionists were angry the next day when they organized a huge rally at the city's Haymarket Square. Towards the end of evening as the last speaker was calling for unity in the push for an eight-hour day, Chicago police marched in formation to clear the area. As they did so, a bomb was thrown from an alley. The ensuing explosion ripped through the crowd. Seven police officers and four workers were killed, and dozens were injured. Following the blast, eight anarchists were arrested, thrown in jail without bail and later convicted of conspiracy. There was evidence that one of the eight may have constructed the incendiary device, but the others, most of whom had not been at the demonstration, were tenuously connected to the crime. Regardless, seven received the death penalty, with the eighth getting a 15-year sentence.

When Darrow arrived in Chicago, there were massive protests against the incarceration of the anarchists, the trials and their outcomes. All seemed so hopeless, but the activism did have some effect. Illinois Governor Richard J. Oglesby (1824–1899) commuted the sentences of two to life in prison. Four others were hanged on 11 November 1887, while one of the accused committed suicide in jail. Darrow thought the whole situation was 'more dangerous to liberty and happiness than all the foolish speeches ever made in America', including those given during the Chicago eight-hour protests (Darrow, 1887).

Depressed and with a failing law practice in a raucous, unforgiving city, Darrow rejected the doubts and the suggestions to go back to Ohio. He refused to admit defeat and instead decided to fight through the misery. He did two things that redirected his life. First, he broadened his professional network beyond the legal world. In retrospect, it may have all seemed so simple; he joined some clubs, namely the exclusive Sunset Club and the highly political Henry George Club. Of the two, the latter was instrumental. Henry George (1839–1897), a towering Gilded Age public figure on both sides of the Atlantic Ocean, was the author of one the century's most notable books: *Progress and Poverty: An Inquiry into the Causes of Industrial Depressions and of Increase of Want with Increase of Wealth*. Published in 1879, George interrogated the relationship between the emerging industrial capitalist economy and the vast wake of poverty and ecological destruction everywhere it appeared. Economic 'progress' produced nightmarish poverty. George offered a simple recipe to address this 'enigma of our times' (George, 1879: 10). Immediately all nations should eliminate all taxes save one, a single tax, on land rent in order to discourage the unbridled accumulation of real estate and encourage the widespread ownership of farms and businesses. George became an overnight star as popular in Ireland, where his book coincided with rent strikes, as he was in Chicago where workers were gathering strength to oppose the industrial capitalism that not only put them in the poor house but also in prisons.

In February 1889, George travelled to Chicago to headline a single tax mass meeting at Central Music Hall. Leaning on his new club friends, Darrow managed to get on the programme as the last speaker of the night. Despite George's rousing and brilliant address, Darrow was able to keep the crowd's attention and have the last word on what the assembled crowd thought was the critical issue of the age: taxation ('The convention which begins at Chicago today', 1889). The next day, his law office was bombarded with clients and well-wishers. He had finally made a splash; he had finally arrived; and he had finally drawn the attention of the man who would be his mentor: John Altgeld.

Befriending Altgeld was the second change that catalysed Darrow's life. The man who drew a nation's attention to penal transformations and the man who desired to be the nation's most famous lawyer were fast inseparable partners and political operators. Altgeld helped Darrow with his desire to make a name for himself in law, and in turn Darrow employed his folksy, gregarious abilities to make allies out of the wealthy with the goal of getting Altgeld elected Governor of Illinois and a kingmaker in the resurgent Democrat Party. Their first triumph was the election of De Witt C. Cregier (1829–1898) as city mayor. Darrow's campaign work was rewarded with a city job as special assessment attorney. When Cregier lost his bid for re-election, Altgeld sent Darrow to the Chicago North Western Railroad, working more directly with Altgeld's corporate allies who were the political prime movers in the state. Darrow did his work well and, in 1892, helped Altgeld realize his dream and become governor. It's here where the protégé began to part ways with his mentor. Darrow expected his compatriot, who had literally written the book on American's inhumane prison system, to immediately pardon the three remaining Haymarket Square prisoners. Governor Altgeld hesitated for months, frustrating Darrow as well as the working-class voters who put him in office. Altgeld waited to free them for fear of any electoral fallout, if not an assassination attempt. For Darrow, the politics of the situation mattered far less than the unjust sentences imposed upon the men. Governor Altgeld eventually pardoned them, providing some comfort to Darrow, but it did not change his mind that Altgeld was wrong about much regarding the nature of crime and punishment in America (Kersten, 2011: 40–50).

It is unsurprising that Darrow disagreed with his mentor. He had always been a contrarian. Reflecting on his life as an iconoclast, he remarked 'I almost always find myself disagreeing with the crowd' and added 'I also know that the truth is many-sided and relative and shifting, and yet it seldom occurs to me that any of my opinions can be wrong' (Darrow, 1929: 13.). Unlike Altgeld, Darrow was not an optimist, never believing in progress and rarely in the idea that reforms could make things better for average people. 'Life is a terrible tragedy all through', America's most famous pessimist once said. In concert with the naturalist Jean-Henri Fabre (1823–1915), he saw life as nothing more than 'a fierce riot of empty bellies' (Darrow, 1923: 23).

Altgeld and Darrow also had very different approaches to the concepts of crime and punishment. Altgeld was a part of an international and historic reform movement that was steeped in the best data that they could acquire (Howard, 1777; Wines, 1878). Darrow did not share that data-driven reform impulse. He was a philosopher, a lyrical lawyer and a sentimentalist who was more concerned about the individual than the group. Rather than statistics and legal reform, Darrow focused on debating and writing books, such as *Crime: Its Cause and Treatment* (1922) and his autobiography (1932). What motivated him towards the abolition of prisons and capital punishment were his cases and the philosophical ideas that he held tightly.

On crime, punishment and environment

For Darrow, in terms of crime and its after-effects, it was vital to consider one basic question: are individuals responsible for their crimes? At the root of the question sat Darrow's notions about human nature: people were just animals, no different from ants or cows or cats (Darrow, 1921: 23). Heredity had very little to do with how people lived their lives (Darrow, 1925). Darrow was in direct opposition to scientific racism and eugenics. Who one's parents were genetically bore no bearing on who a person became. In his famous debate with the American eugenicist Albert E. Wiggam (1871–1957), Darrow told a crowd of 2,000 people in Cleveland's storied Public Auditorium in 1922: 'The child in the cradle, I grant, is purely the product of heredity. Heredity may also determine the ultimate size of the individual, and may determine the quality of the mind, whatever that may be – I don't pretend to know. But after birth – what then?' (Whitehead, 1922: 7).

Darrow believed that one's environment, and whether one had a strong or weak nervous system, made all the difference. There was no free will. There was no means to control an individual's conduct. People were merely biological machines set loose on the earth (Darrow and Smith, 1928). What mattered was this: in the accident of birth, were you born into wealth and privilege? If so, you could expect to live a life without worry of the penal system. If not, then you were likely to be caught up in its maw. Darrow rejected the notion of eugenicists like Wiggam that crime was the product of 'stupidity' and the social Darwinist position that the poor were stupid (Whitehead, 1922: 15). Rather, it was a very logical result of the class structure in the US.

For his understanding of the social environment, Darrow took his cue from Leo Tolstoy (1828–1910), not Altgeld (see Zorin, Chapter 4 in this volume; Cox and Taylor, Chapter 5 in this volume). Statistics and investigatory reports did not animate Darrow's thinking. Like Tolstoy, Darrow saw that 'the world is divided into two classes, those who sow and those who reap, those who toil and those who live upon their fellow-men' (Darrow, 1963: 193). Rejecting his privilege, Tolstoy became an ascetic. 'I came to the following simple conclusion', he wrote, 'that, in order to avoid the suffering and depravity of men, I ought to make other men work for me as little as possible, and to work myself as much as possible.' Putting it another way, Tolstoy said simply: 'if I pity the exhausted horse on whose back I ride, the first thing for me to do, if I really pity him, is to get off of him, and walk' (Darrow, 1963: 197). Neither a count nor a rich man – and too much of a hedonist to become a friar – Darrow saw his job as battling for the common man in court where 'injustice, oppression and wrong are ever fortified and entrenched'; where 'lawyers with specious arguments and endless briefs ... prove that black is white, that wrong is right'; where 'judges in high places ... maintain existing things'; and where 'the state ... protects the strong and subverts the liberties and natural rights of the disinherited and despised' (Darrow, 1963: 199).

According to Darrow, crime and punishment had to be contextualized within this human environment that boiled down to one class oppressing another. At the height of his career in 1922, he encapsulated his thoughts with the publication of *Crime: Its Cause and Treatment*. One can view this book as a protégé's reformulation of Altgeld's *Our Penal Machinery and Its Victims*. However, it lacked the careful reasoning and statistical rigour of his mentor's book. It is best to see it as his closing statement in the indictment of the American legal system. Eschewing the statistical analysis of previous criminological surveys, he focused on answering three core questions: what is crime?; what is the purpose of punishment?; and what is to be done? He argued that 'the laws that control human behavior are as fixed and certain as those that control the physical world' (Darrow, 1922: vi). Humans were machines without free will that spent their lives responding to the external stimuli of Nature. Whether a person led a life that did not encounter the legal system or whether a person was a 'victim', as Altgeld explained, depended on the environment where a person was born. This law also governed the oak tree:

> The acorn will inevitably produce the oak tree and it will grow true to its pattern ... Still if the acorn is planted in good soil, where it is properly nourished and in a spot where it is sufficiently sheltered, the tree will be more likely to become large and symmetrical, than if it is planted in poor soil or in an exposed spot. (Darrow, 1922: 37)

Darrow focused in on the metaphorical swampy, nutrient-starved environments and their effects on humans. In those settings, the rules or 'folkways' that govern life had been written and codified by the rich and powerful. Breaking those rules is a crime which leads to punishment. Thus the criminal is born. According to Darrow, it is not 'hard to understand ... He is one who, from inherited defects or from great misfortune or especially hard circumstances, is not able to make the necessary adjustments to fit him to his environment' (Darrow, 1922: 57; Sumner, 1906). Unable to cope with industrial life or city life or modern social relations, the criminal may have stolen, broken Prohibition laws, had an abortion or murdered a neighbour. Like an oak tree grown crooked, 'some natures are less stable, some nervous systems less perfect, and built up barriers [to breaking the law] are weaker' (Darrow, 1922: 83). Nothing in jail or prison improves the condition. Criminals are punished, Darrow wrote, for 'vengeance', and capriciously at that (Darrow, 1922: 10, 151). The solution was equally self-evident. Drawing on Altgeld and others, Darrow recommended treatment over punishment. Societies should also tackle the inequities of the human environment and create more opportunities and better education. He never thought that all crime could be eradicated or jails would not be needed 'to restrain certain men' (Darrow, 1922: 152). He believed that most of the penal code should be scrapped and most penal institutions closed. To him, those who adjudicate social ills 'should consider that this imposition calls for intelligence, kindliness, tolerance and a large degree of sympathy and understanding' (Darrow, 1922: 285).

Transforming the penal landscape

Like most of Darrow's books, *Crime* did not have the intended impact as readership was sporadic. Darrow did not replicate the magic of Altgeld's *Our Penal Machinery and Its Victims*. However, he did make a mark in the movement of criminal reform in the US. He did it as an influential speaker, whether giving an address or a closing statement in court. In 1902, he arranged to speak before the prisoners of Cook County jail in Chicago. Just the idea that he would address the prisoners caused a stir. Even some of his friends urged him to reconsider. Darrow loved such controversy. The iconoclast doubled down. Not only did he give his address, but he also had it printed 'on rather good paper and in a somewhat expensive form'. 'In this way', he wrote in the preface of the printed edition of the speech, 'the truth does not become cheap and vulgar' (Darrow, 1902a: 10). And his truth was even more radical than Altgeld's. By the turn of the 20th century, Darrow was arguing publicly for the abolition of the death penalty and the transformation of the penal system such that physical restraint and separation would only be for violent offenders. Those who committed nonviolent crimes would have no incarceration. All who encountered the legal system and were responsible for breaking societal norms would have treatment, not vindictive punishment. His first words to the prisoners must have been well received: 'I really do not believe in the least in crime.' Further:

> I do not believe there is any sort of distinction between the real moral condition of people in and out of jail. One is just as good as the other. The people here can no more help being here than the people outside can avoid being outside. I do not believe that people are in jail because they deserve to be. They are in jail simply because they cannot avoid it on account of circumstances which are entirely beyond their control and for which they are in no way responsible. (Darrow, 1902a: 23)

Not stopping for the warden to object, Darrow pressed on to say that 'there ought to be no jails'. The penal machinery only existed because of the 'heartless' people on the outside (Darrow, 1902a: 24). The poor who were incarcerated were no more or less guilty of a crime than the rich who had good lawyers to keep them out. Laws were designed not to help the poor but to protect the property of the rich. Moreover, he said that most of the property crimes that poor people committed were a result of not having enough money to pay for food, fuel, and transportation. Whose fault was that? The individuals kept in poverty or the rapacious gas utility or streetcar company? 'When I ride on the street cars', Darrow elucidated, 'I am held up – I pay. Five cents for a ride that is worth two and a half cents, simply because a body of men have bribed the city council and legislature, so that all the rest of us have to pay tribute to them' (Darrow, 1902a: 25). Jails were filled not with these perpetrators, but their victims. No doubt those listening to him agreed wholeheartedly. He was equally clear on what was to be done:

> The only way in the world to abolish crime and criminals is to abolish the big ones and the little ones together. Make fair conditions of life. Give men a chance to live. Abolish the right of private ownership of land, abolish monopoly, make the world partners in production, partners in the good things of life. Nobody would steal if he could get something of his own some easier way. Nobody will commit burglary when he has a house full. No girl will go out on the streets when she has a comfortable place at home. The man who owns a sweatshop or a department store may not be to blame himself for the condition of his girls, but when he pays them five dollars, three dollars, and two dollars a week, I wonder where he thinks they will get the rest of their money to live. The only way to cure these conditions is by equality. There should be no jails. They do not accomplish what they pretend to accomplish. If you would wipe them out, there would be no more criminals than now. They terrorize nobody. They are a blot upon civilization, and a jail is an [sic] evidence of the lack of charity of the people on the outside who make the jails and fill them with the victims of greed. (Darrow, 1902a: 38–39)

In terms of the abolition of prison, Darrow spent his time and energy as an advocate in the public sphere, on the lecture circuit and in the courtroom. Similarly, he devoted his lawyerly craft and his time outside of court to abolishing the death penalty.

Questioning state-sanctioned murder: the Leopold and Loeb case

Darrow's most notorious capital case was the Leopold and Loeb case. On Wednesday, 21 May 1924, Bobby Franks, a 14-year-old who lived in an affluent section of Chicago, was kidnapped. The main perpetrator, a person who identified himself as George Johnson, called Bobby's mother and demanded cash for his safe return. The Franks assembled the cash, but also contacted the police as they had noticed Bobby was missing even before 'Johnson's' call. Police began canvassing the area for witnesses and clues while the family tried to deliver the payment. The drop fell apart as the instructions were too intricate and highly dependent on the trains running on time, which they did not. At the same time, police found Bobby's brutalized, lifeless body and narrowed in on those who had committed the murder. Within a week, detectives had enough to make two arrests: Nathan

Leopold (1904–1971) and Richard Loeb (1905–1936). Clever, rich and well educated, Leopold and Loeb had been obsessed with committing the perfect murder. They planned to get away with a dramatic, sadistic killing, picking Franks almost randomly. The two teenagers knew him as he lived nearby and disliked him. Franks was younger and smaller. The killers thought they could easily subdue and murder him. As soon as they were arrested, the teenagers confessed. Their parents hired Darrow in an attempt to avoid the death penalty. Darrow had a well-earned reputation of saving the condemned and the damned. Of the hundred or so capital cases that he had, he only lost one, his first: the case of Patrick E. Prendergast (1868–1894), who had murdered Chicago Mayor Carter Harrison Sr. (1825–1893) in 1893. Even then, Darrow was ardently opposed to what he termed 'state-sanctioned murder' (Darrow, 1902b: 11, 57). Through some legal manoeuvring, he was able to pull the trial away from a jury, which almost certainly would have gone for capital punishment, towards Judge John R. Caverly (1861–1939) for summary judgment and sentencing. Darrow's closing statement was 11 hours long and effective:

> I know your Honor stands between the future and the past. I know the future is with me, and what I stand for here; not merely for the lives of these two unfortunate lads, but for all boys and all girls; for all of the young, and as far as possible, for all of the old. I am pleading for life, understanding, charity, kindness, and the infinite mercy that considers all. I am pleading that we overcome cruelty with kindness and hatred with love. I know the future is on my side. Your Honor stands between the past and the future. You may hang these boys; you may hang them by the neck until they are dead. But in doing it you are making it harder for every other boy who in ignorance and darkness must grope his way through the mazes which only childhood knows. In doing it you will make it harder for unborn children. You may save them and make it easier for every child that some time may stand where these boys stand. You will make it easier for every human being with an aspiration and a vision and a hope and a fate. I am pleading for the future; I am pleading for a time when hatred and cruelty will not control the hearts of men. When we can learn by reason and judgment and understanding and faith that all life is worth saving, and that mercy is the highest attribute of man. (Darrow, 1924a: 120–121)

Darrow's successful plea on behalf of Leopold and Loeb and of those facing the death penalty made him even more celebrated and reviled, both of which were good for the debate circuit. One month after he saved the lives of Leopold and Loeb, he debated Judge Alfred J. Talley at the Manhattan Opera House in New York City ('Darrow and Talley on death penalty',

1924: 40). Talley presented the affirmative and more popular view. To him, there was nothing barbaric about state judicial killing. If an individual can kill for self-defence, Talley reasoned, then the state can do so too. If it is acceptable in war, then it is acceptable in peace. He concluded with a pointed attack on Darrow: 'Those who would seek to take away from the State the power to impose capital punishment seek to despoil the symbol of justice' (Haldeman-Julius, 1924: 22). Darrow gave as good as he got, dismissing Talley's philosophical and statistical arguments. All that mattered was sentiment: 'If you love the thought of somebody being killed, why, you are for it. If you hate the thought of somebody being killed, you are against it' (Haldeman-Julius, 1924: 40). Darrow was against it. And he said that he 'would hate to live in a state that I didn't think was better than a murderer' (Haldeman-Julius, 1924: 41; see also Greeley, 1872). Darrow then repeated his thoughts on crime and its treatment. Crime was a construction of the rich to oppress the poor. Nothing more, nothing less. It was about social environment, not about free will or individual responsibility. In his rebuttal, Judge Talley attacked the logical next step in Darrow's argument: 'If I am able to gather alright Mr. Darrow's sentiments upon this subject of crime and punishment', he concluded, 'we should not shut up any criminal in a prison cell' (Haldeman-Julius, 1924: 47). That was indeed the next step.

A hopeful pessimist: Darrow's legacy

Throughout his later years, Darrow remained an ardent advocate of ending capital punishment and prisons. In the twilight of his legal career, he did something quite unusual for him and decided to lead an organization, which was something he had not done before. At the age of 78, he was elected President of the American League to Abolish Capital Punishment (Kersten, 2011: 240). The dream of ending the death penalty did not happen during his lifetime. In fact, the abolition of the death penalty as well as all prisons in the US has been an elusive goal. Certainly, conditions have improved marginally since Darrow's lifetime, and there are reform attempts that recently have brought mental health (or, as Darrow would have said, a weak nervous system), parole and cash bail into focus. But the American press is filled with stories of barbarism, whether it is solitary confinement in supermax prisons, forced prison labour (which some maintain is akin to modern-day slavery), police brutality or the horrors of execution methods which have been notoriously unreliable (Bogel-Burroughs, 2022; Brockell, 2022; McGoogan, 2023; Eisner, 2023; Anderson, 2024; Bogel-Burroughs, 2024). If we could speak with Darrow's ghost today, he would be angry, but not surprised (he was a pessimist), that more progress had not been made during the decades since his death (Coyle and Scott, 2021). That said, he would encourage penal and death penalty abolitionists to reread his writings and take heart in the advances that he and Altgeld made working within the system and outside it. They were both key actors and thinkers, who along with such people as Leo Tolstoy and Enoch Wines provided the intellectual foundations for reformers and penal abolitionists in the 20th and 21st centuries (see also Zorin, Chapter 4 in this volume). Centring their understanding of crime and punishment within social, economic and political contexts, Altgeld and particularly Darrow continue to be read and have remained relevant to debates about prisons and the death penalty (Knopp, 1977; Breyer, 2016). Moreover, and significantly, Darrow's refusal to view criminals and noncriminals differently in any way not only inspires all of us to a greater sense of empathy but also helped to lay the framework for modern sociological perspectives on the environmental aspects of crime and punishment that challenge attempts to pathologize criminals and working-class people (Cohen, 1988). In short, Darrow is still a towering figure for his battles outside of courtrooms as much as inside of them. If he were here today, he would tell lawyers, judges, activists and academics to carry on the battles and challenge those who refuse to see the humanity in everyone. A hopeful pessimist until his dying day, Darrow would have looked at the current situation and likely only quoted Omar Khayyam (1048–1131), a kindred spirit who believed 'so-called sins of men were not crimes, but weaknesses inherent in their being and beyond their power to prevent or overcome' (Darrow, 1899: 14). Rather than selfishness, cruelty and vengeance, Khayyam, like Darrow, counselled charity, forgiveness and love. In the *Rubaiyat*, Darrow's favourite book, the Persian poet penned:

> So I be written in the Book of Love,
> I do not care about that Book above,
> Erase my name or write as you will,
> So I be written in the Book of Love. (Le Gallienne, 1901: 48; Darrow, 1924b: 121)

References

Altgeld, J.P. (1886) *Our Penal Machinery and Its Victims, New and Revised Edition*, Chicago: A.C. McClurg & Company.

Anderson, C. (2024) 'Disentangling the relationship between serious disorder problems and the use of supermax prisons', *Criminology & Public Policy*, 23(1): 77–117.

Barnard, H. (1938) *Eagle Forgotten: The Life of John Peter Altgeld*, Indianapolis: Bobbs-Merrill.

Bogel-Burroughs, N. (2022) 'Death penalty researchers call 2022 "year of the botched execution"', *New York Times*, 16 December. Available from: https://www.nytimes.com/2022/12/16/us/death-penalty-botched-executions.html [Accessed 24 October 2023].

Bogel-Burroughs, N. (2024) 'After a botched execution, Alabama is trying an untested method', *The New York Times*, 23 January. Available from: https://www.nytimes.com/2024/01/23/us/nitrogen-execution-alabama-kenneth-smith.html [Accessed 24 January 2024].

Breyer, S. (2016) *Against the Death Penalty*, Washington DC: Brookings Institution Press.

Brockell, G. (2022) 'LA voters keep "slavery" at Angola Prison, once and still a plantation', *Washington Post*, 10 November. Available from: https://www.washingtonpost.com/history/2022/11/10/angola-prison-louisiana-slave-labor [Accessed 24 October 2023].

Brown, T.J. (1998) *Dorothea Dix: New England Reformer*, Cambridge, MA: Harvard University Press.

Cohen, S. (1988) *Against Criminology*, Oxford: Transaction.

Coyle, M. and Scott, D. (2021) 'The six hues of abolitionism', in M. Coyle and D. Scott (eds) *The International Handbook of Penal Abolition*, Abingdon: Routledge, pp 1–12.

'The convention which begins at Chicago to-day' (1889) *New York Times*, 19 February.

Darrow, C.S. (1887) 'Letter to the editor', *Democratic Standard* (Ashtabula, Ohio), 2 September, Darrow Family Scrapbooks, Scrapbook n°. 1, Newberry Library, Chicago, Illinois.

Darrow, C.S. (1899) *A Persian Pearl and Other Essays*, Chicago: C.L. Ricketts.

Darrow, C.S. (1902a) *Crime and Criminals: Address to the Prisoners in the Cook County Jail*, Chicago: Charles H. Kerr & Company.

Darrow, C.S. (1902b) *Resist Not Evil*, Chicago: Charles H. Kerr & Company.

Darrow, C.S. (1921) *Insects and Men: Instinct and Reason*, Girard, KS: Haldeman-Julius Publications.

Darrow, C.S. (1922) *Crime: Its Cause and Treatment*, New York: Thomas Y. Crowell.

Darrow, C.S. (1924a) *Plea of Clarence Darrow in Defense of Richard Loeb and Nathan Leopold Jr on Trial for Murder*, Chicago: Fine Arts Building.

Darrow, C.S. (1924b) *The Rubaiyat of Omar Khayyam with a Critical Essay by Clarence Darrow*, Girard, KS: E. Haldeman-Julius.

Darrow, C.S. (1925) 'The Edwardses and the Jukeses', *American Mercury*, 6(2): 147–157.

Darrow, C.S. (1929) *What Life Means to Me at Seventy-Two*, Girard, KS: Haldeman-Julius Publications.

Darrow, C.S. (1932) *The Story of My Life*, New York: Charles Scribner's Sons.

Darrow, C.S. (1963 [1902]) 'Leo Tolstoy', in A. Weinberg and L. Weinberg (eds) *Clarence Darrow: Verdicts Out of Court*, Chicago: Ivan R. Dee, Inc., Publishers, pp 186–200.

Darrow, C.S. and Smith, T.V. (1928) *Can the Individual Control His Conduct?*, Girard, KS: Haldeman-Julius Publications.

'Darrow and Talley on death penalty' (1924) *New York Times*, 27 October: 40.

Eisner, C. (2023) 'NPR uncovered secret execution tapes from Virginia, more remain hidden', *NPR: All Things Considered*, 19 January. Available from: https://www.npr.org/2023/01/19/1149547193/secret-execution-tapes-virginia [Accessed 24 October 2023].

George, H. (1879) *Progress and Poverty: An Inquiry into the Causes of Industrial Depressions and of Increase of Want with Increase of Wealth*, New York: Modern Library.

Greeley, H. (2002 [1872]) 'The death penalty is state-sanctioned murder', in M.E. Williams (ed.) *The Death Penalty*, San Diego: Greenhaven Press, pp 39–45.

Haldeman-Julius, E. (1924) *Debate on Capital Punishment: Clarence Darrow Negative, Judge Alfred J. Talley, Affirmative*, Girard, KS: Haldeman-Julius Company.

Howard, J. (1777) *The State of Prisons in England and Wales with Preliminary Observations and an Account of Some Foreign Prisons*, London: William Eyres.

Kersten, A.E. (2011) *Clarence Darrow: American Iconoclast*, New York: Hill & Wang.

Knopp, F.H. (ed.) (1977) *Instead of Prisons*, Syracuse, NY: Critical Resistance.

Le Gallienne, R. (1901) *Rubáiyát of Omar Khayyám: A Paraphrase from Several Literal Translations, New Edition with Fifty Added Quatrains*, New York: John Lane.

Lindberg, R.C. (1996) *Quotable Chicago*, Chicago: Wild Onion Books.

McGoogan, C. (2023) '"You're a slave": inside Louisiana's forced prison labor and a failed overhaul attempt', *Washington Post*, 3 January. Available from: https://www.washingtonpost.com/nation/2023/01/01/louisiana-prison-labor-ballot-slavery [Accessed 24 October 2023].

Sumner, W.G. (1906) *Folkways: A Study of the Sociological Importance of Usages, Manners, Customs, Mores, and Morals*, Boston: Atheneum Press.

Titus, M.V. (1906) *Index to the Reports of the National Prison Association, 1870, 1873, 1874, 1883–1904*. US Senate, 59th Congress, 1st Session, Senate document n°. 210. Washington DC: Government Printing Office.

Whitehead, G.G. (1922) *Environment vs. Heredity: Debate Between Clarence Darrow and Albert Edward Wiggam*, Girard, KS: Haldeman-Julius Publications.

Wines, E.C. (1867) *Report of the Prisons and Reformatories of the US and Canada*, Albany, NY: Van Benthuysen and Sons.

Wines, E.C. (1878) *The Actual State of Prison Reform throughout the Civilized World: A Discourse Pronounced at the Opening of the International Prison Congress of Stockholm, August 20, 1878*, Stockholm: Central-Tryckeriet.

Wines, E.C. (1880) *The State of Prisons and of Child-Saving Institutions in the Civilized World*, Cambridge: John Wilson & Son.

15

Emma Goldman: The Making of a Prison Abolitionist

Penny A. Weiss

Introduction

Emma Goldman opens her major essay on prisons with an excerpt from Dostoevsky's *The Priest and the Devil* (1849), in which the devil chastises the priest for threatening folks with the tortures of hell when, in fact, so many are *already* living in hell. The devil offers examples: a factory worker labouring in the scorching heat of an iron foundry, and a farmworker subject not only to dust and heat and impoverished living conditions, but also to the overseer's whip. But the 'very worst' example is the enchained prisoner: vermin-covered, living in foul air and poorly fed. 'Yes, this is hell', the priest reluctantly agrees (Goldman, 1969: 111).

Imprisonment, to Goldman, is not just wrong, but is among the 'very worst' violations of the human spirit. In this chapter, I inquire into precisely what constituted the hellishness of prisons to Goldman and why she advocated for prison abolition rather than reform: why we can and should look beyond carceral 'solutions' to crime. I believe her insights, and the depth of her commitment, can inform and inspire prison abolitionists today.

Goldman's own experiences with 'criminal justice' systems were numerous and deeply problematic. She understood those encounters through the lens of her anarchism, but, I will argue, she also allowed her anarchism to build on and learn from her experiences at the hands of police and prison officials. While both she and anarchism were considered by the state to be serious threats, she thought the *real* danger was posed by overzealous states that would stop at virtually nothing to enforce obedience to their authority and to veil their own complicity in crime. Since the means these dangerous states regularly rely upon include prisons, it is not so surprising that Goldman became an early prison abolitionist; that stance is consistent with her general analysis of government force as illegitimate, her overriding commitment to individual freedom, and her experiential knowledge of carceral means and ends.

The purpose of prisoners losing their liberty at the hands of the state has been variously (and inconsistently) conceived as protection of the public, punishment of the offender, retribution for victims, deterrence of future crimes and reform of the wrongdoer. Goldman argued that prisons fail *on every count*. Further, throughout most of their history, prisons were 'crowded, diseased, and dangerous' (Thorsteinson, 2017) – guilty of their own crimes. Reform of criminal justice systems has a history almost as long as that of prisons themselves; in the US, it dates back at least to the colonial period, when William Penn (1644–1718) guaranteed citizens the right to a jury trial and reduced the crimes for which one might receive the death penalty. It is still needed today.[1] However, Goldman argued that: 'With all our boasted reforms, our great social changes, and our far-reaching discoveries, human beings continue to be sent to the worst of hells, wherein they are outraged, degraded, and tortured' (Goldman, 1969: 111).

It is not that 'all our boasted reforms' make *no* difference, because they do, as Goldman recognized when she worked from within for better food, medical care and working conditions. She held out some hope that prison officials 'may be taught a little humanity, especially if they realise that their jobs depend upon it' (Goldman, 1969: 121). But for her, reforms do not change the illegitimacy or ineffectiveness of caging, abusing and dehumanizing people. Reforms are limited in terms of what they aspire to accomplish, and problems inherent in a system that violates and exploits cannot be reformed away.

I explore the distinctive character of Goldman's prison abolitionism: an early, decidedly anarchist abolitionism. After establishing the grounds for treating Goldman's own encounters with 'criminal justice' as the basis of her experiential knowledge of the carceral state, I create a history of those experiences, focusing primarily (but not exclusively) on her arrests and imprisonments.[2] I explore what each encounter might have taught or revealed to her, hoping to capture the individual and cumulative effects of this unasked-for education. I show how these lessons later became the arguments in 'Prisons' (Goldman, 1969) on incarceration as a 'social crime'. Then I address Goldman's second abolitionist argument: that prisons are also a 'failure' not only by her standards but also by their own. Finally, I look at the grounds for her hopefulness in thinking prisons are unnecessary. My main goal is to leave the reader with an understanding of why Goldman thought prisons *ought* to be eliminated and why she believed they safely *can* be eliminated. Over a century later, her arguments and passion can enlighten and ignite critics of carceral states.

Emma Goldman and 'criminal justice'

Goldman was many things: relentless agitator, prolific author, trained dressmaker, nurse and midwife, and renowned lecturer, 'the most accomplished, magnetic speaker of her time' (Fee and Garofalo, 2011: 1044). She spoke Russian, German, French, Yiddish and English, and read and wrote in Spanish and Italian. 'One of the greatest intellectual forces of the day', (Rohe, 1912) Goldman contributed to the very development of anarchist philosophy, and brought that philosophy to bear on a host of issues, from women's rights to prisoners' rights, from free speech to free love, and from militarism to capitalism. Untold thousands heard her speak or read her essays.

Goldman was born in Kovno, Russia (now Lithuania) in 1869 to an Orthodox Jewish family, one of six children. Laws restricted Jewish economic activity and physical mobility. Her family struggled with economic hardship, paternal violence and anti-Semitism. Goldman was often considered disobedient, though what she validly and valiantly fought against ranged from molestation by a teacher, to an early arranged marriage, to physical violence by a father who also discouraged her academic ambitions. In others' eyes, she evolved from a young rebel to the infamous 'Red Emma', so threatening that she had to be exiled from the country she had long called home. That youthful spirit of rebellion reflected an acute sensitivity to injustice which focused her considerable energies throughout her life.

As is sadly true of so many female thinkers, biographies of Goldman have long outnumbered and overshadowed serious treatments of her ideas. I offer a selective biography focused on Goldman's major encounters with 'criminal justice', but in this instance, I do so to tie these life events to her ideas: her abolitionism. After all, Goldman herself said, 'it was the prison that had proved the best school' (1970: 148).

Youthful experiences: the early making of an abolitionist

Goldman began learning about the carceral state long before she came face to face with it as an adult. Here I cite two important examples.

In Russia

In her autobiography, Goldman wrote about the 'harshness' she witnessed as a youngster in Russia:

> I was outraged over the official brutality practiced on the peasants in our neighborhood. I wept bitter tears when the young men were conscripted into the army and torn from homes and hearths ...

I was indignant when I discovered that love between young people of Jewish and Gentile origin was considered the crime of crimes. (1970: 386–387)

Under the Russian Empire, Lithuanians were persecuted and both repressive state policies and pogroms against Jews were not uncommon. 'Goldman lived in a world ruled by fear and the ubiquitous secret police, a world in which even the mildest expression of dissent would be summarily crushed' (PBS, n.d.).

In this early education, Goldman came to see the idea that police exist 'to serve and protect' everyone and all communities equally as mythical and intentionally mystifying; instead, as she witnessed, the actions of the Russian police (and the state more generally) targeted and took the heaviest toll on the already marginalized, and served the narrow interests of the already privileged. The police were not only subject to but also enforced prejudices that were pervasive. And she saw that to *enforce* prevailing ideologies and perpetuate existing inequalities, the state regularly uses *force*, as it was (and is) set up as legitimately able to do, against whatever or whomever is seen to threaten it or a plausible conception of the general welfare. 'Her childhood seems to have served her as an object lesson in the brutalizing effects of capriciously exercised authority' (Shulman, 1972: 5).

These early lessons about police and state violence would never be lost or negated. Early on, then, Goldman had reason to suspect that those pursued, caught and encaged by the state might not, in fact, be either wrongdoers or dangers to their communities; instead, they were often dangers to systems of privilege and inequality. From another angle, the number of Lithuanians who, like Goldman, emigrated at the time – perhaps 350,000 to the US alone – highlighted the depth of the human desire for freedom and dignity. Thus, these early experiences provided both the negative (oppression) and positive (freedom) spurs to her work, including her abolitionism.

Haymarket, 1886

When the teenage Goldman arrived in the US, she settled in Rochester, NY, with relatives. She worked in the garment industry, where she experienced, as she had in Russia, poor labour conditions and appalling pay. She easily understood why at least 300,000 workers went on strike on 1 May 1886, determined to establish an eight-hour workday.[3] On 4 May, labourers gathered in Chicago's Haymarket Square to protest against earlier police shootings of striking workers; a sizeable police force attempted to disperse them. A homemade bomb was thrown. Gunfire ensued. Seven police officers and at least four striking workers died, and many were wounded. Anarchists, stalwart defenders of unions, were blamed. A jury found eight of them guilty of conspiracy and sentenced seven to death, four of whom were executed.[4]

Goldman called the Haymarket executions 'the most decisive influence in my existence' (1970: 508) and 'the birth of my social consciousness' (1970: 669). In this political awakening, she learned about anti-union efforts, which included spying on, firing and blacklisting those associated with unionizing; lockouts of workers; the hiring of strikebreakers; and attempts to turn workers against each other. The way in which union organizers and members were treated – from being arrested to being demonized in the media – fed her growing critique of industrial capitalism. She learned more about how business interests were opposed to the interests of workers, and how the former alone were supported and protected by the police.

During the trial, Goldman learned how judicial processes could contribute to mass incarceration. Justice, supposedly blind and impartial, somehow permitted the judge to be openly hostile to the defendants, who were, for example, denied separate trials. Anyone expressing sympathy with the union was exempted from jury duty, while those admittedly prejudiced against anarchists were allowed to serve. The officer leading the investigation fabricated evidence; he was dismissed, but was later reinstated. No actual bomber was tried and nor were clear connections established between the defendants and the bomb thrower. Not all of the convicted had even been present at the time of the bombing. In the absence of conclusive evidence, the defendants' associations, writings and support for the strike were sufficient to convict them.[5] No one who used violence *against* the striking workers was ever tried. Goldman called the verdict 'the worst frame-up in the history of the United States' (1970: 8) and denounced the executions as 'judicial murder' (1970: 124).

Importantly, Goldman also learned from the police using Haymarket to justify disrupting anarchists' meeting places and raiding their homes and offices, without such niceties as search warrants. She learned that the police can, for the most part, abuse their targets with impunity. As in Goldman's youth, the police were linked with terrorizing certain people and the working class in general. All too often, she saw, laws were less a safeguard than a free pass. Seeing that even 'protected' freedoms of speech and assembly meant little in certain situations, she would question the real-world value of legal rights as political solutions. She understood that those who play large and official roles in deciding who should be incarcerated could get away with injustice even while they demonized those they convicted of injustice. In response, she became 'determined to become a revolutionary' (Shulman, 1972: 7).

1883: direct encounters with 'criminal justice'

As an adult, Goldman witnessed many more incidents of police and prison abuse. Moreover, she herself became a victim of them.

Homestead strike and assassination attempt, 1892

The Homestead strike occurred at a steel plant in Pennsylvania owned by Andrew Carnegie and managed by Henry Clay Frick, who had an established reputation for hostility to labour and the workers' strong union. The profitable company wanted to cut wages and deal with workers individually rather than collectively. This strike, too, combined corporate opposition to unions, a lockout, a strike, strikebreakers and violence, this time between the striking workers and the 300 armed guards hired by the company to protect strikebreakers. Repercussions accrued to many as, for instance, Frick evicted the families of strikers from company houses. Goldman and her close colleague Alexander Berkman went to Homestead to support the workers, although she had returned to New York by the time violence broke out, generating a chaotic scene with gunfire resulting in deaths on both sides.

In the aftermath, Berkman decided to assassinate Frick, who had played a leading role in the violence against the strikers and who broke the union. It was conceived as an instance of *attentat:* an act of revolt against the oppressive capitalist system in the hope that it would be a catalyst for revolution. Goldman was left in charge of 'spin' after the act, being left to explain both workers' rights and political violence. Berkman wounded but did not kill Frick, and was convicted of attempted murder; the masses were not, in fact, roused to revolutionary action. Berkman was sentenced to 22 years and served 14. But police were sure that Goldman was involved too. In this direct encounter between Goldman and the police, they raided her apartment in search of evidence they never found, seized her papers and convinced her landlord to evict her.

What did Goldman learn? First, industrial capitalists do not fear to take extreme measures against individual workers or workers' rights, or even against workers' families; they have workers at their mercy.[6] The main lesson: 'capitalism was relentless, the State crushing every individual and social right', while, on the other hand, 'those daring to give voice to the suffering ... were persecuted and jailed' (Goldman, 1970: 525). The police, as she saw in the raid on her apartment, can cast a wide net without much evidence and without negative consequences for them. Neither Carnegie, who wanted wages slashed, nor Frick, who destroyed a powerful union and hired the murderous guards, was charged with any crimes. Goldman would take this deeply to heart: those exploiting thousands are of little interest to the 'criminal justice' system; it was more likely to laud, protect, accommodate and believe them than to investigate, check, charge or replace them. 'Criminal justice', she understood, does not focus on the *real* criminals; this insight informed her abolitionism.

Incitement to riot, unlawful assemblage, 1893

The year 1893 was a time of economic crises: banks failed and the local unemployment rate was over 20 per cent. In Union Square, Goldman gave a speech during which she urged the nearly 3,000 attendees – particularly the unemployed workers among them – to: 'Demand work! If they do not give you work, demand bread. If they deny you both, take them. It is your sacred right!'[7] Undercover officers were present for what they termed this 'incendiary speech'. The New York police pursued and arrested Goldman in Philadelphia, where she was preparing to address another crowd and where, needlessly, 'officers drew their guns and held back the crowd' (Goldman, 1970: 124).

Official procedures that Goldman encountered were, again, educational. She rejected a police officer who offered to drop the charges against her in exchange for informing on others. While out on bail, she was taken back into custody, despite the fact 'that only in cases of murder was such procedure permissible' (Goldman, 1970: 129). At the trial, neither contradictory 'testimony nor that of the witnesses for the defence prevailed against the statements of the detective' (1970: 129), such being the power and credibility of the police. In fact, '[t]he New York Police sought in the Union Square meeting an opportunity to make Emma Goldman an anarchist target'; she herself was 'the victim of police persecution' (Goldman, 1970: 130).

Charges such as 'incendiary speech' are liable to misapplication – or, rather, they are purposefully applied to those advocating *for* the oppressed and subordinated. The 'incendiary' is opposed to the 'harmless'. Goldman, like other union and anarchist organizers, did not want to be 'harmless' – they wanted to harm the systems and practices that injured and exploited, oppressed and discriminated against various groups, whether victims of industrial capitalism, militarism or sexism.

Goldman *wanted* to inflame, to raise consciousness, to motivate people to stand up for themselves and for one another. That, apparently, was a crime. Her arrest taught her the danger of criticizing capitalism or, indeed, 'hold[ing] opinions contrary to what this government prescribes and sanctions in her subjects'.[8] She wrote that 'the farce of my trial had strengthened my opposition to the State' (1970: 130) – lesson learned. Importantly, once imprisoned, she learned things about the incarcerated and incarceration. First, behind bars for ten months, 'I found the cells small, dark, and filthy, the sanitary conditions appalling, and the general attitude toward the convict on the part of prison officials hard and cruel' (Goldman and Berkman, 1920: 5). These, she learned, were 'normal' conditions and standard treatment. She also found that many of her fellow prisoners were not even convicted of any crime, but were awaiting trial, stuck in prison because they could not afford bail. The carceral state differentially impacts the wealthy and the poor. She also learned that the imprisoned were 'capable of sympathy and devotion, of generous impulses', having committed crimes only as a result of their poverty. Instead of seeing them as criminals, she understood them to be 'victims, links in an endless chain of injustice and inequality' (Goldman, 1970: 136). She found no evidence that some 'criminal nature' was the cause of crime. She learned, too, about the virtually unchecked power of prison staff, noting, as she clashed with the matron, that 'she could put me back in my cell, deprive me of my commutation time for good behaviour, and make the rest of my stay very hard' (1970: 138). She witnessed cruelty on a number of occasions and saw convicts 'deprived of food for the slightest infraction' (Goldman, 1970: 147). She herself became acquainted with the horrors and 'impenetrable blackness' (Goldman, 1970: 139) of solitary confinement.

These experiences informed the central arguments of Goldman's essay 'Prisons: a social crime and failure'. There, Goldman powerfully captured the dehumanization of the imprisoned that she witnessed and experienced: 'Robbed of his rights as a human being, degraded to a mere automaton without will or feeling, dependent entirely upon the mercy of brutal keepers, he daily goes through a process of dehumanization, compared with which savage revenge was mere child's play' (1969: 119).

There is no higher value to anarchists in general, or Goldman in particular, than individual freedom. Incarceration not only means that people are unfree in that they are locked up; it also means that their precious individuality is seen as a threat to prison 'order' and they are left at the mercy of others – 'brutal' others. Criminally, everything brilliant and 'radiant' about human life (to use a favourite Goldman term) is systematically denied or beaten out of the imprisoned: 'his will is broken, his soul degraded, his spirit subdued' (Goldman, 1969: 119).

Goldman's prison abolitionism was growing.

Complicity in assassination, 1901

In 1901, Goldman was suspected of involvement in the assassination of US President William McKinley. The assassin, Leon Czolgosz, had attended a Goldman lecture, implicating *her* in the eyes of the law, even though she had been in another city at the time of the assassination. Czolgosz, despite evidence of mental illness, was convicted and executed. Because Goldman defended Czolgosz as a political protester, the portrayal of Goldman as a public enemy began in earnest. Goldman wrote that 'two hundred detectives had been sent out throughout the country to track down Emma Goldman' (1970: 296). She quietly returned to Chicago, where she destroyed letters and papers, lest the police use them against anyone. She was taken into custody there, along with 12 others. There was no evidence of her complicity; in fact, 'she no longer even condoned such deeds' as assassination (Shulman, 1972: 13).

Goldman had yet more to learn: 'I had often heard of the third degree used by the police ... to extort confessions, but I myself had never been subjected to it. I had been arrested a number of times since 1893; no violence, however, had ever been practised on me' (1970: 300).

Now, however, Goldman was threatened 'with the direst things' (1970: 300), and was kept *incommunicado*, part of the state's attempt to break her spirit (1970: 301). In court, however, 'the Buffalo authorities failed to produce evidence to connect [Goldman] with Czolgosz's act' (1970: 310). She was released after having been held in detention for weeks. She later insisted that 'he who remains indifferent to the conditions that result in violent acts of protest cannot escape his share of blame for them' (Goldman, 1970: 560). To her, that indifference was more truly criminal than her speech was.

Goldman gained more knowledge about the workings of the state. For instance, the state could and did cast such a wide net as to capture and criminalize many who were only marginally or incidentally involved in illegalities. Anarchists might have been the least surprised by the state throwing out the liberties it guaranteed in its own constitution, concerned that people not use their freedom to question the state. After all, anarchists argued, governments and laws, particularly in unequal societies, are inherently unjust.

Anarchism, assault, incitement to riot: 1906

In 1903, reeling from the McKinley assassination, Congress passed an Immigration Act, also called the Anarchist Exclusion Act. This barred entry to anarchists and required all immigrants to swear they were not anarchists; beliefs were as forbidden as actions. Goldman described it as 'a law which gives the average officer a right to invade the head and heart of a man, as to what he thinks and feels' (1906a: 127). In 1906, several speakers were arrested at a meeting called to fully process what happened with Czolgosz and to determine whether he was even an anarchist. When others gathered to protest against those arrests and defend free speech, 'several detectives jumped on the platform and placed [one speaker] under arrest, while twenty-five police officers began to club the audience out of the hall' (Goldman, 1906d: 197). Goldman was arrested with nine others and was held under the New York Criminal Anarchy Law 1902, 'which makes almost every Anarchistic utterance a crime' (Goldman, 1906c: 200). She was charged with assault, anarchism and incitement to riot. She believed that the police, rather than the speakers, had caused the disturbance. This time, while she was out on bail, the charges against her were dismissed.

Elements of this episode, too, would find their way into Goldman's 'Prisons' essay, part of prisons' 'social crimes'. Not only is it drastic to put so many behind bars, she argued, but the state acts criminally by using drastic methods to put people there. Drawing on her harassment and arrests, she held that 'although in America a man is supposed to be considered innocent until proven guilty, the instruments of law, the police, carry on a reign of terror, making indiscriminate arrests, beating, clubbing, bullying people, using the barbarous method of the "third degree"' (Goldman, 1969: 119).

The use of such methods by the police is followed by similar means within prisons. Goldman reminded her audiences of the torturous tools the state used against the imprisoned: 'the black-jack, the club, the strait-jacket, the water-cure, the "humming bird" (an electrical contrivance run along the human body), the solitary, the bull-ring, and starvation diet' (Goldman, 1969: 119). New York actually had an Anarchist Police Squad. It became clearer and clearer to Goldman that freedom of speech was going to be restricted to 'the discussion of only such subjects as are popular' (1906d: 197).

Obscenity: 1915 and 1916

New grounds for arrest were issued in 1915 in Portland, Oregon, and in 1916 in New York City: obscenity. Goldman had been speaking about and disseminating information on birth control, in violation of the Comstock Act and its local equivalents. Named after the anti-vice crusader behind it, the Comstock Act banned the transportation of 'obscene' matter via the mail or across state lines. Courts had ruled that the Act prohibited distributing information on contraception. Thousands were prosecuted under the Act and 'served a total of 600 years in prison', while 'millions of books, newspapers, magazines', and other print material were 'burned, under court order' (Friedman and Werbel, 2023). Goldman felt that Comstock exercised 'a control which has proved disastrous to the freedom of the press, as well as the right of privacy of the American citizen' (Friedman and Werbel, 2023).

There was growing interest in the topic of birth control and Goldman offered a nationwide series of talks on it. The 1915 arrest happened in the midst of a speech entitled 'Birth control: how and why small families are best'; in 1916, she was arrested as she prepared to lecture and was 'taken to a filthy station house, then hustled into a patrol wagon, rushed to the Clinton Street jail, [and] there searched in the most vulgar manner' (Goldman, 1916a: 561). 'Persecution of birth-control advocates', including Margaret Sanger, 'went merrily on' (Goldman, 1970: 587). Goldman was just as determined: 'It is not the Birth Control Movement, but the law, which will have to go' (Goldman, 1916b: 577), she wrote. She explained her motivation: 'We do it because we know the desperate condition among the masses of workers and even professional people, when they cannot meet the demands of numerous children' (Goldman, 1916a: 561). Goldman, a nurse and midwife, had long been 'impressed … by the fierce, blind struggle of the women of the poor against frequent pregnancies. Most of them lived in continual dread of conception' (Goldman, 1969: 185). So, once again, she challenged who the real criminal was: 'Is there anything more terrible, more criminal, than ... [to be] condemned to breed ... forced to breed' (Rothman, 2016) no matter what the circumstances?

In the first case, Goldman paid bail and was released. A judge later found her guilty, though witnesses had 'testified that the [questionable] circular was not publicly posted and that it was not generally distributed among the spectators' (*Oregon Journal*, 1915: 529). She paid a fine and was freed. She was found guilty in the second case too; this time, she opted to spend 15 days in the County Penitentiary rather than paying the fine. She intended to use the time to learn more about and from other outcasts.

Concerned with a narrow, conventional 'morality', the state, Goldman learned, cared more about obscenity – real and imagined – than it cared that it was condemning people to intolerable lives. Moreover, it cared more about control over women's bodies and sexuality than about freedoms of expression, speech and religion, or about bodily autonomy or women's equality. Nor would the state be charged or tried for its crimes; she, however, was arrested and convicted for sharing knowledge with people who were hungry for it, and who had a right to free choice and meaningful control over their lives.

In Queens County jail, Goldman's idea 'that the average social offender is made, not born' (Goldman, 1970: 571) was strengthened. She saw that their circumstances were often dire, their employment options limited and their crimes often mere survival tactics. She condemned the inhumanity of imprisonment in starker terms. In 'Letters from prison', she said: 'I am watching human misery. There is no misery so appalling as imprisoned misery ... [T]he irreparable harm is done by the very fact that human beings are locked up, robbed of their identity, their self-respect, their self-hood' (1970: 579). Her prison abolitionism was nearing its peak. Other beliefs that supported her anarchist abolitionism were also confirmed. For example, government coercion would be upheld by courts as legitimate, even when it denied people access to information they wanted and resulted in forced pregnancies; the state was not protecting, but oppressing. She also discovered that there are 'many towns in the United States where free speech had been gagged and its defenders maltreated' (1970: 511). Finally, laws like the Act she had violated – that criminalized her actions – were, all too regularly, merely 'arbitrary official regulations' (1970: 535). Furthermore, these arrests strengthened her support 'for free motherhood, for the right of the child to be born well' (Goldman, 1970: 553); 'police persecution', she said, 'made me surer of myself, more determined to plead for every victim, be it one of social wrong or of moral prejudice' (1970: 555).

Conspiring to obstruct the Draft Act, 1917

The Selective Service Act of 1917 required males aged 21–30 to register for conscription. In June of 1917, a mere two months after the US entered the First World War, President Woodrow Wilson signed the Espionage Act, which, among other things, forbade interfering with the draft – that is, obstructing recruitment. Goldman and other anarchists regarded involuntary conscription 'as a complete denial of every human right, the death-knell to liberty of conscience' (Goldman, 1970: 598). Again, Goldman pointed out legislative complicity in mass incarceration, the criminalizing of what should be legal. Goldman and Berkman organized the No Conscription League of New York; chapters arose in other cities. They organized rallies against the war and against conscription. Police repeatedly assailed their events. The *Mother Earth* offices were raided without a warrant (Goldman, 1970: 610). Goldman and Berkman were finally arrested for conspiring to violate the Draft Act. 'Free expression on the war and conscription had become a rarity', mourned Goldman (1970: 609).

Goldman wrote that 'the prosecution [against her] was resourceful' (1970: 618). The 'evidence' presented included the No-Conscription manifesto, and work published in *Mother Earth* and another anarchist publication, the *Blast*. They presented issues of the journals that *pre-dated* the war, conscription and the Espionage Act, and the judge allowed it. One police officer claimed that he had transcribed a verbatim report of Goldman's speech, including, he said, her call to use violence; his report was easily contradicted by other witnesses, but to no effect. Again without much effect, Goldman adamantly held that she never advised any individual to refuse to serve in the military; she believed that decision, like other decisions, belonged to each individual alone, not to her and not to the state. She said that 'as an anarchist I could not presume to decide the fate of others' (1970: 598). Finally, the 'judge told the jury that Goldman's charges were not a First Amendment issue' (Schroeder, 2018), closing an avenue of defence. Goldman and Berkman were found guilty by the jury after 39 minutes of deliberation. Each was sentenced to two years in prison – the maximum – and fined $10,000. The judge also recommended to immigration authorities that the pair be deported after release. Goldman moved that 'the verdict be set aside as absolutely contrary to the evidence' (1970: 622); the motion was denied. Their appeal was also unsuccessful (Abbott, 1919).

In court, it was 'the evident intention of the Government to turn the prosecution into persecution' (Goldman, 1970: 615). It did not surprise Goldman that the verdict was unjust, or that the worst tools of the state would now be used against her to enforce it, in order to reinforce itself. 'We did not believe in the law and its machinery, and we knew that we could expect no justice' (1970: 613). Characteristically, 'our last evening in

New York was devoted to ... the organization of the Political Prisoners' Amnesty League' (1970: 651).

Now an advanced student, the first lesson the imprisoned Goldman reiterated was that her fellow prisoners – who she now knew better and for longer – 'were recruited from the lowest social strata', the impoverished, and 'most of them had been driven to crime by conditions that had greeted them at birth ... I found no criminals among them, but only unfortunates' (1970: 652–653). She also saw that as a result of the Espionage Act, 'non-combatants and conscientious objectors from every social stratum were filling the jails and prisons' (1970: 640). She understood that many were, like her, unjustly imprisoned, feeding her prison abolitionism.

Goldman now learned more about prison labour. She was forced to work as a seamstress. Having done away with contract labour, the state was now the employer. This didn't change the working conditions, and made the state a 'slave-driver' and a 'scab' (Goldman, 1970: 654), simultaneously oppressing the imprisoned and undermining union labour. She found the arrangement exploitative and saw how demanding quotas imposed on untrained labourers 'kept the inmates in constant trepidation' (1970: 627). 'The shop was dreaded by all the inmates, particularly on account of the foreman', who 'terrorized' them (1970: 653–654). She believed that the working conditions 'caused all the hardships and trouble in the prison' (1970: 686).

These experiences later became more arguments for denouncing prisons as a social crime. Goldman called prison labour a form of slavery, the state becoming the master that coerces, drives, bullies, tortures, brutalizes, terrorises, browbeats, harasses and exploits.[9] The work demanded is not useful job training for life after release (which she supported), nor does it pay enough 'to set aside a little for the day of his release' (Goldman, 1969: 122). Instead, the work is 'mind- and soul-destroying' (Goldman and Berkman, 1920: 7), enormously profitable to companies and the state, but of no use to the imprisoned, other than breaking the monotony of prison life. Goldman's claim is that in this environment, the foreman and ultimately the state are the *real* criminals, taxing prisoners 'beyond their strength' because of the 'enormous profits' of convict labour (Goldman, 1969: 124). 'One's life is made a veritable hell' through this 'criminal thievery' (Goldman and Berkman, 1920: 6).

During this longer prison sentence, Goldman also learned more about the cumulative effects of the daily realities of prison life. In addition to documenting extreme wrongs, she testifies to the quotidian impact of incarceration: 'the depressing effect of my cell. Its dirty grey walls, the lack of light and ventilation' (1970: 656). There's a sense of 'helplessness in prison' (1970: 661) towards those outside the prison walls too: 'the hardest thing to bear in prison is one's utter powerlessness to do aught for one's loved ones in distress' (1970: 675). For those incarcerated for life, in particular, there was 'no hope or cheer for them' (1970: 673).

Alien Exclusion Act violation, 1919

The final time Goldman was arrested, it was for having a questionable immigration status, which meant, as an avowed anarchist, she could be deported. Goldman had secured US citizenship through her ex-husband, Jacob Kershner, a naturalized citizen.[10] So, to render Goldman eligible for deportation, her citizenship was revoked by stripping Kershner (who was missing or deceased) of his: 'J. Edgar Hoover himself directed her deportation hearing' (Shulman, 1972: 16).

Goldman described the state's methods of revoking her citizenship as 'shady' and its usual claims about the sacred right of citizenship 'hollow' (1970: 703). She viewed the Anarchist Exclusion Act as 'utterly tyrannical and diametrically opposed to the fundamental guarantees of a true democracy' (1970: 704). She saw her previously legal publications used as evidence to establish longstanding criminality and to justify banishment. She decried the immigration hearing, as she had other judicial proceedings, as 'a farce' (1970: 704).

Once again confined, now at Ellis Island, she noted that 'the condition of the emigrants ... was nothing short of frightful. Their quarters were congested, the food was abominable, and they were treated like felons ... [T]hey found themselves locked up, ill-treated, and kept in uncertainty for months' (1970: 713). She and Berkman were ultimately deported to Russia with 247 others, all 'radicals' of some variety. Consistent with previous treatment by the state, they left on a boat that was once 'used as a transport in the Spanish-American War', but which had since been 'discarded as unsafe' (Goldman, 1970: 718).

Goldman did not think any of this was anomalous, but was rather the standard operating procedure of the carceral state. 'Today so-called aliens are deported. Tomorrow native Americans will be banished' (*New York Times*, 1919); whoever else the state might turn on, with handcuffs and fisticuffs, with imprisonment and banishment, is similarly unsafe. Goldman had learned, in four decades in the US, that there were but few limits on government abuse; this case fell into a longstanding pattern. Laws that were ineffective, intrusive on freedom, anti-labour, based on the narrowest conception of morality or even unconstitutional were passed year after year. Courts regularly upheld state abuses, blessing them with veneers of legitimacy and necessity. Furthermore, violators of (illegitimate) laws would be convicted on minimal evidence, often fabricated by corrupt police. Biases, including those against immigrants, pacifists, atheists, and anarchists, would too often be indulged by judges and juries, resulting in harsher sentences.

At the end of this process, those incarcerated would find themselves in a version of hell, where their very humanity was dishonoured, their rights and needs disregarded.

Etc.

This list of Goldman's encounters with 'criminal justice' is representative, but far from complete. As she wrote, 'police brutality and outrage against Anarchists have become such an every-day occurrence, that one no longer feels inclined to refer to them' (Goldman, 1908: 363). Truly, there were far too many incidents of police harassment to list.

In 'Prisons', Goldman iterates the four types of criminal as developed by Havelock Ellis: the political, the passional, the insane and the occasional. Goldman saw herself as a political prisoner, 'the victim of an attempt of a more or less despotic government to preserve its own stability' (Goldman, 1969: 119). She considered such people not as anti-social, but as trying to overturn an anti-social order, so that 'the political criminal of our time or place may be the hero, martyr, saint of another' (1969: 120). Unfortunately, Americans think America has no political prisoners, failing, really, to understand the (carceral) state as fully as the anarchist does.

A final, cumulative lesson emerged: 'Surely there must be something wrong with the American Institutions of today; something terribly black and corrupt, if they cannot stand the light of criticism; if they can thrive only when physical force is used to defend them against the light of free discussion' (Goldman, 1902: 98).

A social crime and failure

Speaking and writing about prisons during and after this long list of experiences with the 'criminal justice' system, Goldman made two broad charges against prisons, deeming them both 'a social crime' and 'a failure'. Each claim has several parts, and it is possible to see the roots of these arguments in Goldman's experiences.

'A social crime'

The 'social crime' argument has largely been examined via Goldman's carceral experiences. We have encountered her claims that *prisons are criminal* for so often caging the already downtrodden in order to protect the more privileged; for regularly resorting to varied forms of violence with impunity; for not pursuing the real criminals who oppress whole classes of people; for confining inmates in inhumane conditions; for exploiting inmates' labour, forcing them to work beyond their capacity and dramatically underpaying them; and for being an integral part of the government's aggressive campaign against those who stand up for and exercise their freedom and individuality. The effects include the gradual dehumanization of the imprisoned and perhaps of us all. Goldman saw such wrongs as built into the very nature of prisons; thus, they are capable of only modest reform.

Goldman made an additional argument about prisons as a social crime: the amount spent on prisons is also criminal. She estimated the cost at falling in the range of $1–8 billion a year and held that 'such unheard-of expenditure for the purpose of maintaining vast armies of human beings caged up like wild beasts' was indefensible (Goldman, 1969: 112). In 2016, the US spent around $80 billion on public prisons and jails (McLaughlin et al, 2016: 2), plus another $115 billion on policing. Goldman seems to object to the sheer size of the investment in something so awful – caging our fellow human beings, and to our consequent inability to address other urgent and unmet needs.

Goldman also acknowledged nonmonetary costs of imprisonment: social costs. She mentioned, for example, the 'ruined and poverty-stricken family' (Goldman, 1969: 114) that results from imprisoning one member of it. These costs, too, have grown, but garner less attention: '[T]hese costs do not appear on government budgets, [yet] reduce the aggregate welfare of society' (McLaughlin et al, 2016: 3). It is criminal, then, to spend these exorbitant sums on an enterprise that cruelly punishes not only the convicted but also their children and their neighbourhoods, and that leaves us unable to address other pressing social needs.

The failure of prisons

Goldman's second major abolitionist charge was that prisons are not only 'crimes' but also 'failures', unable to secure *any* of the ends that are used to justify them.

One unkept promise of prisons is that imprisoning some ensures the safety of the rest. However, despite our exorbitant investment in prisons and police forces, and despite record numbers of people behind bars, it turns out that people are still not 'protected': Goldman often said that 'crimes are on the increase' (1969: 112). She insisted that 'it seems ridiculous to prate of the protection society derives from its prisons' (1969: 112). Why ridiculous? 'Prison, a social protection? What monstrous mind ever conceived such an idea? Just as well say that health can be promoted by a widespread contagion' (1969: 111).

The need for 'protection' presumes being endangered. But, as we have seen, Goldman rethinks both the 'dangerousness' of the incarcerated and the 'innocence' of the state and of social conditions. Even today, 'the majority of prisoners have landed in such a horrid place through nothing but immigrant status, gang association, and non-violent drug-related activities, if not through outright political persecution by the U.S. government ... [I]ncarceration in the U.S. is meted out predominantly according to wealth and skin tone' (Saed, 2012: 3).

Profoundly, Goldman's argument goes even further: 'the legal aspects of crime, and the methods of dealing with it, help to *create* the disease which is undermining our entire social life' (Goldman, 1969: 114, emphasis added), akin to how the police repeatedly instigated the violence at her events. Goldman thinks what the state is really doing when it imprisons is 'hid[ing] its own shame and its mistakes behind prison bars' (Goldman and Berkman, 1920: 4), not making anyone safer. Furthermore, those leaving prisons – as 95 per cent of the incarcerated do – are *more* of a danger to the public than they were when they were sentenced. In fact: 'Society might with greater immunity abolish all prisons at once, than to hope for protection from these twentieth-century chambers of horrors' (Goldman, 1969: 120).

The primary causes of crime, Goldman emphasized, are our 'cruel social and economic arrangement[s]' (1969: 115). As long as social conditions mean that many are unable even to feed, house, clothe, and educate their families, society will continue to produce people who must resort to crime: 'Nine crimes out of ten could be traced, directly or indirectly, to our economic and social iniquities, to our system of remorseless exploitation and robbery' (Goldman, 1969: 116). The rest, committed, for example, by the mentally ill, are best dealt with via noncarceral means. Neither group is deterred from their desperate crimes by the incarceration of similar others or the threat of their own incarceration.

Importantly, in attempting to deter crime, what prisons are actually doing – as hinted at earlier – is terrorizing us all: 'Legally and socially the State exercises punishment, not merely as an infliction of pain upon the offender, but also for its terrifying effect upon others' (Goldman, 1969: 118). To an extent, this works, but the state cannot legitimately terrorize the citizenry, and so its efficacy on this ground proves state power to be illegitimate rather than justifying it. Goldman insisted that: 'Order derived through submission and maintained by terror is ... the only 'order' that governments have ever maintained' (Goldman, 1969: 59). In response, she 'targeted all forms of repression – economic, political, and psychological'. Her own experience in prison 'brought about ... a deepening of [her] hatred for any kind of tyranny and oppression'.[11] Addressing *those* would deter crime.

Rehabilitation as a goal of prisons completely misses the point that the majority of crimes have social causes rather than a source in the inadequacy of the criminal: their sinfulness, weakness, or vice. Thus, it is social conditions that need reform more than the incarcerated do. Further, it is perverse to believe and act as if people can be 'tortured "to be made good"' (Goldman, 1969: 119). Like some religions, the state seems to think that the convicted 'sinner' must 'expiate his sins through suffering and pain' (Goldman and Berkman, 1920: 5). However, inhumane conditions and brutal treatment cannot rehabilitate (see also discussion by Bell and Scott, Chapter 1, this volume). Instead, in our time as in Goldman's, such punishment and brutality 'make them become more hardened and anti-social' (1920: 5). For example, solitary confinement, imposed on about 80,000 people every day in US prisons, 'causes devastating harm to physical, mental, and behavioral health and is counterproductive to any goals of safety' (*Solitary Watch*, 2023: 3). Here, as elsewhere, Goldman is led to conclude that 'the State is the real offender' (1920: 7).

Perhaps the oldest justification for punishment – retribution – is supposed to repay a wrong with punishment neither greater nor lesser than the gravity of the crime (Baier, 1977: 38). Goldman likely thought incarceration imposes such misery as to be, most often if not always, out of proportion to the offence; it thus fails to meet the requirements of just retribution. In 1940, when Goldman died, the incarcerated US population was around 265,000, a rate of 201 per 100,000 people; in 2020, the incarcerated numbered 1,675,400, or 505 per 100,000. It has changed little since. At the very least, Goldman would say, we are using the most desperate and drastic tool of the state as a solution to *way* too many problems; such punishment is, consequently, quite often disproportionate to the wrongs committed.

Further, according to Goldman, harsh treatment of the imprisoned is not reluctantly engaged in or only as a last, desperate measure. Instead, the abuses by prison staff amount to 'a cold-blooded, methodical and daily crime' (Goldman and Berkman, 1920: 11); an atmosphere of 'violence and force' pervades (1920: 4), again precluding just retribution. The 'failure' here amounts to another 'crime'. To Goldman, these state acts are *more* criminal – more systematic and quotidian, as well as more cruel – than those committed by the vast majority of the incarcerated. These are human rights violations and are inherent in imprisonment.

Finally, it is not clear that prisons even satisfy the 'primitive' desire for revenge, as the avenging has been 'delegated to an organized machinery' (Goldman, 1969: 118), quite a distance from those directly and indirectly affected by wrongdoing.

So, prisons were supposed to deter potential criminals, but they have not, for conditions create an ongoing need for the majority of crimes: 'Nothing short of a complete reconstruction of society will deliver mankind from the cancer of crime' (Goldman, 1969: 121). Prisons were supposed to rehabilitate the criminally inclined, but instead destroy the good in them: 'the gates of prison hells return to the world an emaciated, deformed, will-less, shipwrecked crew of humanity' (Goldman, 1969: 126). Prisons were supposed to enact just retribution on violators, but in fact punish and terrorize out of proportion to their offences. Prisons were, finally, supposed to make us (feel) safer, but crime continues unabated as long as its real causes fail to be addressed. Together, Goldman concluded, prisons are ineffective and morally unjustifiable, and thus best eliminated: 'prison abuses are conditioned in the very character of prison life and in corrupt politics, so that nothing short of the complete abolition of prisons will ever eradicate the terrible wrongs committed in penal institutions' (Goldman and Berkman, 1920: 10–11).

Why we *can* eliminate prisons

Most of Goldman's arguments speak to the wrong of caging people: the injustice and horror of carceral conditions, and the illegitimate (often unchecked and frequently misused) power of the police and courts. She also addresses the prison's failure to accomplish any of the goals meant to justify it. But might things be even *worse* without prisons? Today, as in Goldman's time, it can be difficult really to believe that prisons aren't necessary, even if they are a necessary evil. In fact, so normalized is today's carceral state that communities try to attract prisons as employment opportunities; that torturous treatment of the 'hardened criminal' is seen as justified, as it once was for those with 'criminal natures'; that police and prison costs dominate local budgets year after year, and candidates for public office repeatedly run as defenders of 'law and order'; that sexual abuses in prison are punchlines for comics and part of what people are threatened with in police dramas; and that prison seems to be *the* solution to wrongdoing, impoverishing our imaginations.

Anarchists might be said to have a reasonably optimistic view of human nature. Many think that abolitionist ideas like those Goldman espoused are, at best, unrealistic – naïve fantasy and wishful thinking – and, at worst, downright dangerous. They do so based on a competing outlook on human nature. Goldman was familiar with appeals to a human nature variously conceived as hostile, competitive, conniving, self-interested and aggressive. In her definitive essay 'Anarchism: what it really stands for', she writes:

> Poor human nature, what horrible crimes have been committed in thy name! Every fool, from king to policeman, from the flatheaded parson to the visionless dabbler in science, presumes to speak authoritatively of human nature. The greater the mental charlatan, the more definitive his insistence on the wickedness and weaknesses of human nature. (1969: 61–62)

Goldman is more hopeful than this, because present conditions do not – cannot – reveal our greater potential: 'how can anyone speak of [human nature] today, with every soul in a prison, with every heart fettered, wounded, and maimed[?]' (Goldman, 1969: 62). If we cramp, confine, mistreat, abuse, mislead and oppress people, we cannot then study them to discover all there is to know about human nature and potentiality. We know what oppression does to some and what privilege does to others. We know what capitalism wants from its workers, as we know what patriarchy demands of each sex. We do not know what we might become if such things, including prisons, were to disappear, as our commitments grow to human rights, freedom, individuality, equality, and the satisfaction of basic human needs. Yet this is what Goldman dared to imagine. And she imagined that under such conditions, 'we believe that we would not have a criminal' (Goldman, 1893).

Goldman makes many analogous arguments, trying to get us to stretch our imaginations. For example, the 'laziness' among workers many expect and see as 'normal' – as expected as crime, given 'human nature' – is not somehow fated and inevitable, either for certain individuals or for any group. Many are disinclined to work hard when working conditions are oppressive and the profits of labour go to others. However, according to Goldman, these same people would be eager to strive, exert, produce, create, experiment, design, care and provide under fair conditions and just circumstances. Our understanding of human nature needs revision; its plasticity, or malleability, should turn our attention from biology to social conditions (see also earlier chapters for further discussion of this claim, such as Tuke, Chapter 2, this volume).

Similarly, while many think love leads to and is best supported by marriage, Goldman regarded marriage as another oppressive institution that often compromised or destroyed love, freedom and individuality. In fact, she argued, love would survive, and even thrive, if the institution of marriage was abolished (Goldman, 1969: 227–239). She found it not only unnecessarily pessimistic, and even cynical, but also unjustified, to think we would, 'by nature', without all the forms of compulsion and punishment, abandon our children, become freeloaders, pursue only our narrow self-interest and quickly resort to violence, as if without compulsory education we would refuse to learn. Changeable social conditions and perfectible human nature could bring us together in voluntary communities, simultaneously nurturing our social capacities and shared interests on one hand, and our precious individuality on the other hand. We know a great deal about the conditions that breed and feed criminal activity, and we know a good amount about what people need to be and to feel respected, justly rewarded, connected and free. We *could* do better. In fact, there are mountains of evidence in favour of 'natural' sociality, love and productivity; virtually all of us have experienced such things in ourselves and in our associations. Wildly, Goldman found evidence that such characteristics and acts are never entirely obliterated, even under the worst of circumstances; after all, she documented their existence in prisons. Imagine, she urged us to consider, what might happen if we actively nurtured such capacities and relationships.

Goldman's argument about the feasibility of abolitionism is, then, partly based on her carceral experiences, just as were her critiques of prisons. Acquainted with 'scores and hundreds' of criminals in many prisons

(Goldman and Berkman, 1920: 4), she found no evidence for seeing any as unredeemable evildoers: 'In all my twenty months of the closest contact with my fellow prisoners, I did not find one I could call depraved, cruel, or hard' (Goldman and Berkman, 1920: 11). Goldman found among her fellow inmates 'more humanity, a greater spirit of co-operation and helpfulness, than I would be likely to find among those who sit in judgment over them and send them to jail' (1916c: 594). There is *reason* to be hopeful.

Goldman thought that most criminals were 'phantoms of [society's] own making' (1969: 111). Not only is there no 'inherent criminal nature', so to speak; 'the average criminal is just the average man, generally speaking … thoroughly normal' (Goldman and Berkman, 1920: 4). It is not a diseased criminal we need to 'fix', but 'diseased social conditions' that necessitate or at least encourage criminal acts among 'children of poverty and desperation' (Goldman and Berkman, 1920: 3). 'Our system … makes the criminal, and then hypocritically pretend[s] that they are saving the system from the criminal' (Goldman, 1916c: 594).

Concluding thoughts

In our day as in Goldman's, jails are but one way in which we dehumanize and subordinate; though they are among the worst, all are objectionable. It is Goldman's profound respect for the individual and her deep commitment to freedom that fed her anarchist abolitionism, fuelled by her sensitivity to and repugnance for injustice and oppression. The battle for freedom and dignity, like freedom and dignity themselves, gave her life meaning, and can make ours meaningful too. It is worth tying abolitionism today to the big ideas behind Goldman's abolitionism; theorizing need not be a distraction. It is as important to tie it to the quotidian realities of life for the imprisoned, as Goldman did. A strong abolitionism requires, and benefits from, both.

We, in the end, are meant to learn from *her* story. We learn just how many tools the state has at its disposal to use against the disfavoured and disadvantaged. Goldman was charged with a host of offences over time: from unlawful assembly, assault and inciting a riot to obscenity, impeding the draft and attempting to overthrow the government. Prisons are overpopulated today with violators of parole and probation (20–30 per cent of the incarcerated) and low-level offenders (about 25 per cent of the jailed population) (Sawyer and Wagner, 2023). The Federal Bureau of Prisons calculates the percentage of imprisoned people serving time for drug offences at 44 per cent of all those incarcerated ('BOP statistics: inmate offenses'). It is not so hard to imagine better solutions to such problems than prisons. In Goldman's lifetime, police tactics were diverse too: they blocked Goldman from speaking, used violence against her and her audiences, ransacked her home and office, lied about her in court and repeatedly arrested her. Such tactics have not disappeared today, and remain powerful tools of the state at social justice rallies, in higher-crime neighbourhoods and against people of colour. Prison officials were complicit, too, in Goldman's life. Despite the special attention she sometimes garnered once incarcerated, Goldman was forced to labour for pennies, denied adequate food, exercise and medical care, put in solitary confinement and left at the mercy of prison officials, who could act with impunity. Prison conditions today have improved for some, but worsened for others. Laws used against Goldman – including the Comstock Act, the Selective Service Act, the Anarchist Exclusion Act and the Espionage Act – show the range of our lives impacted by the states that govern us, the weakness of guardrails that are supposed to protect us against government abuse and overreach, and the presence of prejudices at every stage in the 'criminal justice' system. Goldman's evolution from prisoner to prison abolitionist might inspire us to become stronger defenders of some of the things she stood for, understanding, as she did, the connections between prison abolition and the right to privacy, the right to criticize the government, reproductive freedom, sexual freedom, workers' rights, women's rights, freedom of speech and freedom of assembly. So much is at stake that virtually all of us are affected; we have to see the connections and do the work both of challenging injustice and building more just communities.

One cannot say that Emma Goldman was ahead of her time without acknowledging that it was because she was also so deeply *of* her time. Following in at least some of her footsteps, we, too, can be both enraged and inspired by the realities around us.

Notes

[1] See, for example: Alysia Santo, Joseph Neff and Tom Meagher (2003) 'Guards brutally beat prisoners and lied about it. They weren't fired', *New York Times*, 19 May; Haroon Siddique (2023) 'UN torture expert urges UK government to review indefinite sentences', *The Guardian*, 30 August; Nomin Ujiyediin (2023) 'Missouri prisons ban friends and family from sending books to prisoners', *NPR*, 29 August; John Raby (2023) 'Prosecutors seek plea hearings for two West Virginia jail officers accused in inmate's death', *AP*, 24 August; Ed Pilkington (2023) '"People are dying": Texas prisoners say heatwave turns cells into ovens', *The Guardian*, 31 July.

[2] Goldman not only critiques prisons, but also everyone and everything that *leads* to incarceration: unjust laws that mostly protect wealth and that criminalize what should be tolerated, corrupt law enforcement that acts illegally with impunity, biased judges and courtroom procedures, and more. I respect her approach by focusing here on the prison pipeline, while emphasizing incarceration.

[3] On average, American workers at the time worked just over 60 hours a week in six days on the job, often in unsafe workplaces.

[4] Two had their sentences commuted to life in prison and a third killed himself in jail.

[5] Six years later, those still in jail were pardoned by Illinois Governor Altgeld.

[6] In this instance, workers who later returned to their jobs had to do so as nonunion labourers.

[7] There are several different versions of this speech, but the content is pretty consistent.

[8] Goldman, 1903. This was written in response to the arrest and exile of John Turner.

9. All these verbs are from Goldman's entry in 'Fragment' (Goldman and Berkman, 1920).
10. There was also the possibility that when she was a minor, Goldman acquired citizenship through her father, who was also a naturalized citizen; this does not seem to have been treated as relevant in the court's decision.
11. 'Letter to Claus Timmerman', in *Emma Goldman*, vol. 1, p 193.

References

Abbott, L. (1919) 'The trial and conviction of Emma Goldman and Alexander Berkman', *Mother Earth* (July). Available from: https://dlc.library.columbia.edu/catalog/cul:dncjsxkv5s [Accessed 12 March 2024].

Baier, K. (1977) 'The strengths and limits of the theory of retributive punishment', *Philosophic Exchange* (1)8: 37–53. Available from: http://hdl.handle.net/20.500.12648/3327 [Accessed 12 March 2024].

'BOP statistics: inmate offenses' (n.d.) *Federal Bureau of Prisons*. Available from: https://www.bop.gov/about/statistics/statistics_inmate_offenses.jsp [Accessed 1 December 2023]

Falk, C. (2005) 'Raising her voices: an introduction', in C. Falk, B. Pateman and J. Moran (eds) *Emma Goldman*, vol. 2, Berkeley: University of California Press, pp 1–80.

Falk, C. and Pateman, B. (eds) (2012) *Emma Goldman: A Documentary History of the American Years*, vol. 3, *Light and Shadows, 1910–1916*, Stanford: Stanford University Press.

Falk, C., Pateman, B. and Moran, J. (eds) (2005) *Emma Goldman: A Documentary History of the American Years*, vol. 2, *Making Speech Free, 1902–1909*, Stanford: Stanford University Press.

Fee, E. and Garofalo, M.E. (2011) 'Red Emma (1869–1940): idealistic revolutionary', *American Journal of Public Health*, 101(6): 1044–1045. Available from: https://doi.org/10.2105%2FAJPH.2010.300038 [Accessed 12 March 2024].

Friedman, J. and Werbel, A. (2023) 'The Comstock Law at 150', *The Hill*, 3 March. Available from: https://thehill.com/opinion/education/3882873-the-comstock-law-at-150-a-highly-relevant-cautionary-tale-for-today/ [Accessed 12 March 2024].

Goldman, E. (1902) 'To Lucifer, the lightbearer' [letter], in *Emma Goldman*, vol. 2, pp 97–99.

Goldman, E. (1903) 'The new inquisition', *Free Society* (1 November), in *Emma Goldman*, vol. 2, pp 115–116.

Goldman, E. (1906a) 'A sentimental journal. – Police protection', *Mother Earth* (April), in *Emma Goldman*, vol. 2, pp 186–188.

Goldman, E. (1906c) 'Letter to Jean Spielman', in *Emma Goldman*, vol. 2, pp 200–201.

Goldman, E. (1906d) 'Police brutality', *Mother Earth* (November), in *Emma Goldman*, vol. 2, pp 197–199.

Goldman, E. (1908) 'The latest police outrage', *Mother Earth* (September), in *Emma Goldman*, vol. 2, pp 363–364.

Goldman, E. (1916a) 'Press circular', *Mother Earth*, 15 February, in *Emma Goldman*, vol. 3, pp 560–562.

Goldman, E. (1916b) 'The social aspects of birth control', *Mother Earth* (April), in *Emma Goldman*, vol. 3, pp 573–578.

Goldman, E. (1916c) 'To my friends, old and new', *Mother Earth* (June), in *Emma Goldman*, vol. 3, pp 591–596.

Goldman, E. (1969[1917]) *Anarchism and Other Essays*, New York: Dover Publications.

Goldman, E. (1970[1931]) *Living My Life* (vols 1–3), New York: Dover Publications.

Goldman, E. and Berkman, A. (1920) *A Fragment of the Prison Experiences of Emma Goldman and Alexander Berkman*, New York: Stella Comyn. Available from: https://tile.loc.gov/storage-services/public/gdcmassbookdig/fragmentofprison00paul/fragmentofprison00paul.pdf [Accessed 12 March 2024].

McLaughlin, M., Pettus-Davis, C., Brown, D., Veeh, C. and Renn, T. (2016) 'The economic burden of incarceration in the U.S.' Working Paper #AJI072016, Institute for Advancing Justice Research and Innovation, Washington University in St Louis.

New York Times (1919) 'Deportation defied by Emma Goldman', 28 October. Available from: https://www.nytimes.com/1919/10/28/archives/deportation-defied-by-emma-goldman-anarchist-leader-refuses-to.html [Accessed 12 March 2024].

Oregon Journal (1915) 'Emma Goldman is fined $100 in city court', 8 August, in *Emma Goldman*, vol. 3, p 529.

PBS (n.d.) 'Emma Goldman'. Available from: https://www.pbs.org/wgbh/americanexperience/features/goldman-1869-1940/ [Accessed 12 March 2024].

Rohe, A. (1912) 'Sex problem talks fill hall', *Denver Daily News*, 17 April, in *Emma Goldman*, vol. 3, p 352.

Rothman, L. (2016) 'Read Emma Goldman's 1916 letter defending the need for birth control', *Time*, 11 February. Available from: https://time.com/4208056/emma-goldman-1916-birth-control/ [Accessed 12 March 2024].

Saed (2012) 'Prison abolition as an ecosocialist struggle', *Capitalism Nature Socialism*, 23(1): 1–5. Available from: https://www.tandfonline.com/doi/full/10.1080/10455752.2011.648830 [Accessed 12 March 2024].

Sawyer, W. and Wagner, P. (2023) 'Mass incarceration: the whole pie 2023', *Prison Policy Initiative*, 14 March. Available from: https://www.prisonpolicy.org/reports/pie2023.html [Accessed 12 March 2024].

Schroeder, J. (2018) 'How anarchist Emma Goldman energized the US free-press debate', *Columbia Journalism Review*, 10 December. Available from: https://www.cjr.org/analysis/emma-goldman-first-amendment.php [Accessed 12 March 2024].

Shulman, A.K. (1972) 'Introduction', in A.K. Shulman (ed.) *Red Emma Speaks: Selected Writings and Speeches by Emma Goldman*, New York: Vintage Books, pp 3–25.

Solitary Watch (2023) 'Calculating torture: analysis of federal, state, and local data showing more than 122,000 people in solitary confinement in US prisons and jails', May. Available from: https://solitarywatch.org/wp-content/uploads/2023/05/Calculating-Torture-Report-May-2023-R2.pdf [Accessed 12 March 2024].

Thorsteinson, K. (2017) 'Introduction', *19th Century Prison Reform*. Available from: https://digital.library.cornell.edu/collections/prison-reform [Accessed 12 March 2024].

16

Seeing through the Game: Alexander Berkman and the Modern Prison Abolition Movement

Søren H. Hough

Introduction

Anarchism emerged in resistance not just to government, but to the structures of domination which strip people of their basic rights to liberty and dignity. As the anarchist Marie Goldsmith once wrote: 'To determine what social classes and categories they fight for, the anarchists bring to the forefront the question of who is oppressed and exploited in the given society' (Korn, 1925). It is therefore little surprise that anarchists have universally decried police and prisons as a barbarous tool of the wealthy and powerful to keep the masses under strict surveillance and control. In the anarchist conception of a world free from exploitation and oppression, the police and the cages they operate are nowhere to be found. Although it should be noted that the prison, police and related systems of classical anarchists' lifetimes (in the late 19th and early 20th centuries) were different from what exists today, their critiques nonetheless have salience when examining modern systems bearing the same names and indeed many of the same problems.

The anarchist communist Alexander Berkman (1870–1936) was one such critic of police and prisons. A Russian-born Jewish activist who spent much of his life abroad, Berkman likewise proposed his own vision of an emancipated humanity. Berkman is perhaps primarily known as Emma Goldman's intimate partner and close friend (see Weiss, Chapter 15 in this volume), but was himself a prolific writer and engaged militant. In 1892, he attempted to assassinate the anti-union industrialist Henry Clay Frick in Pittsburgh, Pennsylvania, for which he was imprisoned for 14 years. He also spent time in prison prior to his deportation from America in 1919. Throughout these experiences, Berkman wrote books about his time in incarceration, anarchist theory, and his dismay at the Bolshevik-led outcome of the Russian revolution. In one of these texts, *Prison Memoirs of an Anarchist* (1912), Berkman goes into depth about his experiences. According to the scholar Nolan Bennett, this book presents Berkman's 'ambivalent' anti-prison politics (Bennett, 2023). Bennett details how Berkman struggled to decide whether prisons were merely a means of suppressing radical action or, in fact, an opportunity for education, organizing and solidarity (Bennett, 2023). Bennett explains how, over the course of *Prison Memoirs*, Berkman shifts from a self-flattering romantic understanding of prisons as primarily a means of suppressing the voices of political dissidents to a more holistic and grounded understanding that 'prison is not merely a tool of state persecution: it is an institutional extension of capitalism, the state, and other modern authorities' (Bennett, 2023).

Throughout his life, Berkman wavered between selectively supporting political prisoners like himself and more generally supporting all incarcerated people. At one point, he even stated that ordinary criminals 'are not of my world ... they do not belong to the people' in contrast with revolutionary actors (Bennett, 2023). In another instance, he spoke admiringly of the average incarcerated person, referring to their 'frequently superior initiative, daring and intelligence' even if these traits ultimately constitute 'misdirected energy, effort applied wrongly' (Goldman and Berkman, 1920: 3). He also failed to resolve the conflict between the foundational anarchist principle of the unity of means and ends – that the tools of revolution should align with the society one wishes to create or risk perpetuating exploitation and domination (Baker, 2019) – and the need to address immediate harm. Nevertheless, Bennett notes that Berkman 'offers a unique analysis of an understudied era in carceral development, and the tensions in Berkman's analysis exemplify the complexity and global scope of prison reform debates in the era' (Bennett, 2023). By exposing prison conditions to the public through legal advocacy and by using propaganda (articles and pamphlets), he demonstrated 'how correctional facilities conceal their conditions from the outside' so that they can function without oversight (Bennett, 2023). Despite differences in how prisons operated in the pre-Second World War US versus the modern era, Berkman's analysis nevertheless remains a live concern even today. Prisons in Chicago, Illinois (Ackerman, 2015), Baton Rouge, Louisiana (Vargas, 2023), and Fayette, Pennsylvania (Melamed, 2023), have been exposed in recent years to be operating if not extra-legally, at least beyond public view and in violation of basic human rights.

This chapter investigates how Berkman's anti-prison politics specifically manifest in *Now and After: The ABC of Communist Anarchism* (1929).[1] This text, written nearly 20 years after *Prison Memoirs*, is perhaps his most well-known theoretical work. The book addresses fundamental questions about what an anarchist communist society might look like. Berkman makes his arguments by contrasting what he sees as the elegance of anarchist solutions to anti-social behaviour with the incoherence of the prison model. Amid these arguments, he critiques policing head-on, anticipating responses from an audience likely inured to police and prisons as an inevitable matter of course. In doing so, he prefigures many of the ideas that constitute the modern prison abolition movement and sometimes goes beyond them. At the same time, Berkman leans too far into simplistic analysis and solutions and in doing so falls short of modern abolitionist theory. While he was tied up in a mostly white anarchist milieu, modern abolitionism from figures like Mariame Kaba, Ruth Wilson Gilmore and Angela Davis is significantly rooted in Black feminist thought. We can learn from both Berkman's ideas and his flaws to produce a new synthesis of anarchist and abolitionist ideas. In this process, we can create an analysis which better describes and prescribes than either body of thought could on its own.

Law and punishment

One of the fundamental ideas Berkman champions is that laws, and much less the police, do not keep people safe. He addresses the ostensibly non-anarchist reader by framing the status quo with a partial syllogism: 'if the law really prevents crime, then the more laws the better. By the time we have passed enough laws there will be no more crime' (Berkman, 1972: 78). Then he appeals to the reader's common sense: 'Well, why do you smile? Because you know that it is nonsense. You know that the best the law can do is to *punish* crime; it cannot prevent it' (Berkman, 1972: 78). In his view, the abolition of the law and its police enforcers is a matter of obvious necessity because they are mechanisms of vengeance, not deterrence.

Berkman's argument that laws incur punishment first and foremost links him to modern prison abolitionists (Levin, 2022). He describes the 'atmosphere' of prisons as one of 'violence and force, of force and violence' where 'the spirit of humanity, of understanding, and justice, is a stranger' (Goldman and Berkman, 1920: 4). He asserts that the penal system 'has neither understanding of human motives nor sympathy with human weaknesses' (Goldman and Berkman, 1920: 4). Moreover, he observes that if punishment prevented crime, 'crime would have stopped long ago, for surely the law has done enough punishing. The whole experience of mankind disproves the idea that punishment prevents crime' (Berkman, 1972: 79).

Berkman goes on to note that the severity of the punishment likewise has little impact on whether the crime occurs at all. This perspective lays bare the anarchist view of what prisons really are, an observation repeated by today's abolitionists: a system of state-sanctioned revenge at best and a mode of systemic repression of the marginalized at worst. Moreover, in focusing on punishment, the prison perpetuates itself through a system of recurring vengeance. The prison abolitionist Mariame Kaba says in her book *We Do This 'Til We Free Us* that 'when we demand more prosecutions and punishment this only serves to reinforce a system that must itself be dismantled' (Kaba, 2021:192). Just as anarchists refuse to use government or prisons to achieve revolutionary aims, Kaba in this passage describes punishment itself as a tool to be avoided lest it reproduces indefinitely.

For Berkman, punishment cannot assuage crime because it misunderstands the source of criminal behaviour. Although he acknowledged the existence of 'congenital criminal degenerates whose number is infinitesimal, and who belong in the care of the alienist', he was emphatic that, in general, the '"real criminal" ... does not exist' and that 'the average criminal is just the average man, generally speaking' (Goldman and Berkman, 1920: 4).[2] For Berkman, 'the criminal is made, not born. He is the product of his environment, a child of poverty and desperation, of misery, greed, and ambition' (Goldman and Berkman, 1920: 4). For this reason, a simple punishment system could do little to address anti-social activities.

What, then, does Berkman propose for those who perform anti-social acts in a society free of police, prisons and the state? In the first instance, Berkman asserts that the impetuses towards crime – 'economic conditions ... social inequality ... wrongs and evils of which government and monopoly are the parents' (Berkman, 1972: 189) – would be severely diminished. As a result, much of what is currently considered crime would diminish alongside those impetuses. Yet Berkman is under no illusion that some antisocial behaviour would still exist even in anarchy. In search of a solution, he returns to his premise that crime is a result of deprivation and need. He suggests that the anarchist society would look at anti-social behaviour as the product of historical 'diseased conditions and attitudes' which should be 'treated as an unhealthy state of mind rather than as crime' (Berkman, 1972: 189). More specifically, the anarchists 'would begin by feeding the "criminal" and securing him work' (Berkman, 1972:189) with the long-term goal of rehabilitating the individual back into society.[3]

Berkman's assessment that anti-social behaviour should be treated as a mental health issue should not be misconstrued as an endorsement of the harsh mental asylum system of his time. On the contrary, Berkman described asylums as 'penal institutions' alongside prisons (Goldman and Berkman, 1920: 20), a perspective also held by noted anarchist communist Peter Kropotkin (1887: 350, see also Weide, Chapter 9 in this volume). In 1919, Berkman wrote an open letter to prison warden Fred G. Zerbst about the 'brutality, corruption and incompetence' in the Federal Penitentiary in Atlanta, Georgia. Amid his arguments, Berkman noted that there were 'several investigations of penitentiaries and insane asylums going on at this very moment' (Goldman and Berkman, 1920: 20). Elsewhere, Berkman blamed prisons themselves for exacerbating mental health issues. He cited as an example the inmate A. Popoff, who was beaten to the point of unconsciousness and consigned for two years to a 'dark dungeon', ultimately leading to him becoming a 'raving maniac' (Goldman and Berkman, 1920: 23). Berkman even argued that 'common sense and all human experience prove that the criminal is no more responsible for crime than the crazy man for his insanity' (Goldman and Berkman, 1920: 3). In 1920, he contrasted contemporary views of mental health and criminality, and stressed that 'even the most ignorant man knows that insanity is a disease. But in regard to crime and criminals we are still in the stage of dark-age superstition' (Goldman and Berkman, 1920: 3).

While Berkman outlines a compassionate approach to redressing anti-social behaviour, he fails to prescribe anything like modern systems of transformative justice, retributive justice and other survivor-centred models which have been proposed to take the place of the criminal punishment system by modern prison abolitionists and anarchists (The Escape Committee, 2020: passim). It is worth noting that there is disagreement in the anarchist community about these justice models even today. Where transformative justice focuses on an accountability process, queer and feminist anarchists have challenged whether it is fair to force survivors to relive their trauma by going through these processes with their assailants. They argue for a retributive justice model built on a critical understanding of power relations between the oppressed and their oppressors. This paradigm suggests a place for radical self-defence and community defence in the face of harm (The Escape Committee, 2020: passim).

Nevertheless, Berkman's vision of harm reduction echoes the views of prison abolitionists like Kaba who states that: 'A world without harm isn't possible and isn't what an abolitionist vision purports to achieve' (Kaba, 2021: 120). However, how that harm is addressed contrasts significantly; Kaba says that the Black- and Indigenous-led prison abolition movement is about engendering accountability for transgressions, placing focus on the systems that enabled the harm in the first place and addressing specific harm with specific responses. Through this lens, Kaba can both acknowledge that in an abolitionist society, and indeed in anarchy, crime will necessarily reduce in frequency, while providing a more concrete method for how to address new harms when they inevitably occur. Meanwhile, for Berkman, there is no meaningful notion of repairing harm; the focus is placed on helping the perpetrator rather than those who were affected by the perpetrator's actions.

There is some evidence that Berkman understood his own shortcomings in these areas. In a letter to Goldman of 25 June 1928, Berkman wondered about the utility of prisons. He raised the spectre of murder and rape, and juxtaposed two options: mob rule, which, in his view, will almost certainly see the offender killed; or due process, which creates courts and, by necessity, police and prisons. He explored ways of dealing with racial violence against Jewish and Black communities. He considered real-world scenarios where '[p]eople make a pogrom in Russia; or whites trying to lynch a Negro in America' and asked how a community could stop them without invoking an 'armed force' which may simply recreate the police (Berkman, 2005: 254). In setting out the parameters of this binary choice, he misses an opportunity to propose a model more theoretically aligned with what is now called transformative justice.

In *Now and After*, Berkman's final analysis does present a third option: rehabilitation. He proposes making offenders into 'prisoners in freedom' (Berkman, 1972: 295–296). He suggests that these individuals will be given the option either to live alone and with no access to the resources of the community beyond the bare minimum, or to live among the community and by doing so 'be influenced by its revolutionary environment' (Berkman, 1972: 295). By focusing on liberty as a primary concern, Berkman believes they would eventually 'cease to be a danger to the revolution' (Berkman, 1972: 295). In this passage, he refers to 'counter-revolutionists' without specifying what that term entails, but rapists and those perpetrating pogroms certainly would certainly fit into this broad category. Yet despite his behind-the-scenes qualms about the best course of action, it seems that he settled on a method which would not protect the most vulnerable. He relies on proximity to community and demonstrations of value over ensuring that, for example, serial abusers do not have access to additional victims. Moreover, he fails to mention that by prioritizing the freedoms of the perpetrators, those who experience harm are necessarily limited in their ability to go about their daily lives in safety and security. As modern anarchists have pointed out, 'expulsion does not "solve" the problem, and potentially just passes it onto other groups to deal with' (The Escape Committee, 2020: 109).

In his conclusion to the 1928 letter to Goldman, Berkman concedes to her that rape will likely always exist, even in anarchy. Nevertheless, Berkman is steadfast that it is not worth bringing back police and prisons for the sake of addressing this problem. This is, in itself, a coherent abolitionist position, but lacks significant gender analysis. For example, Berkman's commentary fails to consider that prisons and police rarely, if ever, prevent rape and sexual assault in the first place (Parker, 2022), a point often made by prison abolitionist and feminist activists. In fact, the prison and police system often perpetuates these harms and, as such, would not resolve the issue, and would instead exacerbate it (McLaughlin, 2018).

There is another important component missing in Berkman's vision for resolving offences within an anarchist community. While he agrees that punishment produces more misery and anti-social behaviour rather than less, and although he acknowledges that systemic conditions drive crime in the first place, he relies on the notion that satisfying material needs is enough to curb crime. This is sometimes true; it has been shown that having healthcare (Jácome, 2022) and food assistance (Bailey, 2023) can reduce crime rates, for example. But Berkman overstates the claim: he assesses that: 'Fully 97 per cent of all crime is due directly to our economic institutions. The other 3 per cent are traceable to the artificiality and neurosis of modern life, to the anti-social tendencies cultivated among the weeds in the neglected and mistreated garden of human life' (Goldman and Berkman, 1920: 3). His analysis thus virtually excludes systems of oppression beyond those created by economic concerns: misogyny and racial hatred, to name two obvious examples. The notion that anti-Black racial animus or sexual violence against cis-women and the trans community are borne out of mere material deprivation has been roundly rejected by many Black and feminist scholars.

Instead, scholars and activists have expressed a need for internal critique and improvement among the dominant groups. For example, James Baldwin argued that being white is 'a moral choice' that depends on the 'debasement and definition' of Black people (Baldwin, 1984). For Baldwin, white is a category which is defined in opposition to the 'other' (Baldwin, 1984). The solution to resolving white supremacy thus lies with white people deconstructing whiteness in the first instance. Although Baldwin gives ample room for Black resistance and survival within a system they did not create, there is a fundamental belief of white selfhood among the dominant population that must foremost be rejected. Therefore, although racism may relate to material needs, at its base is a belief in racial hierarchy – or, indeed, in race generally – which perpetuates the othering of Black and Brown people.

Kaba gives a similar prescription for misogyny:

> If violence originated because of unexamined misogyny or sexism learned in the family or broader culture, a community process that invites the person responsible to examine that would be more likely to lead to a positive outcome than incarceration in a cell, where the person is likely to experience more violence. (Kaba, 2021: 120)

Here again, the focus is placed on both the dominant group and the systems that group perpetuates. In Berkman's paradigm, satisfying material conditions would disabuse racist or sexist beliefs and behaviours; for Baldwin and Kaba, the problems go beyond these conditions and call for specific solutions which address their root causes. These perspectives provide an answer that Berkman fails to identify when he asks what should be done about 'the leaders of the mob who persist in exciting race or other hatred' (Berkman, 2005: 254).

When Berkman ponders how to address racist mobs, he feels that the obvious solution would be prison or death with the goal of preventing these individuals from causing further harm. But for him, the looming centrality of means and ends to anarchism complicates his views. He was a vociferous critic of the Bolsheviks in Russia and was thus loath to concede any use for prisons even in a temporary fashion. As he wrote in his letter to Goldman, 'a *transitory period* with punishments, prisons, etc. ... is sure to develop the bolshevik ways and methods' (Berkman, 2005: 254–255). In *Now and After*, as discussed earlier, it is clear that Berkman did not settle on a particular view; he takes a broadly abolitionist perspective while remaining generally vague about what to do about those hurting others.

An abolitionist response to Berkman's conundrum might raise the point that the police and government are themselves the agents of the dominant classes. For example, racist lynch mobs may share overlapping interests, if not outright membership, with the local sheriff's department or government. Indeed, some scholarship suggests that lynch mobs were ultimately supplanted by police violence against landless Black individuals in the American South (Niedermeier, 2019: 22–23). Through this lens, the law becomes a selective weapon used to suppress a particular population. Thus, asking the police to intercede on behalf of Black victims is asking the fox to look after the hen house.

There is some evidence Berkman understood this idea in principle. He saw the police as a structure riddled with the biases of its administrators. He explains that the alleged justice system claims to 'recognize[s] no distinction of station, of influence, of race, creed, or color', but that the 'proposition needs only to be stated to be seen as thoroughly false' (Berkman, 1972: 52). He discusses implicit bias and the false notion that the individuals who make up the legal system can set aside their personal views in the name of fairness. He says that 'justice is administered by human beings' who have 'personal sentiments, opinions, likes, dislikes, and prejudices' (Berkman, 1972: 52–53). He asserts that the individuals who make up the system 'can't get away' from their personal biases 'by merely putting on a judge's gown and sitting on the bench' (Berkman, 1972: 53).

In Berkman's view, the system is as rife with flaws as the humans who comprise it. Despite this understanding, Berkman nevertheless falls for the tempting notion that establishing a police force and prison might resolve issues of racial and gender violence. It is therefore important to complement Berkman's anti-prison politics with correctives from prison abolitionists, feminists and racial theorists who have explored the ways that these systems themselves do harm and how to bypass these tempting 'fixes' while keeping the community safe.

Police are not the community

Berkman observed that the police are not of the community, but rather exist in opposition to it. As he writes in *Prison Memoirs*: 'Government, with its laws, is the common enemy ... The Law! It is the arch-crime of the centuries' (Berkman, 2017: 30). For him, the law and the government are not only not representative of the people, but also act directly against their interests. In *Now and After*, he clarifies that prioritizing 'the whole' at the cost of 'the individual' necessarily reveals the fact that the state cannot simultaneously serve the majority and claim to be one and the same with all of its people (Berkman, 1972: 3). Moreover, Berkman notes that because the state is constructed largely by those in power, it will never hold the powerful to account. This paradigm suggests that it is hard, if not impossible, for a poor person to get justice from a rich wage thief, or indeed a Black person to win a case against a white person who has harmed them. Thus, it follows that if the police enforce the will of the government on the people, they must serve dominant interests and are therefore not truly a part of the community.

This reflects the perspective of Cyril D. Robinson and Richard Scaglion, who describe the 'double, contradictory, and dynamic origin and function' of the police as 'the agent of both the people they police and the dominant class' (Robinson and Scaglion, 1987: 114). They emphasize that the notion that the police are from the community is 'a pervasive and essential prop to concepts of modern policing' which elides the importance of the emergence of specialized police forces — that is, as researcher David H. Bayley defines it, a police force which 'devote[s] all of their attention to the application of physical restraint' (Bayley, 1999: 67). The mythmaking around who the police and the government ultimately serve provides justification for the existence of both interconnected entities.

Kaba offers an important finetuning of this perspective. Not only does the government not protect or represent the people, 'set[ting] itself up as the ultimate arbiter of "fighting for the victims"', but can in fact ignore the wishes of those directly impacted by the transgression. Kaba writes that 'nowhere in those proceedings is the "victim's" real interest. If the victim doesn't agree, for example, with capital punishment, the state supersedes that and says we're still going to kill this person on your behalf. In that instance your personal feeling doesn't matter at all' (Kaba, 2021: 152). Moreover, the government uses victims and survivors as mascots to justify its eye-for-an-eye approach to justice. As Kaba writes, 'when the state wants to justify its vengeance it will say, "We're doing this in the name of the person who was harmed"' (Kaba, 2021: 152). Through Kaba's framing, we can see not only how the government purports to represent the people in the abstract, as Berkman notes, but also on a case-by-case basis, leading to new laws and punishments often bearing the names of the victims in whose supposed honour the legislation was passed.

In *Now and After*, Berkman expands on the role of police in society, particularly in relation to the marginalized. He describes the police – and, crucially, the military – as ordinary powerless members of the community who have been given authority over their fellows: 'But the police and the soldiers, the defenders of "law and order", are not of the capitalist class. They are men from the ranks of the people, poor men who for pay protect the very system that keeps them poor' (Berkman, 1972: 21). Foreshadowing the theoretical contributions of Robinson and Scaglion decades later in 'Origin and evolution of police function' (Robinson and Scaglion, 1987), Berkman gestures at the cruel irony that the police and soldiers themselves have been lured into the contradiction of becoming the violent enforcers of the property-owning class. Indeed, without the police (and associated organizations, like the military and judicial system), property rights would become unenforceable and the owner class would lose a key source of power.

From here, Berkman describes how the state imbues individuals with limited power to encourage a minority of the marginalized to abuse, detain and even kill their fellows:

> It just comes down to this: some of the slaves protect their masters in keeping them and the rest of the people in slavery. In the same way Great Britain, for instance, keeps the Hindoos[4] [*sic*] in India in subjection by a police force of the natives, of the Hindoos [*sic*] themselves. Or as Belgium does with the black men in the Congo. Or as any government does with a subjugated people. It is the same system. (Berkman, 1972: 21)

In this passage, Berkman sees colonialism as intrinsically tied to that of policing, a point echoed in modern abolitionist texts (Chowdhury, 2021: 85–93). In particular, he notes the toxic effect of authority and how individuals can be encouraged to inflict pain on their own communities by giving them the power, as backed by the state, to enact violence – or, as he puts it, 'the government uses one part of the people to aid and protect the capitalists in robbing the whole of the people' (Berkman, 1972: 21).

In this way, Berkman mirrors an ongoing discussion in the Black community around the phenomenon of Black police in America. In this case, members of a population disproportionately targeted by the police and prison system are faced with people from the same background joining the military or police force. This gives the veneer of a community managing itself, obscuring how the state delegates violent enforcement to members of that same community.

Many Black theorists, artists and writers have commented on the twisted nature of taking someone who lives under the regime of white supremacy and the government and giving them the power to enact violence on their neighbours. Baldwin described this in *The Evidence of Things Not Seen*:

> Black policemen were another matter. We used to say, 'If you must call a policeman' – for we hardly ever did – 'for God's sake, try to make

sure it's a White one'. A Black policeman could completely demolish you. He knew far more about you than a White policeman could and you were without defenses before this Black brother in uniform whose entire reason for breathing seemed to be his hope to offer proof that, though he was Black, he was not Black like you. (Baldwin, 1985: 66).

For Baldwin, the Black police officer is desperate to demonstrate to the ruling white class some differentiation between themselves and those who were once their classmates and neighbours. Whereas some other populations have been able to assimilate into whiteness, most Black people cannot. Therefore, an opportunity to join law enforcement provides a means of putting on a new skin, the clothing of a government agent and assuming an elevated role among their former peers. They carry with them the full force of the state, although of course their new position in no way threatens the government or its status quo of capitalism and white supremacy; on the contrary, the Black police officer has to violently implement that programme through their very job.

This perspective has persisted well beyond Baldwin and into popular media. In John Singleton's film *Boyz n the Hood* (1991), Coffey (played by Jessie Lawrence Ferguson), a Black police officer, is markedly more aggressive towards the film's protagonist, Tre Styles (Cuba Gooding Jr.). Two years after that film was released, KRS-One also addressed this phenomenon in the track 'Black Cop':

> Both have black cops in cars profilin
> Hardcore kids in the West got stress
> In the East we are chased by the same black beast
> The black cop is the only real obstacle
> Black slave turned black cop is not logical
> But very psychological, haven't you heard?
> It's the BLACK COP killin black kids in Johannesburg.

These lyrics reiterate Berkman's words and speak to a broader observation from modern prison abolitionists. The question of police violence against marginalized people is less about the specific identities of the officers in question and much more about the systems of racial and marginalized oppression in which the police operate. While there are clear cases of police officers abusing their social status as white men, for example, Derek Chauvin in the May 2020 murder of George Floyd in the US (*New York Times*, 2022) or Wayne Couzens in the March 2021 rape and murder of Sarah Everard in the UK (Dearden, 2022), it can also be the case that the perpetrators are nominally from the same group as the individual they are assaulting. In the case of Tyre Nichols, a Black man murdered by five police officers in January 2023 in the US, all of his killers were Black (Associated Press, 2023). For modern prison abolitionists, and perhaps for Berkman were he alive to observe this case, this comes as no surprise: the system, which bears with it all of the biases of the humans who created it, is itself the culprit. For Berkman in particular, this clearly demonstrates his view that the police and prison system uses the marginalized against themselves.

The police and the owner class

One of Berkman's core ideas about the law and policing is that they operate at the behest of the wealthy, reflecting the position of many anarchists both of his time and today. As he asserts in *Now and After*: 'It is … clear that the law will protect those who have power and influence, the rich and the wealthy, however they got their riches' (Berkman, 1972: 26). Because of this, Berkman observes, there is a glaring double standard of treatment between the owner class – those who hold power through wealth, property and controlling the means of production – and the marginalized. He notes that if a poor individual 'took advantage of some one, cheated some one' in the same manner that a wealthy individual did, the poor person 'did it "illegally", and you call him a criminal' (Berkman, 1972: 26). In identifying the disparity in how the law is applied between these groups, Berkman strikes at the heart of a key police function: enforcing property rights to ensure the owner class never loses its grip on power.

The scholars Robinson and Scaglion highlight the notion of the police as a frontline for a dominant class with unfettered access and control over essential resources – commonly referred to as private property. The police, then, are foot soldiers for this dominant class who are tasked with violently keeping those without access to and control of private property at bay. Because the police draw from the ranks of the marginalized, this paradigm maintains a hierarchical system of haves and have-nots without risking the direct physical involvement of the powerful.

Robinson and Scaglion elaborated on this perspective by laying out a theory of policing in four points:

1. The origin of the specialized police function depends upon the division of communal (kinship) society into dominant and subordinate classes with antagonistic interests.
2. Specialized police agencies are generally characteristic only of societies politically organized as states.
3. In a period of transition the crucial factor in delineating the modern specialized police function is an ongoing attempt at the conversion of the social control (policing) mechanism from an integral part of the community structure to an agent of an emerging dominant class.

4. The police institution is created by the emerging dominant class as an instrument for the preservation of its control over restricted access to basic resources, over the political apparatus governing this access, and over the labor force necessary to provide the surplus upon which the dominant class lives (Robinson and Scaglion, 1987: 113–114).

Berkman discusses a similar notion of the police as a weapon of the dominant class by emphasizing the cycle by which the police and prison system on the one hand cannot resolve crime through punishment, and on the other hand make the problem worse by contributing to the conditions that lead to anti-social and violent behaviour. He describes in a 1906 article entitled 'Prisons and crime' how prisons cost the community enormous sums of money and only make the problem worse: 'The money annually expended for the maintenance of prisons could be invested, with as much profit and less injury, in government bonds of the planet Mars, or sunk in the Atlantic' (Berkman, 1906). He reiterates that the prisons and the society in which they arise are the sources of crime. 'No amount of punishment can obviate crime', he states, 'so long as prevailing conditions, in and out of prison, drive men to it' (Berkman, 1906).

Later, Berkman lays bare the absurdity of expecting laws to resolve anti-social activity, stating: 'It has been established that poverty and unemployment, with their attendant misery and despair, are the chief sources of crime. Is there any law to prevent poverty and unemployment? Is there any law to abolish these main causes of crime?' (Berkman, 1972: 80–81). The implication of his rhetorical question is clear: the laws enforced by the police are mechanisms of punishment and are not intended to address any root issues. Beyond not alleviating immiseration, Berkman intimates that the laws themselves are entrenching the cycle that leads to criminality in the first place: 'Are not all the laws designed to keep up the conditions which produce poverty and misery, and thus manufacture crime all the time?' (Berkman, 1972: 81). Here, he not only connects the law to punishment, but also points to the double standards of the legal system in protection of capitalist interests which engender the criminal activity in the first place.

Berkman takes this idea further by framing anti-social activity as a systemic issue, a core notion of modern prison abolitionism. In *Now and After*, he provides a hypothetical example of a poor child driven to crime by circumstance. He implores the reader:

> Don't you see that the *conditions* of his whole life have made him what he is? And don't you see that the *system* which keeps up such conditions is a greater criminal than the petty thief? The law will step in and punish him, but is it not the same law that permits those

bad conditions to exist and upholds the system that makes criminals? (Berkman, 1972: 27)

Berkman orients the self-perpetuation of the legal punishment system in terms of self-interest. 'It is a profitable business, this law-making', he declares, before asking:

> Is it to the interest of the policeman, the detective, the sheriff, the judge, the lawyer, the prison contractors, wardens, deputies, keepers, and the thousands of others who live by the 'administration of justice' to do away with crime? Supposing there were no criminals, could those 'administrators' hold their jobs? (Berkman, 1972: 83)

In this way, Berkman gestures towards the entrenched bureaucracy and petty self-interest of those who depend on these roles as employment. He repeats arguments of anarchists before him, like Errico Malatesta, who, in his 1891 pamphlet *Anarchy*, analogized the French gendarmes to professional wolf-exterminators in whose interest it is to never quite exterminate all of the wolves lest they put themselves out of business. Malatesta notes that the peasants consider the gendarmes more 'wolf-preservers' than exterminators for this reason, with obvious implications for managing criminality (Malatesta, 2014: 24; see Turcato, Chapter 11 in this volume). For Berkman and Malatesta, a system that exists primarily to hold court and then punish criminals must necessarily have criminals to punish in the first place. Thus there is an intrinsic need to keep the system turning by those who are a part of it.

Berkman described the 'whole social attitude toward the criminal' as 'barbaric stupidity that seeks to hide its own shame and its mistakes behind prison bars' (Goldman and Berkman, 1920: 4). More than 80 years later, the abolitionist and academic Angela Davis would make many of these same points. She writes in *Are Prisons Obsolete?* that: 'The prison has become a black hole into which the detritus of contemporary capitalism is deposited. Mass imprisonment generates profits as it devours social wealth, and thus it tends to reproduce the very conditions that lead people to prison' (Davis, 2003: 16–17). She describes the prison as having an almost organic essence, a sort of tumorous outgrowth that absorbs resources and creates a void into which all things undesirable – in this case, any marginalized individual who steps out of line – are thrown.

On this crucial point, the early 20th-century anarchist perspective aligns well with prison abolitionists of the 21st century. American anarchist Voltairine de Cleyre, an associate of Berkman's, noted that those who work in the government 'exist for the purpose of granting privileges to whoever can pay most for you, and so limiting the freedom of men to employ themselves that they must sell themselves into this frightful slavery or become tramps, beggars, thieves, prostitutes, and murderers' (de Cleyre, 2016: 169). Likewise, Kaba and fellow abolitionist Kelly Hayes discuss how the government 'maintain[s] conditions that generate despair and therefore produce interpersonal violence' (Hayes and Kaba, 2023: 81–82). This systemic understanding of how police and prisons reproduce themselves, shared between prison abolitionists and anarchists, is key to our understanding of its continued existence in spite of its apparent ineffectiveness at reducing crime (The Conversation, 2020).

Police, prisons and the state

One of the most important contributions Berkman makes to abolitionist theory is his holistic view of the prison system as an extension of the society that built it. As he put it, prisons are 'an aggravated counterpart of the outside world' (Berkman, 2017: 66). He argued that police and prisons reflect the capitalist social order which 'law and government are there to protect' (Berkman, 1972: 15). He was clear that 'the government needs laws, police and soldiers, courts and prisons to protect capitalism' and its underlying logic of private property (Berkman, 1972: 20). Many prison abolitionists today likewise speak about the intrinsic violence of the state. Yet there is something to be gained by directly linking police and prison abolition to state abolition as Berkman did. Loss of the legal system and of the police and military necessarily mean not just the end of capitalism, but also of the state itself.

Many modern prison abolitionists have written about the overtly violent and anti-community nature of the state. In their book *Let This Radicalize You*, Kaba and Hayes outline plainly that: 'The state sees communal care as an ideological threat' (Hayes and Kaba, 2023: 82) which crushes mutual aid projects and other efforts to build comradery without state machinery or capitalist input (Hough et al, 2021). Echoing Berkman, they go on to say that:

> State violence around the world is routinely dealt out in such a manner: the state reserves the right to overstep its own laws, and even when it subsequently acknowledges its mistakes, it has already subjected people to the indignity of arrest, deprived them of their liberty, or subjected them to other violence. (Hayes and Kaba, 2023: 249)

Here Kaba and Hayes reiterate that the police serve the powerful, and thus create a system of laws which fall differently on the powerless. The violence and authority of the state give the police an air of legitimacy, but ultimately they serve the same masters as the government itself: those in dominant gender and racial categories and those who own private property.

Abolitionists theories include not just police and prisons, but, in concordance with Berkman, militaries and border patrols as well. This is why many modern abolitionists use the term 'prison industrial complex' (PIC) – that is, the interconnected state-owned and private network of prisons, prison labour, courts, military and other linked systems. Their understanding of the PIC extends beyond mere anti-capitalism as has been suggested by some critics (Wacquant, 2009: 84–87), considering how important factors like racism, sexism and queerphobia drive police violence and incarceration rates (Duff, 2021: passim). PIC abolition does not see police and prisons as a mere means of generating profit, although they can, but as a self-perpetuating exercise of power which can even lose money if they are able to sustain their purpose of subduing the marginalized.

While police, prisons and other entities like the gendarmes were markedly different in Berkman's time, we can see how his broader ideas about these entities foreshadow the PIC as it exists and is understood today. Indeed, even Berkman himself reflected on how as much as the prison system ostensibly changes, it fundamentally remains the same. In 1920, he observed that: 'It is apparent that modern criminology has had a very negligible effect upon the popular mind within the last twenty-five years, for I have found the prisons of today in no essential way different from those of a quarter of a century back' (Goldman and Berkman, 1920: 4). In particular, he highlights how methods of punishment remained altogether stagnant in that time.

In keeping with Berkman's expansive understanding of police and prisons, Black Lives Matter co-founder Patrisse Cullors states in the *Harvard Law Review* '[a]bolition means no borders. Abolition means no Border Patrol. Abolition means no Immigration and Customs Enforcement' (Cullors, 2019: 1691), implying an end of national borders and the states they define. Many activists have also been explicit that prison and police abolition entails socialism, although what form that socialism takes is often left ambiguous. In multiple interviews, Kaba has stated outright that 'capitalism has to go. It has to be abolished' (Why Is This Happening?, 2019) and that the ongoing immiseration of the poor and marginalized, alongside the failures of the liberal democratic government to meet these needs, has uncovered the 'contradictions and the violences of capitalism, bringing things to light in stark relief' (Intercepted, 2020). And yet, despite the logical conclusion of these statements – that the state itself must be abolished alongside capitalism – it is often the case that modern prison and police abolitionists leave this point unsaid (see also the discussion of different conceptions of the state among abolitionists and socialists in Bell and Scott, Chapter 1 in this volume).

This is where Berkman and the broader anarchist programme can provide additional insights to the modern PIC abolition movement. He identified that prisons are not only a series of interconnected violent forces that protect the powerful against the marginalized, but also as an extension of the inherently violent state itself. Therefore, not only must capitalism be uprooted – a system which itself depends on the state to enforce alleged property rights – but so must the state itself. It is more coherent for PIC abolition as a project to also be anti-state, including alleged socialist states both historical and modern. A society which has ostensibly eliminated capitalism but whose police and prisons nevertheless uphold the interests of the powerful (for example, state bureaucrats or military leaders) has failed to abolish policing and its primary functions of maintaining a power hierarchy. Whether abolitionists adopt the term 'anarchist' is irrelevant, but just as all anarchists should be clear in their full opposition to prisons and policing in order to remain consistent, so too must PIC abolitionists be clear on their opposition not just to capitalist government, but to all government. In doing so, they can envision a new world premised on mutual aid and community where people live safe from harm and from the oppressive framework of government authority.

Conclusion: An anarchist abolitionist synthesis

There are many ways in which Alexander Berkman not only prefigured the ideas of the prison abolition movement, but also offered a more complete analysis of the systems in which the prison and police operate. For Berkman, prisons are an extension of the state, an organ of a larger oppressive matrix that must be abolished in its totality. This provides a roadmap to a liberated future that eschews the pitfalls of so-called socialist states. On the other hand, Berkman's plan for confronting harm when it does occur was limited to addressing material conditions and to keeping 'prisoners in freedom'. We can look at modern discussions around both transformative and retributive justice to see how PIC abolitionists and anarchists have gone beyond Berkman's analysis, even if they still struggle to address some of the fundamental contradictions Berkman himself faced.

Today, the anarchist and PIC abolition movements share significant ideological overlap. Some of the most prominent PIC abolitionists, such as Dean Spade and Harsha Walia, have publicly identified as anarchists. Conversely, many anarchists have embraced the ideas put forward by the PIC abolitionist movement in building new racially conscious and feminist visions for a stateless society. A synthesis of anarchist and PIC abolitionist ideas would therefore emphasize the unique elements each tradition brings to the table.

Using the ideas of Berkman and of other anarchists of his time, this synthesis reconceptualizes the theoretical framework of Robinson and Scaglion with four new points which address not only the abolition of policing and prisons, but also their inextricable role in relation to the state:

1. The police are not a part of the owner class, but have been given authority by the government and private capital to violently enforce their will over

the marginalized (for example, women, queer individuals, the poor, rough sleepers and those with mental health issues) and thus are antagonists of the marginalized. Note that the police do not have any meaningful power or authority to disrupt the systems that use them for enforcement. Their power is strictly limited to hemming in and controlling the marginalized.
2. Because the government serves at the pleasure of the owner class – that is, the class that holds power, be it racial, financial or otherwise – the police also serve at the pleasure of the owner class. Law enforcement violence is thus firmly pointed towards the marginalized; the owner class is above and beyond its reach.
3. Without police, property rights become unenforceable except through privatized militaries and police, which ultimately serve the same function. If police and prisons are abolished, so is private property, and along with it a significant portion of the power of the owner classes.
4. Like property rights, the government cannot enforce its borders, laws or authority in the absence of police and associated entities, such as the military. In abolishing the PIC, the state is also abolished. Thus, prison and police abolition entails state abolition.

These principles provide a better understanding of the project of prison and police abolition. The capitalist-propertarian notion of property rights is only enforceable using either state or private police. So are borders, the arbitrary lines established to declare one state distinct from another. The police and their wider network of border patrols and militias exist as a violent mediator between ingroups and outgroups. Whether that is declaring migrants unwelcome because they do not conform to some imagined national or racial identity, or keeping the homeless out of the sight of property owners and politicians, police and prisons exist to reinforce a false peace both within the borders of the state and, through colonial and imperial action, beyond those borders.

This false peace is the very lie which Berkman himself highlighted in the pages of *Now and After*: 'The entire thing is kept up by educating the people to believe that capitalism is right, that the law is just, and that the government must be obeyed. Do you see through this game now?' (Berkman, 1972: 21). For Berkman, these systems are one and the same. These ideas would eventually be echoed by Baldwin, who, in a 1966 essay entitled 'A report from Occupied territory', frames the issue from a Black perspective: 'The law is meant to be my servant and not my master, still less my torturer and my murderer. To respect the law, in the context in which the American Negro finds himself, is simply to surrender his self-respect' (Baldwin and Weems, 1966). As many penal abolitionist scholars have demonstrated, the logic of punishment and intrinsic racial, gender and class bias are deeply embedded in the legal system. Thus, if we are to take prison and police abolition seriously, we should include in its project the abolition of the state as well, lest we play 'the game' and sacrifice the self-respect of the marginalized to their torturers and murderers.

Acknowledgements

The author would like to thank Bill Nowlin for his help in thinking about how to approach this work. He would also like to acknowledge Nolan Bennett and Anya Metzer for reading earlier drafts of this chapter. Their critical eye and invaluable feedback helped strengthen his argument and scholarship.

Notes

1. Also published under the alternate title of *What Is Communist Anarchism?* (Berkman, 1972).
2. Berkman frequently referred to prisoners using masculine language. This is likely due to contemporaneous conventions and to Berkman reflecting on his own time spent in male prisons. However, we can surmise that this language is not intended to elide the experiences of female prisoners. Berkman's own partner, Emma Goldman, was also incarcerated, and the two wrote together frequently about their experiences in the penal system.
3. When Berkman discusses rehabilitation, he is clear that he does not refer to the same methods proposed by the prison system of his time. On the contrary, he notes that, 'Most men still believe that by beating and punishing the criminal, by hanging and electrocution, we can drive the "evil spirit" out of him. This process is called reforming the criminal.' (Goldman and Berkman, 1920: 3).
4. In this passage, Berkman uses what is now considered an antiquated spelling for Hindu to refer broadly to the colonized people of India.

References

Ackerman, S. (2015) 'The disappeared: Chicago police detain Americans at abuse-laden "black site"', *The Guardian*, 24 February. Available from: https://www.theguardian.com/us-news/2015/feb/24/chicago-police-detain-americans-black-site [Accessed 29 February 2024].

Associated Press (2023) 'Memphis police officer pleads guilty in fatal beating of Tyre Nichols', *The Guardian*, 2 November. Available from: https://www.theguardian.com/us-news/2023/nov/02/tyre-nichols-police-officer-guilty-plea [Accessed 29 February 2024].

Bailey, M. et al (2023) 'Is the social safety net a long-term investment? Large-scale evidence from the food stamps program', *Review of Economic Studies*. DOI: 10.1093/restud/rdad063

Baker, Z. (2019) 'Means and ends: the anarchist critique of seizing state power', *The Anarchist Library*. Available from: https://theanarchistlibrary.org/library/anarchopac-means-and-ends [Accessed 29 February 2024].

Baldwin, J. (1984) 'On being white ... and other lies', *Essence*, April.

Baldwin, J. (1985) *The Evidence of Things Not Seen*, New York: Holt, Rinehart & Winston.

Baldwin, J. and Weems, C.M. (1966) 'A report from occupied territory', *The Nation*, 11 July. Available from: https://www.thenation.com/article/archive/report-occupied-territory-2/ [Accessed 24 February 2024].

Bayley, D.H. (1999) 'The development of modern policing', in L.K. Gaines and G.W. Cordner (eds) *Policing Perspectives: An Anthology*, Los Angeles: Roxbury Publishing Company, pp 59–78.

Bennett, N. (2023) 'The ambivalence of Alexander Berkman's anti-prison anarchism', *American Political Science Review*: 1–15. DOI: 10.1017/S0003055423000965

Berkman, A. (1906) 'Prisons and crime', *Mother Earth*, August: 23–29. Available from: https://theanarchistlibrary.org/library/alexander-berkman-prisons-and-crime [Accessed 29 February 2024].

Berkman, A. (1972) *What Is Communist Anarchism?*, New York: Dover Publications.

Berkman, A. (2005) 'Alexander Berkman to Emma Goldman June 25, 1928, PARIS', in G. Fellner (ed.) *Life of an Anarchist: The Alexander Berkman Reader*, New York: Seven Stories Press, pp 254–255.

Berkman, A. (2017) *Prison Memoirs of an Anarchist*, CreateSpace Independent Publishing Platform.

Chowdhury, T. (2021) 'From the colony to the metropole: race, policing and the colonial boomerang', in K. Duff (ed.) *Abolishing the Police*, London: Dog Section Press, pp 85–93.

The Conversation (2020) 'Police solve just 2% of all major crimes', *Snopes*, 20 August. Available from: https://www.snopes.com/news/2020/08/20/police-solve-just-2-of-all-major-crimes/ [Accessed 29 February 2024].

Cullors, P. (2019) 'Abolition and reparations: histories of resistance, transformative justice, and accountability', *Harvard Law Review*, 132(6): 1684–1694.

Davis, A. (2003) *Are Prisons Obsolete?*, New York: Seven Stories Press.

Dearden, L. (2022) 'Sarah Everard murderer Wayne Couzens loses appeal against whole-life prison sentence', *The Independent*, 29 July. Available from: https://www.independent.co.uk/news/uk/crime/sarah-everard-wayne-couzens-appeal-b2133912.html [Accessed 29 February 2024].

De Cleyre, V. (2016) 'The eleventh of November, 1887', in A. Berkman (ed.) *The Selected Works of Voltairine de Cleyre*, Chico, CA: AK Press, pp 164–172.

Duff, K. (ed.) (2021) *Abolishing the Police*, London: Dog Section Press.

The Escape Committee (2020) *What about the Rapists? Anarchist Approaches to Crime and Justice*. 3rd edn, Leeds: Active Distribution.

Goldman, E. and Berkman, A. (1920) *A Fragment of the Prison Experiences of Emma Goldman and Alexander Berkman*, New York: Stella Comyn. Available from: https://www.loc.gov/item/2014656910/ [Accessed 29 February 2024].

Hayes, K. and Kaba, M. (2023) *Let This Radicalize You*, Chicago: Haymarket Books.

Hough, S. et al (2021) 'Mutual aid does nothing alone: a rebuttal to Joanna Wuest', *The Commoner*, 21 January. Available from: https://www.thecommoner.org.uk/mutual-aid-never-does-anything-alone/ [Accessed 29 February 2024].

Intercepted (2020) 'Organizer Mariame Kaba: we need a people's bailout to confront coronavirus', *The Intercept*, 19 March. Available from: https://theintercept.com/2020/03/19/organizer-mariame-kaba-we-need-a-peoples-bailout-to-confront-coronavirus/ [Accessed 29 February 2024].

Jácome, E. (2022) 'Mental health and criminal involvement: evidence from losing Medicaid eligibility', unpublished Working Paper. Available from: https://elisajacome.github.io/Jacome/Jacome_JMP.pdf [Accessed 29 February 2024].

Kaba, M. (2021) *We Do This 'Til We Free Us*. Chicago: Haymarket Books.

Korn, M. (1925) 'К Вопросу о 'Пересмотре' [On the issue of "revision"]', *Дело Труда/Dielo Trouda* [*The Cause of Labor*], November. Available from: https://mariegoldsmith.files.wordpress.com/2023/07/m.-korn-on-the-issue-of-revision.pdf [Accessed 29 February 2024].

Kropotkin, P. (1887) *In Russian and French Prisons*, London: Ward and Downey.

Levin, S. (2022) '"Police don't produce safety": the Black feminist scholars fighting for abolition', *The Guardian*, 29 August. Available from: https://www.theguardian.com/us-news/2022/aug/29/police-defund-abolition-mariame-kaba-andrea-j-ritchie [Accessed 29 February 2024].

Malatesta, E. (2014) *Anarchy*. Wil Johnson and Dog's Tail Books.

McLaughlin, E.C. (2018) 'Police officers in the US were charged with more than 400 rapes over a 9-year period', *CNN*, 19 October. Available from: https://edition.cnn.com/2018/10/19/us/police-sexual-assaults-maryland-scope/index.html [Accessed 29 February 2024].

Melamed, S. (2023) 'Prisoners of Pa's secret system of indefinite isolation sue for release and damages', *Philadelphia Inquirer*, 3 October. Available from: https://www.inquirer.com/news/pennsylvania-prisons-solitary-confinement-lawsuit-stgmu-doc-20231003.html [Accessed 29 February 2024].

New York Times (2022) 'How George Floyd Died, and what happened next', 29 July. Available from: https://www.nytimes.com/article/george-floyd.html [Accessed 29 February 2024].

Niedermeier, S. (2019) *The Color of the Third Degree – Racism, Police Torture, and Civil Rights in the American South, 1930–1955*, Chapel Hill: University of North Carolina Press.

Parker, A. (2022) 'Why do so few rape cases go to court?', *BBC News*, 27 May. Available from: https://www.saunders.co.uk/news/virtually-all-rape-victims-are-denied-justice-here-is-the-roadmap-to-failure/ [Accessed 29 February 2024].

Robinson, C.D. and Scaglion, R. (1987) 'The origin and evolution of the police function in society: notes toward a theory', *Law & Society Review*, 21(1): 109–154.

Vargas, R.A. (2023) 'Louisiana police accused of "unconscionable" abuse in "Brave Cave"', *The Guardian*, 23 September. Available from: https://www.theguardian.com/us-news/2023/sep/23/louisiana-police-brave-cave-baton-rouge-warehouse-torture [Accessed 29 February 2024].

Wacquant, L. (2009) *Prisons of Poverty*, Minneapolis: University of Minnesota Press.

Why Is This Happening? (2019) 'Thinking about how to abolish prisons with Mariame Kaba: podcast & transcript', *NBC News*, 10 April. Available from: https://www.nbcnews.com/think/opinion/thinking-about-how-abolish-prisons-mariame-kaba-podcast-transcript-ncna992721 [Accessed 29 February 2024].

Index

References to figures appear in *italic* type; references to endnotes show both the page number and the note number (95n1).

Numbers

18th century direct action 4–5
19th century abolitionist ideas 50–62
19th century 'Industrial Society' 111
19th century socialists 3

A

'abatement of imprisonment' (Bailey) 110
abolitionism
　anarchism and positivism 202
　political doctrine and moral philosophy x
　in red and black 1, 26, 27n1, 27n9
　role of community 54–56
abolitionist activism 10–11
abolitionist compass (Scott) 115–117
abolitionist frameworks 2
abolitionist imagination 183
abolitionist movements 5, 59
abolitionist praxis 102, 116–117
'abolitionist real utopia' (Scott) 88, 92, 103
　and Edward Carpenter 109, 118
　and Arthur St John 97, 101, 102
　and Erik Olin Wright 112
'abolitionist rhizome' (Scott) xi, xii
abolitionist struggles 221–222
abolitionist theory 102
abolitionist thought x–xii, 16
Abolitionist Voices (Scott) x, xi–xii
absolute abolitionism 25, 117, 118, 121
'absolutist' conscientious objectors 100
abstractionism 231
Acción Libertaria 201, 204n12
Actresses' Franchise League 94
afterlives of slavery xii
L'Agitazione 229
agricultural penal colonies 232
Aiello, Peppe 217–218
Albert, C. 201
'Alexander Berkman to Emma Goldman June 25, 1928, PARIS' (Berkman) 305–306, 308

Alexander II, emperor 68
Alexander III, Tsar 171
Alexander II, Tsar 171
Allen, William 137
Altgeld, John Peter 16, 260–266
　Our Penal Machinery and Its Victims 268, 269
altruism and solidarity (Gori) 235
America 204n9, 243
　see also Canada; United States (US)
American Civil War 243
American Federation of Labor (AFL) 248
American League to Abolish Capital Punishment 272
American Railway Union (ARU) 242, 245, 247–248
American socialism 250–251, 254
amnesties 8
anarchic government 199
Gli anarchici (Lombroso) 239n18
anarchism 189–204
　and bourgeois morality 229
　exploitation and oppression 301
　and legitimate coercion 221
　as a method 208
　and penal abolitionism 202
　prison abolition 182–185
　and science 190, 201–202
　and statism 219
Anarchism and Other Essays (Goldman) 285–286, 292, 294, 296
'Anarchism: what it really stands for' (Goldman) 294
anarchist abolitionism 12, 117–118, 191
Anarchist Black Cross (ABC) 5
anarchist Darwinism 190
anarchist movements 203, 204n15
Anarchist Police Squad (New York) 285
anarchist press 196
Anarchist Red Cross 5
Anarchist Revolutionary Socialist Party 227

anarchists
  in academia 12–13
  anti-authoritarianism 232
  approaches to social defence 216
  benign human nature 218
  denying punishment 201
  evolutionism 202
  and PIC abolition movements 317
  positivism 202
  revolutionaries 182, 183
  and socialist-inspired grassroots
    movements 9
  socialist transformation 26–27
  sources of 'crime' 17
  spontaneous processes 211
  US 284
anarchist thought 2, 109–110, 190, 191–193
anarchy
  equality of conditions 220
  as a method 208, 222
  and racial capitalism 184
Anarchy (Malatesta) 207, 314
La Anarquía 196, 200
Los anarquistas (*The Anarchists*, Lombroso)
  192–193
Ancona, Italy 229
Andreevna, Sofia 76
Anglo-American worldview 185
Anglo-Boer Wars 100
anthropological theory (Lombroso) 192–193
anti-authoritarianism 198, 201, 232
anti-Black racial animus 307
anti-caravan riots 1898 229
anti-carceral utopia (Morris) 128–134
anti-prison protests 4–5
anti-reform reformism 183
anti-social behaviour 181–182, 212–215,
  304–305, 313–314
  see also crime
'anxiety entrepreneurs' 7
apokatastasis 158
appealing sentences 128
Appeal to Reason (Debs) 251
Aptheker, Bettina 127
Are Prisons Obsolete? (Davis) 183, 314
Argentina 230, 231–232, 234
aristocracy 55–56
Ashurst, Henry 59
Aslan, Gabriel 161, 165n10, 166n20
asylums 217–218
Atlanta Federal Penitentiary 242,
  304–305
At the Café (Malatesta) 207
Auburn system 243, 263
autoethnography of prisons 172–173

B

Bailey, Victor 110
Bakunin, Mikhail 171, 184

Baldwin, James 307
  The Evidence of Things Not Seen 310
  'A report from occupied territory' 318
Baldwin, Roger N. 170
The Ballad of Reading Gaol (Wilde) 111
'Ballata di Sante Caserio' (folk song) 236
Bandera Social 194–195, 201–202
El Banquete de la vida (Lorenzo) 200
banquet of life metaphor 200
Barcelona 197
Bardella, Jordan 8
Barker, H.A. 126
Barnes, Harry 244, 255n4
Bax, Ernest Belfort 133–134, 143n8
Bayley, David H. 309
Beccaria, Cesare 209–211, 219, 220, 222n1
Bellamy, Edward 131, 133
benevolence and equity 44
Bennett, Nolan 302
Benthamite panopticon 126
Bentham, Jeremy 33, 47, 52
Berkman, Alexander 17, 24, 25, 109, 281,
  301–319
  analysis of prisons and police 317
  anti-social behaviour 304, 305, 313–314
  attempted assassination of Henry
    Frick 301–302
  colonialism 310
  confronting harm 317
  deportation to Russia 289, 302
  holistic view of prison system 315
  law and punishment 303–308
  liberty and freedom 306
  material deprivation, crime and racist &
    sexist beliefs 307
  police and the owner class 312–315
  police in opposition to the
    community 308–312
  prison conditions 302
  prosecution under the Draft Act 287
  punishment 304
  racist mobs 307–308
  rehabilitation 319n3
  social attitude towards criminals 314
  supporting prisoners 302
  systemic conditions driving crime 307
  utility of prisons 305–306
  vision of harm reduction 305
Berkman, Alexander, publications
  'Alexander Berkman to Emma Goldman
    June 25, 1928, PARIS' 305–306, 308
  *A Fragment of the Prison Experiences of Emma
    Goldman and Alexander Berkman* 282, 293,
    295–296, 303, 305, 307, 314, 316
  Now and After 302–303, 306, 308,
    309–310, 312, 313–314, 315, 318
  Prison Memoirs of an Anarchist 302,
    308–309, 315
  'Prisons and crime' 313

Berlin, I. 19
Berry, D. 14
Between Peasants (Malatesta) 207
Bevir, Mark 92, 143n8
biases 308
biblical references, Matthew 5:34 69
Bideford Prison, Dorset 4
Biden, Joe 7
biological positivist school 120
Biriukov, Pavel 68
birth control 204n11, 285–286
Birth Control Movement 285
Biryukov, Pavel 90
Black Americans 244, 262
Black chattel slavery 185
Black feminist thought 303
Black intellectuals 250
Black Liberation movement 5
Black Lives Matter 10, 316
Black Marxism (Cedric Robinson) 185
Black Panthers 5
Black police 310–312
'Black Radical Tradition' 5
Black Reconstruction in America
  (Du Bois) 185
Black resistance and survival 307
Blair, Tony 6–7
Blanqui, Auguste 126
Blast 287
'Bloody Sunday' demonstration (November
  1887) 16, 125–128, 130, 143n1
Bolsheviks 308
Boone, M. 7
Boos, F.S. 139
Botkin, Vasily 67
Bourdieu, Pierre 140, 143n14
bourgeoisie using 'progressive' theories 192
bourgeois morality 229
bourgeois terminology 201
Boyz n the Hood (film) 311
Brewer, David 249
Bridewell House of Correction, Chicago 262
British Journal of Inebriety 99
British Journal of Nursing 91, 99
British Medical Association 98
British Prisons (Fitzgerald and Sim) 12
Brockway, Fenner 97, 101
Brotherhood farm colony, Purleigh 90, 96
Brotherhood of Locomotive Firemen
  (BLF) 246–247
Brotherhood projects (Fabian Society) 90
Brougham, Henry 60
Brown, Tony 110
Brown, William Jennings 70
Bruce, S. 131–132
Buenos Aires, Argentina 230
Bulffi, Luis 199
Burdett, Francis 4
Burns, John 126–127, 130, 143n1, 143n3

C

Calderón, A. 197
California Model 9
Camden, New Jersey 10
Campaign Against Prison Slavery 12
Canada 91
La Canadenca strike 197
capitalism
  and crime 232, 251–252
  and the criminal 243–245
  'extended order of human cooperation'
    (Hayek) 211
  and interests of the powerful 317
  poverty and destitution 3
  property rights 318
  as relentless 281
  and slavery 255n6
  and socialism 251
capitalist states 26
capital punishment
  anti-authoritarian principles 198
  campaign to end in US 272–273
  executioners as monsters 220
  Haymarket executions 279–280
  legalized murder 79–80
  Leopold and Loeb case 270–272
  no real deterrent effect 220, 233
  as revenge 24
  Vasily Shabunin 68
  see also executioners and
    executions; punishment
Carnegie, Andrew 281
Carnot, Sadi 228
Carpenter, Edward 17, 20, 23, 108–122
  abolitionist real utopia 118, 119
  abolition of short sentences 117
  absolute abolition 118
  anarchist penological thought 109
  coercion and force to protect society 121
  Common Life 109, 115–116
  contingent abolitionism 109, 117–122
  corporal punishment 115, 121
  Criminal Court of Appeal 117
  criminological enquiries 120–121
  criminological interests 142
  Humanitarian League 91
  impoverishment and crime 120
  incarceration and the depravity of
    society 114–115
  indeterminate sentences and rehabilitation 117
  insanity 120
  labour colonies 96
  nationalizing industries and reducing
    unemployment 116
  nature-nurture debate 120
  and *News from Nowhere* (Morris) 142
  'practicality' and 'utopianism' 111
  pragmatic radical political programmes
    118–119

prison and punishment as morally illegitimate 114–115
prisons encouraging recidivism 114
prisons unnecessary 93–94
radical prison reform 118
real abolitionist utopia 112–117
rehabilitation 117, 122n3
'Revenge,' 'Punishment', 'Deterrence' and 'Reclamation' 108
selective criminalization 112–113
self-governing communal societies 116
'Sensible' violence 121
'soft' anarchism 110, 122n1
transparency and accountability 116
'true Democracy' 142
'useful' and 'pleasurable' employment 116
Carpenter, Edward, publications
 'Defence of Criminals' 112, 118, 119, 142
 England's Ideal 116, 122
 Homogenic Love, and Its Place in a Free Society 111
 My Days and Dreams 142
 Towards Democracy 116, 122
 'Transitions to freedom' 116, 119
 see also *Prisons, Police and Punishment* (Carpenter)
Caserio, Sante 228–229, 236, 238n3
Catalonia 8, 203
Caverly, John R. 271
'Celebration of the Birthday of Robert Owen' (*Northern Star*) 59
censorship 174–175
'centrist' administrations 8
Ceuta prison, Spain 198, 204n10
charity (*charité,* Guyau) 155, 157, 161–164
Charles, Fred 111
Chartists and Chartism 5, 59
Chatham prison, England 138
Chauvin, Derek 311
Chekov, Anton 172
Chertkov, Vladimir 69
Chicago 259, 263–264
Chicago North Western Railroad 266
child imprisonment 10
Christianity 163, 164
Christian Neoplatonism 158, 163
Christie, Nils 12, 61
Christ-Logos (Origen of Alexandria) 166n19
Christ's commandments 69, 82
'Civil Law under Socialism' (Bax) 133
Clairvaux, France 174–175
class and privilege 16, 39, 267, 310–311
Classical School of Criminal Law 228
Clemit, Pamela 39
Cleveland, Grover 245, 248
'Clinica o castigo?' (Gori) 232–233, 239n13
Cobbett, William 60
Cobden, Richard 93
Cobden-Sanderson, Annie 93–94

coercion 19–20, 45, 69, 121, 221
'Coercion for London' (Morris) 130
coercive order 211
coercive punishment 24, 70
 see also capital punishment
coercive states 5, 26, 221
Cohen, Stanley 12, 112, 115, 116–117
coherence between ends and means (Malatesta) 208
Cold Bath Fields prison, London 4
Cole, G.D.H. 221
colonialism 197–198, 310
'Commercial age' (Carpenter) 112
commitment to freedom 18–20
Committee for Social Investigation and Reform 98
Committee to Abolish Prison Slavery (CAPS) 11
Common Life (Carpenter) 109, 115–116
common-sense approaches 97
Commonweal (Socialist League) 126–128, 130–131, 133, 134–136, 138
communitarian socialism 60
Community Action on Prison Expansion campaigns 11–12
community-based accountability and justice 44–45, 61
community-based interstitial initiatives 26
community cooperation and responsiveness 20–22
'commutative justice' of 'social contracts' (Guyau) 153
'competing contradiction' (Mathiesen) 207, 222
Comte, Auguste 203n1
concentration camps 100, 132
concentrations of power 15–16, 17
Confederación Nacional del Trabajo (CNT) 182, 197
Conference of the Ladies' National Association 98
A Confession (Tolstoy) 92
Congress of Capolago 227
Congress of Genoa 227
The Conquest of Bread (Kropotkin) 200
'conscious generation' principle 199
conscription (the draft) 287
consequentialist approaches 153
contemplative silence 243
contingent abolitionism 109, 117–122
Contini, Annamaria 157, 165n7
cooperation
 and mutualism 5, 22
 and solidarity 20
cooperative movement 60
corporal punishment 53, 115, 121, 243
 see also punishment
corporate capitalism 245–247, 249–250, 254, 255n10

INDEX

El Corsario 196, 199
Cossutta, Marco 217
Cotin, Eugène 219
Couzens, Wayne 311
Coyle, Michael J. 36, 46
Cregier, De Witt C. 265–266
crime
  and anti-social behaviour 181–182
  bad economic order 194–195
  and capitalism 195–198, 232
  conceptions of 22
  construction of the rich to oppress the poor 272
  'defective-individual' understanding 243
  economic and social iniquities 292
  false problems 228
  hurting the poor 37
  labels 36
  material inequality 17, 35
  moral perspectives and abstractionism 231
  from natural or social causes 212
  objective, definable form 35–36
  people losing their way 243
  and poverty 17, 51, 120, 227–228
  and private property 196
  and punishment 212–219
  punitive cycle 36
  questioning the definition 22
  reforming 95
  and sharing resources fairly 35
  as a social illness 263
  social irrationality 57
  the state as producers 195–198
  structural causes 6
  see also anti-social behaviour; punishment
Crime and Criminals (Darrow) 269–270
Crime and Punishment (Dostoevsky) 79, 80–81
crime and social disadvantage 119
Crime (Darrow) 266, 267–269
'Crime is a socialist issue' (*New Statesman*) 6
crime prevention 58
crimes against property 113
The Criminal and the Community (Devon) 97
criminal behaviour
  bourgeois morality 195
  and the corporate capitalism 254
  and harmful behaviour 22, 37–41
  libertarian society 199–202
  middle class professionals benefiting from 252–253
  pauperism 120
  solutions to 17–18, 198–202
  victims of unfortunate circumstances 51–52
'criminal companies' (YO) 196
Criminal Court of Appeal (Carpenter) 117
criminal harms 22, 40–41
criminal justice
  allocating culpability and blame 113
  and domination 24

historical processes and change 47
instrument of the powerful 16
right-wing discourses 8–9
and structural inequalities 17
Criminalogia Moderna 230–231
criminal sociology 230–233
The Crisis (Owenite periodical) 56–57, *56*
Critical Criminology (van Swaaningen) x
Critical Resistance 10, 13
Critique of the Gotha Programme (Marx) 18
'Critique of the idea of sanction' (Guyau) 146
Cullera, Spain 197
Cullors, Patrisse 316
Cunninghame Graham, R.B. 126–127, 130, 143n1, 143n3
'The Curse of Law' (Bax) 133
Czolgosz, Leon 283

D

Daily News 128
Darrow, Clarence Seward 16, 249, 259–273
  abolishing crime 269–270
  abolishing prisons 270, 272–273
  and John Peter Altgeld 263–266
  battling for the common man 267
  Chicago law practice 265
  coercive punishment and innocent families 24
  crime, punishment and environment 266–268
  crime to oppress the poor 22, 272
  and the death penalty 269, 271–273
  debate with Alfred J. Talley 271–272
  as a hopeful pessimist 273
  Leopold and Loeb case 270–272
  move to Chicago 263–264
  murder trials 271
  people as biological machines 267
  scientific racism and eugenics 266–267
  transforming the penal landscape 269–270
Darrow, Clarence Seward, publications
  Crime 266, 267–269
  Crime and Criminals 269–270
Darwin, Charles 122n2
Darwinism 190, 200
Davidson, Donald 211, 215
Davidson, Thomas 89
Davis, Angela Y. 12
  abolitionist imagination 183
  Are Prisons Obsolete? 314
  Black feminist thought 303
  capitalism and imprisonment 254–255
  'Political prisoners, prisons and Black liberation' 127
  punishment industry 183
Davitt, Michael 126
death penalty *see* capital punishment
Debs, Eugene V. 11, 16, 25, 242–256
  adopting socialism 250
  arrest 248–249

and the ARU 248
background 245–247
corporate responsibility 247
imprisonment 242, 253
prison abolitionist 249–254
railroad work 246
revered by prisoners and working class 253
socialism and prison abolition 245
systemic critique 254–255
Debs, Eugene V., publications
  Appeal to Reason 251
  Walls and Bars 249, 251
debtors' prisons 58–59
de Cleyre, Voltairine 314–315
de Crespigny, William 60
'Defence of Criminals' (Carpenter) 112, 118, 119, 142
defining criminal acts 37
'Defund the Police' movement 255
degeneracy and crime 193–195, 253–254
dehumanizing prisons 23, 25, 111–112, 114, 283
Democratic Party 9
demolishing prisons 198–199, 204n10
deontological principles 154
deserts-based justice 23
Despard, Charlotte 93
determinism 122n2, 147, 194
'Deterrence' (Carpenter) 108
deterrents
  based on fear 20, 95
  imprisonment 98
  punitive incarceration 36–37, 113–114
Devon, James 97
Dickens, Charles 135
'La difesa sociale contro il delitto' (Malatesta) 214, 215
direct action 4, 219
direct knowledge 44
Discipline and Punish (Foucault) 53, 137, 139
diseased social conditions 120
disinterestedness (Guyau) 154
displacement of goals (Malatesta) 208
distributive justice 153–155, 160
The Divine and the Human (Tolstoy) 74, 75–76
divine essence 69
divine providence 78
Dix, Dorothea 244, 261
doing what is right (Tolstoy) 84
Dostoevsky, Fyodor 71, 79, 80–81, 172, 276
Douglas, Moncure 125
Douglass, Frederick 259
'Doukhobor Sectarians' (Spirit-wrestlers) 80, 90–91
Du Bois, W.E.B. 250
  Black Reconstruction in America 185
Duff, Antony 117
Durkheim, Émile 15, 163

Dussel, Enrique 221
'dynamiters' anarchist prisoners 138

E

Early Church Fathers 158, 163
early socialists ('utopian socialists') 13, 17, 21
earthly justice and divine providence 78
Eaton, Gertrude 100
economic violence 196
education 46, 91, 96
Eliot, William Greenleaf 262
elites punishing political opponents 264
Ellis, Havelock 290
employment opportunities 96
Empson, William 140
Empty Cages Collective 11–12
England 172
  Campaign Against Prison Slavery 12
  Poor Law 52, 58
England's Ideal (Carpenter) 116, 122
'English Bastille' (Burdett) 4
'English liberty' 4
English Prisons To-Day (Hobhouse and Brockway) 101
English radicals 4
Enlightenment 190, 203n1
An Enquiry Concerning Political Justice (Godwin) 33–34, 37, 38, 39, 40, 41–42, 46
Epictetus 165n7
Epicurean inspired ideas 159, 163, 165n3
equality 17–18
equality of conditions (Malatesta) 207, 220
equity 18, 44
Esquisse d'une morale sans obligation ni sanction (Guyau) 146, 154, 157, 159, 162, 163, 165n6, 165n7
ethical evaluations 22–25
ethical socialism 89, 92, 102–103
ethical society 96
The Ethics of Epicurus (Guyau) 153–154, 165n3
eugenics 252, 266–267
Eugenics Education Society 98
Eugenics Review 94
Europe 5, 7, 13, 182–183
European Group for the Study of Deviance and Social Control (EG) xiii, 13
European Prison Observatory 11
Europe écologie les verts 10
Everard, Sarah 311
The Evidence of Things Not Seen (Baldwin) 310
evolutionism 190, 202
'Evolution of criminal sociology' (Gori) 231, 238n8
executioners and executions 74–76, 220
  see also capital punishment
exiles 175
experimental educational institutions 91
expiatory forms of punishment (Guyau) 156, 160

INDEX

exploitation and oppression 301
Ex-Services Welfare Society 99

F

Fabbri, Luigi 213
Fabian Society 90
Fabre, Jean-Henri 266
'false universality of bourgeois law' (Morris) 16
families of prisoners 24, 183
far-right parties 7–9
fear 95, 114
fecundity (Guyau) 156–157, 165–166n11
La Federación Igualadina 195
Federation of Organized Trades and Labor Unions 264
Fee, E. 278
Fellowship of New Life 90
Fenno, Colleen 34, 37–38, 43
Ferrari, Livio 13
Ferri, Enrico 192, 200, 204n13, 229, 231, 238n6
First International Eugenics Conference (1912) 97–98
First International Workingmen's Association 171
First World War 99, 190, 287
Fitzgerald, Mike 12
Fleet Prison, London 4
Floyd, George 10, 311
forcible feeding 95, 97
Forero Cuellar, Alejandro 22
foresight (Guyau) 160
The Forged Coupon (Tolstoy) 73, 76–77
Forum for Prison Abolition, Copenhagen 11
Foucault, Michel
  Discipline and Punish 53, 137, 139
  forms of power 163
  'history of the present' 3
  'humanisation' of penalties 161
  judicial punishment 148
  and Nupkins (judges) 135
  prisons as a totalizing institutions 179
  public executions 137–138, 139
  social defence 166n26
Fouillée, Alfred 157, 159
Fourier, Charles xiii–xiv, 27n10, 51
Fox, William Joseph 60
A Fragment of the Prison Experiences of Emma Goldman and Alexander Berkman (Goldman and Berkman) 282, 293, 295–296, 303–305, 307, 314, 316
France
  19th century prison conditions 172, 174
  gendarmes as wolf-exterminators 314
  gilets jaunes protests 8
  Green Party 10
  juvenile incarceration 175
  Peter Kropotkin's imprisonment 172, 174
  law and order 8
  prison population 8

La France Insoumise 10
Franco, Francisco 182
Franks, Bobby 270–272
freedom 18–20
  and dignity 296
  Libertarian socialism 14, 26
  as a method (Malatesta) 207–208, 220–221
  and mutual aid 20
  paradox (Popper) 216
Freedom (anarchist newspaper) 200
free markets 111
'free-rider' problem 210–211
'free will' (*libre arbitre*) 149–151, 152, 158, 267
Frick, Henry Clay 281, 301–302
Friends' project for a New Town 99
Fry, Elizabeth 52, 58
Fry, Margery 89, 100

G

Galleani, Luigi 230, 238n7
Garden Cities 92
Gardner, A.R. 93
Garofalo, M.E. 192, 278
Garrison, William Lloyd 69–70
Gawthorpe, Mary 93
Geikie Cobb, Wm 93
gender equality 17, 56, 61n2
George, Henry 265
George Junior Republic, Freeville, New York 91
gerontocracy 55–56, 59
Giacomelli, Nella 234
Giddens, Anthony 112
Gilded Age 262
gilets jaunes protests 8
Gilmore, Ruth Wilson 12, 176, 183–184, 303
Giner de los Ríos, F. 202
'Gladstone Report' (1895) 113, 119
Global North 6–7
global prison abolitionist coalitions 11–12, 27n6
God Sees the Truth But Waits (Tolstoy) 78
Godwin, William xiii–xiv, 14, 33–47, 52, 113
  characters as a *tabula rasa* 34–35
  collateral casualty of punishment 175
  'crime' and libertarian socialists 22
  involving offenders in consequences of actions 19
  justice, ethics and jurisprudence 23
  legal institutions as criminogenic 16
  prisons as 'seminaries of vice' 23, 41–44
  theory of perfectibility 46
  understanding circumstances of crime 36
  unjust societies 35
Godwin, William, publications
  An Enquiry Concerning Political Justice 33–34, 37, 38, 39, 40, 41–42, 46
  Things as They Are 37–39, 42–44

Golden Gulag (Gilmore) 176
Goldenveizer, Alexander 76
Goldman, Emma xii, 14, 17, 18, 24, 25, 109, 276–298
  Alien Exclusion Act violation 289–290
  anarchism 276–277
  assassination of William McKinley 283–284
  background 278
  capitalism as relentless 281
  criminals as 'phantoms of [society's] own making' 296
  deportation 289
  Draft Act 287–289
  emigration to US 279
  encounters with 'criminal justice' 280–290
  failure of prisons 291–294
  feasibility of abolitionism 295–296
  Haymarket executions 279–280
  'helplessness in prison' 288–289
  Immigration Act (Anarchist Exclusion Act) 284–285
  imprisonment 282–283, 287–289
  incarceration as a 'social crime' 277
  incitement to riot 282–283
  obscenity 285–286
  police harassment 290, 296–297
  as a political prisoner 290
  power in the hands of the elite 15
  primary causes of crime 292
  prison abolitionism 286, 294, 297
  prison conditions 282
  prisons as criminogenic 23
  as 'Red Emma' 278
  repression of political opponents 16
  Russia 278–279, 289
  'social crime' argument 290–291
  Union Square speech 282
  views on marriage 295
Goldman, Emma, publications
  Anarchism and Other Essays 285–286, 292, 294, 296
  'Anarchism: what it really stands for' 294
  A Fragment of the Prison Experiences of Emma Goldman and Alexander Berkman 282, 293, 295–296, 303, 305, 307, 314, 316
  'Letters from prison' 286
  Living My Life 278–290
  'To Lucifer, the lightbearer' 290
  Mother Earth 170, 287
  'To my friends, old and new' 296
  'Prisons: a social crime and failure' 277, 283, 284–285, 290
Goldsmith, Marie 301
Gompers, Samuel 248
Goodwin, Barbara xiii–xiv
'Gordon Riots' 4
Gori, Pietro 17, 24, 226–239
  altruism and solidarity 235
  approaches to criminal matters 236
  Argentina 234
  background 227
  conviction and exile 230
  and the courts 237–238
  criminal lawyer 228
  critical approaches to punishment 237
  harmonious coexistences 235
  and humanity 237, 238
  imprisonment 228
  libertarian socialist 237
  poetic-literary production 235–236
  political activism 234
  pseudonyms 236
  reformist framework 234–235
  sociology of crime 235
  'thieves in gloves' 230
Gori, Pietro, publications
  'Clinica o castigo?' 232–233, 239n13
  'Evolution of criminal sociology' 231, 238n8
  La miseria e i delitti 227–230
  Sociologia anarchica 235
Gosling, H. 103
government within the community 56
Gover, Robert 119–120
grace (Guyau) 157, 164
gradualism (Malatesta) 208
gradual mitigation of punishment (Guyau) 161
Gramsci, Antonio xiii, 26
Grand National Consolidated Trades' Union 58
grassroots movements 12
Gray, John 58–59
Gray, Victor 103n1
Green Party, France 10
Green Party US 9
Greens, European Parliament 9–10
Gregory, J. 60
guards 43, 179
Guelph reformatory farm, Canada 91
guild socialism (Cole) 221
guillotine executions 75
  see also capital punishment
Guyau, Jean-Marie 146–167
  abolitionist views 159
  alternatives to prison 166n28
  challenges to punitive rationalities 155
  charity and *grace* 21, 155–159, 161–164
  critique of penal justice 156, 165n10
  as a 'crypto-Christian'/'neo-Christian' 157
  deontological principle of *disinterestedness* 154
  'determinists' 147
  distributive justice 153–155
  doctrine of *procession* 158–159
  'Epictetus-Plato-Kant' line of thought 150, 165n7
  expiatory forms of punishment 156, 160
  fecundity 156–157, 165–166n11
  foresight 160
  foundations of moral sanction 154–155

INDEX

'free will' (*libre arbitre*) 149–151, 152, 162, 165n6
generosity and *kindness* 163
gradual mitigation of punishment 161
happiness 155
harms of evil acts 24
irreversibility of evil 151–152
life as 'permanent revenge' 156
merit 149–151
moral agency 162–163
moral *anomie* 166n26
moral merit 146, 147, 149, 153–154, 159, 165n6
moral sanctions 152, 153–154, 163, 165n9
natural sanctions 148–149
nature 148, 165n5
Neoplatonist solution to evil 158
order 151–152
penal justice as 'unjust' 148
penal law 159
Platonic/Epicurean happiness 159
prisons as 'schools' 23
punitive expiation 151
radical abolitionist view of penal law 159
reformist 164
revenge 156
rewards for good actions 153
sanction 25, 147–149, 151, 158, 159–163, 166n20
sensibility 147, 150, 165n2
social defence 159–160, 166n26
sources of action 165n6
temporality of action 154
'transportation' 166n28
utilitarian views 164
vengeance 159–160
will and sensibility 162
Guyau, Jean-Marie, publications
'Critique of the idea of sanction' 146
Esquisse d'une morale sans obligation ni sanction 146, 154, 157, 159, 162, 163, 165n6, 165n7
The Ethics of Epicurus 153–154, 165n3

H

Haldeman-Julius, E. 272
Hall, S. 26
Hamilton, C. 7
handloom weavers 4
Hardin, Russell 217
harmful behaviour
 and criminal behaviour 37–40
 freedom and responsibility 19–20
 libertarian socialist beliefs 22–23
 mutualism and communal responsibilities 22–23
 punitive state responses to 9
 therapeutic intervention and reparations 21
harmonious coexistence 235
harms 22–23

Harrison, Carter, Sr 271
Harvard Law Review 316
Hayek, Friedrich 211
Hayes, Kelly 315
Haymarket affair 1886 16, 264–265, 266, 279–280
hegemony (Gramsci) xiii
Henderson, Fred 138–139
Henry George Club 265
Hetherington, Henry 56, 58
hierarchies and elitism 14
historical analysis 3–4
'history of the present' (Foucault) 3
Hobbes, Thomas 209, 210, 212, 219, 221
Hobhouse, Emily 100
Hobhouse, Stephen 97, 100–101
Holah, F. 69–70
Holloway Prison, London 92–93
Holmes, R. 97
Home Office Departmental Committee on Prisons report 1895 113, 119
homeopathic approaches 99
Homestead strike (1892) 281
'homo-duplex' 15
Homogenic Love, and Its Place in a Free Society (Carpenter) 111
homosexuality 108, 111–112, 122
Hoover, J. Edgar 184
Hôpital Militaire Auxiliaire N°. 307, Neuilly 99
Hough, Graham 140
The House of the Dead (Dostoevsky) 172
Howard, Ebenezer 92
Howard, John 33, 41, 47, 261
Howard League for Penal Reform 88
Howitt, Mary 59
Huelga de Vientres (Bulffi) 199
Hulsman, Louk 21, 143n9
human and natural laws 148
human conduct and punishment (Guyau) 148
human diversity 18, 25
'humane exertions' (Fry) 58
humane, sanitary and progressive forms of jail (Howard) 41
'humanisation' of penalties (Foucault) 161
humanistic perspectives (Malatesta) 218–219
Humanitarian League 91–92
humanitarian reform 118
humanitarian rehabilitative ideal 115
human progress and unjust societies 35
humiliating prisoners 43, 177
hunger and misery 196
Hyde Park socialist meeting 1887 128
hyperindividualized explanations of behaviour 243

I

La Idea Libre 197
'idea of sanction' (Guyau) 147–148
ideas of justice 45–46
Illinois State Supreme Court 248

331

'immediatism' 3
immigrants 244, 254
imprisonment
  coercive power 70
  and crime rates 45
  as a deterrent 98
  as immoral 34
  improving society 45–46
  non-payment of fines 262
  psychological distress 42
  and rejecting punishment 95
  see also prisons
Incarcerated Workers Organizing Committee (IWOC) 10–11
'incendiary speech' 282
Independent Labour Party (ILP) 93, 119
indeterminacy in social interaction 217
indeterminate sentences 96, 117
Indiana State Assembly 247
individualism 14
industrialization and technical advance 51
Industrial Workers of the World (IWW, the Wobblies) 11, 242
inequality
  capitalist society 226–227
  critique of 16–18
  prisons 127
  private property 196
  punishment 21
  source of 'crime' 17, 35
  understanding of wrongdoing 95
  see also social inequality
Ingersoll, Robert 259
Inquiry into the Principles of the Distribution of Wealth (Owen) 57
In Russian and French Prisons (Kropotkin) 118, 170, 171, 173, 177, 180, 181–182
insanity 120, 192
Instead of Prisons (Knopp) 61
institutional power 203
'institutional violence' 43
Insurrectionary Army of the Ukraine 182
intentional communities 60
The Intercept 316
'International Conference of Penal Abolition' (ICOPA) 27n6
International Sound Films Ltd 94
International Suffrage Shop 94
International Working Men's Association 171
invisibility of abolitionist sentiments xi
Irish gangs 243–244
Iron Column (Spanish Civil War) 182
irreversibility of evil (Guyau) 151–152
Italian anarchists 219
Italy 228

J

Jacobins 4
Janet, Paul 151
Jay, Martin 131
Jenkins, Philip 110, 122n2
Jessop, B. 26
Jesus Christ 69, 82
Jones, Ernest 126
Jones, Huws 89
Jullien, Marc-Antoine 53
The Jungle (Sinclair) 247
Jura Federation 171
jury selection 280
justice
  antithetical to human good 46
  communities settling issues 44–45, 61
  Libertarian socialist visions 14
  and punishment 21
  reciprocity (Malatesta) 213–214
  rich grinding poor into submission 38–39
  and social harm 20–21
'Justice' (Kropotkin) 47
Justice, Power, and Resistance (EG journal) xiii
Justicia! 197

K

Kaba, Mariame 303, 315, 316
  We Do This 'Til We Free Us 304, 305, 307, 309
Kant, Immanuel 147, 165n3, 165n7
Kantor, Chaim-Wolf 69, 71
Kaufman, Louisa Susan 125
Kelsen, Hans 211, 221
Kennan, George 79
Kerr, W. 68, 77
Kershner, Jacob 289
Khayyam, Omar 273
killing 35–36
  see also murders and murderers
The Kingdom of God Is Within You (Tolstoy) 74–75, 84–85, 92
Kinna, Ruth 109, 111
Kirk Session, Scottish Presbyterian church 54, 55
kleptomaniacs 113
  see also mental health issues
Knights of Labor 264
Knopp, Faye Honey 61
Kropotkin, Pyotr (Peter) xiii, xiv, 12, 14, 19, 25, 84, 169–185, 233
  abolitionist autoethnography of the prison 172–176
  abolition of prisons 109–110
  anarchist discourse of evolutionism 202
  anti-social behaviour and crime 181–182
  background 170–172
  'Bloody Sunday' demonstration 126
  coercive punishment and innocent families 24, 175–176, 183
  and Darwinism 190, 191, 200
  fear of punishment 114
  futility of reforms 180

INDEX

and William Godwin 47
incarceration 114, 171
indoctrination of children 183–184
inequality & poverty and crime 17
'Justice' 47
the law pillaging society 180–181
legislation enacted by elites 16
'Massacre of Innocents' 174
mutual aid 20, 21
prison reform 175–179
prisons as 'universities of crime' 23
reorganizing society 118
Russia's penal system 117–118
scientific methodology 177–178
social revolution 180, 182
sources 169–170
Spanish anarchist thought 198
and Arthur St John 89, 93, 98, 99
superior moral sense of the community 23
sycophancy of statism 181
theoretical principles 176–182
Kropotkin, Pyotr (Peter), publications 170
The Conquest of Bread 200
'Law and authority' 113, 170, 180–181, 183–184
Mutual Aid 200, 203n3
The Nineteenth Century 191, 203n3
'Prisons and their moral influence on prisoners' 170
'Prisons: universities of crime' 170
In Russian and French Prisons 118, 170, 171, 173, 174, 177, 180, 181–182

L

Labour Party 7
Labour Research Department 100
Lacassagne, Alexandre 120
Lamarck, Jean-Baptiste 122n2
Lanark, Scotland 54
Lancashire weavers 4
'language' (Davidson) 211
Larkin, Michael 136–137
'The latest police outrage' (Goldman) 290
the law
 American Negroes' self-respect 318
 anti-social activities 313
 and class domination 16
 equality as a myth 17
 false universality of 128
 punishing crime 303
 for the state to pillage society 180–181
 suppressing people 308
'Law and authority' (Kropotkin) 113, 170, 180–181, 183–184
Law and Liberty League 126
Lecture on Human Happiness (Grey) 58
Lefebvre, Henri 42–43
legalitarian socialists 227
legal/legitimate coercion 2, 221

Le Gallienne, R. 273
legal system
 biases 308, 318
 as criminogenic 16
 legislation and the elites 16
 logic of punishment 318
Lenin, Vladimir 184
Leopold, Nathan 270–272
'less eligibility' principle 127, 143n4
'Letters from prison' (Goldman) 286
Letter to an American on Non-resistance (Tolstoy) 84
Let This Radicalize You (Kaba and Hayes) 315
Leviathan (Hobbes) 209
Lewell-Buck, Emma 10
liberal democracies 13, 17, 316
'Liberalism v. Socialism' (Bax) 133
libertarian ideals and ideology 202, 234
libertarian militancy 236
libertarian socialism xiii, 13–25, 24–25
 academic scholarship 13
 and cooperation 20, 22
 critique of power 15
 defining 14
 equality and freedom 18–19
 European social movements 5
 freedom and voluntary associations 26
 freedom, justice and democracy 14
 and human nature 15
 and Peter Kropotkin 182–183
 mutualism 22–23
 penal abolition 5–6, 14–15
 prison and legal coercion 2
 revival 12
 social and economic inequalities 16–17
libertarian society 199–202
El Libertario 204n9
liberty (Berkman) 306
 see also freedom
Lincoln, Abraham 251
Lithuania 279
Living My Life (Goldman) 278–290
Loader, Ian 112
local governance 54
Loeb, Richard 270–272
Logan, A. 89, 99
Logos 158, 166n19
Lombroso, Cesare
 anthropological theory 192–193
 biological positivist school 120
 and Pietro Gori 231
 Ricardo Mella's critique 192–193
 no friend of anarchists 234, 239n18
 Martinez Ruiz's critique 192
 Arthur St John's critique 96–97, 103
Lombroso, Cesare, publications
 Gli anarchici 239n18
 Los anarquistas (*The Anarchists*) 192–193
 L'uomo delinquente 231

333

London 127
London Evening Standard 95
Looking Backward (Bellamy) 131, 133
Lorenzo, Anselmo 25, 191, 198, 200, 201
Lovett, William 56, 60
Ludlow, J.M. 58

M

Macron, Emmanuel 8
mainstream socialist voices 8–10
Mainwaring, Sam 136
Makhno, Nestor 5
'Makhnovist insurgency' 5
Malatesta, Errico 14, 17, 19, 23, 25, 207–222, 229, 233
  and abolitionism today 220–222
  abolitionist struggle 221–222
  abolition of prisons as a necessity 109
  anarchism 207–209
  anarchist practices 219–220
  anarchy and 'crime' 214–216
  anti-social behaviour 212–214
  crime and punishment 212–219
  criticisms 216–219
  critique of the state 209–211
  displacement of goals 208
  distributed model for social norms 214–215
  equality of conditions 207, 220
  First International 227
  freedom as a method 207–208, 220–221
  gradualism 208
  humanistic perspectives 218–219
  indeterminacy in social interaction 217
  interdependence of punishment and the state 221
  justice and reciprocity 213–214
  morality 211
  penal issues 220
  punishment 213
  social defence 215, 217
  social orders 211–212
  universal norms 211
  vengeance 213
  violence 213
  voluntarism 208
Malatesta, Errico, publications
  Anarchy 207, 314
  At the Café 207
  'La difesa sociale contro il delitto' 214, 215
  Between Peasants 207
Malthusianism 199, 204n11
Manchester Board of Health 53–54
Manchester martyrs 136–137
'Manifesto for a new penal culture' (European Prison Observatory) 11
Manitoba and Northwestern Railway Company 91
marginalized people 34, 309–310, 311–312
marriage 295

Marshall, P. 14, 17, 20
Marxist abolitionism 12, 184–185
Marxist political revolutions 182
Marx, Karl 18, 171
Marylebone Police Court 134
'Massacre of Innocents' (Kropotkin) 174
massacres 204n9
mass incarceration 280
material inequality 35
Mathiesen, Thomas 12, 36, 207, 222
Maurice, F.D. 58
Maxwell St John, Leonora (Maxwell-Müller) 91, 93, 99
McGowen, Randall 41
McKinley, William 283
'mechanism of fear' (Poulantzas) 26
medical model of crime 232–233
Mee, Jon 40
Mélenchon, Jean-Luc 10
Mella, Ricardo 17, 25, 192–193, 195, 204n4
Melvile, Emily 40
Men's League for Women's Suffrage 94
mental health issues 42, 99, 113, 304–305
merit (Guyau) 149–151
Merlino, Francesco Saverio 215, 217, 227
Merrill, George 108
Merzouk, Nahel 8
method of fear 217, 221
method of freedom 19, 208, 217, 219–221, 221
methodological individualism 208, 218–219
Metropolitan Police 111, 126
Mexican Revolution 182
middle class professionals 252–253
The Midland Herald 91
Mikhailov, Mikhail Larionovitch 171
the military 75, 316
military tribunals 68
Mill, John Stuart 60, 132
Mills, Herbert 90
Milner, Frederic 99
minimally coercive community-based solutions 21
La miseria e i delitti (Gori) 227–230
Modern Criminology 234
modern prison abolitionists 315
Molinari, Luigi 234
Montessori education 96
Montjuic trials 196–197, 204n8
moral agency 149–155, 162–163
moral autonomy 69
moral compass 22–25
moral depravity 23
  see also capital punishment
moral dignity 69
moral education 19
La morale, l'art et la religion d'après Guyau (Fouillée) 157
morality 149, 211, 286
morality of duty (Guyau) 153–154

INDEX

moral merit (Guyau) 146, 147, 149, 153–154, 159, 165n6
moral outrage against the 'other' 7
moral perspectives of crime 231
moral redemption 72
moral regeneration 73, 74, 79
moral sanction 151, 152, 153–154, 163
moral social order 211–212, 214
moral upstanding citizenry 243, 252
Morelly, Étienne- Gabriel 18
More, Thomas 131–132
Morgan, John Minter 51, 57–58
Morris, William 14, 60, 125–144
  abolitionism 134, 138
  anti-carceral utopia 128–134
  Bloody Sunday demonstrations 125–128, 130
  emotional life in utopia 140–141
  'false universality of bourgeois law' 16
  fear as a deterrence 20
  law and class domination 16
  law for rich and poor 128
  Marylebone Police Court 134
  'Nupkins' (judges) 135–136
  palliative measures for social reform 128
  political trials 138
  prison system and poverty 127
  revolutionary social transformation 128
  socialist agitation 131
  substantive freedom 132
  'true Communism' 133
  utopian defamiliarization 129, 130
  'utopian socialists' 21
  utopian vision 133–134, 142
Morris, William, publications
  'Coercion for London' 130
  Foreword to *Utopia* (Thomas More, Kelmscott Press 1893*)* 131–132
  News from Nowhere 92, 125–126, 128–132, 134, 135, 139–143
  Nupkins Awakened 135–136
  The Pilgrims of Hope 135–136
  The Tables Turned 135–136
mortals making laws 68
Mother Earth (periodical) 170, 287
Movimento NO PRISON 13
Mowbray, Charles 138–139
Muhammad, Khahlil 253
murders and murderers 71–72
  see also killing
mutual aid 20, 21–22
Mutual Aid (Kropotkin) 200, 203n3
mutualism 5, 14, 20, 22
My Days and Dreams (Carpenter) 142

N

Nagel, M. 60
National Committee of the United States Green Party 9
National Conference on the Prevention of Destitution (1912) 88, 97
nationalizing industries 116, 251
National Prison Association (NPA) 261
natural abolitionism 55, 57
natural and human laws 148–149
natural aristocracies 56
natural causes of crime 212
natural crime (Garofalo) 192
nature 148–149, 165n5
nature-nurture debate 120
necessitarianism 50, 51, 53, 61n1
Nechaev, Sergei (Netchaieff) 172
needs-based justice 23
negative anthropology 218
negative disciplinary measures 52, 53
  see also corporal punishment; imprisonment
'negative freedoms' 19
negative liberty (John Stuart Mill) 132
neo-Malthusianism 199–200, 204n11, 204n12
Neoplatonism 158, 163
Netherlands 7
Newgate Prison, London 52
New Harmony Gazette 55
New Labour 6
New Lanark, Scotland 51, 52–54, 55
Newman, M. 15
'New Moral World' 56, 57
News from Nowhere (Morris) 92, 125–126, 128–132, 134, 135, 139–143
Newsom, Gavin 9
New Statesman 6
A New View of Society (Owen) 50, 51, 52, 57
A New Way with Crime (Brockway) 101
New York 243
  Anarchist Police Squad 285
  Criminal Anarchy Law 1902 284
New York Times 289, 311
Nicholas II, tsar 80
Nichols, Tyre 311–312
Nietzsche, Friedrich 147, 157
Nikolaevich, Lev 76
Nineteen Eighty-Four (Orwell) 132
The Nineteenth Century 191, 203n3
Nineteenth Century (journal) 170
No Conscription League of New York 287
non-authoritarian socialists xiii, 15, 24, 26–27
noncoercive solutions to harmful behaviour 22–23
'non-coercive states' 26, 221
'#No New Jails' movement 9
'Non-governmental society' (Carpenter) 116, 118, 122n4
non-payment of fines 262
nonpenal real utopias xiii
'No prison' manifesto (Ferrari and Pavarini) 13
North America 243
  see also Canada; United States (US)
Northern Star 59

Norway 7
Notes from the House of the Dead (Tolstoy) 79
Now and After (Berkman) 302–303, 306, 308, 309–310, 312, 313–314, 315, 318
Nupkins Awakened (Morris) 135–136
'Nupkins' (judges) 135

O

obedience to the law 183–184
O'Brien, Michael 136–137
O'Brien, William 16
Ocasio-Cortez, Alexandria 9
offenders *see* prisoners
Oglesby, Richard J. 264
On Crimes and Punishments (Beccaria) 209, 222n1
one-solution-fits-all approaches 18
opening new markets 197–198
Opere 235
oppression 35, 195, 294–295
Oration on the Dignity of Man (Pico della Mirandola) 218
order 151–152
Oregon Journal 286
organic degeneration 194–195
'Organizer Mariame Kaba' (*The Intercept*) 316
Origen of Alexandria 158, 166n18, 166n19
Orwell, George 5, 132
Our Penal Machinery and Its Victims (Altgeld) 260–261, 268, 269
Owenites (Owenite movement) 50
  The Crisis periodical 56, 56
  early British socialists 51
  impact on abolitionist movement 59, 60
  'New Moral World' 56
  penal abolitionism 56–61
  society without prisons or punishment 59
Owen, Robert xiii–xiv, 14, 17, 20, 50–62
  abolitionist thought 51–54
  communitarian socialism 60
  communities 53–55, 59, 60–61
  'Father of British socialism' 59
  gerontocracy 55–56, 59
  natural abolitionism 55, 57
  rational environments 52, 55
  and the reform movement 59–60
  self-regulation 53–54
  'social system'/'science of society' 54–55
  'Villages of Cooperation' 52, 54–55, 57, 58, 59, 60
  well-balanced surveillance 53
Owen, Robert, publications
  Inquiry into the Principles of the Distribution of Wealth 57
  A New View of Society 50, 51, 52, 57
  Report to the County of Lanark 59–60

P

Palmer, A. Mitchell 184
Pankhurst, Emmeline 93

Pankhurst, Sylvia 92–93
'paradox of freedom' (Popper) 216, 218
Paris, France 67
parishes 58
Partido Communista de Espana 182
Partido Liberal Mexicano 182
passive resistance 84
pauperism 120
Pavarini, Massimo 13
Penal Abolitionism (Ruggiero) x
penal incarceration *see* prisons
penal positivism 233
Penal Reform League (PRL) 88–89
penal reforms 47, 55, 58, 95
  see also prison reforms
Pennsylvania system 243, 263
Penn, William 277
penological enquiries 109
Pensieri Ribelli 227, 238n1
Pentonville prison, London 125, 126, 129, 143n5
'The People's Justice Guarantee' (Pressley) 9
Pepinsky, Harold 12
perfectibility (Godwin) 46
personal courage 84
Peter and Paul Fortress, St Petersburg 171, 174
Petrov, Avvakum 172
Philosophie pénale (Tarde) 158
Pianosa penal colony, Italy 232
The Pickwick Papers (Dickens) 135
Pico della Mirandola, Giovanni 218
The Pilgrims of Hope (Morris) 135–136
Pinta, S. 14
plantation agriculture 245, 255n6
Plato 216
police
  abolishing 116, 315–319
  actions against anarchists 203, 204n15, 280
  agents of the dominant classes 308
  biases 308
  dangerous to society 218
  and marginalized people 309–312
  mediator of ingroups and outgroups 318
  myth of protecting everyone 279
  not keeping people safe 303
  operations against anarchist movements 203, 204n15
  in opposition to the community 308–309
  and the owner class 310, 312–315
  role in society 309–310
  serving the powerful 315
  tactics against Emma Goldman 296–297
  "third degree" questioning 284, 285
police harassment 290
'The police system' (Carpenter) 116
political and social ideologies 190
'Political prisoners, prisons and Black liberation' (Davis) 127
political trials 138, 228–229

political violence 189–190
The Politics of Abolition (Mathiesen) 12
the poor
  criminal behaviour 35, 120
  as delinquents 35
  law skewed unfairly against 113
  middle class of professionals benefiting from 252–253
  prisoners 34
  as stupid 267
  victims of unfortunate circumstances 51–52
Poor Law 52, 58
Popper, Karl 216
popular justice movements 4
population growth and resources (Malthus) 204n11
Portland, Oregon 285
El Porvenir del Obrero 196
'positive freedoms' (Berlin) 19
positive science 191
positivism 2, 190–191, 202, 203n1
positivist criminology 191–193, 194
Poulantzas, N. 26
poverty
  and capitalism 3
  and crime 17, 51, 120, 227–228
power xi, 15–18, 43
power hierarchies 317
The Power of Darkness (Tolstoy) 72–73
practical solutions and opportunities (St John) 96–97
Prat, Josep 203n3
Prendergast, Patrick E. 271
'El presidiario' (*Bandera Social*) 201–202, 204n14
Pressley, Ayanna 9
pre-trial incarceration 263
preventative policing measures 58
The Priest and the Devil (Dostoyevsky) 276
Prieto, Francisco 204n10
prison abolition *see* penal abolitionism
prison conditions 92–93, 282–283, 297, 302
Prison, Detention and Punishment Working Group 13
prisoners 296
  dehumanizing 95
  enduring violence and humiliation 43
  enemies of society 177
  physical and psychological pain 43
  poor and marginalized 34
  'reclaimed' by society 115
  reintroduction into society 61, 178–179
  therapeutic intervention 21
  treated according to needs in society 95
  see also rehabilitation
prisoner unions 11
prison guards 43
'prison industrial complex' (PIC) 316–317
prison labour 11, 288

Prison Memoirs of an Anarchist (Berkman) 302, 308–309, 315
prison population 6–8, 293, 296
'Prison reform' (Carpenter) 116–117
Prison Reform League (PRL) 92–102
  early years 98–99
  feminist input 99–100
  First World War 99
  force feeding 97
  and the Howard Association 100
  lobbying and propaganda 102
  objects 94
  utopian politics and practical projects 99
  see also St John, Arthur
prison reforms 41–42, 47, 55, 118, 261–263, 277
  see also penal reforms
prisons
  anathema to socialist ethics 2
  anti-social and criminogenic 23
  Argentina 231–232
  as a black hole 314
  corruption 179
  as criminal 23
  criticism by anarchists 198
  dehumanizing 23, 25, 111–112, 114, 283
  deterring crime 36, 113–114, 178, 293
  effect of 232–233
  eliminating 294–296
  exercise in violence 203
  exploitation and inequality 127
  extension of the state 317
  futility of reform 180
  maintaining social inequalities 25
  making criminals 262
  nonpenal confinement 88
  one-solution-fits-all approach 18
  organs of oppression 182
  'outgrowth of the capitalist system for the poor' (Debs) 253
  and poverty 127
  principle of revenge 177
  and public executions 137
  reasons to reject 25
  reflection and refuge 24
  reforming criminals 113–114
  reformist and abolitionist approaches 83
  rehabilitating criminally inclined 293
  reinforcing criminal (in)justice system 34
  reproducing themselves 315
  restrictions on personal freedom 233
  'school of crime' 151
  self-preservation 177
  'seminaries of vice' (Godwin) 23, 41–44
  as a social crime 288
  social landscape 102–103
  as solution to harmful behaviour 23
  state-sanctioned revenge 303–304
  as totalizing institutions 179

toxic environments 23–24
transportation as alternative 166n28
 as unnecessary 93–94
 see also imprisonment
'Prisons and crime' (Berkman) 313
'Prisons and their moral influence on prisoners' (Kropotkin) 170
'Prisons: a social crime and failure' (Goldman) 277, 283, 284–285, 290
prison sentences 58, 117
Prisons, Police and Punishment (Carpenter) 108, 110, 142
 absolute abolition 118
 corporal punishment 115, 121
 deficiencies of criminal justice 119
 'Non-governmental society' 116, 118, 122n4
 'The police system' 116
 prison and punishment as morally illegitimate 115–116
 'Prison reform' 116–117, 122n3
 selective criminalization of 'Commercial age' 112–113
 utopian dreams and practical penal reform 122
 Oscar Wilde's imprisonment 111
 see also Carpenter, Edward
'Prisons: universities of crime' (Kropotkin) 170
Prison System Enquiry 100
'prison time' (Lefebvre) 42–43
prison visits 176
private property
 abolition 133–134, 180–181
 and communistic societies 57
 as criminogenic 16, 196
 inequality 196
 laws protecting the rich 254
 and the police 116
 selective criminalization 112–113
privilege 294–295
probation 91, 95–96, 296
El Productor 203n3
profit and crime 251–252, 255
Progress and Poverty (George) 265
progressive-era reform 253–254, 256n17
proletarian classes 199
property disputes 38–39, 133
proportionality of exchange 154
Proudhon, Pierre-Joseph 20–21, 113, 171
public executions 67, 136–137, 137
'public imprisonment' 41
Pullman, George 248
Pullman Strike 1894 245, 248–249
punishment
 alternatives to 44–46
 corporal punishment 53, 115, 121
 and crime 212–219
 as a deterrent 36–37
 embedded in legal system 318–319
 ethical legitimacy 37

execution of the law 151
having no benefit 33–34
historical transformation 161
immorality 151
inequality 21
inflicted by public authorities 209
and justice 21
medical model of crime 232
moral agency and sensibility 149–155
as morally illegitimate 150
not obviating the crime 313
not preventing crime 303
prisons' central power in 203
safeguarding liberty 209
serving as an example 37
sinful (criminal) behaviour. 243
and *social defence* 159
socialist issue 6–13
and society 159–162
and the state 209–210, 221
see also capital punishment; crime; rehabilitation
'Punishment' (Carpenter) 108
punishment industry 183
punitive expiation 151
punitive justice 33, 36, 151, 155
'punitive turn' in penal policy 6–7
Purleigh Brotherhood farm colony 96
pyramid of violence 76

Q

Quakers (Society of Friends) 90, 99, 100
Queens County jail, New York 286
Queenwood community (Hampshire) 59
queer and feminist anarchists 305
Quelch, Harry 136

R

race 248
racial capitalism 184
racist mobs 307–308
radical freedom of the anarchist idea 230
radical prison reform 115, 118
Rafanelli, Leda 234
The Raid (Tolstoy) 67
railroads 245–249, 251, 255n6
Ramelli, Ilaria 158
rape 306
Rassemblement national 8
rational environments (Owen) 52, 55
real abolitionist utopia (Carpenter) 112–117
'real utopias' (Wright) 96
recidivism 114, 177
reciprocity 153, 160
'Reclamation' (Carpenter) 108
reconciliation through education 61
'Recuperative Hostel for Sailors and Soldiers, invalided from HM services with Nerve Strain' (*British Journal of Nursing*) 99

INDEX

Re Debs (US Supreme Court) 249
'A Reformatory for Girls and Young Women' (St John) 98
Reformer's Year Book 94
rehabilitation
  Alexander Berkman 319n3
  Edward Carpenter 117, 122n3
  in contemplative silence 243
  'gentlest punishments' (Thompson) 57
  inhumane prisons conditions 293
  and practical employment schemes 96
  San Quentin state prison 9
  Arthur St John 96
  see also prisoners; punishment
reintroduction of offenders 61, 178–179
Religion and Crime (Morgan) 58
reoffending 54, 57, 262
reorganizing society 17, 118
repentance 72
'A report from occupied territory' (Baldwin and Weems) 318
Report of the Departmental Committee on Prisons (Home Office, 1895) 113, 119
Report to the County of Lanark (Owen) 59–60
reproduction 199
Republican Spain 94
residential rehabilitation 96
residual delinquency 232
restorative justice 34, 45
Resurrection (Tolstoy) 66, 80–83, 93
retribution 293
revenge 156, 177, 233, 293
'Revenge' (Carpenter) 108
reverence for the law 181
revolutions 84, 182, 198–199, 204n10
rewards 153–154
Richeux, Francis 67
rich using the law 37, 38–39
right *and* left hands of the state 140, 143n14
right-wing parties 7–9
Robbers (Schiller) 72
robbery and theft 37
Robert, D. 58
Robinson, Cedric 185
Robinson, Cyril D. 309, 310, 312–313, 317–318
Rochdale, England 4
Rope Street New Bailey Prison, England 4
Rose, G. 88–89
Rothman, David 244
Rothschild family 196
Rousseau, Jean-Jacques 131
Rowbotham, Sheila 110, 118–119
Rubaiyat (Khayyam) 273
Rubini, Gennaro 219
Ruggiero, Vincenzo x, 36–37
Ruiz, Martínez 25, 192–193, 199, 204n4
Russia 67, 117–118, 171, 278–279
Russian Revolution 182

S

Saint-Simon, Henri de xiii–xiv, 14, 27n10, 51
Sakhalin Island (Chekov) 172
Salt, Henry 92
Salud y Fuerza 204n12
Salvatore, Nick 246, 249
Sánchez, Pedro 8
sanction (Guyau) 147–149, 151, 158, 159–163, 166n20
Sandburg, Carl 264
Sanger, Margaret 285
San Quentin state prison, US 9
Sarjeant, Douglas Jerrold 59
Saskatchewan, Canada 91
satisfying material needs 307
Scaglion, Richard 309, 310, 312–313, 317–318
Schiller, Friedrich 72
'School in prison' (*Daily News*) 128
'school of crime' 151
science 190, 201–202
scientific racism 266–267
Scotland 12
Scott, David Gordon
  abolitionist compass 115–117
  'abolitionist real utopia' 88, 92, 97, 102, 103, 109, 112
  'abolitionist rhizome' xi, xii
  Abolitionist Voices x, xi–xii
  criminal law allocating culpability 113
  language of anti-hegemonic and anti-prison thinking 203
  legitimacy of the coercive state 221
  positive relationships nurturing offenders 42
  'prison time' (Lefebvre) 42–43
  punishment as morally illegitimate 114
  radical alternatives 115
  'Speaking the language of state violence' 83
  suffering of imprisonment 44
  violence against women 40
Scottish Presbyterian church 54, 55
Scuola 193
'security populism' (Hamilton) 7
selective criminalization 112–113
self-interest 314
self-regulation (Owen) 53–54
Semana Trágica (Tragic Week) 197
'seminaries of vice' (Godwin) 23, 41
Semple, D. 99
sensibility (Guyau) 147, 149–155, 165n2
'Sensible' violence (Carpenter) 121
Serbian Relief Fund 99
Seruya, Sime 94
settling disputes 133
sexual violence 306, 307
Shabunin, Vasily 68–69, 77
sharing resources fairly 35

Sheffield debtors prison, England 4
Sheffield Socialist Society 108
shellshock victims 99
Sherman Anti-Trust Act 249
Shulman, A.K. 279, 283
Siberia 79, 171, 173, 174, 175
Siberia and the Exile System (Kennan) 79
Sidgwick, Henry 147
Sierra Chica prison, Argentina 231
'silent monitors' 53
Sim, Joe 12
sincere repentance 71–72
Sinclair, Upton 247
sinful behaviour 72, 243, 292
Singleton, John 311
sinners expiating their sins 292–293
slavery 185, 255n6
social and economic relations 111
social benefits 33–34
social conditions 15, 95, 120, 212
  see also poverty
'social crime' argument 290–291
social Darwinism 122n2, 190, 252, 267
social defence 161, 166n26, 215, 217
social disease and medicine 263
social disharmony 114
social duty 215
social environments 120–121, 267
social harmony 55
social harms 16, 20–21, 22, 196
social inequality 195, 220–221
  see also inequality
socialism xiii, 54–56, 244–245, 250–251, 316
socialist criminology 110, 122n2, 238
Socialist League 126, 139
socialist movements 118–119
Socialist Party of America (SPA) 246, 250–251
socialist society 2, 23, 133, 134, 221
Socialist Workers' Party 227
social medicine 263
social order (Malatesta) 211–212
social organization 193–195
social revolutions (Kropotkin) 180, 182
Social Science and Utopia (Goodwin) xiii–xiv
Society for the Abolition of Capital Punishment (SACP) 59
Society of Friends (Quakers) 90, 99, 100
Sociologia anarchica (Gori) 235
Sociología Criminal (Ruiz) 192
Sociological Review 94–95, 101
Sociological Society 91
soldiers 310
solidarity 20, 207–208, 220–221, 235
solitary confinement 41–42, 243, 293
solutions to criminality 17–18, 198–202
South America 230–231
Southwark Prison, London 4
Spade, Dean 21, 317

Spain 8, 189–204
  anarchist collectives 5
  Civil War 182
  general strike 1902 197
  police actions against anarchists 203, 204n15
Spanish abolitionist anarchism 191
Spanish anarchists 191–192, 193, 197, 198
Spanish Revolution 182
'Speaking the language of state violence' (Scott) 83
Spirit-wrestlers ('Doukhobor Sectarians') 80, 90–91
spontaneous processes 211
stages of knowledge 190, 203n1
Starmer, Keir 7
the state
  abolition of 198–202
  and capitalism and crime 195–198
  courts upholding abuses 289
  exercising power with public hangings 136–137
  Enrico Malatesta's critique 209–211, 221
  not holding the powerful to account 309
  power to punish 203
  prisons as revenge and repression 303–304
  and punishment 209–210, 221
  as a 'slave- driver' and 'scab' 288
State of Prisons (Wines) 261
state-sanctioned murder 270–272
  see also capital punishment
state violence 196–197, 315
statism 209–210, 219
Statism and Anarchy (Bakunin) 184
status, class and privilege 39, 113
St John, Arthur 20, 87–103
  abolitionist real utopian arguments 101
  approaches 103
  background and military career 89
  communal utopianism 20
  critique of Cesare Lombroso 96–97, 103
  'Doukhobor Sectarians' 90–91
  ethical socialism 102
  First International Eugenics Conference 97–98
  First World War 99
  gradualist steps towards transformative action 94
  harmful effects of imprisonment 97
  Honorary Secretary of PWL 94
  idealism and pragmatism 95
  influences 89–90
  and Peter Kropotkin 93
  marriage 91
  Montessori education 96
  National Conference on Destitution 97
  needs-based justice 23
  offenders treated according to needs in society 95

practical solutions and opportunities 96–97
probation 95–96
rehabilitation and employment schemes 96
suffrage campaigners 93
and Leo Tolstoy 20, 90–91, 99
see also Prison Reform League (PRL)
St John, Arthur, publications
  'A Reformatory for Girls and Young Women' 98
  Why Not Now? 87–88, 101–102
St Louis' primary prison 262
St Petersburg 171–172
St Petersburg House of Detention 171
strikes 248–249, 250
The Struggle to Be Human (Tift and Sullivan) 12
substantive equality 17
substantive freedom 132
suffrage campaigners 93
suffragette prisoners 95
Sullivan, Dennis 12
Sunset Club 265
'survival of the fittest' (Darwin) 122n2
Switzerland 172
sycophancy of statism (Kropotkin) 181
sympathy 160
systemic crimes 37

T

The Tables Turned (Morris) 135–136
Talley, Alfred J. 271–272
Tarde, Gabriel 158, 159, 192
Taunton gaol, England 4
taxes 265
Taylor, Ian 110–111
Tchertkoff, V. 69–70
temporality of action (Guyau) 154
Terre Haute, Indiana 246, 247
theft 37
theory of perfectibility (Godwin) 46
theory of policing (Robinson and Scaglion) 312–313
theory of violence (Tolstoy) 25, 70–79
'thieves in gloves' (Gori) 230
Things as They Are (Godwin) 37–40, 42–44
"third degree" police questioning 284, 285
Thompson, E.P. 129
Thompson, William 51, 56, 57, 60
Throreau, Henry David 89
Tidcombe, M. 97
Tierra del Fuego, Argentina 231
Tierra y Libertad 195, 197
Tift, Larry 12
Todd-Kvam, J. 7
Together Against Punishment (TAP) 12
Tolpuddle Martyrs 58
Tolstoyan idealism 100
Tolstoy, Leo 14, 66–85
  abolitionist approach to prisons 83
  as an ascetic 267

communal utopianism 20
and death 71
doing what is right 84
'Doukhobor Sectarians' 90
impact on radical politics 89–90
intellectual foundations for reformers 273
mad people 71
moral depravity of executions 23
morality of inflicting pain 22, 24
moral redemption of criminals 21
and the penal system 79–83
rejecting violence 71
rejection of the state 83
reorientation of human societies 92
social environment 267
social philosophy 79
and Arthur St John 20, 90–91, 99
theory of violence 25, 70–79
unjust social orders 84
Tolstoy, Leo, publications
  A Confession 92
  The Divine and the Human 74, 75–76
  The Forged Coupon 73, 76–77
  God Sees the Truth But Waits 78
  Letter to an American on Non-resistance 84
  Resurrection 66, 80–83, 93
  War and Peace 75, 77–78
  What Do I Believe 69, 82
  What Is to Be Done? 92
  What Then Must We Do? 67–68
Tolstoy, Sergey 84
'To Lucifer, the lightbearer' (Goldman) 290
'To my friends, old and new' (Goldman) 296
Tonkin campaign 197
torture 137–138, 196, 285
total abolitionism 234
'total transparency' (Rousseau) 131
'tough on crime' (Democratic Party) 9
Towards Democracy (Carpenter) 116, 122
Trafalgar Square march (November 1887) 111–112
Tramonto del diritto penale 234
transformative justice 305
transgressing social norms 111–112, 113, 122
'Transitions to freedom' (Carpenter) 116, 119
transparency 116, 131–132
transportation 166n28
trials 39
La Tribuna Libre 197
Trotsky, Leon 184
'true Communism' (Morris) 133
'true Democracy' (Carpenter) 142
tsars 76–77
Tuke, Ruby 23
Turati, Filippo 227
turnkeys 43, 179
Tussey, J. 251–252
tyrannical landlords 38

U

UK 11–12
  Houses of Parliament debates 10
the 'unfinished' (Mathiesen) 222
UN High Commissioner of Human Rights is (OHCHR) 8
United Services College 89
United States (US)
  abolition of slavery 185
  activism 10–11
  anti-chattel-slavery tradition xii
  anti-violence and abolitionist movements 10
  arrests 260–261
  birth control 285–286
  Black police 310–312
  as a carceral state 289–290
  Commerce Clause 249
  Committee to Abolish Prison Slavery (CAPS) 11
  Comstock Act 285, 297
  conscription (the draft) 287
  corporate capitalism 247, 255n10
  cost of penal infrastructure 261–262, 291
  criminals recalibrating moral centre 243
  crisis of state victimization and penal system 260
  Democrats 7, 9
  Espionage Act 1917 287, 297
  Federal Bureau of Prisons 296
  Gilded Age 262
  immigrants 243
  Immigration Act 1906 (Anarchist Exclusion Act) 284, 289, 297
  inhumane prisons 262–263
  Irish gangs 243–244
  jury selection 280
  moral upstanding citizenry 243, 252
  National Prison Association (NPA) 261
  penal abolitionism 11
  political prisoners 290
  presidential campaigns 251
  prisoner unions 11
  prison labour systems 263
  prison population 7, 293
  prisons manifestation of Dante's hell 261
  prison system and colonial period 277
  programmes for assessment and probation 91
  railroads 245–249, 251, 255n6
  recidivism rates 262
  re-entry of prisoners into society 178
  repression of political opponents 16
  Selective Service Act 1917 (Draft Act) 287, 297
  Sherman Anti-Trust Act 249
  socialist-inspired penal abolition 5
  standardization of sentencing 263
  working conditions 279, 297n3
United States Supreme Court, *Re Debs* 249

universal charity (Guyau) 156
universal grace (*grâce*, Guyau) 155
universal happiness and improvement 44
universal salvation 163
'universities of crime' (Kropotkin) 177
unjust societies (Godwin) 35
unlimited freedom (Popper) 216
unredeemable evildoers 296
unstamped press movement 58, 62n4
L'uomo delinquente (Lombroso) 231
upper-class shoplifters 113
Utopia (More) 131–132
utopian defamiliarization (Morris) 129, 130
utopian imagination 88
utopianism
  Prison Reform League (PRL) 99
  self-governing, communal society 116
  socialist movements 118
  visual discourse 131
'utopian socialists' (early socialists) 13, 17, 21

V

Valerianovna, Elizaveta 76
Vandalia Railroad 246
Vanderbilt, Cornelius 247
van Swaaningen, Rene x, 7
vengeance 159–160, 213, 309
victims and survivors 309
Victorian prison system 138
'Villages of Cooperation' (Owen) 52, 54–55, 57, 58, 59, 60
violence
  abolition of violent punishment 58
  and bourgeois morality 229
  and coercion 69
  criminal justice system 43–44
  establishing oppression and exploitation 213
  as inconceivable and indefensible 70
  morally reprehensible 25
  private property as seed of 196
  theory of (Leo Tolstoy) 25, 70–79
  toxic effect of authority 310–311
  against women 40
violent revolutions 84
visual discourses 131
voluntarism (Malatesta) 208
voluntary associations 26
Vulcan Advocate 98

W

Walia, Harsha 317
Walls and Bars (Debs) 249, 251
Walsall Anarchist bomb plotters 111–112
war and colonialism 197–198
War and Peace (Tolstoy) 75, 77–78
The War Hospital at Neuilly (Semple) 99
Warren, Charles 126
Warrensville, Ohio 91
Washington, Booker T. 250

Weber, Max 221, 264
We Do This 'Til We Free Us (Kaba) 304, 305, 307, 309
Weems, C.M. 318
well-balanced surveillance (Owen) 53
Wells-Barnett, Ida B. 250
We (Zamyatin) 132
What Do I Believe (Tolstoy) 69, 82
What Is Communist Anarchism? (Berkman) see *Now and After* (Berkman)
What Is to Be Done? (Tolstoy) 92
What Then Must We Do? (Tolstoy) 67–68
Wheeler, Anna Doyle 60
white anarchists 303
white defined in opposition to the 'other' (Baldwin) 307
Whitehead, G.G. 267
white supremacy 307, 310
Whitman, Walt 108
Why Not Now? (St John) 87–88, 101–102
Wiggam, Albert E. 267
Wilde, Oscar 111–112, 122, 142
Wilkes, John 4
will and sensibility 162
will/desire and evolution 122n2
Williams, John (Jack) 136–137, 138
Williams, Raymond 140
Wilson, Woodrow 287
Wines, Enoch Cobb 261, 273
withering of the bourgeois state 140
witnesses 39–40
'womb strike' (Bulffi) 199
women
  enslavement at home 199
  sidelined by radicals xii
  suffrage and direct action 92–93
  victims of male harm 40
Women's Franchise 94
Women's Freedom League (WFL) 93, 94
Women's Tax Resistance League 100
Women's Training Colony (WTC) 98, 99
Woodstock penitentiary, US 249
'World Without Prisons' 27n6
Wright, A. 19
Wright, Erik Olin xiii, 96, 112
wrongful convictions 38
Wysocki, Joseph D. 10

Y

YO 196

Z

Zamyatin, Yevgeny 132
Zerbst, Fred G. 304–305
Zuriaga, Rafael 204n12

www.ingramcontent.com/pod-product-compliance
Lightning Source LLC
Chambersburg PA
CBHW051525020426
42333CB00016B/1779